CALLED TO RECKON

CALLED TO RECKON

REPLACING HISTORY AND RECLAIMING MISSION AT A MIDWESTERN COLLEGE

Edited by Jane E. Simonsen

Southern Illinois University Press
Carbondale

Southern Illinois University Press
Mail Code 6806; Southern Illinois University;
Morris Library, 605 Agriculture Dr., Carbondale, IL 62901
siupress.com

Printed in the United States of America

First printed November 2025.

This project was made possible by a Reframing the Institutional Saga grant from the Network for Vocation in Undergraduate Education (NetVUE), administered by the Council of Independent Colleges (CIC) with support from the Lilly Endowment, Inc.

Jacket and cover illustration: Old Main Augustana, cropped, *left*. Augustana College Special Collections, image CD-00067 large soft. Old Main Augustana, cropped, *right*. Wikipedia Commons by Smallbones.

ISBN 978-0-8093-3985-3 (paperback)
ISBN 978-0-8093-3989-1 (cloth)
ISBN 978-0-8093-3986-0 (ebook)

The manufacturer's authorized representative in the EU for product safety: Mare Nostrum Group B.V., Mauritskade 21D, 1091 GC Amsterdam, The Netherlands. gpsr@mare-nostrum.co.uk

Printed on recycled paper ♻

SIU
Southern Illinois University System

CONTENTS

List of Illustrations vii
Foreword by Steven Bahls ix
Acknowledgments xv

Introduction: Naming Our Ghosts 1
Harrison Phillis and Jane E. Simonsen

1. Toward Right Relations with Neighboring Nations 20
Jane E. Simonsen

2. Serving Students and Neighbors: Community Implications of Campus Expansion 52
Sarah Lashley

3. Performing Blackness: A History in Three Acts 85
Lauren Hammond-Ford and Jane E. Simonsen

4. Empowering Marginalized Voices: A Journey Toward Diversity, Equity, Inclusion, and Justice 128
Monica M. Smith

5. Contested Counterspaces: Creating Latinos/x Unidos at a Midwestern College 164
Christopher Strunk and Lizandra Gomez-Ramirez

6. Queering the Landscape: Radical Hospitality at the "Good Life" College 191
Robert Burke

7. Toward a Pedagogy of Accompaniment: Transformative Community, Spiritual Formation, and Augustana's Useable Past 226
Mark Safstrom

8. The Value(s) of Lutheran Liberal Arts in a Neoliberal Age 270
Jason A. Mahn

Epilogue 312
Andrea Kathryn Talentino

Bibliography 319
Contributors 339
Index 343

ILLUSTRATIONS

Figures

Fig. 1.1 Boundary Line marker, Augustana Campus 21
Fig. 1.2 Augustana at Wells and Superior Streets, Chicago, circa 1860 31
Fig. 1.3 Vine Deloria Jr. at Augustana College graduation, 1971 41
Fig. 2.1 Campus property in 1875 55
Fig. 2.2 University/College Zone of Rock Island 75
Fig. 3.1 Jesse Routte, seminary graduation photo, 1933 88
Fig. 3.2 Mashood Àjàlá, Cosmopolitan Club photo, 1949 102
Fig. 3.3 Black Power Symposium, 1969 113
Fig. 4.1 Dr. John Hildreth with student 135
Fig. 4.2 Augustana students react to O. J. Simpson verdict, 1995 148
Fig. 4.3 Vigil for Lives Lost, 2020 154
Fig. 5.1 Group photo of members of Latinos Unidos in front of the Casa Latina sign, 1999 165
Fig. 5.2 Consuelo Martinez photo in front of Casa Latina mural 174
Fig. 5.3 Tribute to Our Lady of Guadalupe flyer, 2016 180
Fig. 5.4 Ayotzinapa vigil, 2017 183
Fig. 6.1 Lighthouse banner, 1990 203
Fig. 6.2 "Say No to Hate" rally, 2005 206
Fig. 6.3 "Gay? Fine by Me" solidarity event, 2006 207
Fig. 7.1 Cross being removed from Sorensen Hall, 2022 228
Fig. 7.2 Professor Jules Mauritzson 242
Fig. 7.3 President Gustav Andreen 243
Fig. 7.4 Professor Edward Fry Bartholomew 251

Fig. 7.5 Professor Parkander teaching an English class in Cable Hall, Old Main 254
Fig. 7.6 Coach Lenny Kallis with Richie Erickson, 1951 256
Fig. 7.7 Augustana Girls' Athletic Association, 1934 257
Fig. 8.1 Dean of Students Betsey Brodahl meeting with a student 271
Fig. 8.2 David Staples, college graduation photo, 2024 305

Tables

Table. 2.1 Rock Island Demographic Information 58
Table. 2.2 Rock Island Population Change over Time 58
Table. 2.3 Rock Island Demographic Change over Time 60
Table. 2.4 Faculty and Staff Residence over Time 62
Table. 2.5 Augustana Student Enrollment over Time 63
Table. 2.6 Transitional Living Areas Acquired Since 1992 64

FOREWORD

Called to Reckon is an important addition to the books recording the history of Augustana College. I commend it to all members of the Augustana community. It adds to the already fine literature about Augustana College through the voices of those whose stories have not been adequately considered and recorded by the college.

I am fond of challenging Augustana students to "turn the crystal" in order to view difficult issues through the eyes of others. I invoke the image of children holding a crystal close to their eyes, rotating it to view the room from different angles. I imagine holding the crystal up, catching a ray of the sun, and projecting bright light on some part of the room. This volume turns the crystal by holding Augustana's history up to the light, illuminating facets of that history not previously considered. Thus, this volume may be challenging to readers familiar with the histories written by Augustana's past presidents. It takes an approach that some might consider critical of Augustana and other predominantly white institutions, but I invite those readers to consider the passion and respect each author has for the college. Augustana is strong enough to weather criticism. Indeed, the philosophy behind turning the crystal is consistent with Augustana's mission as a liberal arts college that encourages all to consider multiple perspectives, question assumptions, and consider a marketplace of ideas from which the best may gain traction.

I hope this book encourages constructive thinking about Augustana's history. My colleague Lendol Calder, a professor of history, has argued that the best way to explore history is through the concept of "uncoverage."[1] Too often, history is viewed as something to be covered rather than an opportunity to think critically about how history is told, and by whom. This volume uncovers aspects of the untold history of Augustana. Other histories of Augustana focus on the college's ability to overcome trying financial times, challenging relationships with the church, and changing student demographics. While the courage of Augustana's leadership is an important part of Augustana's history, it is only a part of it. This volume adds to the story of Augustana by examining historically underrepresented communities.

Though the authors of the chapters in this book tell stories different from those of the authors of previous Augustana histories, there is a common thread. This is an expectation that Augustana responds well to the needs of all its constituencies. Faculty consider themselves to be the keepers of the liberal arts traditions of Augustana. Staff and administrators see themselves as owning student welfare and growth within their areas of responsibility. Students expect their considerable investment in an Augustana education to result in a welcoming place where they can flourish. Alumni take great pride in their education and expect Augustana to maintain a commitment to a high-quality education through its liberal arts traditions. The greater Quad Cities expects Augustana to contribute to the community. Each constituency is passionate about the college, and that is one of the college's greatest strengths. The passion of so many constituents at Augustana keeps the college introspective and strong.

Several chapters refer to the college's "Five Faith Commitments," which appear at the end of this foreword. The idea of developing the Five Faith Commitments came from the 2003 presidential search that led to my appointment. Before the search was launched, the Augustana Board of Trustees changed the requirement that the president be Lutheran to the less stringent prerequisite that the president be a member of a denomination with ecumenical agreements with the ELCA (Evangelical Lutheran Church in America). This decision was controversial, with one member resigning over the decision.

During the interview process, it became clear to me that Augustana was struggling to define its church relationship. As part of the interview process, I asked dozens of members of the Augustana community what that church relationship meant. The board chair and I appointed a task force to help define this relationship. The task force's work took place at about the same time that the ELCA appointed a working group to develop a *Social Statement on Education*, the initial draft of which indicated that Lutheran colleges should endeavor to have a critical mass of Lutherans as students and employees.[2] When most college presidents expressed strong opposition to this provision, believing that Lutheranism should not be defined as counting heads, it was dropped. The resulting statement contains only generalities on Lutheran higher education and is thus of little value in illuminating the Five Faith Commitments. Because the ELCA's expectation for its colleges was quite general, the document named "commitments," not "covenants." The Five Faith Commitments are not an agreement with the ELCA; rather, they are the college's unilateral commitment to the ELCA and the college's faculty, staff, and students. Because they are a commitment, not a covenant, the Augustana community is able to interpret and reinterpret them in ways that mature over time.[3] The chapters in this book will aid in that process.

The Five Faith Commitments endeavored to answer what the nature of Augustana's Lutheran-ness is. I believe they made good progress toward doing that. I did not expect the commitments to open a new set of discussions. How does Augustana need to evolve considering the bold assurances of its faith commitments? How should Augustana, as a corporate body, live out its dedication to social justice? How can Augustana embrace students from diverse religious backgrounds, helping them grow in mind, body, and spirit, just as Augustana has historically helped Lutheran students? What does it mean to help students distinguish between vocational discernment and career choices? At times I thought the commitments raised more questions than they answered. But that is consistent with Augustana's goal of helping students discern. Augustana, too, works to discern its institutional calling. The chapters in this volume wrestle with the questions not fully answered in the Five Faith Commitments.

Another common thread of this and previous volumes is Augustana's effort to maintain its mission in the face of change. In his account of Augustana, Dr. Conrad Bergendoff told the story of a Swedish-speaking college grappling with what its roots meant as Swedish immigration slowed to a trickle.[4] Dr. Thomas Tredway wrote the story of a college that had been "of Lutherans for Lutherans" becoming a liberal arts college firmly rooted in the Lutheran tradition.[5] Each is a history of the college confronting change, sometimes elegantly and sometimes inelegantly. The willingness to adapt to societal change is a hallmark of the saga of Augustana. During my years as Augustana's president, faculty approved changes to curriculum and the addition of majors demanded by students. Staff and administrators continuously improved programs. Board members pushed the college to look over the horizon in order to keep the college strong. Alumni are sometimes bewildered by changes they see at Augustana, but more often than not they are proud to see change as long as it is consistent with the college's traditions of ensuring that students grow in mind, body, and spirit.

Change at Augustana has not been easy, as several of these chapters point out. Like all institutions struggling to adapt, Augustana experiences institutional resistance to change. But most members of the Augustana community believe that the college can and should evolve to become stronger. Shared governance at Augustana may slow change, but it also helps ensure that decisions are made carefully and not prematurely. Shared governance is most effective when all voices, including dissenting voices, are heard. It is my hope that this volume will be widely read by all involved in shared governance to stimulate discussion at Augustana and elsewhere.

Change is often driven by students, some of whom have authored chapters in this volume. Students over the decades have expected the college to evolve to meet their needs. I recall a conversation with a student, Lydia Ruelas Duran, in the first year of my presidency, in which she exhorted me to develop actionable plans to make Augustana more diverse. I recall similar meetings at the Black Culture House. In each case, when I asked what they would do, they developed thoughtful, actionable proposals for change, as is common with Augustana students. I found myself broadening my horizons because of these conversations with students. I hope this book will help many more do the same.

My thanks go to Dr. Jason Mahn, who envisioned this important project, to NetVUE and the Council of Independent Colleges for supporting this project, and to Dr. Jane Simonsen for her tireless efforts to ensure that this book adds to Augustana's institutional saga. May this important volume not only help us hear the historically unheard voices represented in its chapters but also encourage us to seek out other unheard voices to enrich other histories.

The Five Faith Commitments of Augustana College

1. INTERFAITH ENGAGEMENT: Augustana College celebrates God's regard for the worth and dignity of all persons.
2. SOCIAL JUSTICE: Augustana College encourages the development of a campus community that seeks justice, loves kindness, and acts with love and humility.
3. SPIRITUAL EXPLORATION: Augustana College provides a context in which every student might ask meaningful questions about life, morality and spiritual practice.
4. REASONED EXAMINATION: Augustana College encourages our campus community to wrestle with ways in which faith and reason challenge and enrich each other.
5. VOCATIONAL DISCERNMENT: Augustana College affirms that work and career—indeed, all human effort—are aspects of an understanding of vocation, a concept the Lutheran tradition in higher education helps illuminate.

Steven Bahls, President Emeritus
of Augustana College

Notes

1. Calder, "Uncoverage."
2. Evangelical Lutheran Church in America, *Social Statement*.
3. Steven Bahls has been a leader within the Network of ELCA Colleges and Universities and created Augustana's Presidential Center for Faith and Learning. Augustana is a member of the Council of Independent Colleges and its flagship NetVUE, or Network for Vocation in Undergraduate Education.
4. Bergendoff, *Profession of Faith*.
5. Tredway, *Coming of Age*.

ACKNOWLEDGMENTS

The authors wish to thank the Network for Vocation in Undergraduate Education for the "Reframing the Institutional Saga" grant that supported the research, conversation, and fellowship essential to this book. We are also grateful to the Augustana College Office of the President, the Swanson Fund for Social Thought, and the Presidential Center for Faith and Learning for their endorsement of and dedication to this project. The work of Augustana College Special Collections librarians past and present created the bedrock on which our stories are built. In particular, we thank Micaela Terronez and Harrison Phillis, whose enthusiasm, resourcefulness, and curiosity has inflected every essay in this volume.

CALLED TO RECKON

INTRODUCTION
Naming Our Ghosts

HARRISON PHILLIS AND JANE E. SIMONSEN

A college that is more than a century and a half old accumulates stories. Whether collected in archives, set down in institutional histories, or passed on between generations of students and faculty, stories help to define a community. They remind tellers and listeners of those who came before, provide origins that root people in place, and help to craft a shared sense of identity.

But institutional memory can fail—must fail, in fact, to create the sense of progress and coherence crucial to so many histories. These failures become fault lines, cracks in the landscape of the past through which wandering stories and voices drift, like restless, unnamed ghosts. Some say that ghost stories do more than imagine that the departed return to rectify unredressed crimes: they link communities to places that have been the sites of collective invasions and national traumas. The specters of enslaved people and Indians commonly appear in homes and on landscapes, often respectively, in American ghost stories. Colleen Boyd and Coll Thrush, investigating the phenomenon of "Indian ghosts," write that legends of hauntings "disrupt dominant and official historical narratives" and are one method through which societies simultaneously grapple with and dismiss "patterns in the history of conquest" such as slavery and land dispossession.[1] Tiya Miles, in her study of how "dark tourism" capitalizes on histories of slavery, describes these tales as a "cultural process" through which groups communicate ideas about events "excluded from active, embraced memory." Miles explains that ghost stories "call to mind disturbing historical knowledge that we feel compelled to face, but they also contain the threat of that knowledge by marking it as unbelievable."[2] Ghost stories lurk just below the surface of official histories.

Augustana College, like many long established institutions, has its hauntings. It was founded in 1860 by the Augustana Synod of the Lutheran Church in America as a seminary serving immigrant Swedes in Chicago. It had moved to Paxton, Illinois, for a decade before the first building opened, in 1875, at its current location a half mile south of the Mississippi River where it bends west through Rock Island, Illinois. Gradually adding undergraduate degrees, Augustana continued to train mostly ministers, serving Swedish immigrants and their children from Chicago, Minnesota, Wisconsin, and Kansas. In its new location, though, it attracted more women and American-born students and grew along with rising national college enrollment in the latter half of the twentieth century. In 1967, the seminary moved to Chicago, leaving the campus to host only the traditional four-year liberal arts college.

Today, the campus covers 115 acres, with an imposing, domed Old Main, a grassy Quad, and dorms above a wooded ravine. It is often named one of the nation's most beautiful campuses. It has an undergraduate population of about 2,500 students, and while the college is affiliated with the Evangelical Lutheran Church in America (ELCA), the vast majority of its students are not Lutheran. More Black students began attending in the 1960s, followed by Latinx students in the 1980s and '90s. Between 1980 and 2005, the number of domestic students of color fluctuated between 5 and 10 percent of the student body; after 2006, this number rose steadily, even dramatically. The international student population was almost nonexistent until the late 1990s. Since 2014, however, the number of international students has more than quadrupled. As of 2024, 45 percent of the student body identified as either a domestic student of color (24.4 percent) or an international student (19.9 percent).[3] One story of the college, then, is that of physical and cultural growth, enlarging its footprint and embracing new and diverse populations. But most triumphal stories, Miles reminds us, have their ghostly doubles. What stories might our ghosts tell us?

Andreen Hall, a dormitory finished in 1937, is rumored to host at least three ghosts. Students have claimed to hear furniture moving, to see lights flickering and faucets turning on, and to witness the unexplained opening and closing of doors. That ghostly sightings are informed by shared anxieties is clear: in the early 2000s, all three of the ghosts reported in the *Augustana Observer*, the campus newspaper, were mysterious male figures in the halls of a women's dorm.[4] According to a 1969 article in the *Observer*, reports of ghosts in Andreen had surfaced the previous year. The author, who called themselves "rabbit," explained that "this year the conditions have gotten worse and more people are believing their Ouija boards concerning ghosts in Andreen Hall."[5] While "rabbit's" voice is edged in irony, the reports of paranormal activity in the dorm were likely due to campus concern around shared living spaces that was linked to broader power struggles.

In 1969, the campus was steeped in unrest: student leaders were campaigning for a Student Bill of Rights, which protested restrictive dorm policies, especially for women. Women were reporting feeling unsafe on campus due to several break-ins. The Vietnam War draft was looming. The new Afro-American Society was pressing for greater attention to civil rights, and the campus had just hosted a Black Power Symposium two weeks before the story ran. In 1968, three Black student protesters had been shot and killed by the Highway Patrol at South Carolina State University, and by the end of the 1969–70 academic year, four students would be gunned down at Kent State University by members of the Reserve Officer Training Corps (ROTC). Just days later, two Black students were killed by state patrolmen at Jackson State University in Mississippi. Augustana College, like most colleges across the nation, roiled with confusion over how to confront student activism and state-sponsored violence.[6]

Unsettling presences arise in unsettling times. One of the ghosts of Andreen who apparently made his presence felt in the turbulent year of 1969 was reputedly that of Chauncey Lee Morton Jr., shot and killed in a dorm room by a friend a decade earlier. Morton was one of a mere handful of students of color—perhaps as few as three or four—when he arrived at Augustana in January of 1958. A resident of Chicago's Hyde Park and a member of Salem Lutheran Church, an old Swedish Lutheran church that integrated along with its neighborhood in the early 1950s, Morton had graduated from Chicago's Parker High School in January and enrolled at Augustana for the spring semester. He was an aspiring premed student who hoped to follow in the steps of his father, a physician who served southside Chicago's Black community at Provident Hospital.[7] Morton participated in track and field at Augustana and curated a weekly segment of jazz music on WAUG, the college's student radio station.[8] His involvement suggests he was not afraid to take part in college activities, despite there being little support for students of color. Nevertheless, it must have been jarring to leave the Black community in southside Chicago for a predominantly—almost exclusively—white college.

While at Augustana, Morton befriended Richard Buchholtz, a fellow student in Andreen. Buchholz, who was white, bespectacled, and youthful looking, wrestled at Augustana and had been a member of the South Shore High School ROTC.[9] South Shore, mostly white when it opened in 1940, was integrating by the time Buchholtz attended in the late 1950s. The two first-years were described by Morton's roommate, Lynn Christian, as the best of friends, and this sentiment was echoed by their peers.[10] Both were known to have taken part in the masculine postwar culture of "phrigging," or pranking, on campus—a ritual of belonging that likely would have tempted two young men attempting to find their places in a new environment. Not two weeks before his death, Morton, Buchholtz, and five other Augustana College students had stolen a parade float from St. Ambrose College, across the river in Davenport, Iowa. The float was burned sometime on October 12; the owner of the trailer was seeking $250 in damages.

Both Morton and Buchholtz were also gun owners. Morton had falsified his age when the two had purchased .22 caliber pistols from a Rock Island sporting goods store a few weeks earlier, and Buchholtz's ROTC experience would have made him familiar with firearms. Buchholtz told authorities that they would sometimes use the guns to fire blanks in the dorms to startle residents. He also described a kind of dormitory "horseplay" that involved one student placing a gun against the head of another and pulling the trigger. In the room where Morton was shot, authorities discovered holes from .22 caliber bullets in the window screen and others in the wall, which had been taped over or filled. According to Buchholtz, on the afternoon of October 24, 1958, they were meeting in Morton's room to discuss repairs to the stolen trailer. Whether "playing" or arguing, Morton and Buchholtz struggled over the gun; Buchholtz shot Morton, who was pronounced dead upon arrival at Moline Public Hospital at 4:45 p.m., and then hid the gun in nearby Lincoln Park.[11] When the *Chicago Defender*, the nation's leading Black newspaper, contacted Morton's parents, they were "too distraught to give the Defender a statement about the tragic shooting."[12]

While Buchholtz was charged with manslaughter and appeared before a grand jury, it dismissed the charges, deciding that Morton's death was the unintentional result of a "friendly scuffle."[13] Other than acknowledging that Morton was a "Negro," race did not enter into the conversation; perhaps the young men's friendship made it impossible for the community to imagine that race might have influenced their relationship, even under the stress of being implicated for phrigging. For their part, college officials denied allegations that young men used firearms to disrupt the constraints of dorm life, hewing to a story in which Buchholtz was both innocent and untrustworthy. A press release refuted published claims: "Publicity which indicates that horseplay with guns was a common occurrence in the dormitory is contrary to fact, and must be understood as a statement from a person who has already told conflicting stories of his own unfortunate accident."[14]

The college held a memorial service on Tuesday, October 28. Morton's counselor spoke, and the dean of the college, George Arbaugh, delivered a response. The day before the service, the *Augustana Observer* printed a message with the title "In Memoriam": "The Augustana Observer, on behalf of the administration, faculty, and students wishes to express its deepest sympathy to the family and friends of Chauncey Morton. We know that sources of solace are far too few to all concerned with this tragic death."[15] While Buchholtz was asked to leave the college for the remainder of the school year, the college noted, "Future re-instatement will depend on factors not yet determined."[16] Though he never returned to Augustana, Buchholtz was not permanently expelled, nor was he ever convicted of a crime. His innocence, and the college's, was preserved.

Immediately following the shooting, political science professor Stanley Erickson, who served as a Rock Island alderman, urged the city to enact more stringent measures to prevent the sale of firearms to minors, citing Morton's death as motivation.[17] Still, the few Black students on campus at the time must have been terrified and silenced. Perhaps they and their parents were thinking of the angry white mobs who had rioted in 1951 in the Chicago suburb of Cicero in response to the presence of a single Black family. Or they may have remembered the ruined body of Emmett Till, a fellow Chicagoan the same age as Morton, whose 1955 murder in Mississippi set a match to the civil rights movement. While their white classmates probably accepted the story of horseplay gone awry, it would have been difficult for a Black person, in 1958, to see the shooting death of a Black man by a white one, and his subsequent exoneration, as anything but racially charged. It had happened too many times, and the courtroom was rarely a place where justice was served.

On campus, neither a white student's exoneration for killing a Black student nor the striking news of a death caused by gun violence seems to have caused further public discussion, and the specifics of the case, like the bullet holes in the wall, were patched over. Ten years later, in the heat of discussing civil and student rights, Morton was only a nameless, unsettling presence, perhaps stirred up by new fears of the confrontation with race, violence, and justice that had been buried a decade before. When women living in Westerlin Hall gathered to discuss racial mixing in 1968, concerns about integration were charged with anxiety about interracial dating: "most of the white girls are used to living in all-white communities, and consequently feel strange when they're around Negroes and think that they must be overly friendly to them. If they find they don't like a black person, they are uncertain if it is because of his personality [or] merely his skin color." By the early 2000s, Morton's first name had been recovered, but the women of Andreen, perhaps subconsciously calling on the gendered and racialized scripts that had legitimated so many lynchings, understood Morton's death to be the result of a spat over a girl. There was no mention of race, and the weapon was a "show gun."[18] The rapid acquittal of a white student on murder charges and an "unfortunate accident" explanation allowed the historical record to go unmarred. To this day, Morton's death does not appear on publicly available lists of incidents of gun violence on school grounds.

As Tiya Miles and others have shown, memories of violence do not always make their way into a community's official history, but they persist as vestiges of unredressed traumas, however distorted they are or difficult to see, and emerge at moments of crisis. In this respect, that reports of hauntings emerged in 1968, and intensified in

’69, should not surprise us. Only three months before Derek Chauvin murdered George Floyd in Minneapolis, Augustana student Paige Sheppard wrote in the *Observer* that it was time that Morton’s story was framed not as a ghost story but as a possible hate crime. Sheppard linked Morton’s killing to vandalism at Augustana’s Black Culture House two years before, in 2018, in which the perpetrators referred to the KKK and left a sign stating, “Black Lives Are Just Matter.” Sheppard was outraged that, in 1958, the college had “mourned the death of a student but not the taking of his life” and that she had been unaware that racist vandalism occurred just months before she arrived on campus. Mikaylo Kelly, a Black Student Union member, remarked that the “term ‘Institutional Memory’ comes to mind. It refers to how it’s very convenient for institutions to not keep these really intense, uncomfortable, tragic, shameful incidents alive.” The violence, in other words, is not just in the act but also in the forgetting.[19]

Decisions about what stories to include in histories happen all the time, and our choices tell us much about what our values are. The Haitian historian Michel-Rolph Troulliot, in *Silencing the Past: Power and the Production of History*, points out that the word *history* has a slippery meaning: it refers not only to “what happened” but also to “that which is said to have happened.” History is not only the facts of past lives and events but also the stories told about those events to give them meaning.[20] Storytelling, of course, involves choices. What characters will be the focus? From whose perspective will the story be told? What actions are most central in moving the plot forward? Which events constitute the climax, and which the resolution? What communities select and deem to be “recorded history” not only reflects, but in fact creates, their origin stories, their values, and their identities. The result is that experiences that are intrinsic to some people’s ways of being in the world, including both intergenerational trauma and methods of survival and resistance, may exist in official repositories only as “archival silences.”

Indiana Miami/Eastern Shawnee rhetorician Malea Powell emphasizes that for American Indians, archival collections are tools of surveillance. For Black scholar Saidiya Hartman, they are methods of social control from which lives and stories must be liberated.[21] Often, we must either leave the archive, read against it, or record new information in order to hear any of those voices, because the space of an archive—like that of a nation—may exclude voices, experiences, and bodies that challenge its imagined coherence. With this in mind, new generations of archivists are actively working to increase the involvement of those communities whose histories they aim to document. At Augustana, this movement is apparent in the efforts of Special Collections librarians (including Harrison Phillis, one of the authors of this introduction) to help student groups preserve and maintain their histories, to introduce students to those materials, to digitize materials to make them available to the public, and to work with classes to collect oral histories and interrogate archival silences. In recent years, Special Collections librarians have given presentations to student groups like the Black Student Union in order to maintain transparency and foster communication and collaboration moving forward.

Stories, then, just like the boundaries of a nation or a campus, change over time and in response to those who assemble them. The story of Augustana College has been told before, most notably by two past presidents, Conrad Bergendoff and Thomas Tredway. In 1969, Bergendoff, president of the college from 1935 until 1962, published *Augustana, a Profession of Faith: A History of Augustana College, 1860–1935*. Even as the campus grappled with new social realities, the book framed the college's history as a story of immigrant perseverance. The lead characters were the Swedish Lutheran pastors, presidents, and professors who struggled to make ends meet while putting down roots in and adapting to their new location. It is a story of faith, endurance, and financial ingenuity. In *Coming of Age: A History of Augustana College, 1935–1975*, President Tredway (1975–2003) chronicled the college's adaptation to demographic and social changes, especially in the postwar era. Tredway, himself a powerful instigator and mitigator of these changes, charted the course of the college during years when its Swedish Lutheran identity was less apparent in its students or faculty, stressing how the college weathered war, expansion, and social unrest through commitment to its liberal arts values.[22]

While Tredway's history reflects the growing diversity of the college, he relied primarily on the records of administrators and governing bodies. Ann Boaden's *Light and Leaven: Women Who Shaped Augustana's First Century* (2011) was the first college history to focus on a historically minoritized group. Beginning with the question "Where are the women?" Boaden, a longtime professor of English and creative writing at Augustana, told the stories of influential women students, faculty, and administrators, framing them as both barometers and agents of change. Boaden dealt with a lack of primary sources in reconstructing the lives of even the most prominent women at the college, many of whom fit well within the college's historical demographic (white, middle class, Lutheran). To tell their stories, Boaden called on her creative writing skills to animate her subjects, making hers, in part, a speculative history.[23]

Boaden reflected on the power of stories for *Intersections*, a publication of the Network of ELCA Colleges and Universities (NECU) in 2014. Comparing stories to wells of "living water" that nourish each of us, she urged readers to "identify, claim, and proclaim" those wells from which they draw their sustenance—dark, mysterious, unsettling as they may be—in order that they might "see more clearly, more respectfully" into the deep wells of others' identities and traditions. Boaden asserts that as a teacher, tapping into these wells goes beyond "in-depth interfaith conversations. It's what such conversations can do to create an institutional vision, a bone-deep (or well-deep) identity, one that substitutes a tolerantly dismissive 'whatever' for an intentionally engaged 'what.' I believe that such an identity enhances our ability to educate self and other, strengthens us in our quest to take our place and so to help students take their places in the world with discernment, confidence, and 'dauntless love.'"[24] Like Boaden, the authors of this volume recognize the value of stories that sustain us, and they see that to understand institutional identity and vision, we must locate wells of collective identity in ways that are honest and that claim those uncomfortable parts of the past—including roots in a faith tradition that both nourishes and, as Boaden puts it, "demands that the chaos be fully admitted."[25] To draw from the wells that supply us and turn those sources back into the living water of a usable past, we must dredge up layers of history.

In the summer of 2020, Augustana College was one of many organizations going through a reckoning, assessing what stories have been prioritized and which have been marginalized in defining its history, mission, and identity. A team of researchers—faculty, administrators, and alumni—applied for and received a major "Reframing the Institutional Saga" grant from the Network of Vocation in Undergraduate Education (NetVUE).[26] Over the past two decades, Augustana has affirmed that its many innovations and transformations are rooted in its historical identity as a Lutheran liberal arts institution. Among NECU institutions, this affirmation is articulated in *Rooted and Open*, a statement authored by a four-person writing team (including Dr. Jason Mahn, director of Augustana's Presidential Center for Faith and Learning and one of the authors in this volume), which was adopted by NECU's Board of Directors in January 2017. As its name suggests, the document considers how rootedness in the Lutheran theological tradition blossoms into an openness to change that results from religious, racial, ethnic, and other forms of diversification. The document states that students are "called and empowered—to serve the neighbor—so that all may flourish."[27] Augustana's articulation of its institutional identity makes a similar distinction between broadly inclusive "faith commitments" and the Lutheran theology that grounds them. Educators and students join the Lutheran calling, whether or not they are Lutheran.

While we recognize the value of these statements, we also recognize that, just as national histories are far more complicated, uneven, and often shameful than affirmations of national values let on, statements of values and mission do not emerge directly and cleanly from an institution's history. In other words, we cannot draw a straight line from the founders' vision of service and neighbor-love—which was shaped by their place-making experiences as Swedish immigrants in the mid-nineteenth-century American Midwest—to the visions of social justice that the college aspires to today. *Rooted and Open* and Augustana's "Five Faith Commitments" *articulate* institutional vocations, but in celebrating these worthy goals, they may obscure the ways the college has been implicated in white settler colonialism, valuing racial harmony over anti-racist work, contributing to an extractive and unsustainable economy, insulating itself from the struggles and needs of the communities surrounding it, or maintaining other habits that are decidedly *not* neighborly. They do not show how growth will be painful, including the productive pain of recognizing the college, in the words of Dr. Monica Smith, Augustana's former chief diversity officer, as a historically, predominantly, and *persistently* white institution (PPWI).[28]

Other institutions that received the NetVUE grant are sharing the results of similar efforts. Some have expanded their archival collections, such as Warren Wilson College in North Carolina, which is undertaking an oral history project. Some have developed classroom curricula or produced digital projects. Southwestern University in Georgetown, Texas, for example, created the website Placing Memory, featuring stories of lesser-known individuals, desegregation histories, and story-maps of queer spaces, gendered spaces, and its historical ties to Methodism and slavery. Wagner College in New York is developing original songs and performances; several institutions are producing collections of reflective and historical essays. Augsburg University's recent volume *Through Truth to Freedom: Reconciling a University's Past, Present, and Future* reflects deeply on that institution's location in downtown Minneapolis, considering its own Lutheran identity in light of its location on Dakota lands and the ongoing work to link its mission to that of the city around it.[29]

The present volume contributes to this work of institutional reckoning but has the goal of going beyond self-reflection to interrogate the narrative of Augustana as a "place apart." The story is rooted in the college's historical identity as an immigrant institution but rests on an imagined separation between the campus and the real world. Augustana is not a land-grant institution, its buildings were not constructed with stolen labor, and it is not a particularly wealthy institution. The college need not confront the brutality of slavery in the stone faces of its founders. But unlike at larger universities or those in more urban areas, Augustana students do not walk by and through public spaces daily. The campus does not economically or physically infiltrate Rock Island's public spaces, so students need not confront the faces and spaces of their near neighbors. This is one reason why faculty and students alike refer to campus both fondly and critically as the "Augie bubble," a place that promotes the safety and well-being of its students by drawing a curtain around the campus. The term "Augie bubble" seems to have begun circulating about the year 2000 in response to tension between the college's historical whiteness and an increasing national emphasis on multicultural diversity, and this sensibility still frames its use today.[30] As student Ava Jackson wrote in 2023, "I've found a place where I feel safe. . . . I have felt more secure in my identity, yet have trouble seeing this apply to all students. The Augie bubble may be tight but is selective in acceptance."[31] The campus community seems to recognize that the term is both comforting and deeply misleading. It knows that the term emerges from the disconnect between the college's persistent institutional whiteness and the racial, ethnic, and economic diversity on campus and in the communities around it. Just as the response to Morton's killing demonstrated, comfort is often premised on burying troubling truths. These remain just beyond the bubble in ways that exclude those who are unable to leave their experiences and identities behind in order to enter.

Reframing an institutional saga must include the critical, or even repentant, work of analyzing how storytelling about the past may reflect a distorted and superficial identity. In the case of Augustana College, many archival sources, including student publications, yearbooks, and administrative documents, shore up the college's "property in whiteness" by centering activities, priorities, and concerns that are historically rooted in cultural practices prioritized by Euro-American cultural groups (Greek life, athletics, managerial practices, etc.) even when these included non-white students.[32] Our investigations involved sifting through archival collections in order to locate narratives about the campus as place (in the world, in America, in the region, in the Quad Cities), creating opportunities for renewal and reckoning. We sought to bring forward the voices of students and members of the broader community, to highlight moments of tension in the negotiations between neighbors who share space, and to articulate stories that may have been silenced in past efforts to shore up accepted meanings of this place.

In the first two chapters, we investigate Augustana College as an immigrant institution that stands on Native lands and that currently shares space with neighbors in Rock Island. In "Toward Right Relations with Neighboring Nations," historian Jane E. Simonsen considers some of the college's geographic and ideological entanglements with settler colonialism. She traces how the land on which the campus stands came to be owned by the college and suggests how the immigrant institution's tendency to hold the nation's history of conquest and colonization at arm's length was tested during the difficult post–Civil War years. Turning to twentieth-century American Indian critiques, Simonsen considers how Indigenous models of relationality intersect with the mission of the college. In "Serving Students and Neighbors," Sarah Lashley, a professor of environmental studies, turns from the expressed motives and vision of the college to its operative motives and the challenges of neighborliness "on the ground." Lashley looks at interactions between the campus and the community of Rock Island with respect to the physical expansion of campus in order to understand how the college has balanced serving the needs of its students with serving its diverse neighbors.

The next four chapters turn to the ways that students from historically underrepresented groups navigated a PPWI both by creating their own methods of placemaking and by challenging the college, sometimes successfully and sometimes less so, to change itself to accommodate them. In "Performing Blackness," historians Lauren Hammond-Ford and Jane E. Simonsen tell three stories that illustrate the growing presence and power of Black students on campus between 1925 and 1975: that of Augustana's first Black graduate, Jesse Routte; of Mashood Adisa Olabisi Àjàlá, a Nigerian student whose tenacious resolve to navigate impediments during his tumultuous year at Augustana, 1949–1950, set the stage for his later audacity as a world traveler; and of the 1969 Black Power Symposium, in which the newly formed Black Student Union pushed the college to confront racism as part of its mission. "Empowering Marginalized Voices," by Monica M. Smith, former vice president for diversity, equity, and inclusion (DEI), chronicles the difficult but hopeful journey toward DEI at Augustana since 1969. Using interviews with current and former students and faculty as well as archival research, Smith contends that powerful "disruptors" have challenged this PPWI to persist in its commitment to deep belonging for all who call it home and asserts that Lutheran principles and the school's Five Faith Commitments chart the way forward. Chapter 5, "Contested Counterspaces," by geographer Christopher Strunk and alumna Lizandra Gomez-Ramirez ('17), documents the history of Latinos/x Unidos (LU), a student group founded in 1992. They use interviews with former and current students to show how LU has become a "counterspace" that offers opportunities for students to connect with others who share similar experiences even as it has also been a contested space that reveals debates around tradition, political activism, ethnicity, race, gender identity, and relationships with communities in the Quad Cities. Alumnus Robert Burke ('20), in "Queering the Landscape," surveys the college's institutional relationship with queer existence in the post-Stonewall era. Going against the conventional narrative of an alliance between secular enlightenment and LGBTQ progressivism, Burke reveals a more nuanced story of secular management that was mediated by alliances between LGBTQ activists and campus leaders, including pastoral proponents of the "good life" as one that includes gender and sexual diversity.

The final two chapters look both backward and forward to suggest ways to reconfigure and renew the institutional mission of a Lutheran liberal arts school to become a place of inclusion, belonging, and justice. Mark Safstrom, a professor of Scandinavian studies, argues in "Toward a Pedagogy of Accompaniment" that far from being monolithic, the college's Swedish Lutheran identity has always been contested and complex, as faculty and students navigated the uncertainty of creating a place that existed between "two homelands." Safstrom shows how this bi-location informed the college's immigrant identity and educational goals in its early years, and he suggests ways that this framework might offer a "usable past" for new types of bi-location. In chapter 8, "The Value(s) of Lutheran Liberal Arts in a Neoliberal Age," professor of religion Jason A. Mahn situates the rise of "education *for* vocation," as a central professed goal of many liberal arts colleges, next to the precipitous rise of neoliberalism, a default worldview that relegates deliberation about values, goods, and final ends to market forces and consumer choices. He suggests that in spite of the ongoing risk of the college becoming another mechanism for raising a person's market value, heeding the Lutheran liberal arts call to holistic education for the sake of wholeness is essentially a matter of social and ecological justice.

While we attempted to include new voices, events, and stories of Augustana College in this volume, we recognize that there are still stories yet to be told. We have not, for example, adequately attended to Augustana's long relationship with Asia and Asian people. As a location for some of the synod's early mission work, China was the home country of the college's first international students, and Lutheran missionaries there were caught up in the Revolution of 1911. Former Special Collections librarian Emma Saito Lincoln created, in 2018, an online exhibit about Ruth Kumata, a Japanese American who evaded internment in World War II by enrolling at Augustana, but this book does not include the experiences and contributions of Asian and Asian American students who have attended Augustana since the early twentieth century. With the exception of Nigerian student Àjàlá, we have not included the international student experience at Augustana. Though some chapters acknowledge social class, we have not included moments that starkly illuminate distinctions between faculty and staff, such as a parodic protest, in 1990, against the staff's exclusion from the faculty dining area (offering secretaries "guided tours of the Wilson Center" to see "actual faculty eating").[33] Moreover, the increase in contingent faculty since 2000 has, without a doubt, created new social divisions that differ from those of the college in years past. The college has only recently begun to consider how campus geography and its physical structures have long been a barrier to students, faculty, and staff with physical disabilities. Finally, we know that depression, anxiety, and addiction have plagued the community from the start. The father of Augustana's fourth president, Gustav Andreen, took his own life in the woods behind the campus back when Andreen was still a student, a year before he graduated in 1881. Such stories, often buried deeper than most, may never be recovered.

The work of reckoning with untold stories, then, is ongoing, and we hope others will be inspired to seek out histories that need to be told. We recognize that the stories we recount here are not *the* history of the college, but *a* history of the college, and that this history, as every history, serves a present need. As we face widening social rifts and environmental calamity in the third decade of the twenty-first century, we all need to profess our foundational beliefs as well as examine past practices to know more fully what it means to condemn them—and to understand what action that condemnation requires of us. Like the authors of the Augsburg Confession from which the college takes its name, members of this college community must affirm not only what we believe to be true but also what acts, because of these beliefs, we will no longer engage in or tolerate in others.

What, then, should the shooting death of a young Black man on the Augustana campus in 1958 require of the community today? In December of 2020, as the college struggled to get its bearings amid the shockwaves of a global pandemic and a national racial reckoning prompted by the murder of George Floyd, the vice president for diversity, equity, and inclusion, Dr. Monica Smith, held a community conversation about how the college responded to Buchholtz's murder of Chauncey Morton. Smith shared much of the story that Harrison Phillis has researched and described in this introduction and then raised questions for consideration: How might the college have responded differently if Morton had been white and Buchholtz Black? What responsibility do students have to hold one another accountable for dangerous behavior? What responsibility does the college have to consider how the legacy of unequal legal treatment has an impact on our perceptions of violence and legal decisions today? How might we make assumptions about "Black Anger" and "White Guilt" secondary to the goal of reconciliation? Smith asked, "How does the Augustana community of today approach reconciliation in the tragedy of Chauncey Morton?"[34]

We hope that this volume begins the task of reckoning with historical instances in which silence has preserved a superficial equilibrium at the cost of authentic reconciliation. We begin with naming our ghosts in order to recognize their stories as deeply rooted in this place that all of us, for a while, call home. Chauncey Morton is one, whose complex identity as a middle-class, Black, gun-owning, Midwestern Lutheran at a predominantly white liberal arts college does not fit neatly into any story we have yet told. Buchholtz is another—perhaps one of the many young white men entering college in the postwar era who was taught that guns were tools for retaining masculinity and power in an era rife with challenges to these. We must also name their friendship: recognizing that this friendship did exist; that sharing space with others, perhaps even caring about them as people, does not insulate us from perpetuating the ignorance, fear, and violence fueled by systemic racism; and that redemption is possible. We also name those values—including the Lutheran, Christian, and liberal arts values of many of those who enacted decisive and powerful changes—that we may also have consigned to the deep wells of the past rather than confront, examine, and draw from so that they might better nourish us and this place. In naming our ghosts, we bring them into our story and so more fully name ourselves.

Notes

1. Boyd and Thrush, *Phantom Past*, ix, 62.

2. Miles, *Tales from the Haunted South*, 15.

3. Augustana Office of Institutional Research, Demographic data.

4. Sarah Murray, "Ghosts of Andreen Hall," October 24, 2003. An account from 1998 speculates that a ghost named "Fred" died in a game of Russian roulette. In 2007, a resident explained that "a student named Chauncey killed himself in the East Wing." In 2009, "Chauncey" is described as the "resident ghost" of Andreen. Justin List, "Halloween Prompts Memories of Trick-or-Treating Costumes," October 30, 1998; "Upperclassmen Let Out the Truth About Augustana's Landmarks," September 14, 2007; "Campus Housing Tells All," March 27, 2009.

5. Rabbit, "Last Friday Night Writer's Club," *Augustana Observer*, November 6, 1969.

6. Frank, "Storms of 69–70."

7. "Probe Slaying of College Boy: Chicagoan Victim of Dorm Tragedy," *Chicago Defender* (daily edition), October 27, 1958; Albert G. Barnett, "Open House Held at First Negro-Owned Cancer Clinic," *Chicago Defender*, December 16, 1961; Juanita Bratcher, "Provident Honors Dr. Morton," *Chicago Defender* (weekend edition), May 2, 1987.

8. "Ten O'Clock Tonight: WAUG Returns to Air," *Augustana Observer*, February 17, 1958; *Rockety-I* yearbook, 1958, 40, 50.

9. "Bullseye Brigade."

10. "Pal Quizzed in Death of Augustana Student," *Rock Island Argus*, October 25, 1958.

11. "Grand Jury Will Study College Shooting Case," *Rock Island Argus*, October 29, 1958; "Youth Held in Shooting Taken for Lie Detector Test," *Rock Island Argus*, October 28, 1958; "Lie Test Report Awaited; Shooting Probe Continues," *Rock Island Argus*, October 28, 1958."

12. "Probe Slaying."

13. "Buchholtz Awaits Decision of Grand Jury in November," *Augustana Observer*, October 30, 1958.

14. "Augie Youth Free on Bond in Shooting," *Rock Island Argus*, October 30, 1958.

15. "In Memoriam," *Augustana Observer*, October 27, 1958.

16. "Augie Youth Free."

17. Erickson proposed that an ordinance be put in place that would fine minors under the age of twenty-one from five dollars to two hundred dollars for possessing a concealable firearm. In his view, putting preventive measures in place would help to ensure that situations involving gun violence could be prevented. Other council members disagreed with him; one of whom, by the name of Glen Wood, is quoted saying, "I don't think the ordinance is the answer . . . The problem is in permitting those kids to shoot the guns up there." "Augie Youth Free."

18. "Women Residents Discuss Problems," *Augustana Observer*, October 30, 1968; Murray, "Ghosts of Andreen."

19. Paige Shepard, "It's Called a Hate Crime, Not a Ghost Story," *Augustana Observer*, February 20, 2020.

20. Troulliot, *Silencing the Past*, 2–3.

21. Powell, "Dreaming Charles Eastman"; Hartman, *Wayward Lives*.

22. Bergendoff, *Profession of Faith*; Tredway, *Coming of Age*.

23. Boaden, *Light and Leaven*.

24. Boaden, "Well, Well," 46.

25. Boaden, "Well, Well," 47.

26. NECU was founded in 2016 after decades of close cooperation among the twenty-seven institutions composing the network. Augustana is also an active member of the Council of Independent Colleges and its flagship network NetVUE.

27. Jodock et al., *Rooted and Open*.

28. Smith, "Making Diversity Matter," 8.

29. Southwestern University, "Placing Memory."

30. Early mentions of the bubble occurred in spring 2000, including Catherine Huck's letter to the editor in which she expressed her disappointment with the college's diversity efforts. Huck, letter to the editor, *Augustana Observer*, April 21, 2000; Adam Malak, "Amnesty International Sponsors Week for Considering Children Involved in Wars," *Augustana Observer*, April 14, 2000.

31. Jackson, "Augie Bubble."

32. Harris, "Whiteness as Property." For an examination of how student publications at Midwestern colleges have historically shored up whiteness, see Stewart, "Whiteness as Collective Memory."

33. "Memo," *Augustana Observer*, April 26, 1990. With respect to social class, it may be relevant to mention that one of the other ghosts of Andreen is often reported to be a male custodian, whose presence in the halls has been coded as invasive.

34. Monica Smith, "Community Conversation about the Death of Chauncey Morton," unpublished notes shared with authors, December 1, 2020.

1
TOWARD RIGHT RELATIONS WITH NEIGHBORING NATIONS

JANE E. SIMONSEN

On May 3, 1941, the Augustana Historical Society, together with members of the State Historical Society of Illinois, met on the campus of Augustana College to dedicate a bronze tablet memorializing the 1816 creation of the "Indian Boundary Line" between lands ceded to the US government and those that remained unceded.[1] It is not clear whether students, perhaps more concerned with end-of-year banquets, open houses, and the "Augustana Olympics," were present to observe the moment when the boulder on which the tablet was laid became part of the campus landscape, nestled into the hillside below the seminary buildings (Fig. 1.1). By the same time the next year, the college was preoccupied by a war of territorial conquest in Europe, and the marker may have become merely a quaint reminder of events long past. Still today, students, faculty, and staff may walk by this marker hundreds of times without ever stopping to consider the rock, the plaque, or the implications of living and learning on conquered land. Entwined as they are with histories of conquest that dominant groups often prefer to forget, such boundary lines have left only a faint mark on most Americans' geographical consciousness.

But not all. Not two decades after the marker was placed, a member of the Yankton Dakota nation and fourth-generation Episcopalian entered the seminary on Zion Hill. Perhaps that seminarian, Vine Deloria Jr., contemplated the marker as he sat in classes, learning what he later called a "hopeful bolstering of ancient dogmas and doctrines" that he regarded as "virtually useless for solving the brutal problems of everyday life." He recalled keeping his mouth shut in a classroom shared with young men he thought of as less in awe of the mysteries and power of the divine than as seeking validation of "the

Fig. 1.1. Indian Boundary Line historical marker, Augustana College, Rock Island. Photograph by Jane Simonsen.

universal nature of their religious experience."[2] His later writings, in their particular mixture of theology, history, politics, and cultural critique, suggest that the Indian Boundary marker is part of a broader tendency on the part of Western cultures to attempt to pin the vitality of experience—wonder, spirituality, energy, and relationship with each other and the world—to unchanging and universal representations, whether a church, a monument, a doctrine, a political border, a national identity, or the face of God.

For many Americans, marking and defining are linked to the need to root oneself in place, politics, and history, even when that history is framed as progressive. It is possible to see the Indian Boundary Line marker as an early form of the land acknowledgments that have been adopted at many colleges and universities. The text describes how the land on which the campus lies was relinquished to the US government in 1804 by the Sauk and Meskwaki and, twelve years later, by the affiliated nations of the Three Fires Confederacy—the Potawatomi, Ottawa, and Ojibwa. But like so many settler markers and monuments, this information creates an origin story that links the campus, established by Swedish immigrants many decades after the treaty signings, to a story of political relations between the United States and its Native neighbors that ultimately resulted in this land being incorporated into the new nation. The inconspicuous marker may lead us to conclude that the disappearance of such boundaries is part of a positive, progress-oriented story of inclusion in which difference and distinction have been overcome and immigrants share place, vision, and values with Americans in general.

But we might ask, as Deloria and many other Indigenous people have, who is served when histories of difference are acknowledged as appeals to existing ideals, whether of Christian atonement or American progress? In this chapter, I suggest that reckoning with the college's historical relations with Native nations troubles definitions of inclusion as universally good. I begin by telling a story of how the land on which the campus stands came to be owned by the college and how that story represents a broader historical transition that devalued kincentric place relations in favor of abstract, economic ones.[3] I then investigate the late nineteenth-century emergence of Augustana's identity as an American rather than a Swedish institution, focusing on the story of the college's first "American" professor, Andrew Woods Williamson. His life reveals the complications of one incarnation of inclusion—missionary idealism. In contrast is Vine Deloria Jr.'s critique of missionaries and his recommendation that activism emerge from the particularities of place and community. Finally, I consider how Indigenous ideals of relationality provide models for negotiating relationships with place, history, and neighboring nations by reclaiming the identity of migrants on the land, for whom the phrase "to treat with" can mean not conquest but balance, and perhaps even healing.

CROSSING A LINE

The Indian Boundary Line was originally negotiated by Illinois territorial governor (and slaveholder) Ninian Edwards after the conclusion of the War of 1812. The war's end solidified American power over land earlier claimed by the British but still occupied by multiple and diverse Native nations that were negotiating new political realities, in part by forging intertribal alliances.[4] As the American victory knocked down an already-ajar door to white settlement in the northern part of the Illinois Territory, Edwards sought to establish a clear border between US territory and unceded lands that lay within the tract acquired from the Sauk and Meskwaki nations in 1804,[5] in a deal made sweeter by the offer of bounty lands to war veterans. This boundary was created by an 1816 treaty with the Three Fires Confederacy whereby its leaders agreed to "relinquish to the United States, all their right, claim, and title" to a triangle of land south of a line stretching due west from the southernmost point of Lake Michigan to the Mississippi River and between the Mississippi and the Illinois Rivers. By 1816, this territory was partially occupied by settlers with their eyes on statehood; Edwards hoped that the promise of peaceful relations with Indigenous nations would entice more settlers to come. Safety was just as important to the leaders of the Three Fires Confederacy, who trusted that the government would protect their access to the region's natural gifts. In its negotiations with the US government, the confederacy maintained the right to keep the northern part of the Northwest Territory—from the southern boundary running through the current campus, up through the rich mining lands of what is now southern Wisconsin, and all the way to the Canadian border. The affiliated tribes were to be paid collectively with $1,000 worth of goods every year for the next twelve years. Given that the land included the mineral deposits of southern Wisconsin, whose value was already clear to white prospectors, the trifling amount paid to the three nations in 1829 was, according to findings in a 1967 lawsuit by the Citizens Band of Potawatomi, "unconscionable."[6]

A year after the treaty signing, Edwards arranged to survey the tract, a move that acting Secretary of War George Graham (and later commissioner of the General Land Offices under Andrew Jackson) touted as "very much facilitat[ing] the migrations to the Illinois Territory." The line was surveyed in 1819 and again in 1821; by 1823, white squatters, some bringing enslaved men and women with them, had breached the line in pursuit of lead in the rolling hills around present-day Galena, Illinois.[7] These incursions led to an uptick in resistance by the Ho-Chunk, Menominee, and Ojibwa nations that culminated in 1827 with US military intervention (the so-called Winnebago War) and the incarceration of several Ho-Chunk leaders.[8]

Members of the Sauk and Meskwaki nations had continued to live in their villages along the Mississippi and Rock Rivers in accordance with the 1804 treaty, but white settlers began to arrive in larger numbers after the Ho-Chunk uprising—young miners lured by lead and coal as well as farming families from Kentucky and Virginia, who started squatting on Rocky (now Arsenal) Island and along the eastern banks of the Mississippi in anticipation of the government offering the treaty lands for public sale. Early white settler John W. Spencer recalled heading north to the mines from Greene County, Illinois, in 1827 and noting the good land around Rock Island. In the fall of 1828, he heard a rumor from another would-be settler, Rinnah Wells, that "the Indians had left their old village at Rock Island." By December, Spencer and Wells were squatting at the large village of Saukenuk, a town made up of a shifting population of various tribal nations and home to several thousand people in summer. The residents had gone west to their winter hunting ground, leaving their wickiups and food caches behind, as they had always done. The settlers moved into the well-constructed homes that they found in the village and started to fence and plant corn in the women's fields.[9]

When the Sauks and Meskwakis returned to their homes in the spring of 1829, they found them quite literally occupied. Feeling deeply betrayed, the Sauk leader Black Hawk and others sought remediation from French Potawatomi translator Antoine LeClaire, from trader George Davenport, and from their agent, Thomas Forsyth. LeClaire and Davenport counseled them to leave; the 1804 treaty, which remains disputed to this day, stipulated that the ceded land remained open to them only at the government's discretion. As soon as white folks wanted it, in other words, Indigenous residents would be evicted. Davenport, who had lived on Rock Island since 1816 and traded with Native groups living along the upper Mississippi, knew that the tide of white settlement was on the way. Indeed, that summer, the principals of the Three Fires Confederacy sat again with white men, this time in Prairie du Chien, and ceded to the US government the lands north of the boundary line and between the Rock and Wisconsin Rivers, including the northern portion of today's campus.[10]

When the federal government, under the new leadership of Andrew Jackson, offered treaty lands for public sale in the fall of 1829,

Davenport traveled to Springfield and bought most of township 17N, containing much of what is now the city of Rock Island as well as the portion of today's campus lying south of the Indian Boundary Line. At the time, his purchase included the town of Saukenuk and many of the surrounding fields where women planted and cached the corn, beans, and squash that sustained their community both physically and spiritually. Davenport attempted to justify his purchase to the Sauk leader Black Hawk, with whom he had long had good relations, but Black Hawk—and perhaps even more so, the women of the community—were insulted and angry. Settler J. W. Spencer recalled that in one of the meetings in which General Edmund Gaines and other white officials tried to convince the Sauk and Meskwaki to leave the village, an Elder "introduced herself to the General, and said she was a granddaughter of a prominent chief, and then began to speak of the sale of the lands. She said, 'the men could not sell the cornfields, for they belonged to the women—they had made them.' She said, 'it was very hard work to dig up the ground,' and putting her hand on her back, she said, 'it made their backs ache.' Another reason she gave was, 'that if the men had sold them they would have told them of it, which they had never done.'"[11]

The women—like their mothers before them—had mixed their labor with the soil and indeed felt that connection in their very bodies. Such a connection could not be sold. The woman's description of what it meant to be rooted in place should have been understandable to settlers, who defined their own land claims in similarly embodied ways, albeit market-oriented: squatters' rights were predicated on profitable "improvements" made by mixing labor with the land in ways that made it more valuable on the market—tilling the soil, erecting fences, building homes. The women, she explained, had done these things; the land knew their hands. But in the eyes of the US government, the community-sustaining work of Native women did not justify ownership in a profit-oriented nation.

For Black Hawk, this betrayal ran deep. In his autobiography, his bitterness toward Davenport, Forsyth, and LeClaire is clear: "The reason was now plain to me why he [Davenport] urged us to remove. His object, we thought, was to get our lands. We concluded that if we were removed by force, that the trader, agent and others must be the cause, and that if they were found guilty of having driven us from our village they should be killed. The trader stood foremost on this list."[12] Writing about Davenport in the 1880s, Black Hawk War chronicler Perry Armstrong seemed to have felt compelled to justify the trader's crusade to purchase the land as an effort to look out for his friends. "His plan was as bold as it was gigantic," Armstrong claimed. "It was no less than the purchase of the lands on the peninsula, embracing all the cultivated lands of the Sauks, together with the site of Saukenuk itself. . . . *For the sole purpose of preserving the site of Saukenuk, Black Hawk's Watch Tower and the improved farms of the Sauk Nation to their use.*"[13]

It is possible that Davenport thought the Sauk people would stay, continuing to grow corn in their village and trading at his post. But Davenport also knew a good investment when he saw one—the timbered land was valuable and the bottomlands rich, while the fur trade was faltering and over-mining was driving down the price of lead. He knew that the Sauk and Meskwaki people were many thousands of dollars in debt to him. And he knew that he did not have their consent to this plan: it was a private investment in public lands, not a treaty. While a significant number of Sauk and Meskwaki people *also* saw the writing on the wall and moved to their villages west of the Mississippi, Black Hawk and a few hundred of his allies resisted, resulting in an armed effort to resist government seizure of treaty lands. Locals, if they know it at all, call it the Black Hawk War; Meskwaki historian Johnathan Buffalo, noting that when Black Hawk returned to the Rock River he was not intending to go to war but only to come home, calls it a massacre.[14] And indeed, in August of 1832, after a summer of resistance, more than two hundred of Black Hawk's relatives, including many women, children, and Elders, were shot along and in the waters of the Mississippi as they attempted to cross back into unceded land.

After the government forced the Sauk and Meskwaki out of Illinois, speculators moved in. Historian Regena Schantz writes that developers were eager to acquire the whole wedge of land between the Rock and Mississippi Rivers on which Saukenuk had stood: "an entire peninsula . . . perfect for industry."[15] Lumber companies, coal mine prospectors, and grist mill operators set up, many of them squatting on the island, harvesting its trees and using its waterpower. Davenport,

Spencer, and other early white settlers began speculating with the lands they had acquired. After Davenport's death in 1845, his sons, George and Bailey, became bankers and landowners on both sides of the river. Bailey sunk coal mines uphill from Saukenuk at what is now called Black Hawk State Historic Site; the Denkmanns, Weyerhausers, Spencers, Mitchells, and Lyndes built industries, lumber mills, and banks. P. L. Cable, who with his friend Phil Mitchell invested in coal mines and eventually built up the legendary Rock Island Line, later gave a $25,000 gift for the construction of Augustana's Old Main; rumored to be a Confederate sympathizer, Cable had four Black servants whom he reputedly purchased in Kentucky before moving to Illinois, where he freed them.[16]

As for the part of section 36 of township 18N, where the north half of Augustana's campus is now, much of it was sold at the Public Lands Office at Galena in 1836 to several US military veterans, many of whom were early settlers and likely had trade dealings with Sauk and Meskwaki people: Henry McNeil [McNeal], William Lathrop, and Joel and David Thompson, all of whom fought in the Black Hawk War, and Samuel Burtis, likely a veteran of the War of 1812. McNeil and Joel Thompson were locals who signed an 1831 petition to the governor of Illinois to oust the Sauks and Meskwakis; both mustered into the militia unit known as the "Rock River Rangers" at Fort Armstrong in June of 1832, along with many others who had occupied Saukenuk and its surroundings several years earlier. McNeil later married squatter Rinnah Wells's daughter. Lathrop and David Thompson mustered into the militia up the Rock River at Hennepin, Illinois. On March 11 and March 25, 1836, respectively, Burtis and David Thompson bought, for $1.25 per acre, just over fifty acres each of the east half of the southeast fraction of section 36 lying north of the Indian Boundary Line. The federal government received $127.60 for the acreage on which Augustana now stands; that year, as part of President Andrew Jackson's effort to pay down the national debt, sales of public lands wrested from Native nations accounted for 48 percent of US government earnings.[17]

When Burtis died four years later, he no longer owned the land. He and two of his sons had purchased multiple tracts in the area, and David Thompson lived in nearby Henry County. Despite having family in the area, all of the men likely purchased the land for profit rather than to settle there.[18] At some point, the fraction lying north of the Boundary Line passed into the hands of Henry Palmer Hull, vice president of the Rock Island Savings Bank, whose obituary described him as "a capitalist and one of the most well-to-do citizens of the city."[19] At the time of his death, he owned lucrative stock in the bank, the Rock Island Plow Company, and the Tri-City Railway Company, among others.[20] In 1871, the Augustana board of directors' Real Estate Committee began to consider how its land investments in Paxton, Illinois, might fund a move to Rock Island. Two years later, the board bought nineteen acres of this land—considered "very cheap" at $10,000—from Hull and called it Zion Hill, a name that marked the end of their unsettled, immigrant wanderings.[21]

Thus, the land on which Augustana stands was acquired through a combination of coercion, debt-inducing trade relations, violence, confiscation of nature's resources, federal land sales, and speculation. In the process, the homes, farms, and hunting grounds of the Sauk, Meskwaki, Potawatomi, Ojibwa, and Ottawa people were transformed from places to live, dense with plant and animal relatives, into property to sell. In this respect, the history of the piece of Illinois on which the campus was built is not unlike that of most institutions on American soil. But the very commonality of this story should give us pause. The Indian Boundary Line, far from making Augustana special, weaves the campus into a national story, a network of boundary lines, each with its own history of conquest, co-optation, and removal. When it dedicated the Boundary Line marker in 1941, the Historical Society may have wished to pin this place to a grander, more national story of progress through democratic treaty-making. Today, we might define this history as settler-colonialist. But to do that alone is to gloss over the particular nature of relationships between neighbors: the shifting and negotiating of agreements and alliances that were tribally specific and sometimes surprisingly personal. Merely shifting from a triumphal narrative to a rueful one incorporates the Augustana story into a narrative that is more contrite but is no less generically American. And for some decades, the Swedes who founded Augustana did not consider themselves to be part of those American stories at all.

MOVING TOWARD MISSION

The founders of the Augustana Synod immigrated to the Midwest during the years when Native land dispossession opened the doors to white settlement and when the nation's investment in slavery was driving the country toward war. Swedish immigrants thus found themselves encountering questions about what their nationality and their faith required of them with respect to neighbor-love, particularly in relation to Black and Native people. For some immigrants, this neighborliness was geographic, as northern Europeans moved into lands that were still occupied by Native nations. For others, neighbor-love took the form of mission work. Between 1850 and 1900, Augustana worked to define its location geographically, in order to serve Swedish immigrant communities, but also to locate itself in the landscape of American Protestant religion, which was increasingly embracing mission work. While many Midwestern Swedes attempted to hold themselves apart from the twin evils of slavery and continental conquest, the college struggled to find a balance between cultivating a sense of mission and the moral entanglements that fervent faith required in that time and place. The experiences of the college's first "American" professor, Andrew Woods Williamson, who grew up on a mission serving the Dakota people, reflect the tensions implicit in nineteenth-century missionary idealism.

Swedes contemplating a move to the Midwest in the nineteenth century almost certainly would have known of their countrywoman Fredrika Bremer's popular account of her travels there in 1850. Setting out from Chicago to view the rolling prairies to the west, she exulted in what she saw as a landscape of vast possibility: "The sun-bright soil remained here still in its primeval greatness and magnificence, unchecked by human hands, covered with its flowers, protected and watched alone by the eye of the sun." Illinois was a land of industrious and generally agreeable farmers, though Chicago seemed to her to be made up primarily of people who were there to "make money and not to live." The Swedes she met in Chicago, including the pastor of the Swedish Episcopalian congregation there, Gustav Unonius, had endured great hardships and had worked hard to overcome them, and the pale, blue-eyed Swedish and Norwegian children who had gathered in his church for schooling were "for the most part children of persons in low circumstances." Though Bremer stayed with Juliette and John Kinzie, who had both been deeply enmeshed in the Midwest fur trade (John served as agent to the Ho-Chunk people in the aftermath of the 1829 war), she viewed relations between Native people and whites as remnants of a romantic past, as "beautiful drama" that needed to be recorded before it was forgotten.[22]

Historian Gunlög Fur suggests that Bremer's views represent those of other nineteenth-century Swedish immigrants who distanced themselves from the "abhorrent practices of the Anglo-American race" toward Native and enslaved peoples. Indeed, the founders of Augustana were pushing back against the "americanism" and "nationalism" of frontier states like Illinois in order to distance Swedish identity from these American moral horrors: for instance, Lars Paul Esbjörn's decision, in 1860, to open Augustana Seminary in Chicago was prompted in part by his frustration with Swedes like Unonius, an Episcopalian, who were willing to affiliate with a church that tolerated slavery and with the religiously expansive American revival movement (Fig. 1.2). Facing the diversity of Protestant groups in the United States, the Augustana Swedes became more theologically conservative than they had been at home, breaking from the "New Lutherans" to create the Augustana Synod even as the nation began to split in two over slavery.[23] When the Civil War erupted a year later, the seminary's pool of students shrank, and leaders began to contemplate planting a rural "colony" to host the seminary and anchor a Swedish community. Though Esbjörn found this plan troublingly "American," in 1863, Augustana College bought land in Paxton, Illinois, on those open, rolling prairies that Bremer had extolled. Maria Erling underscores that the move to Paxton was motivated by financial stress, referring to this time as one of "speculative ventures in land holding and colony building."[24] While the Augustana founders may have wanted to distance themselves from the New Lutherans in Chicago, the move to "open land" came precisely at a time when Swedish immigrants were reeling from the violent repercussions of settling on other nations' homelands.

Just before the move to Paxton, the Synod was shaken by an event that had a deep impact on Midwestern Scandinavians. In the US-Dakota

Fig. 1.2. Augustana at Wells and Superior Streets, Chicago, circa 1860. From *After Seventy Years.* Rock Island, IL: Augustana College and Theological Seminary, 1931. Courtesy of Augustana College Special Collections, Rock Island, Illinois.

War of the summer of 1862, Swedish, Norwegian, and German settlers in southern Minnesota bore the brunt of the Dakota people's violent retaliation against federal policies that made them dependent on stingy government handouts. The nation was shocked, regarding these settlers as innocent victims of Native neighbors who had inexplicably turned against them. More sympathetic Swedes like Eric Norelius of the Augustana Synod, who chastised Christians for not treating Native people better, still appealed to the myth of innocent pioneers and ignorant "heathens," noting that the Indians did not "know any better."[25] The move to Paxton occurred the same year that those Dakota men who had not been executed were incarcerated at a prison camp in Davenport, Iowa, across the Mississippi from Rock Island. Their families were exiled to South Dakota and, later, Nebraska.

Moving to a rural area likely fit with the college's desire to cultivate a traditional Swedish Lutheran church in America that was distinct from Protestant denominations with historical ties to slavery and colonization; it also moved the seminarians farther from a growing movement toward "foreign" mission work that was centered in Chicago. After the Civil War, the Synod grew more receptive to the idea of religious outreach, concentrating mostly on "home" or "inner" missions: work among newly arrived Scandinavians. But in 1874, just as Augustana was resettling in Rock Island, the Synod's mission committee began to discuss outreach to American Indians, and five years later, Augustana graduate Matthias Wahlstrom was sent to Anadarko, Oklahoma, charged with setting up a mission to the Comanche. It was a failure in every way: the young pastor was beset by illness, hostile white settlers, fear of Indians, and weak financial and spiritual support from the Synod. His attempt lasted less than a year. Erling reads this brief foray as a sign of broader conflict between idealistic, mission-oriented revivalism and ethnic conservatism but also as a strategic move into missions that was less about the salvation of souls than an attempt to institutionalize mission work in competition with American Protestant denominations.[26]

In 1880, the same year that Wahlstrom abandoned mission work to teach at another Augustana Synod college, Gustavus Adolphus, Augustana hired the man remembered as the college's first "American" professor, Andrew Woods Williamson, whose body and mind were marked by the tragedies that grew out of the nation's commitments to colonization and slavery. The son of Virginia slave owners turned abolitionist missionaries, Williamson was born at his parents' Presbyterian mission on the shores of Lac qui Parle (Lake that Speaks), Minnesota, in 1838. While he must have spoken Dakota fluently, he could not speak Swedish at all.[27] Neither Swedish nor Lutheran and steeped in "foreign" mission work, Williamson's history of radical outreach was part of his American identity as well.

Williamson came to Augustana from Gustavus Adolphus College, which had relocated to St. Peter, Minnesota, in 1876, a decade after that community had been shocked by the nearby Dakota uprising. Courted by "Americans" in St. Peter, Gustavus aspired to open its doors to English speakers.[28] But that goal could not compromise its Lutheranism. When Williamson began in 1877, one of three faculty, his Americanness likely enhanced the academy's ability to serve a more diverse (non-Swedish) population. A mathematician and physicist, Williamson was a deeply pious man who conducted prayer at the college in English, worked to learn more about Lutheranism, and saw his teaching as a call from God. He was willing to convert, but there was no English-speaking Lutheran church in St. Peter. The board of trustees was not content with willingness. It was one thing to be American—and in Williamson's case, the product of family histories that linked him to both slavery and land dispossession—but quite another not to be Lutheran. In an effort to preserve its ethno-religious identity in the face of americanizing influences, the board of trustees declared in 1880 that all faculty needed to be members of the Lutheran Church. Gustavus's President Jonas Nyquist was nonplussed: not only was he losing a dedicated teacher, but he had also hoped that by retaining Williamson, he might "not only get the house full of students, but also a lot of Americans." Retaining Williamson and hiring a Lutheran American would bring in additional tuition dollars, Nyquist told the board, suggesting a bit of civil disobedience in the name of diversity. If just a few members were willing to "break the law," he reasoned, it would benefit the college.[29]

Augustana must have been more open to the idea of noncompliance, or perhaps it saw a professor with a missionary background as in keeping with institutional ideals. In 1880, Williamson joined the Augustana faculty and, not long after, converted to Lutheranism and became a founding member of the English-speaking Grace Lutheran Church in Moline. His conversion and commitment to worshiping in his own language may have been shaped by his parents' decades-long efforts to convert the Dakota by translating the Bible into their language. Williamson would have had ample opportunity to be reminded of these efforts, for not two decades earlier, his father had moved to Davenport, Iowa, to convert the Dakota prisoners who were interned there from 1863 to 1866. For them, conversion was likely motivated by trauma and by their relations with one another and with Williamson's father.[30]

Williamson's parents, Margaret and Thomas Williamson, had lived with and worked among the Sisseton-Wahpeton bands of Dakota since the 1830s. When the Civil War began in 1861, Andrew Williamson joined the Union Army. He was assigned to Fort Ridgely, not far from his old home in southern Minnesota, possibly because he could speak the language of the eastern Santee Dakota, who, because the US government had broken its treaty, were starving and restless. In the summer of 1862, their frustration ignited in violence against those immigrant settlers with whom many had shared food and neighborly relations. Fed-up young Dakota men turned their anger first against the Broberg and Lundborg families—new immigrants from Västergötland—and others followed their lead, heading to Fort Ridgely to seize supplies. Williamson helped defend the fort and was there a few weeks later when hundreds of Dakota men, including a few Sisseton-Wahpeton, possibly Williamson's childhood companions, were marched to Mankato. Thirty-eight were executed there in the nation's largest mass hanging. The rest were sentenced to internment at Camp Kearny within Davenport's Camp McClellan. Williamson's family followed them there, conducting Bible studies among the shackled men until the missionaries were banished from the camp for allegedly absolving prisoners of guilt.[31]

Williamson, the Dakota people, and the nation were all broken by the war. After his Minnesota service, Williamson served as a second lieutenant for one of the newly mustered Black regiments, the 71st Colored Infantry, created at Natchez, Mississippi. In the 1850s, when abolitionism was far more radical than mere antislavery, he had attended the abolitionist colleges Knox and Marietta. By war's end, he was blind in one eye from a head injury and had been laid low by "swamp fever" (probably cerebral malaria), which left him with permanent neurological disabilities that resulted in some erratic behaviors. At Augustana, Williamson was known as "kind and queer," living alone at the edge of campus, talking to himself, and carrying a pocketful of peanuts for snacking. Some students speculated that he was odd because he had never married, while others may have wondered at a professor who, unlike their Swedish professors, had "grown up among Indians."[32]

Though he taught math and physics, Williamson was broadly trained in languages and humanistic inquiry.[33] Two years after his arrival at Augustana, Williamson published "The Dakotan Languages, and Their Relations to Other Languages," a meticulous study of the linguistic structure of the four branches of Dakota. The object of the article was to compare the Dakotan languages to Indo-European tongues and to find them related; it was a search for common linguistic roots, what he called "radical words." His analysis indicated that the "Dakotas did not separate from the Teutonic family till long after the latter separated from the South European family. The fact that the Dakota resembles the Icelandic and Gothic in vocabulary and in structure much more than it resembles the older Latin, points in the same direction."[34] Williamson's structural analysis reflected his scientific approach but, at the same time, hinted at a desire to find a close basis for a relationship with the Dakota people, a yearning, almost, to demonstrate the ways that they were "like white people"—sharing ancestry with the Teutonic, Icelandic, and Gothic peoples. His investigation suggested that Williamson sought common roots in order to establish connections that transcended cultural differences.

So too with Christianity. For Williamson, as for many Americans involved in nineteenth-century missions, the Christian God was both the common root and the universal to which all people could and should have access; those who had lost their way could be saved if shown the path. Conversion involved struggle, and Williamson's childhood was marked by his parents' dogged attempts to bring the Dakota into the fold and the equally persistent resolution of the Dakota to retain their culture, religion, and agricultural practices. Thomas Williamson and his partner, Stephen Riggs, were somewhat remarkable for their effort not only to learn Dakota but also to create a written language for translating hymns and the Bible. If their methods were particular, though, their belief in Christianity as universal underlay all of their endeavors, as it did for many American Christians hoping to heal the nation's wounds. This sort of universalism may have served as Williamson's justification for converting to Lutheranism after growing up immersed in a radical branch of Presbyterianism. Perhaps Williamson found that the common roots of Protestantism allowed him to find a home in a Lutheran community. Perhaps like his father, he believed that new conditions necessitated accommodation: if the seeming inevitability of Euro-American settlement required the Dakota to lose their tribal identity and accept the Christian faith to become part of the whole, what should prevent a Presbyterian in a Lutheran community from altering his faith accordingly?

Williamson likely knew enough about Indigenous people to understand that survival requires mutually sustaining relationships. He had intimate knowledge of the Dakota prisoners' conversion. Perhaps desperate for community in the midst of sickness, death, and crippling separation from kin, they, like Williamson, may have found solace in Bible study in their own language. Many survivors learned to read and write in captivity, using their new skills to communicate with loved ones. Sara-Eva Carlson speculates that their conversion may even have been a form of negotiation with their missionary: to convert was to form a relationship that allowed them to leverage his assistance.[35] During their years of incarceration, Thomas Williamson traveled to Washington to entreat Lincoln and then President Johnson to commute the sentences of the remaining prisoners, the last of whom was freed in 1866.

Andrew Williamson was mission-focused his whole life. While he did not follow his father's and brother's path as missionaries, he continued to speak about foreign mission work on campus and support the americanization of the Lutheran church in the community, working with others to turn his English-speaking church into "a mighty power, influence and example within the Synod."[36] He seems to have been able to sustain his idealism in spite of knowing that conviction can lead to war. Raised in the midst of ideological conflict, Williamson witnessed firsthand the horror of war fought over deeply clashing worldviews. Louis Menand, writing of the broken optimism of abolitionist-turned-soldier Oliver Wendell Holmes Jr., explains that the Civil War convinced the future Supreme Court justice that when societies "take up arms to impose their conception of civility on others, they sacrifice their moral advantage." Violence in the name of morality, Holmes concluded, was "slavery's twin."[37]

Between 1860 and Williamson's death in 1906, Augustana was attempting to negotiate the implications of being a school for immigrants to a nation that was struggling with the moral stains of slavery and colonization. Doubling down on Swedish Lutheran identity preserved a sense of innocence, even as these immigrants attempted to set up colonies in order to root their faith and institutions in a new land. Williamson's arrival at Augustana coincided with the Synod's attempts to endorse foreign mission work as an institutional orientation, rather than as a radical pursuit to save the souls of Native Americans, and more broadly with the tricky question of what it meant to be an "American" college. After his death, Augustana students paid tribute to him by noting that "we are slowly changing from being a Swedish-Lutheran to an American church. . . . It was well that we had this American at such a prominent place among us at the very beginning of this change going on with us. If we have much of the Williamson character in our synod, we need not fear Americanization." Yet students and colleagues also recalled that Williamson, as a man who sacrificed much to live his Christian life, had "never married" and "had no home of his own": "For the support of church, of mission, of Sunday schools and of poor students he spent most all of his income, without asking for reward in this life."[38] Like the Dakota he was raised among, he gave freely of all he had to his neighbors.

Yet as the kind and quirky professor walked the campus with his pockets full of peanuts, a tendency toward abstract thinking, and his wounded body, he may have reminded students, the children of immigrants, of the marriage between violence and idealism in the Americanness they themselves may have been drawn toward. Remaining conservative in its theology spared the college from the conquest of Indigenous souls that is part of some denominations' pasts. But it also may have contributed to an ethnic insularity that made it more difficult to understand how to share common ground with Native nations.

In 1886, Williamson, perhaps grateful for the acceptance that Augustana had extended to him, donated to the college a six-acre parcel of land. That land, on which student dormitories stand, runs along both sides of the wooded ravine now filled by the Slough. Its northern border is the Indian Boundary Line.[39] While the founders purchased the portion of the campus that had been, until 1829, unceded land, it was Williamson who helped the campus expand its footprint into "American" territory.

"WE TALK, YOU LISTEN"

About a century after the college's founding, Vine Deloria Jr. arrived on Zion Hill to begin his course of study at the Augustana Seminary. Like Williamson, he was the son of a missionary to the Dakota people. Unlike Williamson, the new seminarian *was* Dakota. He was born among the Yankton Dakota near the Standing Rock reservation, where the US government sent them in 1858. His choice to attend the seminary was rather unplanned: he had headed west with his new wife to begin graduate school in Washington state but discovered that he did not have enough funds to enroll. He may have contacted Augustana, where his wife's parents had attended school in the 1930s; they must have offered good terms, because the young couple turned around, headed back to the Midwest, and moved in with his wife's Swedish grandmother at her home in Moline, just a mile or so east of campus. He attended seminary by day and earned a living as a welder in the evening hours.[40]

Deloria Jr. was the great-grandson of Tipi Sapa (Philip Deloria), an Episcopalian minister born in 1853, who is recognized as the first Native missionary to his own people in the United States. His grandson, Deloria's father, worked for years as a minister, first in South Dakota and later at a predominantly white church in Iowa. Active in the Episcopal Church as a young man, Deloria Jr. intended to follow in his father's and grandfather's footsteps in becoming a minister. But at some point during his time at the Augustana Seminary, he began to see his commitment to American Indian sovereignty and self-determination as incommensurable with Christianity. He would later recall his time in Rock Island as crucial to his burgeoning disillusionment: "For me, at least, Christianity has been a sham to cover the white man's shortcomings. Yet I spent four years in a seminary finding out for myself where Christianity had fallen short."[41] After graduating from the seminary in 1962, he was elected director of the National Congress of American Indians (NCAI); in 1967, he published *Custer Died for Your Sins*, one of the best-known books by a Native American author. It excoriated the missionary enterprise, defining its focus on redemption as a mechanism for ignoring past and present violence, and it advocated a return to Indigenous religion as a way to reclaim Indigenous sovereignty. Deloria went on to become a lawyer, scholar, prolific writer, American Indian civil rights leader, and the widely recognized founder of American Indian studies. In 1974, *Time* magazine named him a "Theological Superstar of the Future," an honor that amused him and befuddled others.[42]

Certainly, Deloria did not need the Boundary Line marker to remind him of the federal government's abysmal failure to uphold its end of treaty agreements. In *Custer Died for Your Sins*, he stresses the importance of treaties in establishing boundary lines but not in marking settler ownership. Instead, treaties validate the Indian title to land and, by association, the Indian identity, culture, and beliefs that are forged in relation with that land. Perhaps he *was* thinking of the marker when he cited treaties with the Three Fires Confederacy and the 1804 treaty with the Sauk and Meskwaki as explicit expressions of the government's agreement with Native nations. In 1789, just after claiming these nations' homelands as part of the Northwest Territory, the government confirmed the boundary between ceded and unceded lands as "a division line between the lands of the United States of America, and the lands of said nations, forever . . . to live and hunt upon, and otherwise to occupy as they shall see fit." Fifteen years later, the US government promised it would "never interrupt the said tribes in the possession of the lands which they rightfully claim, but will on the contrary protect them in the quiet enjoyment of the same."[43] Treaties were covenants, in which Native nations agreed to allow white settlement on some of their lands in order to live in harmony with newcomers and to engage in their cultural practices free from interference. But by the mid-nineteenth century, the US government had abandoned such agreements between equals, substituting "race" for "nation" and then redefining members of Native nations as "uncivilized races" in need of political and economic incorporation through the violent disciplining of bodies, minds, souls, and lands. The tragedy of Dakota internment was only one of many disastrous outcomes of this policy.

Termination was another. When Deloria arrived at Augustana Seminary, federal policy had shifted, riding the wave of post–World War II americanization of various ethnic minorities to enact "Termination" policies. These were strategies to end federal recognition of Native nations, to give states jurisdiction over tribal lands and citizens, and to sever individuals from their cultures and lands by relocating them to urban areas where they would, the government hoped, have no choice but to be absorbed into the American mainstream. Like missionaries, government agencies and officials defined "inclusion" as a public good; likewise, inclusion did not require mainstream American culture to change as a result. Indigenous activism grew in response to these policies. Ironically, the political frustration of Indigenous veterans, especially, was amplified by the very relocation that the government hoped would destroy sovereignty. Members of diverse nations in cities such as Minneapolis, Chicago, and Oakland began to collectively organize and resist. Even before better-known events such as the seizure of Alcatraz Island in 1969 and the armed resistance at Wounded Knee in 1973, members of NCAI met in Chicago in June 1961 to draft the "Declaration of Indian Purpose" that insisted on their "right to choose [their] way of life" and laid out proposals on health, housing, education, and their rights to land and natural resources that called on the federal government to honor treaties.[44] This conference reinvigorated NCAI, which had been founded in 1944, and as its executive director from 1964 to 1967, Deloria helped to expand the national membership and to advance the cause of tribal sovereignty before the federal government.

A decade after completing his course of study at Augustana Seminary, Deloria returned to the Rock Island campus, this time as the speaker at the May 30, 1971, commencement ceremony (Fig. 1.3). In addition to his NCAI service, he had published two books, *Custer Died for Your Sins* (1969) and *We Talk, You Listen* (1970), and had earned a law degree from the University of Colorado.[45] Deloria graciously accepted the invitation to attend graduation, to receive an honorary degree, and to give the commencement speech. In his address, titled "The System Today," he warned students that the "system"—the social, political, and economic frameworks that produce relationships between individuals and groups—"does not automatically produce justice. Only active intelligent citizens produce justice." A summary of the speech published in the local paper described Deloria's reference to political interest groups, in which he noted that "the cry has gone out that any meaningful progress depends on a destruction of the present system of government and its replacement with a more humane system in which war, racism, poverty and disease do not exist." Deloria's next sentence, however, is almost lost in a review that stressed students' ability to "change the system": he cautioned his audience that the cry to destroy the system reflected "an idealism so abstract as to render it meaningless."[46]

This sentiment was at the heart of his recently published book *We Talk, You Listen*. In it, he lobbed a powerful critique at almost every activist group of the civil rights era—women's liberationists, Black

Fig. 1.3. Vine Deloria Jr. speaking at commencement, 1971. Augustana College Photograph Collection, C-F04374. Courtesy of Augustana College Special Collections, Rock Island, Illinois.

nationalists, war hawks, antiwar protesters—for creating an unwinnable "war of ideas" in which "non-tribals" used abstract ideals to justify their actions in the name of progress. Even religion, as he discovered in seminary, was part of the fray, in which "religious sensitivity is expressed as rigorous adherence to the values of racial and ethnic groups—secularization of religious feeling in political action." Each of these groups, he argued, was protesting the system in service of an ideal that, if universalized and politicized as these groups desired, would become profoundly disconnected from experience, place, and community. Identity and experience are not abstract, he maintained. Instead, they are history-, culture-, and place-specific, and spiritual beliefs and expressions must emerge from and sustain those relationships if they are to mean anything at all. Deloria suggested that a solution might be a reinvestment in what he called "tribalism": a conservative commitment to deeply rooted cultural practices that rely on communal decision-making and resource-sharing, often place-based, in ways that foster the survival of the community. Rather than imposing these practices on their neighbors, communities could find common cause by finding points of connection—"tangent lines" where the needs of one community align with the needs of others.[47]

Deloria's proposal reads like a community-based version of the definition of vocation widely recognized among Lutheran institutions, created by Frederick Buechner in 1973, which has its own version of specificity: "The place God calls you to is the place where your deep gladness and the world's deep hunger meet."[48] Deloria was skeptical of the term *vocation*, which in his experience required learning existing knowledge rather than exploring timely questions that emerged from what was *not* yet known. Deloria's "tribalist" version clarifies that the world's "deep hunger" is a product of ever-changing circumstances, and "deep gladness" is deep, not because it stretches up and out toward an abstract ideal, but because it is deeply rooted in the experience of relationality. We are not called to conquer the world in our efforts to find locations to do good work. To find points of intersection, we are called to recognize and respect the sovereignty of communities with whom we might not share common identities but with whom we should seek common cause. This is sovereignty: not of individuals but of communities empowered to cultivate thriving lives for themselves and their neighbors through respectful negotiation, where value is not something to be calculated or added but to be sought out, kept, and cultivated.

Here we might consider not only Deloria but also his wife, Barbara Nystrom, as a product of this place on the Indian Boundary Line. Her parents' home was not a mile from the former internment camp in a neighborhood still called McClellan Heights after the Civil War–era camp. She was a librarian like her mother, Mildred, the daughter of German immigrants, who attended Augustana in the 1930s and who married fellow student Eugene Nystrom, the son of Swedish immigrants to Moline. When Deloria spoke at graduation, he and his wife stayed with Mildred, who attended as well.[49] The Delorias' son Phil Deloria credits his mother with saving a box full of drawings created by his great-aunt, Mary Sully, a self-taught early twentieth-century artist whose work articulates modern ideas using Indigenous designs. Of his mother, Phil Deloria writes, she "was the daughter of a librarian . . . born with a commitment to saving and storing things. She looked through the drawings—over one hundred of the three-part images—and tried to make sense of them. She failed but decided that she liked them anyway."[50] Barbara Nystrom Deloria, her son suggests, responded according to her vocational tendency to preserve and record but stopped short of imposing meaning. In the same way, perhaps, she had acted as her husband's editor and manager, helping to communicate ideas outside her experience. Phil Deloria's description of his mother as the "quiet guardian of Mary Sully's legacy" imagines her act of saving those materials as holding on to a mystery, believing in the value of something that she herself was not equipped to understand.[51]

WALKING THE WORLD

While the English word *treaty* as a political negotiation developed first, a second use later emerged—to treat as to heal. Indigenous leaders remind us that their ancestors and relatives signed treaties and exchanged wampum belts in attempts to restore balance in response to changing conditions. When American Indians refer to the breaking of treaties, then, they are not always arguing that those treaties were never valid (though some were not) but may be referring to the failure of the federal government to uphold its part of the agreement. This generally includes obligations to provide appropriate education, health care, and housing; to support tribal nations in their management of water, timber, and other resources; and to guarantee the rights of those nations to practice sustainable forms of agriculture and harvesting of animal life. Settler societies and their governments felt justified in breaking these treaties because they elevated universals—Christianity, resource extraction, and the accumulation of wealth by individuals—above site-specific relationships that emerge from mutual need in the face of changing conditions. In its relations with tribal nations, the US government was generally motivated by abstract notions of "the good"—individualism, the progressive flow of time, a God unattached to time or place. The Boundary Line marker, especially when regarded together with other such markers in the Midwest and elsewhere, performs a similar function, pinning the site of the college to the abstract goals it references: ownership, expansion, the forward march of "civilization." But as a monument to a treaty-signing, it also represents a set of obligations that, though broken, might be repaired. Despite their histories of land dispossession and the rigid systems that have long structured Western education, institutions of higher learning are well situated to consider how to shed certainty for the generative experience of encountering the stranger.

In grappling with the legacy and ongoing destructiveness of colonial priorities, institutions may begin by asking how well their missions have served them in confronting what Deloria Jr. called the "brutal problems of everyday life." The faith of Augustana's founders led them to immigrate, seeking places where Swedish Lutheran communities could thrive while rightly resisting the deep moral failings of the American system of government land seizures and slave labor. Yet the places where Augustana (like so many other colleges in the United States) planted and cultivated those new communities were and are marked by violent histories in ways that the land, and those displaced from it, cannot forget. The outwardly directed, missionizing spirit, which thrived among Protestant churches in the United States, led the Augustana Synod, and the college, to test out a new role for itself. In immigrating to a nation deeply divided by race and committed to individuality and profit, Swedish Lutherans were compelled to shed some of their own communal values in order to navigate a new place.[52] But the project of extending its faith to neighbors who neither asked for nor required it was a failure. Mission, as an institutional strategy, required neither humility nor openness to change, and for Wahlstrom as for Williamson, their radical faith impeded other communities' capacities to flourish.

If we listen to the voices of Indigenous theorists (and I include among these both academic theorists and the activists and knowledge-holders who have been generous enough to share that knowledge with outsiders), they will help us to see that the Euro-American way of seeing land as commodity, and history as something to commemorate, can blind us to the living and evolving story-archive of the places where we have established ourselves. Augustana College, as many others, has inherited an educational practice of filtering out ways of knowing and living that are deemed unscholarly or unprofitable. There is a reason that education was paired with private property ownership in the US government's assimilation policy: the educational system stresses acquisition and profit, examination and control. In their fascinating study of the co-evolution of forms of writing such as mapmaking, accounting, and education, Hoskin and MacVe note that these ways of recording information result in a form of "human bookkeeping" that prepares students to bend to forms of abstract control (the distant but powerful CEO who rules through mass emails and productivity reports, for example) and moves them ever farther away from embodied, relational, and respectful ways of knowing.[53]

For institutions oriented toward whiteness (regardless of the race, ethnicity, or nationality of their students), the hurdles to unsettling approaches to education are significant. Westerners generally regard educational achievements as unconnected to place—plants, animals, geographic features, and even human groups can be "objects of study" rather than teachers with wisdom to share. Most educational institutions likewise have ethical barriers to co-opting Indigenous ways of knowing just as we have already incorporated their lands and waters. Teachers cannot simply adopt Indigenous knowledge and experience by writing them into the syllabus. Reincorporating these forms of knowledge has been difficult even for Indigenous people, especially given that colonization resulted not only in violence and land dispossession but also in cultural dispossession and genocide through residential schooling, relocation and urbanization, and blood quantum policies. Leanne Betasamosake Simpson, a Michi Saagiig Nishnaabeg teacher-activist, writes of her own struggle to shift from academic knowledge-seeking to "Nishnaabeg intelligence" by learning from Elders: "I kept asking them about governance, and they would talk about trapping. I would ask them about treaties, and they would take me fishing. . . . I could see only *practice*. I couldn't see their *theory* until decades later. I couldn't see intelligence until I learned *how* to see it by engaging in Nishnaabeg practices for the next two decades."[54]

Simpson concludes that Indigenous knowledge cannot exist within settler spaces, including institutions of higher learning. What she calls a project of "radical resurgence" means refusing settler ways of knowing, using, and controlling; a return, for Indigenous people, to ways of being and acting that can function as a "doorway" leading from the "enclosure of settler colonialism and into Indigenous worlds."[55] For Potawatomi writer and biologist Robin Wall Kimmerer, author of *Braiding Sweetgrass*, these ways of knowing might coexist, but only when we stop relying on controlling plants and animals and instead center our relationships with them, asking questions that enrich human and nonhuman inhabitants. Both writers use Anishinaabeg origin stories as touchstones, not for a sense of certainty, but to describe a way of being in the world that centers change, adaptation, and renewal. Skywoman, for Kimmerer, provides us with a set of guidelines for reciprocity with our natural world: falling into this world from another, pregnant and alone but with her pockets full of seeds, Skywoman proceeded to ensure flourishing not just for herself but also for the future of the world into which she had fallen.[56]

Kimmerer describes Skywoman and her progeny, the human residents on Turtle Island, as "immigrants" who managed to establish "indigenous" relations with the world through their commitment to relations of respect and reciprocity with the plant and animal nations already living there. Simpson explains that Nanabush (or Nanabozho), sometimes described as a "trickster figure" but whom Simpson regards as "our first intellectual" and "first researcher," is a model for "walking the world through a 'liberal lens.'" Nanabush walked through the world twice, first to talk to, share with, and understand the lives, experiences, and practices of all beings in the world—not to conquer them but to generate new knowledge and ceremony: a "collective consciousness" of a wider world. Then Nanabush did it again, this time with Wolf as their companion, and the knowledge gained in companionship with another Being was different. Simpson calls the resulting—and ongoing—practice "Nishnaabeg internationalism," that is, a way of being in the world that recognizes the place we are as not only our home but as the home, as well, of other beings whose knowledge, behaviors, and ethics we are bound to understand and respect.[57]

Like Simpson, I am skeptical that any nonindigenous institution of higher learning can authentically or ethically claim Indigenous wisdom. But I resist the common alternative—the settler alternative—which is to ignore and exclude our neighbors' histories and knowledges if we cannot claim or mark them like artifacts in a cabinet of curiosities. I also resist the universality of settler values, which are, in the long march of time, recent creations that mark a radical departure from even traditional Western ideas of what constitutes a thriving society. What might it mean to stand humbly but eagerly alongside uncolonized but neighboring intelligences? To acknowledge that we are travelers in a world not our own and are bound to respect it while we reside on this place? Most students who attend college stay for a fleeting few years, passing through on their way to some other place, tumbling from this world into another, prepared not with unchanging Certainty but with an idea of how to learn more and their pockets full of seeds. Might colleges and universities consider the geographic and temporal boundaries that frame student experience as tangent lines, where not only histories, but present realities, intersect with the many human and nonhuman neighboring nations with whom we are obligated to establish right relations?

The story of Nanabush, who travels the world with humility, openness, and curiosity, suggests that it is not only communities descended from immigrants who must embrace the experience of being guests in a strange and compelling land. Colleges and universities need not co-opt the story of Nanabush to amplify the educational narrative that we are all travelers seeking ways to survive in places we inhabit but do not own, and therefore we owe respect to and right treatment of our neighbors. We must take seriously our duty to walk the world, engaging in conversation with its human and nonhuman nations, and to create new ceremonies and new wisdom by learning with and from them. This is not to say that we should ignore, or be absolved of, the violence engendered by religious and capitalist forms of conquest. While many Indigenous people struggle to reconnect to and revive cultural traditions that were broken by years of conquest, those of us on the other side of the Indian Boundary Line should consider what in our own belief and value systems has been broken by the systems and values we continue to uphold when we fail to question or resist them. We should seek opportunities to "walk the world" both on campus and around the globe—as immigrants, as neighbors, as treaty-seekers—working to find ways for different communities to collaborate in our caring for place, even as they operate at different registers.

This chapter is an attempt at honest storytelling about who profited from past relationships with the land. Other institutions, including ECLA institutions, have moved on to action. In 2021, Lawrence University in Appleton, Wisconsin, worked with architect Chris Cornelius

(Oneida) and Indigenous students to install a large public artwork in a central location on campus. Called *Otāēciah* (Crane), it is meant to make Indigenous history and presence more visible. Gustavus Adolphus College in St. Peter, Minnesota, has formed a President's Council for Indigenous Relations, with the goal not only to build relationships with Dakota communities and educate students about Indigenous histories but also to "examine and reimagine institutional practices in response to Dakota relationships, partnerships, and research." Augsburg University offers a program in Indigenous studies; in addition to offering specialized services for American Indian students, it now offers an endowed scholarship for American Indian students, including those from out of state. St. Olaf College in Northfield, Minnesota, will begin offering financial aid through the St. Olaf Indigenous Student Affordability Commitment in 2025. This pledge, like Augsburg's, extends eligibility to children and grandchildren of enrolled tribal members, since blood quantum requirements for enrollment (the legacy of federal definitions of indigeneity) often exclude individuals of mixed tribal heritage.[58] Without measures like these, institutions, including Augustana, risk repeating the errors of treaty-makers of the past, merely marking a moment in history without committing to the acts necessary to sustain right relations.

In his short essay "A Good Day to Die," Deloria Jr. grapples grudgingly with the topic of vocation that he was asked to write about. Claiming that he found the Western idea of vocation too stodgy, he says it calls to mind the fixed pathway he associated negatively with his Augustana Seminary experience. For Deloria, encounter with the holy was the start of a mysterious journey, not a tidy conclusion to a course of study. Settling upon the image of Crazy Horse as the model of what it means to have a vocation, Deloria upends the idea of tradition and inflexible attachment to ideals that many Euro-Americans associate with Indigenous people. Deloria explains that the Oglala Lakota leader's battle cry, "It's a good day to die!," was not an exhortation to die for an existing creed but to courageously unsettle one's own identity in the course of living, "to ride into one's community with a challenge to its presuppositions, presuppositions which one cherishes and from which one's identity is received."[59] Such challenges need not be violent, for when it is created with honesty and a commitment to action, a treaty is a form of reconciliation.

Notes

1. "Illinois Historical Meetings Here Today," *Augustana Observer*, May 1, 1941; "Dedicate Boundary Marker on Augustana Campus," *Moline Daily Dispatch*, May 3, 1941; Barbara Smith, "Smith Discusses Democratic Way," *Moline Daily Dispatch*, May 3, 1941, 12. The topic of that year's conference was "American Democracy in Historical Perspective."

2. Deloria Jr., "Good Day to Die," 85–86.

3. Enrique Salmón defines *kincentric* as physical and spiritual integration with "life in all forms" that is maintained through language, ritual, and thought. "Kincentric Ecology," 1328.

4. For more on resistance to white settlement in Illinois following the War of 1812, see Jung, "American Indian Resistance."

5. The Sauks and Meskwakis allegedly relinquished their territory in Illinois at the 1804 Treaty of St. Louis. The Sauk leader Black Hawk disputed the government's understanding of this agreement in his 1832 autobiography, and Sauk and Meskwaki people have continued to authenticate this version of events. Ma-ka-tai-me-she-kia-kiak, *Life of Black Hawk*, 27–29; Ratified Indian Treaty 43.

6. Ratified Indian Treaty 82; Citizen Band of Potawatomi v. United States.

7. Davis, "The Indian Boundary Line," 37.

8. Jung, "Spirited Resistance."

9. Spencer, "Reminiscences," 11. White settlement at Saukenuk began just as Andrew Jackson, who campaigned in part on promises to open public lands to white settlement, was elected president, in November 1828.

10. Ma-ka-tai-me-she-kia-kiak, *Life of Black Hawk*, 85–93.

11. Illinois State Archives, "Illinois Public Land"; Spencer, "Reminiscences," 46.

12. Ma-ka-tai-me-she-kia-kiak, *Life of Black Hawk*, 94.

13. Armstrong, *Black Hawk War*, 144. Italics in original.

14. Brown, "They Don't Even," 66.

15. Schantz, *Trader*, 263.

16. In the US Census, James Dickinson is listed as an "old black servant" whose condition was "can't smile." Ellen Tsagaris, "The Cables," 4.

17. Illinois State Archives, "Illinois Public Land"; Anderson and Martin, "Public Domain," 905.

18. Burtis Sr., Will Records.

19. "Henry P. Hull, Old Resident, Answers Call," *Rock Island Argus*, December 17, 1919; Henry Hull Estate.

20. Schantz, *Trader*, 263.

21. Augustana College Board, "Record of Proceedings." Symbolic for Swedish Lutheran immigrants, the name Zion refers to Jerusalem throughout the Hebrew scriptures, the ultimate destination of the wilderness wanderings of the people of Israel (e.g., Psalm 2:6 "I have set my king on Zion, my holy hill"). Paxton, Illinois, lies on land acquired from the Potawatomi shortly after the Black Hawk War, in October 1832, as part of Jackson's Indian removal efforts.

22. Bremer, *Homes*, 604–13.

23. Fur, "Indians and Immigrants," 60; Bergendoff, *Profession of Faith*, 115–16. See also Nelson, "Unity, Ecumenicity, and Difference," and Forsberg et al., "Theological Pilgrimage."

24. Erling, "Wrestling," 135.

25. Quoted in Fur, "Immigrants and Indians," 64.

26. Erling, "Wrestling."

27. Sebelius, *Master Builders*, 97–104.

28. Lund, "Educational Experience,"17.

29. Lund, "Educational Experience," 30.

30. Carlson, "They Tell Their Story," 271.

31. Glewwe, "Life of a Legend."

32. Sebelius, *Master Builders*, 97.

33. Lund, "Educational Experiences," 19–21.

34. Williamson, "Dakotan Languages."

35. Carlson, "They Tell Their Story," 271.

36. Trinity Church, *Manual and Directory*.

37. Menand, *Metaphysical Club*, 45.

38. Tributes to Williamson.

39. Brolander, *Historical Survey*, 5.

40. Philip Deloria, interview with author, February 4, 2022; Deloria Jr., "Good Day," 84.

41. Deloria Jr., *Custer Died*, 124.

42. James Treat, in his introduction to the collected writings of Deloria Jr., *For This Land*, 1, notes that respected Lutheran theologian Martin A.

Marty suggested that the list of theologians included "token" members of various minority groups.

43. Deloria Jr., *Custer Died*, 36.

44. American Indian Chicago Conference, *Declaration.*

45. One Augustana administrator's notes on Deloria's accomplishments suggest that there may have been some concern—possibly on the part of the faculty or board—that his several degrees in different fields (a BS from Iowa State, an MDiv from Augustana Seminary, and a JD)—may have indicated some instability on his part. "At present [he] is a student," the notes read, with a parenthetical addendum that "this was a serious decision—he is in his forties [Deloria was thirty-eight]—realized that legal matters are of great importance in connection with his work with the Indian problems." Whether thinking of Deloria's being a student or an Indian, the writer was apparently compelled to add, "He is very stable—not immature at all." Untitled memo, Commencement 1969–71, 36, CWS.

46. "Augie Commencement: Today's System Said Not Wrong but How It Is Permitted to Run," *Rock Island Argus*, May 31, 1971.

47. Deloria Jr., *We Talk*, 18, 13. Perhaps recalling his time at Augustana and sharing a home with his Swedish-speaking relative, Deloria notes that "vestiges of sovereignty and tribalism" still exist among urban immigrant groups—Poles, Swedes, and Irish" (122).

48. Buechner, *Wishful Thinking*, 118.

49. Letter from Deloria to Sorensen, May 3, 1971, Commencement 1969–71, 36, CWS.

50. Deloria, *Becoming*, 7, 21.

51. Deloria, *Becoming*, vi.

52. I am grateful to Mark Safstrom, a fellow contributor to this volume, for this observation.

53. Hoskin and MacVe, "Accounting," 125–30.

54. Simpson, *As We Have Always Done*, 19.

55. Simpson, *As We Have Always Done*, 217.

56. Kimmerer, *Braiding Sweetgrass.*

57. Kimmerer, *Braiding Sweetgrass*, 3–10; Simpson, *As We Have Always Done*, 57–58.

58. Augsburg University, "American Indian Full Tuition"; Gustavus Adolphus College, "President's Council for Indigenous Relations"; Kat Dodge, "St. Olaf Announces."

59. Deloria Jr., "Good Day," 91.

SERVING STUDENTS AND NEIGHBORS
Community Implications of Campus Expansion

SARAH LASHLEY

Sonja Knudsen moved to her 34th Street home in Rock Island in 1975, a year after receiving tenure at Augustana College. Immediately after receiving tenure, she had taken a leave of absence to teach in Denmark for a year, she recalls. While she was away, a colleague notified her that the house was available and thought it would be of interest. She had bought the house unseen. When she first arrived home, she recalls being greeted by a giant sign reading, "Mid Campus Headquarters of PUG Fraternity," strung across the low-slung stucco house across the street. Over the subsequent years, that house and others in the neighborhood hosted a number of loud parties that left the yards strewn with litter. At times, the music was so loud that the floors of her home shook. Over time, Augustana College purchased and demolished a few of the nearby houses to make way for new campus facilities. She was not sad to see a couple of them go.

Of course, it was not all nuisance. Living so close to campus allowed Knudsen to get to know students. She recalls a student who asked permission to store his motorcycle in her garage. She obliged, and when the air conditioner unit fell out of her window, he replaced it for her. Furthermore, she was close to her campus office, which moved around before settling in Denkmann Hall. She was also surrounded by colleagues. Referring to the street as "faculty alley," she noted that colleagues from the Departments of English, Geology, Art, Speech, Music, Philosophy, History, and others filled the homes on the street at different times.

Over time, though, the neighborhood changed. Most faculty moved to other areas in the Quad Cities. While there are still other single-family homeowners in the neighborhood, there is not much sense of community among the residents. The college bought additional homes, transitioning some to student housing and demolishing others to make way for campus buildings and parking lots.

Today, the neighborhood is much quieter. She credits the college's housing policies and oversight with much of the change. She notes that a planter and a reflector have gone missing from her yard, most likely the result of student mischief, and students sometimes park in front of her driveway. She also notes that students cut across the street at the corner of 10th Avenue and 34th Street without looking for oncoming cars; she's even stopped students to remind them to be safe, but these issues are minor. Indeed, during the school year, she appreciates the bustle of activity, which helps to prevent feelings of isolation. These feelings were acute during the COVID-19 pandemic, when students left campus in a hurry and the neighborhood grew quiet, although she observed deer, foxes, and other wildlife taking their place.

Sonja is clear that she does not perceive an antagonistic relationship between neighbors and students of the college. Her story helps to elucidate how the relationships between Augustana College and the Rock Island community are reciprocal. The policies and practices of the college and its students influence the dynamics of the community. At the same time, neighbors near the college care for the safety and development of students as they transition to adulthood. They help to cultivate a sense of civic responsibility and neighborliness in students. This pattern of reciprocity highlights the deep interconnections between a campus and town. However, Sonja's story also acknowledges that the interconnections can produce tensions at times. Indeed, although there are no gates to campus, it may sometimes seem gated to those not affiliated with the college. She suggests that inviting neighbors to come to hear campus speakers or to events like the International Dinner could help them feel more welcome. Such invitations could encourage students to interact more with neighbors and, overall, provide more opportunities for all to get to know one another.

PURPOSE

Since the founding of the college's Rock Island campus in 1875, the student body has increased from approximately 85 to 2,500 students.[1] Correspondingly, the college acquired land to support this growth, culminating in the college's current 115-acre campus. As Sonja's story illustrates, though, the growth of Augustana's campus does not simply have implications for its students, faculty, and staff. It also has implications for the college's Rock Island neighbors, city functioning, and college relations with the city and its residents. The purpose of this chapter is to identify these implications, the tensions that arise from them, and the way our college balances serving its mission of offering a challenging education that develops the mind, spirit, and body with serving our city neighbors. Many of the viewpoints featured in this chapter come from interviews the author conducted with current and former college personnel, city leadership, and community members. In the spirit of neighborliness, the chapter asks how we can extend our circle of concern and attend to the needs of both campus and community.

As lessons from other studies of college and community relations have shown, this balance is uneasy. Like most colleges and universities, Augustana College is interested in supporting community-engaged student learning, campus safety, and overall student well-being, all of which rely on a thriving surrounding community. However, the experiences of Augustana College are rooted in our position as a small, residential college located in a post-industrial Midwestern city. The college does not possess the financial resources to unilaterally shape the surrounding community, nor is it located in a large urban center. Thus, while this chapter illustrates the uneasiness of college and community relationships that is common to these kinds of studies, it is also uniquely Augustana.

SITUATING THE COLLEGE

Augustana College

Founded in Chicago, Illinois, in 1860, Augustana College moved to Paxton, Illinois, before settling into its Rock Island location. The initial 18-3/4 acres upon which the college sits, bound by 7th Avenue on the north and the Indian Boundary Line on the south, and stretching from 35th Street on the west to 38th Street on the east, was purchased from H. P. Hull in 1873 (Fig. 2.1). The significance of the Indian Boundary Line to Augustana's campus is explored in chapter 1, by

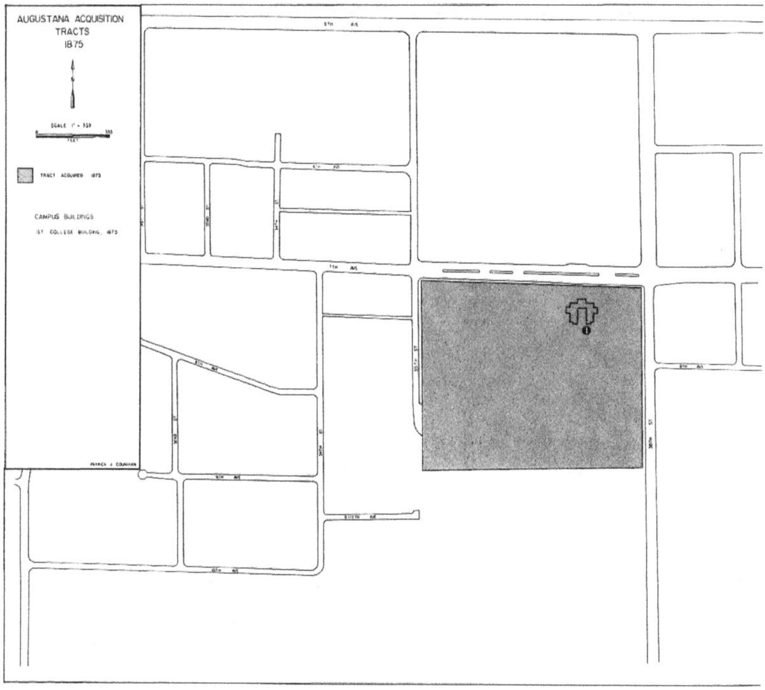

Fig. 2.1. Campus property in 1875. From Glen Brolander, *An Historical Survey of the Augustana College Campus*, Augustana Historical Society Publications, 1985.

Dr. Jane Simonsen. When the campus's first building was ready for occupancy in 1875, the college made the move from Paxton. Since then, the physical college has grown and changed to accommodate its student body and support its academic programs. As Glen Brolander, who served as the chief financial officer from 1961 to 1992, wrote, "The physical plant of an educational institution which recognizes its obligations to provide a quality program in tone with current needs must be constantly changing."[2]

Much of the college's growth is documented in his 1992 historical atlas and topical description. Thus, rather than repeat his detailed work, I will simply note that the large tracts of land upon which our campus sits today were largely acquired by the early 1960s. By this time, Augustana's campus stretched from 5th Avenue on the north, 12th Avenue to the south, 38th Street to the east, and 30th Street to the west. The notable exceptions are the acquisition of the Seminary and Book Concern properties in 1966 and 1967, respectively, which resulted from the merger of the Augustana Seminary with Central Lutheran Seminary, Suomi Theological Seminary, Grand View Theological Seminary, and Chicago Lutheran Seminary into the Lutheran School of Theology at Chicago, where it subsequently moved.[3] It is important to note, though, that the acquisition of the seminary property represents a reacquisition of property, since the property was part of the campus prior to the seminary's split from the college in 1948. Since the 1960s, the growth of the physical campus has occurred when smaller parcels of land, mostly located along the periphery of residential neighborhoods, were acquired. This growth has largely been dictated by two forces: the college's site location and its Master Plan.

The college's expansion is driven by its site location. Located along the floodplain zone of the Mississippi River, the college's 115-acre campus is locked in by residential neighborhoods to the east, west, and south, most of which were developed in the early twentieth century, and by former industrial activities to the north. Further, as noted in a planning document, much of the surrounding undeveloped land is owned for park space, available as an occasional lot, or is one piece of underutilized commercial development.[4] Consequently, college land acquisition is more difficult today and, by necessity, has become more opportunity-oriented.

The growth of Augustana's campus is also directed by the philosophy set forth in the college's Master Plan. A master plan is a document used to indicate where academic and residential buildings, open spaces, utilities, and other components of a campus's physical plant will be located. In contrast to a campus map, which is a representation of current facilities, a master plan is an adaptable representation of where future facilities may be located. According to planners Linda Dalton and James Davis, "The plan must be adaptable to changing conditions and take into account both challenges and opportunities, while providing adequate guidance so important concepts are sustained and not compromised to attain lesser short-term advantages over more significant long-term benefits."[5] While grant opportunities, donor interests, and college needs may influence the ordering and prioritizing of campus facilities, the college's Master Plan helps to ensure that a long-term perspective is leveraged in decision-making.

With the assistance of BLDD Architects and Sasaki Associates, Augustana College last underwent an intensive master planning process in 2004. The purpose of the planning process was twofold: "Identify and address existing capital investment needs and plan for the growth as described in the College's recently completed Strategic Plan."[6] The strategic plan included goals related to enriching academic programs, enhancing student life and co-curricular activities, welcoming diverse students, growing the endowment, and strengthening relationships with alumni and external constituencies. The planning process engaged different constituencies of the college, including faculty, staff, students, and administrators. Of significance for the college's neighbors, through the master planning process, academic facilities were centralized nearest to the Lower Quad while residential areas were largely brought together on the hilltops surrounding the Slough, which are in the southern and western areas of campus. As part of this process, Carlsson Evald Hall was renovated and transitioned from a dormitory to an academic building.

Since the development of the 2004 Master Plan, under the leadership of the chief financial officer, the college has reviewed its campus planning priorities on a five-year cycle. At the time of writing, the most recent significant evaluation took place in 2019 and plans for an updated Master Plan were being made.

Rock Island

Located along the Mississippi River, the city of Rock Island is home to approximately thirty-seven thousand people (Table 2.1). The city makes up the southwestern quadrant of the greater Quad Cities region, which also includes Moline, Illinois, and Davenport and Bettendorf, Iowa. As a result of social and economic pressures, Rock Island's population has been on the decline since the 1970 census (Table 2.2).

Once a manufacturing powerhouse, the city of Rock Island faced a harsh economic downturn in the 1980s. A *Chicago Tribune* article published in 1987 read, "Community leaders in the Quad Cities area are like river bottom residents after a Mississippi flood. While surveying the wreckage, they're taking tentative steps to rebuild. But the catastrophe that devastated this bistate area wasn't high water. It was a manmade disaster—the collapse of the farm equipment manufacturing

Table 2.1: Rock Island Demographic Information

Indicator	*Rock Island*	*Illinois*
Population Estimate	37,108	12,671,469
White	59%	76.3%
Black	19.2%	14.7%
Asian	4.3%	6.1%
Hispanic or Latino	11.6%	18%
Rate of Owner-Occupied Housing	61.4%	66.3%
Median Value of Owner-Occupied House	$106,300	$202,100
Vacant Housing Units	10.9%	9.11%
Bachelor's Degree or Higher	22.2%	35.5%
Median Household Income	$48,120	$68,428
Persons in Poverty	21.5%	11%
Population per Square Mile	2,199.4	230.8

Source: United States Census Bureau. 2020 Decennial Census. Accessed May 29, 2023. https://data.census.gov/profile/Rock_Island_city;_Illinois?g=160XX00US1765078.

Table 2.2: Rock Island Population Change over Time

Year	*Population*	*Percentage Change*
1950	48,710	13.9
1960	51,863	6.5
1970	50,166	–3.3
1980	46.821	–6.7
1990	40,552	–13.4
2000	39,684	–2.1
2010	39,018	–1.7
2020	37,108	–4.9

Source: Social Explorer. Social Explorer Dataset: US Census Bureau. Accessed October 24, 2022. https://www.socialexplorer.com/us-census-data.

industry. The decade-long decline of farm equipment makers wiped out 40 percent of the Quad Cities' manufacturing jobs. The downturn shook the confidence of a region that in the 1970s smugly called itself the recession-proof farm equipment capital of the world."[7] Indeed, the closure of International Harvester's facilities along with the downsizing of the facilities of John Deere and Company and J. I. Case shook the economic foundations of Rock Island and its surroundings. From 1979 to 1984, manufacturing employment in the Quad Cities dropped from fifty thousand to thirty-six thousand positions.[8] This downturn compounded the social fractures already evident.

Though the city was facing a declining population and economic challenges in the 1980s, social fractures resulting from racial tensions had emerged the decade prior. Not only was the total population of Rock Island on the decline, but the racial makeup of the city was changing (Table 2.3). While the percentage of whites in the city declined from 89.7 percent in 1970 to 59 percent in 2020, the percentage of Blacks in the city increased from 10 percent to 19.23 percent. Similarly, the percentage of Hispanics in the city increased from 3.4 percent in 1980 to 11.58 percent in 2020. This pattern suggests that Rock Island followed national trends of whites leaving diversifying areas in the post–World War II era.

Racial tensions became apparent during the Rocky Riots, ten days of conflict at Rock Island High School that stemmed from the unfair treatment of Black students. The riots began on October 6, 1972, with a disturbance at the Friday night football game. According to an article published later in the *Quad-City Times*, the disturbances began when students surrounded three police officers who were trying to remove a Black student from a reserved seating area. As the officers attempted to escort the student to the stadium exit, they were taunted, spat on, and physically attacked by students in the crowd—both Black and white.[9] When the situation appeared to be deteriorating, twenty-five additional officers were sent to the scene, and a chemical spray was used on the crowd. One student was hospitalized, and another sixteen people were arrested.[10] This incident set off ten days of skirmishes and discussions at the school. An account of the events written in a history of the high school concludes, "Rocky was

Table 2.3: Rock Island Demographic Change over Time

Race	*1970 (%)*	*1980 (%)*	*1990 (%)*	*2000 (%)*	*2010 (%)*	*2020 (%)*
White	45,094 (89.7)	37,926 (80.6)	31,802 (78.4)	29,485 (74.3)	26,464 (67.8)	21,910 (59.0)
Black	5,038 (10.0)	7,067 (15.0)	6,879 (17.0)	6,741 (17.0)	6,987 (17.9)	7,135 (19.23)
Hispanic		1,581 (3.4)	1,531 (3.8)	2,341 (5.9)	3,664 (9.4)	4,297 (11.58)
American Indian and Alaska Native		306 (0.7)	83 (0.2)	87 (0.2)	84 (0.2)	63 (0.2)
Asian			230 (0.6)	290 (0.7)	680 (1.7)	1,603 (4.3)
Native Hawaiian and Pacific Islander				17 (0)	8 (0)	12 (0)
Multi				670 (1.7)	1,067 (2.7)	1,928 (5.2)
Other	118 (0.2)	156 (0.3)	27 (0.1)	53 (0.1)	66 (0.2)	160 (0.4)

Source: Social Explorer. Social Explorer Dataset: US Census Bureau. Accessed October 24, 2022. https://www.socialexplorer.com/us-census-data.

Note: The United States Census has changed how it collects racial and ethnic data over time. Thus data are not available for all demographic categories in all years.

forever changed by that autumn of 1972. To this day, security teams roam the halls. Gates were installed to close off sections of the building, if the need should ever again arise. Enrollment at local private schools increased."[11]

Outmigration

The movement of Augustana's faculty and staff followed the same outmigration pattern observed more broadly in the region (Table 2.4). According to the college's faculty and staff directory, Cosmo, throughout the 1950s and early 1960s, the overwhelming majority of Augustana's faculty and staff resided in the city of Rock Island. However, by the late 1960s, this number began to decrease such that by the close of the twentieth century, only 40 percent of the college's faculty and staff resided within the city. By the 2018–19 academic year, the percentage had fallen to 21.1 for those living in Rock Island.

The outmigration that began in the 1970s has continued. Several explanations have been given for this continued outmigration, including higher rates of taxation in Rock Island, public perception of Rock Island as a "tougher" town, and stagnant or even declining property values.[12] Perceptions of the city's public schools may also have played a role; one college staff member recalled being advised by an employee of Rock Island–Milan School District to move outside the district. Finally, the increasing number of dual-career families means that residential choices are more complicated, as families may choose to split commute times or locate near only one spouse's place of employment. In all likelihood, no singular explanation can account for these changes. Instead, the complex interactions of changing economies, household structures, and race relations influenced the outmigration. No matter how we explain it, though, the population decline has left Rock Island, like many other post-industrial towns, with a declining tax base, budget challenges, and vacant properties.[13]

Even as the population of Rock Island shifted, in terms of both numbers and composition, student enrollment at Augustana College remained consistent with national trends.[14] Student enrollment exhibited some variability in the 1980s before growing to its peak around 2010 (Table 2.5).

Table 2.4: Faculty and Staff Residence over Time

Location	*1951–52*	*1960–61*	*1969–70*	*1980–81*	*1990–91*	*1999–2000*	*2010–11*	*2018–19*
Rock Island	63	91	148	222	239	183	190	127
	(84%)	(84%)	(61%)	(58%)	(53%)	(40%)	(28%)	(21%)
Moline	6	9	32	58	65	79	93	68
Davenport	4	6	14	35	49	54	65	70
Bettendorf	0	0	5	14	32	30	50	44
East Moline	2	1	4	7	11	9	22	14
Other	0	1	19	33	40	83	121	96
Inconclusive	0	0	21	11	12	24	148	183
Total	75	108	243	380	448	462	689	602

Source: Cosmo: Faculty and Staff Directory. Augustana College, n.d.

Table 2.5: Augustana Student Enrollment over Time

Year	*Total Student Enrollment*
1980	2,434
1985	2,160
1990	2,253
1995	2,197
2000	2,230
2005	2,386
2010	2,532
2015	2,478
2020	2,389

EXPANDING OUR FOOTPRINT

In the past thirty years, dozens of properties have been acquired by the college. To identify all properties owned by Augustana College, a search was done using the online property database of the Rock Island County Assessment Office. These properties were then cross-referenced with the college's property deeds to identify, where possible, the year the property was purchased, its purchase price, and from whom the property was acquired. While not all properties could be identified and cross-referenced, enough data were collected to help us understand acquisition patterns.

For example, since 1992, multiple properties were acquired and transformed into transitional living areas, which are college-owned apartments and houses that provide junior students with a more independent, yet supportive, living arrangement (Table 2.6). Nine properties along 6th Avenue that were acquired in 2006 and 2010 now host Augie Acres, the college's student-run urban farm. Finally, at least two dozen properties have been converted into parking lots, primarily for athletic facilities and residence halls.

The means of finding desirable properties and the purposes for which they were acquired have varied. The properties were largely bought to secure the college's footprint for potential future development. According

Table 2.6: Transitional Living Areas Acquired Since 1992

Year	*Address*	*TLA*
1992	731 34th Street	Heimdall House
1998	753 34th Street	Lundahl House
1999	3801 8th Avenue	Bremer House
1999	3203 10th Avenue	Zander House
2000	602 39th Street	Bellman House
2001	3400 7th Avenue	Lutheran House
2002	3235 8th Avenue	Freya House
2002	3429 7th Avenue	Branting House
2002	721 34th Street	Delling House
2003	3233 10th Avenue	Loki House
2003	816 34th Street	Thor House
2003	1117–1119 35th Street	Karsten House
2005	1204 35th Street	Lindgren House
2006	1111 37th Street	Tyr House
2006	750 35th Street	Levander House
2006	1113 35th Street	Milles House
2007	3052 9th Avenue	Erfara House
2007	1118 35th Street	Midgard House
2007	3048 9th Avenue	Sanning House
2007	3051 10th Avenue	Zorn House
2007	3054 9th Avenue	Ansvar House
2011	3437 7th Avenue	Skadi House
2011	1120 35th Street	Wicksell House
2012	610 39th Street	Austin House
2012	1116 35th Street	Jansson House
2013	1110 35th Street	Ribbick House

to the former dean of students, Evelyn Campbell, as quoted in the *Augustana Observer*, "There is a strategic purpose to purchase property for Augustana College. The purpose is to expand Augustana College for future growth for academic buildings and/or playing fields."[15] According to the same article, "Augustana College does not go out looking for properties to purchase. However, if the property has a house on it, the college is very likely to purchase it. Usually, the people of the neighboring community tell Augustana College when they want to sell and are the first to contact the college with regards to buying it."[16] College leadership confirmed that the college rarely seeks out opportunities to purchase properties. Rather, the college is likely to seize opportunities to buy properties when they provide contiguous land ownership or reduce the presence of abandoned properties.

In one interesting story of acquisition, the City of Rock Island gifted multiple properties along 6th Avenue to the college. According to one former city planner, the homes on those lots sat on the edge of a slope that became unstable. So the city acquired and demolished the homes, leaving them with empty lots. Rebuilding on those lots would come at a premium given the lots' instability. To keep the city from owning and maintaining additional vacant lots, the city gifted the properties to the college, which used them to build Augie Acres.

These processes of land acquisition set Augustana College apart from some other colleges and universities. In these acquisitions, Augustana College is the known purchaser or recipient of the property. This transparency differs from some institutional acquisition wherein the college's or university's identity is shrouded to the buyer. For example, in an effort to construct the Trinity Heights project in Hartford, Connecticut, Trinity College used a third-party realty company to prevent price inflation.[17]

A HISTORY OF POSITIVE IMPACT

Augustana College has a long history of community engagement. Faculty and staff serve on city committees and commissions, students grow their knowledge through internships with local organizations, and city and college staffs share expertise and resources. Moreover, the college is one of the largest employers in the city and has a reputation and history of maintaining and beautifying its properties.

According to data from the Quad Cities Chamber of Commerce, with approximately 650 employees, Augustana is the third largest employer within the city of Rock Island. The largest employers are the Rock Island Arsenal (6,500 employees) and UnityPoint Health (4,700 employees). In addition to employment, the college stimulates the local economy through demand for goods and services. With use of the simple calculation of budget times 1.8, which is the median multiplier effect for four-year colleges, Augustana's overall economic impact can be estimated at $144 million.[18] Thus, Augustana certainly makes a positive economic impact on the area. However, the college's impact is not simply about economic stimulus; it is also about contributions to intellectual and social capital.

Augustana College has a history of community-engaged learning, including internships, community-based learning courses, and service. For example, founded in 2013, the Upper Mississippi Center "mobilizes Augustana's faculty and students to help communities solve social, economic, and environmental challenges."[19] By partnering with local entities to address important environmental questions and issues, the college builds and sustains enduring relationships with partners. Under the guidance of faculty mentors, students have assessed watershed quality for the City of Davenport, developed a Sustainable Urban Forest Management Plan for the City of Clinton, Iowa, and advised Rock Island's Parks Department on the best way to manage urban parks in a more natural, and less resource-intensive, way. Furthermore, for decades, students have interned with local organizations, such as John Deere, Rock Island Arsenal, World Relief, and MetroLINK, the public transit provider in the Illinois Quad Cities, among others. Finally, the college has a long-standing relationship with Longfellow Liberal Arts, an elementary school reimagined by district and college leaders in 2008 to focus on creative problem-solving, imagination, and collaboration.[20]

Through the development of these long-term partnerships, the college has worked to overcome the institution-centric models of experiential learning common throughout higher education. In such models, service opportunities are initiated by the institution and have positive outcomes for its students, but the community organization shoulders the burden of the work.[21] For example, in 2008, Augustana College developed a Community Connection event that was held as part of the college's Fall Connection orientation program for several years. A predecessor to Welcome Week, Fall Connection was a new student orientation program that took place prior to the start of the fall term. The orientation was designed to help students adjust to college life by introducing them to the college's liberal arts mission, faculty, campus, and community.[22] Community Connection was an event held during orientation wherein students completed service projects with local organizations, including food pantries, Habitat for Humanity, Quad City Botanical Center, Painting for a Purpose, and others. Students also participated in neighborhood cleanups. While only about half of the incoming class choose to participate in the event in the first couple of years, the event was popular with students.[23] "This was my favorite part of orientation because I love serving others, and Augustana should continue to provide opportunities for us to serve the community," wrote an *Observer* columnist.[24] While these types of one-off events tend to serve students' interests by growing their civic agency, they may not align with community organizations' true needs. As Darby Ray writes, "Unfortunately, these institutions fail to appreciate the toll such events can take on off-campus partners, who have to scramble to come up with projects and work sites and who often wind up working extra hours to open their agency's doors for these events."[25] Thus, with this recognition in combination with staffing changes, Augustana ended the program around 2014.

Although some connections are frequently not visible to most members of the college and Rock Island communities, the college and city have a history of finding creative ways to partner. For example, one college staff member described how city police and fire protection may use vacant Augustana houses for training drills. Another noted how the college and city partnered to refinish a road along the edge of campus. The college was interested in adding parking on the east side of the street while the city was interested in repaving the road. The two entities engaged in a joint planning and cost-sharing program to meet both of their interests. In another example, in 2023, the city and college partnered to improve tennis facilities. Under the partnership,

Augustana College entered a ten-year lease, with annual payments of one dollar and an option to renew, on city-owned land located within Lincoln Park.[26] The college constructed six regulation tennis courts, bleachers, restrooms, and parking on the land. While the college's varsity teams have priority access during the competitive season, the facilities are otherwise available for college and community use.[27] Prior to this arrangement, the college's tennis courts were located behind Evald Hall and in need of upgrading. However, the courts could not simply be resurfaced, and the location of steam and power lines beneath the facility made a full-scale renovation challenging. This partnership provided the space for upgraded facilities. Moreover, this partnership provides city residents with access to high-quality tennis courts and allows the city to invest in facilities at parks across the city. Finally, one city representative acknowledged that college ownership of properties also reduces the number of vacant and unmaintained parcels in the area, as the college has a reputation for maintaining its properties.

The positive intentions and impacts of the college on the community are rarely disputed. However, the relationships between the college and city are complex, and in this complexity, challenges to balancing the college's and city's interests arise. For example, in acquiring property for future use, the college necessarily changes the makeup and dynamics of the community.

BALANCING COLLEGE AND COMMUNITY INTERESTS

There is a long history of writing about the benefits and tensions between a college and the city where it resides. The differences in socioeconomic makeup of the college and the town, the self-contained nature of residential colleges, and the economic contributions and drains that colleges make to towns are the focus of much of the writing.[28] These attributes and differences often lead to a perceived dualism between colleges and towns. Indeed, in this case, Augustana College is perceived to be a place of privilege and, in turn, its students are perceived to be wealthy. In contrast, Rock Island is perceived to be a socially vulnerable and economically depressed city, despite the college's efforts to highlight its social, cultural, and environmental amenities. Further, within the history of liberal arts colleges, the campus experience has been sold as a refuge from the messiness of everyday life, a sanctuary for renewal and reflection.[29] Thus, colleges can be tempted to insulate their campuses and close off their boundaries with the community, as has happened at places such as Rhodes College (Memphis, Tennessee), Millsaps College (Jackson, Mississippi), and many others. In such instances, colleges may figuratively and/or literally turn their backs on their surroundings. Drawing on interviews with current and former college personnel, city leadership, and community members, this section explores the complexity of Augustana's relationship with Rock Island by identifying a few sources of tension between the college and city and the strategies used to manage those tensions.

Residence Life Behaviors, Policies, and Expansion

The lines between college and community are blurred along the southern and western boundaries of campus. In these areas, student residences, whether owned by the college or local landlords, are interspersed with those of short- and long-term residents of Rock Island. Thus, the residential policies and practices of the college, behaviors of the student body, and concerns of community members are tightly bound.

The parties at Augustana College throughout the 1970s, 1980s, and 1990s were notorious among neighbors living near campus. As recalled in this chapter's opening, the music was loud and student behavior disruptive. College and city staff recall numerous resident complaints: noise, public urination, and excessive garbage, largely beer cans and cups, being strewn around the neighborhood. According to an *Augustana Observer* article from the late 1980s, "[One community member's house] is surrounded by houses with college students. Every time there is a party, people freely urinate in their yards with no concern for their property or feelings . . . Still another felt that things had gotten so bad that he was going to install a fence around his yard."[30]

The college and city, working in collaboration, made efforts to address the complaints. For example, in spring 1985, a police liaison committee worked together to address issues of housing, parties, and safety. Advised by then dean of students, Jack Hullett, and chaired by a senior student, the committee worked with local police to establish a list of guidelines designed for minimizing police intervention at parties.[31] Some years later, a series of community relations meetings were hosted by the college during the 1988–89 academic year. Sponsored by the college's Student Government Association (SGA) and moderated by Hullett, the forum offered an opportunity for community members and students residing off campus to discuss the issue of partying.[32] Signaling the significance of these issues, both candidates for SGA president that same year included improving campus-community relations regarding off-campus parties in their campaign platforms.[33]

Despite these efforts, and much to the frustration of neighbors, the parties seemingly continued unchecked. In response, the Coalition of Rock Island Homeowners fought to put a referendum limiting the number of unrelated people living in a house to three on the November 1990 ballot. Although the Rock Island Housing Board had rejected the idea months prior, residents garnered the 2,500 signatures necessary to put the referendum on the ballot. One member of the coalition who attended a public forum about the proposed law was quoted as saying that students tell her, "I don't care what happens to this neighborhood or property because I don't really live here."[34] The referendum passed with a vote of 6,498 voters in favor and 3,591 voters against.

As one former city staff member recalled, City Council was not inclined to enforce the ordinance because they did not think it would solve the underlying problem of student behavior. Further, enforcement of such an ordinance would be limited, and significantly, the ordinance would have to be applied across the city. Nonetheless, because the referendum passed, council members felt the need to be responsive to constituents.[35] Consequently, the ordinance was instituted in 1991 and is still in effect in 2024. While city and college staff agree that it did not have much effect beyond increasing the number of variances to the ordinance requested by the college and nearby landlords, the referendum signaled community frustration with student behavior and the college's tacit acceptance of it.

Efforts were also made to increase opportunities for students and local residents to interact with one another under positive circumstances. Initiated in 1997, the 6th Ward Neighborhoods/Augustana College Task Force was formed at the insistence of neighbors with the purpose of "continually improving the communication and relationships between students and the community."[36] Formed in response to complaints about parties, parking, and alcohol, the group hosted neighborhood welcome picnics, created an "Off Campus Survival Guide" to provide advice to students on being good neighbors, and initiated a "Good Neighbor Award" for those contributing positively to the neighborhood. Gatherings occurred through at least 2001.[37]

Several initiatives undertaken by the college are perceived to have aided in the reduction of complaints since the 1990s. Importantly, former Dean Evelyn Campbell, whose tenure began in 1991, recalls taking a much stronger stance on discipline. In addition, and of particular significance to the growth of the college's footprint, are the changes in campus residential opportunities for junior students and the expanded view of residential life's role in student learning and development.

First-year, sophomore, and junior students are required to live in college-owned housing. Seniors are encouraged to live off campus. First-year and sophomore students typically reside in traditional residence halls, while the college provides transitional living areas (TLAs), formerly known as lease-option housing, to junior students.[38] As described by a student journalist, "TLA provides houses and suite style apartments which provide kitchen facilities, cable, internet, and custodial services . . . Transitional Living Areas are kept in good shape, are provided with security, and are found at many good locations on campus."[39] However, for many years, there was a significant shortage of TLA housing.

During the 1999–2000 academic year, there were 458 juniors but only 280 TLA spaces.[40] During the 2003–2004 academic year, there were only enough TLA spaces for 68 percent of the enrolled juniors.[41] Remaining junior students had to live in a traditional residence hall. A spring 2005 editorial read, "Let's face it: Augustana has a housing problem. Such a high number of juniors forced to spend a third year in dorms is a big problem."[42] This disparity and discontentment, along with the growing student body and availability of local properties, prompted the acquisition and construction of additional TLA housing. Throughout the late 1990s and early 2000s, the college acquired multiple residential properties that were transformed into TLAs (Table 2.6).

These acquisitions in combination with the construction and opening of two residence halls, Swanson Commons in 2006 and Parkander in 2007, made TLA housing available to every junior student.[43]

While the implementation and expansion of the TLA program was a way to provide more modern facilities and to equalize housing opportunities, it has since become an important part of an intentional set of programming designed to facilitate student development and learning through residential life experience. Each year of residential experience at Augustana is designed to meet needs and enhance student development. According to an informational brochure from the Office of Student Life, the first-year residential experience is designed to help students feel at home at Augustana through the building of social connections. The second year is designed to help students reflect on who they are, who they want to be, and life goals. According to the brochure, "The third year will focus on transitions and more independence, so you are ready to move with friends into off-campus housing in the neighborhood as a senior."[44] Furthermore, as students complete their third, and final, year of residence in college-owned housing, they are expected to complete a program initially called "Transitions . . . Living Off-Campus."

Initiated in spring 2006, the program is designed to provide students with information and perspectives that can help them effectively transition to off-campus housing. Held as an in-person event for many years, the training moved to a video format in 2020 due to the logistical challenges of finding common times for presenters and students at the onset of the COVID-19 global pandemic. The current training not only includes remarks from the dean of students and director of residence life but also from Tom Phillis, the director of public safety, and Bruce Crowe, the housing and property maintenance inspector for the City of Rock Island. They address important issues, such as whom to call in an emergency, property safety requirements, parking considerations, landlord and tenant responsibilities, getting to know neighbors, and hosting responsibly. Students take a short quiz at the end of the video to ensure their comprehension of key points.

In addition to formal training required by the college, the *Augustana Observer* has published numerous articles about exploring and living off campus. For example, an article published in September 2009 highlighted advice from landlords on being a good neighbor.[45] Advice included communicating with landlords, purchasing renter's insurance, being a good representative of Augustana, introducing oneself and being available to neighbors, and respecting the property and neighbors: "All landlords reiterated the same basic principle: respect. Respect the property, respect the neighbors, and respect the neighborhood." An article published a few months earlier had introduced students to the nearby Greenbush and Keystone neighborhoods, featuring places to eat and volunteer.[46]

While complaints about student behavior may have decreased, locals, former city staff, and college personnel perceive that student housing has contributed to a shift in neighborhood housing dynamics. Census data are not available at the street-level scale needed to affirm this perception, but the unanimous perception among interviewees was that houses in the area had transitioned from single-family-owned homes to rental properties. The array of landlords is diverse. According to interviewees, some properties have been purchased by alumni, with a few purchased to serve as houses for local Greek organizations. Others have been purchased by family members as homes for their student during their time at Augustana and then retained as a rental. Others are purchased by local and out-of-town landlords as investments. Finally, a few are transitioned to rentals as elderly family members die. Further, as documented earlier in the chapter, many homes have been purchased by the college and transitioned into college-owned housing. A few interviewees, including city and college staff, speculated that the decrease in community complaints is simply a result of this neighborhood transition; renters, whether they are affiliated with the college or not, may be less invested in the neighborhood and less likely to lodge a complaint.

Although the number of complaints over student behavior has decreased, they do still occur. Indeed, among resident complaints about the college made to a local elected official, student parties still top the list. Also significant are complaints about property upkeep. Issues of landlord negligence have been a persistent problem. Complaints from students regarding the lack of landlord responsiveness date back decades. In an article published in the *Augustana Observer* in 1990, students claimed that landlords were slow to address problems, if they addressed them at all. One student is quoted as saying, "We have windows that won't open, no heat in one room, and a board is blocking off our basement so the city can't read our meters."[47] Another says, "We were missing fire alarms, and the carpets were ruined, so we had to pull it all up and clean and paint the floors ourselves."[48]

These issues continue today. Although students are notified of their landlord's responsibilities and whom to contact for dispute resolution during the transitional living training described above, resolving issues is still difficult. Moreover, landlord unresponsiveness does not only affect students. The lack of upkeep also degrades the appearances of the homes and, in turn, the neighborhood. Of course, this issue is not unique to the campus area. Community organizers in the city's West End, a disadvantaged neighborhood west of the college with many rental properties, note a similar frustration with landlord inaction. As a consequence, several interviewees would like for the city to better enforce existing property codes.

Property Tax Exemption

Most colleges and universities in the United States are tax exempt because of their educational mission. As described by the American Association of Universities, "The educational purposes of universities and colleges—teaching, research, and public service—have been recognized in federal law as critical to the well-being of our democratic society. Higher education institutions are in turn exempted from income tax so they can make the most of their revenues."[49] Of significance for municipal entities, this exemption includes property taxes.

As Augustana College has acquired property, including residences, these properties were taken off the property tax rolls. The only exception is when the college rents the properties to non-students; then the college does pay property taxes on those residential units. Thus, while Augustana College benefits from city-provided services, such as the maintenance of roads and police and fire protection, the college does not generate income for the city through property taxes.

For some residents of Rock Island, this arrangement seems inequitable. As described by one interviewee, residents resent, from their perspective, having to pay a larger share of property taxes while also experiencing depressed home values due, in part, to nearby student rentals. A former township staff member recalled how residents would walk into her office with magazine articles about college activities, demanding that she do something to force the college to pay property taxes. These individuals would be frustrated that the college could afford to build a new football stadium or invest in other campus facilities but did not pay its share of taxes. In the eyes of these residents, there was a direct relationship between the college's exemption and their high tax bills.

Augustana College leaders are aware of the tensions raised by the college's tax exemption status. Current and former college staff all agreed that the college does have a responsibility to attend to the needs of the community and noted the ways that the college and city do partner, some of which were described above. For example, one college staff member pointed to how the college invested both money and personnel time in partnering with the Rock Island–Milan School District to reimagine Longfellow Elementary in 2008 and prevent its closure.[50] Many of these ways of attending to the community, though, are invisible to those not directly involved.

Transparent Communication

Each president of Augustana College has leveraged their expertise and experience for the betterment of the college. In recent years, Thomas Tredway, who served as an instructor of history and academic dean before being appointed president, was acquainted with the college's academic programs and strengthened the college's liberal arts focus, faculty, and facilities. Under his leadership (1975–2003), new academic facilities, including a library and two new buildings for biology, chemistry, physics, computer science, and mathematics, were constructed, the endowment grew twentyfold, and both the number of faculty and the number of faculty holding terminal degrees increased.[51] According to those with whom he worked, he was an accessible president to the campus community, the kind who would share conversation with students over beer, but who kept his attention focused on the college. He did not serve on community boards and preferred to handle college and student issues internally.

Reportedly, during this time, there was little sustained and transparent communication between the college's administration and city staff. As one college staff member recalled, the primary engagement of the college with the city was through the vice president of business and finance's participation in the Development Association of Rock Island. According to former city staff members, the college shared few of its intentions and plans with city personnel or the Rock Island community. Instead, there was a perceived expectation among the college's administration that the city would simply acquiesce to any need or plans of the college. One former city staff member described the college as a bully to the city, a bully that drew its power from its economic contributions to the city. There was a sense among neighbors that their viewpoints were dismissed and that the college had free rein to do what it wanted.

One key concern among city staff and neighbors was a sense that they did not know what to expect from the college. Given that the student body had increased (Table 2.5), city residents wondered when and where the college might expand. A former city staff member recalls that the college had a development plan but declined to share it with the city. Thus, in response to the concern over future college growth, the city proposed and approved a special College/University Zone in the 1990s (Fig. 2.2). The purpose of this zoning was to define a reasonable growth area for the college. This zoning provided the college with flexibility and the opportunity for growth by allowing it to make select land-use planning decisions without applying for a variance from the city's board of zoning appeals. At the same time, the zone boundaries provided neighboring residents with a sense of the parameters of the college's growth and control. While the zoning innovation helped to reduce community anxiety, it did not address the wish for transparent communication. Thus, when Steven Bahls assumed the college presidency in 2003, he was advised that increased transparency with the city was needed. He took this advice seriously, making active engagement with the city an enduring part of his legacy.

As explained by one interviewee, President Bahls's experience as a practicing lawyer and law school dean helped him understand the need to interface with the surrounding community. During his tenure (2003–2022), he served as a board member for multiple local organizations, including the Putnam Museum of Natural Science, Genesis Health System, United Way of the Quad Cities, Quad Cities Cultural

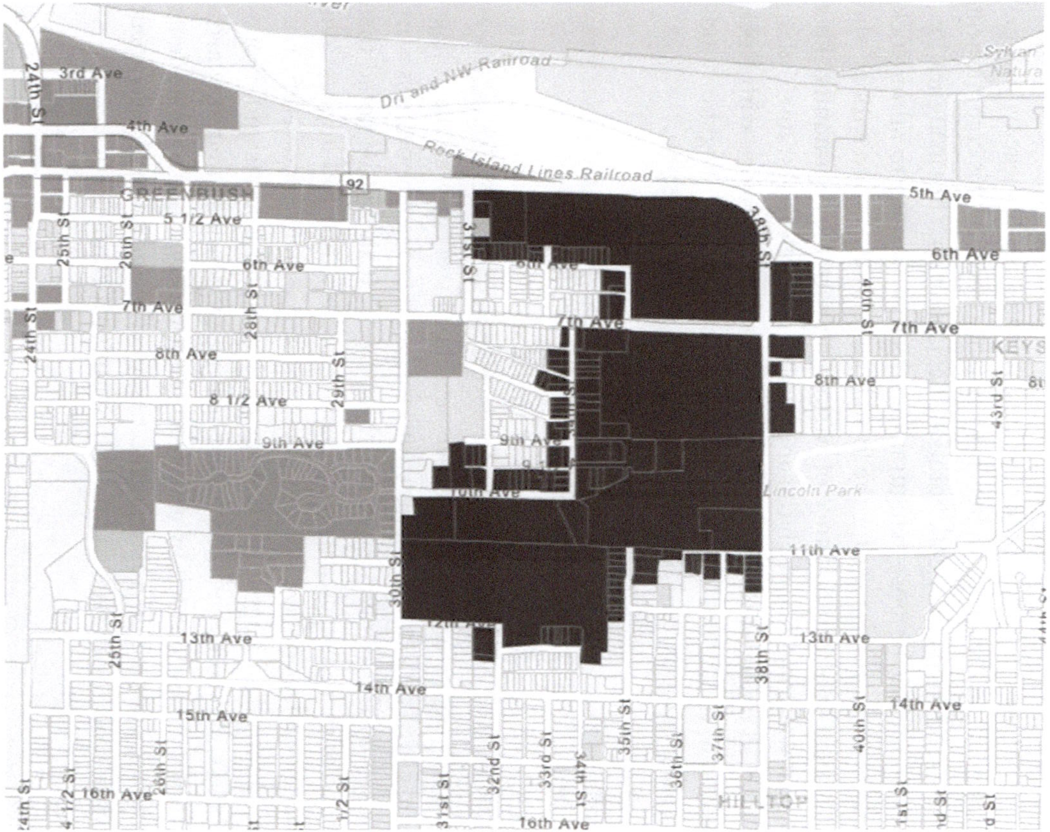

Fig. 2.2. University/College Zone of Rock Island. *Black*: university; *dark gray*: community business, planned development; *light gray*: residential/neighborhood business. City of Rock Island GIS Department, Public Zoning Districts Map, October 1, 2014. https://rock-island-hub-example-rigov.hub.arcgis.com/apps/2a03f88524a94f40a3dafd42c1b982cd/explore.

Trust, the Quad City Symphony Orchestra Association, and the Quad Cities Chamber of Commerce. He was also a chair of Q2030, the regional economic and cultural planning committee. He is remembered for attending community events, such as ribbon cuttings, and sitting on expert panels. For his part, he recalls hosting planning meetings with city colleagues at his home and encouraging faculty, staff, and members of his cabinet to be active in the community. Through his engagement, he helped the community to understand the college's mission, priorities, and plans, building a legacy of increased trust. His philosophy of transparent communication and community engagement helped set the stage for effective college-community collaboration.

From the beginning of her tenure at Augustana College, which began in 2022, President Andrea Talentino has affirmed this commitment to college-community collaboration. Beginning with her inauguration, which included a post-inauguration street party open to all in Rock Island and a fundraiser for the local high school's resource room, she has signaled the importance of partnering with the community. This signal was amplified with the approval of the college's strategic plan. Adopted in 2024, the plan calls for the college to "work with Rock Island to contribute to neighborhood vitality, enhance neighborhoods around campus, and be an engaged presence in the region."[52]

BUILDING NEIGHBORLINESS

While there is little disagreement that the college has played an important and beneficial role in the development of Rock Island, there are still opportunities to improve neighborliness between the college and city. The following suggestions for enhanced neighborliness were raised by those interviewed for this project. It should be noted that none of these suggestions have been vetted for their full implications for the college or city, nor are any of the suggestions endorsed by representatives of Augustana College or the City of Rock Island. Nonetheless, they provide ideas for navigating the tensions that may arise from the pressures felt by colleges and universities to attract students and provide meaningful opportunities for civic and career development when working in true partnership with local communities.

Incentives for Faculty and Staff

Multiple interviewees expressed a desire to reverse the trend of Augustana College faculty and staff residing outside Rock Island. Many recalled a time when the surrounding neighborhoods were filled with Augustana faculty and staff. One recalled riding his bike around town with the children of Augie faculty. These memories were accompanied by a sense of community between the neighborhoods and campus. Thus, several suggestions were made for increasing the number of Augustana College faculty and staff residing in Rock Island. For example, given the older housing stock in the city, the college might offer no-interest home improvement loans. Such an offering could help faculty and staff repair or renovate an older home. Another suggestion was to offer down-payment assistance wherein the college would contribute several thousand dollars to the down payment on a home purchased in the city. Finally, it was suggested that the college better advertise its partnership with the Development Association of Rock Island and its homebuyer assistance program called Live-Work Rock Island. These incentives, it is thought, would benefit the city by improving housing stock and steadying the tax base.

Payments in Lieu of Taxes

Although the college has given back to the community through different means, such as supporting the restructuring of Longfellow school and using college-owned homes for fire and police training, these benefits are targeted and not necessarily observed by the public. Thus, it was suggested by residents that Augustana College follow the example of other institutions, albeit wealthier ones, by making an annual payment in lieu of taxes. These payments could help to fund publicly supported services, such as schools, libraries, fire, police, and infrastructure.

College-Community Programming

Several individuals expressed the desire to create opportunities for greater interaction between students and community members. It was suggested that the college make campus events more accessible to Rock Island neighbors by advertising speakers and special events more broadly. Others expressed a desire to get to know their student neighbors through jointly planned picnics and service days, such as those organized by the 6th Ward Neighborhoods/Augustana College Task Force in the early 2000s.[53] Those events reportedly strengthened relationships between students and neighbors. Others wished to see students more involved in local politics. For example, students could attend neighborhood association meetings and register voters. An elected representative expressed a desire to hear more about student needs and concerns and suggested holding office hours on campus. Finally, others saw an opportunity for students to serve their aging neighbors by volunteering to do small tasks, such as taking trash cans to the curb. All of these suggestions are designed to break down the social barriers between the college and community.

Enacting these suggestions will necessitate addressing how welcome others feel on campus. Although Augustana College does not have gates or walls surrounding it, there are still perceptual barriers that influence the permeability of our campus border, as was noted in the opening vignette. Coauthors Lauren Hammond-Ford and Jane Simonsen and coauthors Christopher Strunk and Lizandra Gomez-Ramirez address these themes in their chapters on performing Blackness and the history of Latinos/x Unidos, respectively.

Joint College-City Planning

Augustana College, the City of Rock Island, and residents of both all want Rock Island to be a safe and vibrant place to live, work, play, and learn. Indeed, both the college and city have an active interest in the economic and land development of Rock Island. The city wants to attract businesses to bolster employment, recreation, and social opportunities. Augustana College wants to attract students to the college and provide a safe environment for engaged learning. Multiple college staff noted that when declining an offer of admission from the college, many prospective students comment on the condition of the surrounding area. Consequently, it was suggested that the college and city follow the example of other small college towns and engage in joint planning processes and private-public partnerships to advance their mutual interests.

From the perspective of neighborliness, the success of these endeavors relies on the development of a true partnership. It is important to follow the models set by institutions such as the University of Winnipeg and the University of Buffalo Medical School, wherein the interests of the community, as articulated by those affected, are lifted up alongside those of the institution.[54] In these examples, local concerns regarding affordable housing, employment, and cultural respect were addressed alongside the university's needs for housing and learning spaces. The universities avoided the use of community engagement rhetoric simply to develop support, including financial resources, for campus-driven priorities.

When asked what it means to be a good neighbor, college and city representatives shared similar perspectives. Being a good neighbor means giving back, treating others how one wants to be treated, opening lines of communication, and working through differences. Throughout the college's recent history, these ideals have wavered. However, in acknowledging this history, as well as past and present tensions, and intentionally working alongside our Rock Island neighbors at the individual and institutional scales, we can work toward the ideal of neighborliness. In so doing, we are working toward the well-being of our students and our neighbors.[55]

Notes

1. Bergendoff, *Profession of Faith.*
2. Brolander, *Historical Survey* (1992).
3. Harold Skillrud, *Decade of Decision.*
4. Augustana College and BLDD Architects and Sasaki Associates, "Campus Assessment."
5. Dalton and Davis, "Campus Master Planning."
6. Augustana College Board of Trustees, "Authentically Augustana."
7. Goozner, "Quad Cities Try."
8. Steven Greenhouse, "Bitter Time for Quad Cities," *New York Times*, December 25, 1984, https://www.nytimes.com/1984/12/25/business/bitter-time-for-quad-cities.html.
9. Alma Gaul, "Rocky Comes Alive in New Book," *Quad-City Times*, August 15, 2016, https://qctimes.com/news/local/education/rocky-comes-alive-in-new-book/article_5911b2fe-36af-5401-ad67-38290fd4f20a.html.
10. Frazer et al., *Rock Solid: Our History.*

11. Frazer et al., *Rock Solid: Our History.*

12. Graham Ambrose, "Quad-Cities Population Loss Is a Decades-Old Problem That Lacks a Single Cause, or Solution," *Dispatch Argus*, August 7, 2019, https://qconline.com/article_855f95c2-8327-5b6f-84aa-6697803194f6.html.

13. Russo and Linkon, "Social Costs."

14. National Center for Education Statistics, "College Enrollment."

15. Faye Marek, "Transitional Living Areas Promote Independence," *Augustana Observer*, September 22, 2011.

16. Marek, "Transitional Living."

17. Baldwin, *In the Shadow.*

18. Leslie and Slaughter, "Higher Education."

19. Augustana College, "Upper Mississippi Center."

20. Rae, "Teaching the Whole Child."

21. Stoecker and Tryon, *Unheard Voices.*

22. Augustana College Catalog 2008, "Academic Policies."

23. Erin Gehn, "First-Years Engage in Community," *Augustana Observer*, September 3, 2009.

24. Nicole Swanberg, "Fall Connection Hits the Right Notes," *Augustana Observer*, September 2, 2010.

25. Ray, "Self, World."

26. Grace Kinnicutt, "Augustana Building Six Tennis Courts at Lincoln Park," *Quad-City Times*, March 1, 2023, https://qctimes.com/news/local/augustana-building-six-tennis-courts-at-lincoln-park/article_94fefb06-7eab-5055-9d1c-2328d04cceaf.html.

27. Charlie Roiland and Allie Rial, "Relocation of Augustana's Tennis Courts Cause a Racket," *Augustana Observer*, March 23, 2023, https://augustanaobserver.com/34985/features/relocation-of-augustanas-tennis-courts-causes-a-racket/.

28. Bruning et al., "Town–Gown Relationships"; Massey et al., "Partnering"; Gavazzi, "Campus and Community"; O'Mara, "Beyond Town and Gown."

29. Baldwin, *In the Shadow.*

30. Tarum Malkani, "Community Relations Meeting Discusses Parties," *Augustana Observer*, October 12, 1988.

31. Jacqui Foertsch, "Liaison Committee Establishes Dialogue," *Augustana Observer*, April 6, 1986.

32. Malkani, "Community Relations."

33. Marcy Geighes, "Two Tickets Compete in SGA Election," *Augustana Observer*, March 23, 1988.

34. Dave Heitz, "Rock Island Will Limit the Number of Unrelated Persons Living in a House," *Augustana Observer*, April 12, 1991.

35. Heitz, "Rock Island Will Limit."

36. Tara Crandall, "Group Makes Better Neighbors," *Augustana Observer*, September 29, 2000.

37. Aaron Shaffer, "Connections 2002 Members Train Seniors to Be Alumni," *Augustana Observer*, October 19, 2001.

38. Richard Nelson, "Efforts Continue to Create Ideal Transitional Living Area Housing," *Augustana Observer*, December 18, 1998.

39. Emily Rizzulo, "Augie Juniors Choose TLA, Others Decide to Find a Place of Their Own," *Augustana Observer*, October 14, 2005.

40. Stephanie Wennmacher, "Realities of On-Campus Student Housing Explained by Residential Life Before Sign-up Day," *Augustana Observer*, April 7, 2000.

41. Alanna Boyd, "No Changes in Senior Housing Slated for Next Year," *Augustana Observer*, January 24, 2003.

42. Tom Foss, "Juniors in Dorms Should Have Options," *Augustana Observer*, April 29, 2005.

43. Rebecca Arnold, "New Projects on Campus Named After Prominent Augustana Women," *Quad-City Times*, June 23, 2007, https://qctimes.com/news/local/rock-island/new-projects-on-campus-named-after-prominent-augustana-women/article_3f9a0768-9020-5c6e-b9c8-a9e4da0f1f24.html; Stephanie De Pasquale, "New Dorm Allows Alcohol," *Augustana Observer*, May 5, 2006.

44. Office of Residential Life, "Living on Campus."

45. Andrew Shaffer, "Be a Good Tenant and Neighbor," *Augustana Observer*, September 17, 2009.

46. Sarah Johnson, "Augie, Meet Greenbush," *Augustana Observer*, April 3, 2009.

47. Kristin Everett, "Students Say They Are Fed Up with Negligent Landlords," *Augustana Observer*, October 12, 1990.

48. Everett, "Students Say."

49. Association of American Universities, "Tax-Exempt Status."

50. Rae, "Teaching the Whole Child."

51. "J. Thomas Tredway."

52. Augustana College, "Bold and Boundless."

53. Crandall, "Group Makes Better Neighbors"; Shaffer, "Connections 2002 Members Train Seniors to Be Alumni."

54. Baldwin, *In the Shadow*.

55. I would like to thank Peyton Heisch ('23) and Lazlow Ziebel ('25) for their research assistance. I would also like to thank the numerous current and former city staff, neighborhood residents, and college personnel who took time from their already full days to talk with me about college-city relationships and neighborliness.

PERFORMING BLACKNESS
A History in Three Acts

LAUREN HAMMOND-FORD AND JANE E. SIMONSEN

The Black Culture House, which serves as a formal and informal gathering space for Augustana students, sits on a rise overlooking 34th Street. It is situated near the other "culture houses" (Casa Latina and the Asian Pacific Islander Desi House) and not far from the upper entrance to the Center for Student Life, where students stream in from dorms for mealtimes and study hours. Today it is a sanctuary for students of color, primarily members of the Black Student Union and African Student Association, yet it is located near the social heart of campus. Established in 1969 as part of the national Black campus movement, the house was originally located at the edge of campus, as a point of contact between Black students and the Black community of Rock Island. Moved in the late 1980s to accommodate a new library, the house today is surrounded by student housing, campus buildings, and parking lots that enclose it within the campus "bubble" that many students still understand as "white space."

The presence of students of color at a small, historically Swedish, private college associated with the Lutheran Church has changed the institution. From the 1920s on, Black American and African students have altered policies and practices of the institution to accommodate their identities, beliefs, and experiences. While many studies of Black student activism focus on the period between 1965 and 1975 and primarily on the experience of students at public universities and in large urban areas, understanding the forms that Black student activism has taken at Augustana College requires a longer view, attuned to the nuanced ways that students at a small, religiously affiliated, predominantly white institution in a mid-sized city encountered and altered white space through the historically and culturally specific performances of Black identity.

In this chapter, we tell the stories of two individuals and one campus group, describing how each brought with them experiences formed by political and cultural realities that had previously seemed beyond the concerns of the college. Their interactions with campus institutions and authorities lay bare the particular forms that both "whiteness" and "blackness" took at Augustana College in the 1920s, the post–World War II era, and the civil rights era. Sometimes willingly and sometimes unwillingly, formally or informally, their conduct, appearance, and presence pushed the college to confront, with increasing urgency, spiritual and political ideas that had emerged from other histories and contexts: Black Lutheranism, African nationalism, and Black Power. These challenges unmasked the whiteness of places and practices that a predominantly white college community had assumed to be open to all.

ACT I: WIDENING THE CIRCLE, 1925–1932

In the fall of 1947, the social experiment of a Black Lutheran pastor named Jesse Routte made headlines across the United States and around the world. Traveling from his home in Queens, New York, to serve as wedding officiant for his brother Louis in Mobile, Alabama, he decided to alter his appearance, donning a rented purple turban and, according to several accounts, "speaking with a slight Swedish accent." His identity play confounded those who encountered him in the "white car" of the train and in whites-only restaurants. He reported being treated like a "visiting dignitary" and said he encountered none of the racism that he had been met with on an earlier trip to Mobile. "I felt like a paratrooper behind enemy lines," he recalled. While Routte said that the turban insulated him from being "insulted and pushed around" as he had been on his previous visit, he clearly meant to use ambiguous self-presentation to cross racial boundaries in a segregated city, deliberately entering white spaces and pressing gatekeepers—headwaiters, police, politicians—to confess to maintaining those boundaries. He claimed that a police captain told him that there was no race problem in Mobile: "if we have any trouble with a [Black person], we just knock him down." When reports of his experiment were published in New York, a cross was burned on his family's lawn in Long Island.[1]

Routte's high-profile experiment with turbaned travel has attracted the interest of commentators since. In "The Importance of Being Turbaned," Paul A. Kramer, whose research on the turban was also featured on NPR's *Code Switch*, proposes that Routte's subterfuge was the opposite of passing for white, in that it "projected and confounded blackness by rendering it illegible."[2] Routte's well-publicized identity play, however, has overshadowed Routte's no-less-subversive performances in the 1920s as the only Black student at Augustana College, where he learned to mimic a Swedish accent. More significantly, he used his musical performances and his Lutheran faith as wrappers of respectability to gain him—and later, others—entry to white spaces bound not by law but by custom, sometimes referred to as the "Other Jim Crow."

Augustana alumna Emma Nordmeyer has pointed out that as an undergraduate at the college, Routte "disrupted racial stability" on campus, using his performances to "create his own black space within a white institution."[3] Entering Augustana College during the era of the Great Migration and New Negro activism, Routte's insistent visibility forced the college to consider Black culture not as it was imagined by white people but as embodied in a Black person. At the same time, Routte was changed by the college. In his attempt to carve out space for himself in places that were primarily if not exclusively white by claiming an intellectual and spiritual identity that was accepted, even embraced, by white progressives, he began to forge an identity perhaps as perplexing and ultimately challenging to Midwesterners as the turban was to Southerners: a Black Lutheran pastor.[4]

During his undergraduate and seminary years at Augustana, Routte not only adopted forms of Black masculinity that gave him access to the spaces and privileges of a liberal arts education, but he also began to challenge Midwestern Lutherans to understand that addressing racial inequalities was part of their mission. His daughter Eneid Routté-Gómez recollected that her father saw "breaking down the massive walls of racial hatred" as his pastoral duty and that her parents were "engaged in a character-producing war against prejudice."[5] Working from within the Lutheran church was critical to Routte's lifelong commitment to an activism that was focused more on systemic change than individual transformation (Fig. 3.1).

D-L Stewart argues that student publications at historically white campuses have protected whiteness through the invisibility of non-white bodies, racialized imagery, and a lack of explicit attention to civil rights.[6] Prior to Routte's arrival in 1925, Black bodies appeared in the pages of the *Augustana Observer* primarily as jokes. The very first issue, in 1902, included an introduction to the paper as a "just and true reflection of student sentiment"; immediately below it was a joke premised on the imagined ignorance of a Black Southern church congregation (presumably *not* Lutheran) that wished to procure an advanced degree for its pastor.[7] Indeed, racist jokes were a feature of the paper's back pages into the 1920s, suggesting that such jokes functioned as the newspaper's "kitchen," where Black bodies have been forced to serve and amuse while remaining dehumanized and hidden. The nation's "race problem" was addressed in serious ways in the newspaper, but members of the campus community regarded "the Negro question" as a Southern concern and one for Southerners to solve. The deep racial divides of the first decades of the twentieth century—formal and informal segregation, lynching, and the resurgence of the Klan that was led by Midwestern states—seem not to have been frequently discussed. Students and faculty may have understood the whiteness of the college not as exclusivity but as insulation from

Fig 3.1. Jesse Routte, seminary graduation photo. Augustana *Rockety-I* yearbook, 1933. Courtesy of Augustana College Special Collections, Rock Island, Illinois.

the problems of more diverse communities. In 1906, the two primary campus debate organizations held a formal debate on the question of whether "the Negro should be expelled" from the United States. While the club arguing in the negative won, the judges lauded them for the soundness of their claim, not its morality.[8]

Arts and service organizations mobilized ideas of blackness for entertainment and edification. In 1922, the Augustana Woman's Club held a concert of "negro songs" performed by members "dressed to represent negro minstrels." Two years later, the club put on a play in which a white student's performance as "Gyp, a colored servant girl" was praised for her use of "the negro dialect" and "characteristic actions."[9] And in February of 1913, Augustana Seminary's senior class was invited to dine at the home of Professor Lindberg, where they were serenaded by two members performing a "genuine negro duet." While the songs struck the audience as expressing some essence of Black identity, the seminarians performing them were white.[10]

Music may have been the primary mode through which ideas about Black identity and culture were communicated on campus. The prominence of the Music Conservatory meant frequent concerts; these included Black musical traditions alongside Euro-American sacred songs. In the 1920s, choir and concert band programs often included one or two spirituals. Songs like "Hear Ye, Israel" and spirituals such as those arranged by Black composers Nathaniel Dett and Harry Burleigh were likely understood to be sufficiently religious but also to represent "American culture" in their use of Black vernacular. Recitals also incorporated non-sacred songs meant to evoke other cultures: in 1927, costumed students performed songs like "Uncle Remus," "A Chinese Fantasy," and "Mr. Wing Foo." When the concert band went on a European tour in the summer of 1928, it included "Indian song, Negro spirituals, and other typically American music" alongside Bach and Beethoven; later, one student reported that the band received criticism for presuming that a Black musical form should be performed alongside the classical European masters.[11] Both at home and abroad, then, Augustana audiences regarded Black music and dialect—whether caricatures or in spirituals written by Black composers—primarily as representing an ethnic "type" that was both authentic and available for appropriation.

Ideas about Black American identity were also communicated through the Augustana Synod's home mission work. In 1923, missionary August Aden gave a lecture titled "The Little Africa in the Black Belt of the United States," arguing that mission work was necessary to address "the Negro problem" in the South. Despite the fact that many Black Southerners were Christian, the title of his lecture suggests that this work would be similar to "foreign" mission work.[12] Later that year, Augustana sent seven students, all white, to the national convention of the Student Volunteer Movement. Of more than 6,500 participants, 400 were international students and 124 were Black. While these delegates were in the minority, they seem to have been heard: "race relations were considered of the utmost importance by the delegates, as most frankly stated they face them on their own campus." Domestic race relations were the top priority, outweighing war and international relations, and delegates formed a committee charged with addressing these problems. The group, which included white students representing different US regions, a Filipino student, and a Black student, discussed "the race problem from different points of view, all agreeing that the only solution would come through the principles of Christianity."[13] Two Augustana attendees and their faculty advisor, C. A. Blomgren, discussed the conference at Zion Lutheran Church in Rock Island. While much of the presentation focused on foreign missions, Blomgren noted that "the great exodus of negroes to the north" in recent years (an exodus he attributed to the boll weevil rather than to political violence and poverty) meant that "we must now shoulder a part of the burden." Perhaps alluding to the early twentieth-century notion of the "white man's burden" of helping less "civilized" races, he concluded that "we need a great acquaintance with these problems."[14]

The Great Migration seems to have raised campus awareness of race as a "problem" in its own community.[15] It was during these years that Jesse Routte and a few other Black students began their study at Augustana. When the campus debate societies, in 1921, wrangled over the "Problem of the New Negro," they may or may not have been considering that within a few years, a tiny number of "New Negroes"—confident, educated, and proud of their Blackness—would be arriving on their own campus.[16] Jesse Routte was part of this vanguard, using artistic expression to articulate Black history and consciousness and forcing the campus community to encounter Black identity as embodied in a Black person. Transplanting his roots in Black communities and the African Methodist Episcopal (AME) Church into his new faith, he claimed a mission-focused Lutheran identity for himself, and Augustana was his first field.

Routte enrolled as a first-year student at the Music Conservatory in the fall of 1925. Born in Missouri, his father, Louis Routte, was a laborer who became a clergyman in the AME Church. The family lived in Macon, Missouri, and later Kewaunee, Illinois, moving around 1910 to Iowa, a slightly more progressive state on race issues, when Routte was about five. Routte's father served churches in Dubuque, Boone, and Fort Madison, Iowa. When the elder Routte died in the influenza pandemic of 1918, his mother, Lula, mobilized her three musical boys to support the family through performances. The family was living with her brother in Rock Island in 1919 when Routte and his brothers were guests at a charity dinner held by the Rotarians just before his brother Frederick Douglass died. Routte worked for a cleaning company through his high school years, often going without meals. He graduated from Rock Island High School in 1925, apparently the only Black member of the senior class. His employer, Archibald Beverlin, recognized Routte's drive and agreed to fund his college education under "certain terms," which Routte never specified.[17]

Routte arrived at Augustana to find that, as he later put it, "the air was chilly." He credited his professors with helping him "handle the situation," and by the middle of his sophomore year, he was described as "popular" on campus. Acceptance was likely the result of substantial effort on his part. He told the *Observer* that he believed "kindness is the key that unlocks many hardened hearts" and described himself as dedicated to improving his own social standing in order to serve and assist other Black people.[18] His words suggest that he was familiar with the ideas of Black intellectuals such as W. E. B. Du Bois, who asserted that racial uplift must come through race consciousness and solidarity. If Routte found a cold reception when he arrived, he set about warming the air not only by making himself visible but also by bringing other Black students and guests to campus. The next fall, he was joined by another Black student, George Smith. Smith had moved from Missouri to attend high school in Macomb, Illinois, where, like Routte, he was active in oratory and debate. He met Routte through a local club called Mu . . . Lit . . . So . . . (Music, Literature, Social) that Smith had helped to organize. He explained that he was at Augustana because "Jesse Routte brought me here" and that Routte had praised the "Christian spirit" and good instruction. No doubt Routte believed that Augustana was a place where they could succeed; certainly, having another ambitious young Black man on campus would have made his own journey less lonely. Smith, though, was working the night shift as a porter and mechanic at a hotel in Davenport to pay for his education. Perhaps the effort was too much, because Smith did not appear in the yearbook for that year.[19]

Routte may have sought to bring other Black students to campus to find community with them, but he also found something of value at Augustana: he was drawn to Lutheranism. He likely attended the AME church in Rock Island (he took his middle name, Wayman, from it), but according to his son, Luther, Routte appreciated the more staid style of worship he found at Augustana.[20] While others at the college may have been more interested in "foreign missions" or the "Little Africa" of the South, Routte clearly saw a future for Black folks in Midwestern Lutheran churches. Even if the atmosphere of the college could be cold at times, Routte saw Lutheranism as more than this. Perhaps, like Lenny Duncan, a Black, queer, former Lutheran pastor who authored the 2017 book *Dear Church*, he believed the Lutheran Church needed *him* in order to live out its Christian values in a deeply racist nation.[21]

Indeed, as Routte began to amplify his presence on campus in a partnership that may have been strategic for both him and the college, he began to follow the tradition of Black racial uplift that suggested that social goals could be achieved through the ministry. In the fall of 1927, he offered a series of concerts at local churches, beginning with First Lutheran and Grace Lutheran Churches in Rock Island. He would sing a program, which included "two sacred numbers and one Negro spiritual," at a different church every Sunday until the end of the year. College officials helped to arrange the concerts, which they likely saw as a recruiting tool, but Routte explained that they were linked to his service goals, since "he intends to become a social worker after being graduated from Augustana . . . Possibly he will enter the ministry."[22]

His musical choices were canny: interest in Black spirituals was high on campus and around the nation, and the religious messages in this music provided entry for a Black man into white spaces. Pairing traditional sacred music with language rooted in Black experience, Routte eased himself in front of white audiences, a process Nordmeyer links to "signifyin'"—using terms and vernacular from subcultures to disrupt social norms.[23] Routte himself later told his children that when he encountered racism, he searched for common ground in order to "disarm" the antagonist, and that while "the Swedes draw a tight circle around themselves . . . I drew a larger circle around them, and drew them in."[24] Music and faith likely provided that common ground. The following fall, other Black musicians joined him on campus. A Lyceum tour featured Black singers, and Routte invited other Black performers from Rock Island to campus to perform for members of the student government association. Routte sang spirituals accompanied by pianist Maurine Houston while Cornelia Davis, "an accomplished elocutionist," did several readings. The event took place two days after a concert to dedicate the Music Conservatory's new location was held, but the Black musicians were not part of the dedication ceremony.[25] They may not have been consigned to the kitchen but were not invited to the table.

In his senior year, however, Routte began combining his performances with public speaking about Black history and culture, possibly drawing on his experience in the AME Church as a safe place for Black people to teach one another history not taught elsewhere. Spirituals may have warmed his audience to his lecture topic, "Progress of the Negro Since 1863," the year of the Emancipation Proclamation. By the time of his spring graduation, he had given fifteen of these lectures and added a certificate in oral expression to his Music Conservatory certificate.[26] Routte was not only entering but attempting to transform Lutheran spaces to make place for Black folks like himself: this was mission work to white Lutherans. Faculty, whether or not they recognized their own churches as targets for this Black missionary, likely reinforced his interests, given the Synod's growing focus on "inner missions" work that, according to faculty member E. F. Bartholomew, focused on "the Street"—ministry to immigrants and others in order to "make the gospel a mighty factor in the life of the streets, a power of God unto salvation to the tens of thousands and hundreds of thousands who live their lives on the streets, who have no other home, no other school, no other sanctuary."[27]

A conference on inner missions was held at the college in November 1928; maybe this galvanized Routte, as during the holiday break, he traveled to Chicago. There, he followed Du Bois's lead, serving as a "social investigator" for the Augustana Synod's Inner Mission.[28] That winter, Routte canvassed six hundred Black families, reporting on their poverty, social situations, and lack of access to schools; he directed the choir and helped with their Christmas program.[29] The experience may have solidified his sense that racial uplift could come through Lutheran outreach. The Inner Mission was pleased with his work; indeed, historian Hazel V. Carby suggests that whites have historically been quicker to accept those "race men" who signify a particular kind of respectable, intellectual Black masculinity, holding them up as representatives of their race.[30]

But as one of four students to give a graduation recital that spring, Routte's artistic choices suggest that he used his role as representative to complicate Black identity for his white audience. The recital took place in the chapel, where, accompanied by Black musicians Houston and Frederick Swanson, he interspersed spirituals arranged by Burleigh, including "Deep River" and "Steal Away to Jesus," with poems by Black writers Paul Laurence Dunbar, Frances E. Watkins Harper, and Chicago native Fenton Johnson. He included a few vernacular poems such as "Keep A-Pluggin' Away" and "Dey Am Right" alongside literary works that celebrated Black culture in standard English. He seems to have read the entirety of Dunbar's short story "The Mortification of the Flesh," which embeds a critique of wealth in its Christian symbolism and local-color literary form.[31]

Routte likely chose these selections carefully and deliberately. Both Dunbar and Harper embed themes of protest within poems that reinforce ideas common to white Protestants, such as linking work to heavenly rewards. "Keep A-Pluggin' Away," for example, promotes diligence as the key to overcoming difficulties: "If the hills are high before / And the paths are hard to climb/Keep a-pluggin' away./And remember that successes/Come to him who bides his time,—/Keep a-pluggin' away." Yet the poem also suggests that the difficulties faced by the narrator are social rather than natural obstacles, as it is not the narrator's lack of hard work that stands in his way but rather the "sneers" of others. The promise of a "brighter day" in Heaven uses Christian imagery to evoke the idea that toil and perseverance are not rewarded equally for all: literary scholar Margaret Ronda notes that many of Dunbar's works suggest what is now called "institutional racism."[32]

Routte may have been aware that Black intellectuals of the 1920s such as James Weldon Johnson had critiqued Dunbar for his use of dialect in some "Black" poems and mimicking the "white voice" in his Standard English work. But scholars since have argued that Dunbar and other Black writers at the turn of the century were deliberately combining the refined and regal mode of poems like "Vashti" and "Ode to Ethiopia," with its Biblical allusions and language ("Be proud, my race, in mind and soul/Thy name is writ on Glory's scroll"), with dialect poems to explore different modes of Black identity and experience. While one form carried "cultural authority," the other served to "uplift" the realities of Black life: labor, family life, faith, struggle.[33] While Routte would have been guided by his instructors, it is difficult to imagine that these selections, all by Black writers and composers, were not entirely his own, chosen to reflect his own realities and priorities as a young man who used the authority of the Lutheran faith to create space for his own reality.

At his graduation, he was recognized as the first Black graduate of Augustana, with a degree in economics and commerce; moreover, he was the first Black person to enter Augustana Seminary. In the summer between his graduation and entering seminary, Routte went on tour around the Midwest, lecturing almost daily for three months. He presented at churches and Luther League meetings from Indiana to Michigan with his agenda of educating the public about the "homely" and "Christian" culture of Black Americans and "boosting Augustana." During his years at seminary, he broadened his topics to the artistic contributions of Black Americans and his perspective on the "Negro Problem." Pastors praised him for the "deep earnestness and conviction" with which he presented his message.[34] Routte was expanding his identity as a Black musician in becoming a Black Lutheran minister.

Routte's efforts during his time at Augustana did not banish racism from the campus, nor did they lead to a substantial population of Black students. His younger brother Louis followed him a few years later in graduating from the college and the Seminary. Louis played piano and guitar, acted in plays, and worked his way through school by operating a campus shoeshine stand.[35] By 1935, the Routtes and a seminary graduate from Hunan Province, China, named Ching Wang were the only non-white students to have graduated from Augustana; ten years later, the Routtes were still the only Black graduates.[36] Indeed, other Protestant denominations had excluded Black people, giving rise to AME in 1816. The persistent whiteness of Lutheran churches of the Midwest in the early twentieth century meant that in spite of his outreach, Routte was not offered leadership in any churches there. Embraced though he was as a representative of his race, Lutheran leaders determined that he was not ready to represent the faith—or perhaps the faith was not ready for him.

Routte's first placement was at Transfiguration Lutheran Church in Harlem, New York, which served a population of West Indian migrants: Black folks, who, to his surprise, had grown up Lutheran and wanted a Black pastor. There, he met his wife, Enid Gómez, who was born in the former Danish colony of St. Thomas (now US Virgin Islands) but identified as Puerto Rican and was a graduate student at Columbia University. In 1933, he helped found Holy Trinity Lutheran Church in Jamaica, Queens, in the heart of the West Indian community, and he continued his social outreach programs there for decades.[37] He returned to Augustana at least twice. In 1942 he sang at chapel and spoke to classes. A decade later, he shared with the Human Relations Club his "memories of his struggles for recognition on the Augie campus" and "challenged the group to actively support the ideals of the organization."[38]

Perhaps it was rewarding for him finally to have an audience receptive to hearing the realities of his experience. Perhaps he was thinking of his graduation recital more than two decades earlier, when his solos truly did represent a lone voice on campus. During his years at Augustana, Routte bravely put himself in front of white audiences to challenge Lutheran congregations to "widen the circle" by including Black people and their experiences; at the same time, he imagined an activist role for Lutheran missions in Black communities. But while churches welcomed him as a cultural spokesman, it seemed that no white Midwestern church was ready to let him lead. Indeed, there was no safe space from racism in the United States. After the murder of Emmett Till, Routte's wife and two of his children went to stay with her family in Puerto Rico, where his daughter remained, becoming a well-known Afro-Caribbean journalist. Writing in 1986, she recollected that "it was not any easy road that my parents chose to walk, run and charge along in the cause of civil rights. It was a road fraught with the fear and terror engendered by innocence and ignorance. But as my mother put it, there had to be a beginning. . . . That's my contract with my children. I have to make a better place in this world for them and while I'm doing it I'm doing it for others."[39]

For Jesse Routte as for his wife, Enid, there had to be a beginning. In electing to leave the historically Black AME church and enter into what Elijah Anderson calls the "deep White space" of an all-white college, Routte may have found success by bending the ideals of Lutheran education toward the needs of the Black community, pushing the college to acknowledge its existence through his artistic and historical presentations.[40] In the end, though, the college—and the church—shored up its property in whiteness by encouraging Routte in the idea that Black communities rather than white ones needed changing. Routte would eventually take his activism elsewhere, infamously using his acumen as a performer in a turban to reveal the boundaries of other white spaces. Perhaps he was thinking of Langston Hughes's 1926 poem "I, Too," as he continued this struggle: "Tomorrow/I'll be at the table/When company comes. . . . They'll see how beautiful I am/And be ashamed."[41]

ACT II: THE TRAVELER, 1949–1951

In the summer of 2022, Nigerian rap artist Oladips released a song that quickly became a hit in Nigeria and beyond. "Àjàlá Travel" takes its title from a song by another Nigerian musician, Ebenezer Obey, who released a song titled "Àjàlá the Traveler" as part of his Juju album

Board Members in 1972. The lyrics became part of Nigerian pop culture in the years that followed: "Àjàlá travel all over the world / Àjàlá travel / Àjàlá travel / Àjàlá travel all over the world." Indeed, the name came to stand for a person who refused to settle down, and the phrase "Àjàlá travel," used as a noun, stood for a certain kind of restless movement.[42]

Àjàlá was a real person, Mashood Adisa Olabisi Àjàlá, who became famous in the 1950s and '60s for his excursions, usually by motor scooter, "all over the world." His account of his globetrotting, published in 1963 as *An African Abroad*, brought him notoriety that lasted well beyond the book's brief original print run.[43] His run-ins with Jordanian border patrol agents, meeting with Soviet leader Nikita Khrushchev, audience with Israeli Prime Minister Golda Meir, and his international womanizing became the stuff of legend. But, as Nigerian scholar Senayon Olaoluwa argues, Àjàlá's audacious tourism in the era of African liberation movements also exemplified his physical and political "subversions of power." Àjàlá put his life on the literal line to undermine state power at various civic and international borders and to wrangle audiences with the world's most powerful leaders. Olaoluwa explains that in addition to Àjàlá's overt "self-fashioning" as an agbada-wearing Nigerian in ways that exhibited his transnational identity, his willingness to confront state authorities confirms Routte's experience of encountering border-policing in places far from national borders.[44] Even more deliberately than Routte, though, Àjàlá used personal relationships with his hosts to reveal and undermine that authority.

He dedicated his memoir to a list of "the many friends I have made during my journey, and particularly to the following people who have helped me in various ways." Along with his mother and individuals from Switzerland to Burma is listed "Dean Johnson, Rock Island, Illinois, U.S.A." This was Harry S. B. Johnson, a former pastor and professor of Greek who served as the dean of men at Augustana College from 1945 until 1964. How did Dean Harry Johnson end up on Àjàlá's list of friends? Àjàlá's first destination as a traveler was Augustana College, and his first piece of journalism in the United States was likely published in the *Augustana Observer* with the soon-to-be-infamous byline "M. A. Olabisi Ajala."

An examination of Àjàlá's time in Rock Island and his continuing ties to Augustana College after he relocated to Chicago help to provide insight into the experiences of an international student in the Midwest during the early postwar period, when the college made increased efforts to open itself to the world and Nigeria was facing political and financial turmoil. At the same time, it reveals the Augustana-era Àjàlá as a man already on a mission to challenge representations of Africa and Africans, cultivate advantageous friendships, and cross boundaries. Johnson's record of his many dealings with Àjàlá details a complex relationship, in which both Johnson and Àjàlá attempted to deal with local and international red tape; their correspondence suggests that Àjàlá was addressing his own vulnerability by using a familiar Nigerian strategy of cultivating the patronage of the person most likely to help him achieve his goals: in this case, Johnson. He would take this strategy with him around the world.

Àjàlá arrived in New York City by boat on September 20, 1949. At 4:09 p.m., he found himself in desperate straits and frantically wired Augustana's then-president Conrad Bergendoff. While Àjàlá had been accepted at Augustana College and was awarded a partial tuition scholarship and a work-study position, he had exhausted all his financial resources getting from Lagos, Nigeria, to New York City and still needed money to make the trek across half the country to Rock Island. He wrote, "Urgently request advance of funds to enable me to reach college pending receipt of remittances from home."[45] Mildred A. Busch, a teacher at Hunter College High School, stepped in to provide the young man with the necessary funds and even cabled Harry Johnson to ask that someone meet the young Nigerian at the Rock Island train station. Àjàlá was off to a rocky start.[46]

This image of a young, desperate Àjàlá trying to reach Augustana stands in stark contrast to the popularized image of him as the international playboy who fathered children with multiple women in various nations, traveled to eighty-seven countries, and acted in the 1953 Hollywood film *White Witch Doctor.* Perhaps this is because the academic year that he spent at Augustana College is rarely mentioned in popular or scholarly accounts of Àjàlá, most of which date his arrival in the United States to 1952, as a premedical student at the University of Chicago. To a degree, this is understandable, as his financial situation was insecure; Àjàlá may have been embarrassed to discuss his first year in the United States, when both he and the college were attempting to negotiate new balances of power between the United States and other nations as well as the effects of rising African nationalism in Nigeria and elsewhere. This situation spurred on the college's interest in international exchange, but it also created new pressures for these students.

The year before Àjàlá's arrival at Augustana, the Student Union began to host the "Friendship Fair," an all-college gathering whose proceeds were donated to "bring one or two foreign students to Augustana to study." Both the fair and support for international students were meant to "show the fundamental friendly attitude of Augie."[47] The first fair clearly meant to repair ties broken by World War II: the plan was to invite two Austrian students from the University of Vienna.[48] The Austrians, Leonhard Ceconi and Margaret Bauer, arrived in fall of 1949, grateful for the "idealistic enthusiasm" and "friendly attitude and joyfulness" of Augustana students. The *Observer* described the exchange as helping Austrian students, noting that being a good neighbor "brightens our own lives."[49]

The Friendship Fair and emphasis on study abroad occurred during the early years of the Cold War as the United States attempted to expose the world to the American way of life and to repair broken relations. Àjàlá was not a recipient of Friendship Fair funding, but he arrived on campus at the same time as the Austrians, along with a student from China and one from Poland. It is unclear how Àjàlá made the connection to Augustana; the college may have indicated to the Institute of International Education that it was interested in hosting a Nigerian.[50] He was not Lutheran. His father was Muslim, and Àjàlá attended the Lagos Baptist Academy and the Anglican boys' high school in Íbàdàn. His memoir is vague on motive, stating only that he went to America because "I had several ideas about life and my future, and I felt that to achieve them I would have to leave the Nigerian society." He wrote that he went to New York in 1948, against the wishes of his father but funded by an uncle; letters to and from Johnson, however, indicate that he arrived in 1949 and that his trip was paid for by a lawyer in Lagos, Samuel Okanade Ayila Kester.[51] Mildred Busch, who helped him make his way to Rock Island, was a member of Christ Lutheran Church in Mount Vernon, New York, and may have had connections to the Augustana Synod. The college granted Àjàlá a "one-year Lutheran scholarship" and indicated that he was "the first and only African to be admitted into our college on tuition scholarship."[52]

Augustana's air of openness and friendliness toward foreign students may have appealed to Àjàlá. He later described being involved in intramural swimming, running, and tennis and being invited into professors' homes. Faculty provided him with warm clothing during the frigid Midwestern winter, and he said he was "spared the embarrassment of racial bias." But there were frustrations: with registration red tape, unfamiliar cafeteria food, and people's inability to pronounce his name. Instead, students gave him a nickname: Mexi. While Àjàlá did not seem to mind this nickname, it was likely meant to set him apart from the handful of African American students. Not African American but clearly not white, he was "Mexi." When he mentioned appreciating the help of friends, he expressed his special thanks to "my Negro friends in Davenport, Moline, and Rock Island," suggesting that he looked beyond campus to find community with other people of color.[53]

Àjàlá was part of the international Cosmopolitan Club (Fig. 3.2), yet he seems to have kept a lower profile on campus than some of the other exchange students: Austrian Ceconi spoke in chapel, as did Eunice Djao of Hong Kong, who seems to have been especially active. She joined the Sigma Mu Alpha music fraternity, took part in an art club fundraiser in which students modeled "costumes from various countries," and participated in the Augustana Foreign Mission Society fundraiser, displaying her "native costumes" and singing "some of her oriental songs."[54] Àjàlá had already left Augustana by the time of the Mission Society fundraiser in the spring of 1951, but the characterization of Africa and Africans at events such as these, where students spoke about mission work alongside artifacts representing the "dark continent," likely troubled him.[55] The "mission tea" with displays of items such as knives and "witch-doctor" masks seemed to be a feature of the spring and fall mission weeks at Augustana, where Africa was often discussed. In October 1949, the week's theme was "White unto the Harvest."[56] Àjàlá had moved into Andreen Hall just a few weeks earlier.

Fig. 3.2. Mashood Àjàlá (*front row, second from right*) as member of the Cosmopolitan Club, 1949. Augustana *Rockety-I* yearbook, 1950. Courtesy of Augustana College Special Collections, Rock Island, Illinois.

These exhibits, some clearly meant to show the "primitivity" of the African people, would have grated on Àjàlá, who had come of age in a time of rising nationalism and campaigns for self-governance in Nigeria and elsewhere. He left home in the midst of labor strikes and colonial backlash; ethnic factions were struggling for control of nationalist movements. He may have had political motives for his study in the United States, since he preferred not to study in Great Britain, the colonizing power, and allegedly told Augustana administrators that he hoped his American education would help him to "instigate political revolt against British rule" upon his return.[57] He clearly came prepared to educate others about Nigeria: one of his first acts on campus was to alert Johnson of his intent to deliver a public lecture. Titled "As an African—From Nigeria," it was to be "of an informal nature." Johnson quickly discouraged him, writing that while "I am sure that all of us want to hear about your native land . . . I think it wise for you to defer this lecture for several months until you have become better acquainted with our language."[58] Àjàlá, a British subject, wrote and spoke in English already. Perhaps Johnson was not acquainted with him enough to know this, but if he was already aware of the young Nigerian's revolutionary energies, he might have felt that Augustana was not quite ready for Àjàlá.

It seems that he never was able to deliver this lecture on campus, since he quickly became mired in financial struggles that occupied much of his psychic space—and Johnson's. Àjàlá was penniless in the United States, and no funds arrived from his sponsor. While the college arranged for him to work in the cafeteria and covered his fall tuition, he had nothing left for books, lab fees, or other expenses; moreover, if he planned to stay another semester, he would need to come up with nearly $600. Rather than making Àjàlá leave, Johnson began writing letters to potential sponsors: the Nigerian Secretariat, the American Consul-General in Lagos, the Institute for International Education, a businessman friend of Àjàlá's family, Àjàlá's brother and father. By January, no money had arrived from any quarter; worse, Àjàlá learned that his sponsor had died in December.[59]

Àjàlá was writing letters of his own, though. He began contacting historically Black colleges and universities in the South, and soon inquiries about his academic record and "Christian character" arrived on Johnson's desk from Fisk University and Knoxville College. Àjàlá had indicated that he was hoping to move to a warmer climate and that he wanted to be at a Black institution. J. Reed Miller, the president of Knoxville College, after noting that he hoped his inquiry would not jeopardize Àjàlá's standing and that "my mother was a Lutheran and I feel quite at home among the people of your group," indicated diplomatically that "sometimes Negro young people feel more at home among their own people."[60] Johnson struggled to answer as diplomatically. He may have genuinely liked Àjàlá but could not attest to his academic and financial credentials. To Miller, he wrote, "Mr. Ajala is a very acceptable person. . . . I have been unable to decide whether his trouble with his studies is due to lack of ability or to problems of adjustment only." He agreed that Àjàlá might do better "among his own people" and explained that his dire straits were due to his sponsor's death, but he warned Reed and Harold Smith, of Fisk, that Àjàlá would need financial support and expressed his doubts about Àjàlá's ability to "adjust to the American educational system."[61] Johnson seemed uncertain about what it meant for an African in America to be among "his own people": Was it nationality or skin tone that mattered?

While Johnson did not say as much to his fellow administrators, he knew Àjàlá was suffering. Àjàlá must have written to his family friend, Adeniji, to say he was considering suicide rather than face deportation. Adeniji sternly advised him against it, noting that death would "rightly mark you a cowardly living young man, and inexperienced. If you are on adventure and happen to meet obstacles and difficulties it is for you to know how to get rid of them. . . . I therefore advise you very strongly to arise and advance forward to pick up the mantle of courage to get what you want by dint of hard working, expand your social status among the men of Uncle-Sam, whom I believe are always prepared to help all shrewd business people."[62]

Àjàlá's brother, however, had a different response to the suicide threat: "You had better die than come back to Nigeria empty-handedly. . . . It is a complete disgrace for a person who left not more than six months ago with the aim of studying to return to Nigeria in such a way." He informed Àjàlá that others were working on his behalf and that Àjàlá should continue to plead his case to his father, who, though he was "the most nefarious man in the world," was still their father. He admonished his brother to "struggle very hard" as there is "no wall so high that it cannot be climbed at last." Otherwise, it would be better to die by suicide and "leave your parents to mourn your death."[63]

Perhaps knowing that Àjàlá was in such mental anguish pushed Johnson to continue working on his behalf. Johnson himself wrote to Àjàlá's father, assuring him that his son was making progress. Johnson invoked the biblical story of the prodigal son, writing "you have a son in a far-off country in need of help, and I am sure that you will never regret extending him a helping hand." Johnson's letter must have accompanied one that Àjàlá wrote to his father, in which the son invoked not the Bible but Allah: "I tried to use the little bit of wisdom Allah has given me to help me to arrange my education. . . . Because I want to be of service to my country, I must get my education where I can be made the most useful citizen."[64]

Even as Àjàlá was struggling with self-destructive thoughts and fears of deportation, he finally followed through on his aim to educate the campus about his home. There is no evidence of a lecture, but in mid-March 1950, Àjàlá's lengthy article, "Augustana Student Explains . . . Africa Not an Uncultured, Dark Continent," appeared in the *Augustana Observer*. The article is a taste of the sharp observation, conversational flair, and unflinching social criticism that would characterize his later writing. In bold print, he states his intentions: "my motive is to repudiate and uproot the general misconception held by many Americanized Europeans, Negroes, and Asiatics that Africa is a continent where the natives are of low intelligence and are rubbing shoulders with animals." He debunks the myth of the "dark continent" held by "every Tom, Dick, and Harry," enlightening his readers about the diversity of cultures, languages, and nations in Africa; he explained that the University of Sankoré in Mali predated Oxford and that Sudan had existed as a wealthy and peaceful empire when tribal wars had raged in medieval Europe. He acknowledged the political turmoil in Africa, claimed that Americans would do well to pay attention to these revolutions, and suggested that African nations would soon take a greater place on the world stage.[65] Àjàlá had found his way to the media, creating what was possibly the first of many press releases attacking preconceptions about Africans.

It is possible that his desire to assert his identity as an African among Americans—including a small number of African Americans—at Augustana also led him to change his self-presentation on campus. In an October *Observer* photograph, he appears alongside other international students about to attend their first American football game; all of them are receiving "gridiron tips" from the team captain. Àjàlá leans back, aloof, hands in pockets, wearing a collegiate sweater, slacks, and tie. By the end of the year, however, he appears in a Yoruba agbada in a group photo of first-year students in the yearbook. While he seems to have spurned any opportunity to dress in "native costume" for campus events like the Friendship Fair, in his yearbook photo, he asserted his West African identity against those of white and Black students at the college.[66]

His more overt self-presentation as a Nigerian at Augustana may have been a response to the presence of state power limiting his choices. His lack of funds and weak academic record meant he would not be able to remain in the United States—he needed to be in school, working, or both. Àjàlá went to Chicago several times in the spring of 1950 to deal with immigration paperwork, and by summer he had moved there. Johnson had contacted the pastor of Bronzeville's Olivet Baptist Church, the oldest Black Baptist church in Chicago, and Reverend J. H. Jackson found a job for Àjàlá as an orderly at Provident Hospital, a facility founded by and serving the Black community of Chicago. As Johnson dashed off letters to the Immigration and Naturalization Service, Department of Justice, and the Nigerian Consulate, which was offering to provide assistance to Nigerian students in the United States who had been affected by the economic crisis at home, Àjàlá moved into a Chicago YMCA, with plans to pay off his debt to Augustana and return as soon as possible.[67]

In Chicago he encountered racial rather than national barriers. His wages at Provident were low, and he struggled to pay his expenses in a city where "everybody go the way of laissez faire." By the end of summer, he had not sent any money to Johnson. He managed to get an orderly job at an all-white hospital, where his wages were nearly 50 percent higher. He sent his pay stubs to Johnson as proof. He applied to Loyola University and asked Johnson, whom he strategically commended for his "conspicuous and notable part in the building of my educational general existence," to explain his low grades: "you are aware of the reasons for that, on which I will appreciate having your testimony and recommendation of me." While Johnson was willing to do so, the registrar refused to send a transcript until Àjàlá made a payment. In September, he sent fourteen dollars; Johnson obliged with a letter to Loyola in which he explained Àjàlá's loss of sponsorship but not his low grades. When Loyola turned Àjàlá down, Johnson returned the money.[68]

Àjàlá responded, as he had for months, by turning to his relationship with Johnson, but both seemed to be aware that Àjàlá's ties to Augustana were no longer going to sustain him. "At the moment, I am totally confused as to my academic situation," he wrote. "I need your brotherly advice." Choosing to be more fatherly than brotherly, Johnson gave Àjàlá a version of what he had told his fellow administrators for months. Johnson told him this was a matter that required Àjàlá to "search out your own heart and mind." He did not believe the young Nigerian had the "native ability" to be successful in college. "I do not question your ambition nor do I question your desire to do all in your power to secure an education. I do question whether or not you will be able to complete your work no matter how hard you try," Johnson wrote. He stressed that his seemingly cruel comment came from a place of love. If he had repeatedly failed to get into college, Johnson suggested, he would "take it as an indication that college work was not intended for me and would seek to further my personal ambitions though other channels."[69] The words did sting. Though Àjàlá later thanked Johnson for his honesty, he reaffirmed his ambition, and by that summer, he had cultivated an alliance with a new patron, a white doctor from Illinois named David Engelking.[70]

Augustana administrators were done with Nigerians. Johnson wrote the British Embassy to that effect; when Àjàlá applied to George Williams College in Chicago, Augustana admissions director Herbert Glynn wrote to the registrar there to warn them. Admitting Àjàlá had caused a "deluge" of applications from other Nigerians, but he had been such a headache—his bill remained unpaid—that Glynn vowed not to accept another. As for Àjàlá, he was "a case for the immigration authorities."[71] Àjàlá's yearlong transgression of the economic, academic, and political boundaries that defined membership at Augustana caused such trouble that even when Nigerian authorities tried to smooth the way for Nigerian students in the United States, the college slammed the door. Augustana continued sponsoring foreign students through 1951, but by 1953, Friendship Fair funds were repurposed to repay the Student Union's debt.[72]

But Àjàlá was just getting started. The man whom Olaoluwa describes as "compulsively enamored of power" and able to cross boundaries precisely because of a "creative strategy that is veiled by innocence" was clearly emerging during his time at Augustana, where his friendship with Johnson ensured his ability to stay on campus.[73] Upon arrival in Chicago, he must have made his way to the office of the *Chicago Defender*, at that time the nation's most prominent Black newspaper, and briefly held a job there. By May 1950, the *Defender*'s Lutrelle Palmer had already written a profile of him. Subsequent articles about him appeared in the *Defender*, which later described him as "the most colorful character to hit the Chicago scene."[74] During a short stint at DePaul University, he joined its newspaper staff. By the next year, he was a premed student at Roosevelt College. But in 1952, out of a need for money, visibility, power, or all three, he abandoned study for the sort of risk taking that would characterize his journalistic career.

In 1952, he donned his agbada—which later became his attire of choice as a traveler—for a bicycle tour across the United States funded by his "Africa Today" lectures in churches in cities such as Joliet, Springfield, St. Louis, and Denver. During his trek, he was robbed once and briefly jailed for attempting to stay at a whites-only YMCA.[75] In Los Angeles, he got a supporting role in the film *White Witch Doctor* starring Robert Mitchum. His exploits there were literally straight out of Hollywood: a nurse sued him for child support, he was arrested for passing bad checks, he went on a hunger strike, and he climbed a radio tower to evade immigration authorities, calling down that he would jump to his death rather than be deported to Nigeria. Ramping up claims for asylum that he had made in 1950, he professed that to be returned would result not just in shame but in "tribal execution."[76] His history—and perhaps more importantly, his future—suggest that this stunt was less a threat to his own life than a highly visible, physical form of resistance to geopolitical boundaries that surrounded the bodies of transnational travelers wherever they went.

ACT III: A CRITICAL MASS, 1968–1978

When Martin Luther King Jr. was assassinated on April 4, 1968, his death seemed to cause barely a ripple on the Augustana campus. The new campus chaplain, Robert Sorensen (no relation to the college president at the time), led a memorial service that was attended by nearly all the Black students on campus (about twenty-five) but only a tiny fraction of white students, faculty, and administrators—despite the fact that classes had been canceled. In a letter to campus about what he saw as a "disgrace for Augustana," Sorensen reminded his audience of Augustana's Lutheran heritage and emphasized that King's murder was a tragedy for "all Christians who happen to be Americans." A student, Lynne Curtis, echoed Sorensen's sentiment by contrasting the paltry turnout to the crowds of mourners in Atlanta. "I am sad and very sorry that Augustana would not honor such a man or pray for such a dream," Curtis wrote. Finally, another letter writer, R. P., lambasted both the campus and the nation for the "cancerous condition" of racism that, the author remonstrated, was just as present in the hate speech of Northern radio disc jockeys and city governments as it was in the South. The author denounced the "racial antipathy" exhibited by many who would call themselves Christians but who refused to recognize the ways their faith called them to act on civil rights abuses.[77]

This lack of response to King's death galvanized Black students and supporters to challenge white complacency and to look, as elsewhere in the nation, to the Black Power movement for a language to articulate and politicize their identities as Black students on a white campus. Studies of the Black campus movement generally suggest that by adopting the strategies of the Black Power movement, student groups constructed themselves as formidable oppositional forces that pressured administrators to respond. At many large, public, urban institutions, students were able to join forces with other ethnic minorities and with community organizations. Black students were also challenging long-standing ideas of institutional identity at smaller colleges, where the size, religious affiliation, and relative isolation of campus and community may have fostered a more coherent but less flexible campus identity. Lauren Araiza, in her study of the Black Power movement at tiny Mills College for women in Oakland, California, demonstrates that Black students there were not only opposing institutionalized racism but were defying community and campus ideas of what a "Mills girl" was.[78] Oakland, unlike Rock Island, was a center of Black nationalism in the 1960s, but between 1968 and 1972, Black students at Augustana used public expressions of Black Power to ignite critical conversations about how well the college could live out its Christian mission if it continued to insulate itself from the struggles of its Black neighbors. While religion is not often considered with respect to the Black campus movement, students at Augustana seem to have imported ideals from the Black church that framed Jesus as a revolutionary who challenged political power structures and asked followers to do the same.

Shortly after King's murder, Black students at Augustana formed the Afro-American Society (AAS), the first organization on campus founded specifically to address their concerns. In doing so, they joined the national Black campus movement that developed in the mid-1960s in which Black student groups carved out formal and informal spaces to discuss political beliefs and engage in practices and behaviors that were in opposition to, and even consciously critical of, the white majority. In 1969–1970, almost half of the twenty-four members of the AAS were from Chicago and would likely have been familiar with, if not participants in, the public school boycotts between 1966 and 1968 that protested racial segregation in Chicago schools and demanded both physical improvements and curricular changes.[79] The AAS, later called the Black Student Union (BSU), followed this strategy and that of many other campus groups in creating a sense of collective identity that led to a set of demands for change: increased recruitment of Black students, more Black professors, courses that focused on Black culture and history, and policies that held students, faculty, and staff accountable for racist acts.[80]

Many members of the AAS responded to alienation through a separatist strategy, marking a departure from earlier Black students' efforts to be included in existing Augustana campus groups and events, from Greek organizations to the annual Swedish Sankta Lucia festival. Separatism challenged the language of "acceptance" that dovetailed with progressive Lutheran attitudes but rarely exposed the ways campus life was structured around historically white culture and values. The administration reported that, in 1968–1969, Black students had begun to "withdraw from the campus community as a whole," preferring "black-oriented" activities. Some, allegedly at the insistence of AAS leaders, actively avoided campus events and even quit activities such as band, drama, and athletics. According to BSU leader Joe Looney, this created divisions within the group, as some feared being tagged as "Uncle Toms" while others resisted, demanding the right to "determine their own destiny."[81] In late 1968, student Cathy Johnson observed that white students were befuddled at the "segregationist" orientation of the AAS. They failed to understand AAS actions as necessary to the "growing pains of black pride" and responded by "recoiling in misunderstanding" upon having the experience of being rejected themselves.[82] Black students were also likely struggling to rectify cultural separatism with their isolation on campus. Unlike student groups in

Chicago or Oakland, Augustana did not have strong ties with the local Black community for students to draw on.[83] Still, by the end of 1969, the AAS had developed a policy that empowered Black students to make their own social choices while making the organization the public face of the Black student body.

Members' statements as well as campus reactions to those statements suggest that while the organization's goals were political, white students often read their efforts as merely performative. In an October issue of the *Observer*, the AAS declared that "the Afro-American Society is on the move" and that they were "tired of being on the outside looking in." They warned the campus that "the black students at Augie are wide awake. They are going to pull the campus out of a deep, blinded sleep. . . . WE ARE ON THE MOVE!"[84] Using the language of the Black Power movement, the letter provoked a range of responses from white faculty and students, who may not have situated the AAS's representational politics within this context. Psychology professor Jack Hullett wrote the *Observer* to laud the AAS for pointing out "de facto segregation (mental and physical)" on the campus but also to note that their request to "get" a Black faculty member "smacks of tokenism, and I choke on it." A self-identified "white student, paying full tuition and room and board," asked how Black students could see themselves as "outsiders" when they regularly participated in sports, complaining that these athletes were "getting a free ride." Another student, John Greenwood, challenged the AAS to do more than mere posturing—wearing "Afro clothes," buttons, and spouting rhetoric rather than "changing minds, attitudes, and prejudices."[85] While it is tempting to see this debate as simple resistance to Black students' call for change, it shows a range of positions, as faculty and students sought to determine how the movement fit into existing values at the college, both liberal and conservative. Greenwood was a member of the leftist Youth International Party (YIP), which was involved in a campaign for housing security in Rock Island's largely Black West End, while Hullett gave racial sensitivity training to the Rock Island police force and would later serve on the board of the Black Culture House.[86]

While the majority at Augustana may have seen the AAS as being simply disruptive to campus norms, others understood it as part of a national movement.[87] White student leftist Bill Sampson first defined

Black Power in the student newspaper as a political, educational, and economic strategy; by fall of 1968, three Augustana students joined others from various colleges and universities at a conference on institutionalized racism at the University of Notre Dame, where they strategized about ways to combat racist structures at their schools.[88] The demands of the AAS at Augustana followed an organized national agenda to integrate Black culture into campuses and curricula. Professors Ross Paulson and Harold Bell recognized this effort, pointing out to the campus community that in asking that their own history be taught, members of the AAS were "following the path taken by countless immigrant ethnic groups in the past century," including Swedes at Augustana. Responding directly to Hullett, his colleagues reinforced the claim of Black studies advocates that "the study of history is a means of overcoming alienation and of achieving self-identification."[89]

While Paulson and Bell attempted to draw a connection between appreciating Swedish history and including Black history, individuals both on campus and off felt that Black Power unsettled the identity of Augustana as a Lutheran institution. Starting in fall, 1968, the AAS organized, along with a few white students, a "Black Power Symposium" held in February 1969 (Fig. 3.3). Officially titled "Confrontation '69," the symposium was meant to showcase various methods emerging from the Black community to promote political, educational, and economic empowerment and pride. Prominent leaders of the movement Dick Gregory, Adam Clayton Powell, and Roy Innis were invited, but other speakers included teacher Roy Morrison and several Black ministers: a young and recently ordained Jesse Jackson and C. S. Smith of the historic Bethel AME Church in Davenport, Iowa, who was an advocate of Black Power and a leader in the local aid organization Project NOW.[90] When Augustana announced the event and its roster of speakers, some Quad Citians, parents, and alumni were quick to express their displeasure. Sorensen defended the event on the grounds of free speech, noting that student organizers were in charge and pointing out that Senator Strom Thurmond, a segregationist and opponent of civil rights, had spoken on campus the previous year. Views expressed at the event were not the institution's, Sorensen explained. Thurmond's presence had elicited silent protest from some attendees; a week later, the student Representative Assembly noted that while it "approved of the chance to hear this dim voice from the past," it stated that "his racism is wholly untenable." Those who objected to the symposium, however, claimed that Gregory and Powell were "crooks" and political insurgents who might incite unrest. One writer averred that "police should be allowed to shoot any group that takes over the Dean's office in a college." Several alumni called upon the college to consider its Christian mission; the parents of a student wrote in to express dismay and claimed the symposium was evidence that "Augustana's usefulness to God and the Christian community was slipping fast."[91]

When faced with a public debate among Black leaders over different paths toward civil rights, some members of Augustana and the broader community opted to evade questions of white Christians' responsibility for achieving racial equality by entrenching themselves in the question of whether a Christian college should host speakers who were

Fig. 3.3. Roy Innis with students at the Augustana Black Power Symposium, February 1969. Augustana College Photograph Collection, C-F03913. Courtesy of Augustana College Special Collections, Rock Island, Illinois.

"immoral." Rather than using a more overtly racist story that would defend the campus as a "white space," dissenters defined Gregory and Powell as threats to the campus as a Christian space, calling on liberal ideals of separation of politics and faith. In so doing, however, these objectors demonstrated their lack of understanding that Christian spaces had historically served as places of safety and of protest for Black Americans. Gregory, who drew the most concern, was an entertainer who not only collaborated with Black church leaders on social justice measures but frequently critiqued Euro-Americans' use of religion as an instrument of power over non-white bodies. Vaughn Booker argues that Gregory, influenced by both Christian nonviolence and the social critiques emerging from the Black church, used comedy to offer commentaries on the Bible that challenged both Black and white Christians to see the "absurdity in their mournful worship of Jesus without meaningful engagement with current social sins."[92] Critics, in other words, entrenched themselves in a version of Christianity that not only excluded Gregory but generally ignored the presence of Black pastors from Chicago and Davenport who represented liberatory theological traditions emerging from historical Black experiences.[93]

The symposium was one visible manifestation of the confrontations that developed as the college tried to define what racial equality might look like on a white, church-related campus. Many of these revolved around a simmering discussion of what some saw as the "tokenism" that Hullett had challenged and the need for substantial institutional commitment to creating an anti-racist environment. In the lead-up to the Black Power Symposium, Reverend C. S. Smith of Davenport expressed his anger at white people's ongoing efforts to deny Black people's "right to exist." Their "riots and such are to help you understand that tokenisms won't work—tokenisms such as Augustana's four scholarships for four blacks. Obviously, you do not understand what we think and cannot understand what we want, which is what you must do rather than place tokens in our hands."[94] Indeed, the college likely saw the AAS's initial requests, such as hiring Black faculty and offering scholarships, as actionable items to quell dissent rather than part of a national call to acknowledge the validity and vitality of Black culture and history. Responding to Black students' request for a Black faculty member, Sorensen had apprised them of the college's fruitless efforts to do that, offering that "one of the members of the Augustana College Board of Directors is a Negro Pastor from Chicago."[95]

This was Robbin Skyles of St. James Lutheran Church, Illinois's first Black Lutheran church, who had also urged the college to think beyond questions of admitting Black students to consider what fostering Black students *as part of the* broader Black community would actually mean. In a document titled "Priorities in Relation to the Community at Large and in Relation to the Student from the Disadvantaged Community," Skyles urged the college to consider its Lutheran identity in relation to its Black neighbors, suggesting that the college should adapt in response to external factors. It should look to more "unorthodox criteria" in admitting some students from under-resourced schools—not grades but attitudes such as "determination," "growth potential," "integrity," and "dreams." He noted that Black students might take time to "demonstrate their full self-confidence" in an "all-white situation" and warned that "success" for minority students might not mean graduating. Presumably on behalf of his congregation, he advised that mission funds that had "religiously been sent abroad for so many years be spent on our black neighbors here at home" in order to help "the church to purge itself of its ancient American hypocrisy which focused upon sin and evil in foreign lands while steadfastly ignoring or denying the dehumanization and exclusion which result in the active and deep-rooted racism of this country."[96] This undated report may have been prompted by discussion among other Black Lutherans in Chicago. In a September 1969 letter to Sorensen and Skyles, Troy Hedrick, pastor of Christ the Mediator Church, pointed out ways that the college had failed its Black neighbors: "I do not feel that the college has kept its promises to seriously consider the ways in which it can assist the church in the urban situation of today." The college had agreed to start a Center for Urban Studies that was meant to "be a resource for the church as well as a training center for persons attending the college," but Black deacons in Chicago were not convinced that the college was serious about its "responsibility in dealing with White Racism and the Urban Crisis."[97]

The failure of the college to make meaningful connections with its Black neighbors in ways that would sustain both the campus and the community seems to confirm a warning to "white Christian liberals" that visiting professor of religion Stanley Hauerwas, who had arrived on campus in fall of 1968, issued at the time of the symposium. Their response to Black Power, he wrote, "has been mainly one of some resentment and almost complete bewilderment. . . . They feel as if the starved dog they tried to feed has suddenly bitten the hand of his benefactor." He was intrigued by the way the movement moved away from civil rights strategies that seemed to require Black people to be *more* moral than white people and challenged white liberals to stop using their feelings of guilt as "proof of their morality" in the face of social and political inequalities that required more than "good intentions." Hauerwas, who left Augustana for Duke University and became one of the nation's most prominent theologians, worried, however, that the Black Power movement, which he associated primarily with political spaces, could never satisfy the deeply spiritual human need to find meaning in life.[98]

Hauerwas remains wary of links between Christianity and politics today. Many Black faith leaders such as Jemar Tisby, though, claim a long tradition of bringing "faith into the public square for the common good and flourishing of all humanity," pushing back against the idea that ending racism is a political rather than spiritual imperative.[99] Others linked the imperative of ending racism on campus to the spiritual needs of Black and white students. Campus pastor Richard Swanson amplified the concerns of the AAS in a 1969 memo to Sorensen. With some sarcasm, he pointed out the error in the college's assumption that "admission to the White educational enterprise would be a most welcome gift to the Black Folk." Merely allowing them to partake in "glories" such as athletics and lectures by white academics would do little to help Black students to cultivate their own identities. He urged a "Blackness-supportive environment" that would allow "Blackness to survive" at a white institution. The AAS's list of demands, he argued, was not just a list of changes to be made: these were required to allow Black students to thrive in mission-oriented ways that had been historically available to white students. To view education as a gift to Black people without changing that education in order to nourish their souls as well was, Swanson charged, itself a form of racism we often now recognize as "the white savior complex."[100]

Swanson's letter was part of a campaign to make Black students and Black culture more visible on campus by creating a Black Culture House: what *Observer* reporter Deb Skromme described as "an oasis in a sea of white."[101] Despite directives from the Board of Education that prohibited the building from being exclusive to Black students, the AAS and BSU successfully created a space that not only served their needs but also followed the precedent of Freedom Schools. Black students held cultural events there throughout the year, and as part of an effort to "bridge the communication gap" between Black Augustana students and Black community members, they collaborated with the Rock Island Youth Council on a tutoring program for elementary through high school students. Later on, they added programming on Black history.[102] The Black Culture House also served as a home base for recruitment and retention efforts by and for Black students that began in 1968.

After the AAS had asked administrators to recruit more Black students, it suggested that members could recruit in Rock Island schools. While the AAS rightly pointed out that this was not its work to do, two members eventually agreed to help the admissions office. In the summer of 1971, these student recruiters were paid for their work.[103] And the work had results: while the number of Black students fell short of the goal of 10 percent of the student body, their population quadrupled between spring 1968, when the AAS formed, and May 1973, from 25 to 112.[104] After its founding, the Black Culture House served as a locus for the student-led Black Student Orientation. Members would take students on a tour of campus, help them fill out their registration materials, and introduce them to the organization. There were barbecues in nearby Lincoln Park, a dance, and an all-day open house. The members cautioned new students to have no illusions about what it was like to a be a Black student at a white liberal arts college in a small town. "If you're looking for something big and exciting," Augustana was not the right place. But a small college offered the advantage of close relationships with faculty, with the Black community in Rock Island, and with one another. "Augustana is what you make it to be," wrote AAS President Kenneth Mason in 1969. "We . . . have attempted to make it what we thought was for the good of all, both Black and White."[105]

Many white critics of the Black campus movement, at Augustana and elsewhere, may not have been aware of the role of Black churches in creating spaces and programming where Black history, culture, and humanity was affirmed or have known that for many Black Americans, political positions that appeared radical were rooted in the gospel and other faith traditions. Theologian James Cone wrote in 1969's *Black Theology and Black Power* that the liberation of Black people was one of the deepest expressions of Christian theology.[106] Although the college began to make progress on curricular and structural changes after 1969, Black students remained frustrated in their attempts to push the college from a position of liberal-minded accommodation of their needs to do the more difficult work of nourishing their souls. Even as the campus made space for Black culture and denounced racism, it struggled to embrace dismantling racist structures as part of its mission as a Lutheran institution rather than as a matter of secular politics.

Eight years after the Black Power Symposium, members of the BSU expressed their frustration with the white majority in a poem published in the student newspaper. They were explicit about the lack of respect and collegiality that continued to lead to acts of blatant bigotry on campus. White students blamed them, they said, for being the ones who "get all the financial aid / A free college ticket that's government paid / A Black house with a color TV, a record player and a carpet made of suede / All of this is what the school paid to keep us from making them afraid." They resisted being called "militants" or separatists when "the social life at this school is made for you" and invited white students to try coming to *their* events: "come join us next time we throw an all school dance / Come be a part of the rhythm grace and debonair of the rubber band dance / Come feel the spiritual fire of the Gospel Choir / Make this school a real learning experience."[107]

Augustana's BSU, like other organizations of the Black campus movement, is often associated with a list of demands—for a Black professor, a Black history course, admissions outreach, a safe space on campus, and policies to punish racist acts. As the poets suggested, though, the administration's eventual assent to these demands may have been a way to placate Black students that was in keeping with the school's liberal arts mission. Harder to change, they found, was a climate in which Black students were admitted yet were not fully included in the institution's mission to nourish mind, body, *and* spirit. Their growing numbers gave them a sense of community and increasing visibility, but their advocacy demonstrates a longing that went beyond their demands. They and their supporters insisted not only that Black bodies be admitted but also that Black culture, history, and faith have a role in directing the institution's future. They forged links between the campus and the Black community in Rock Island, provoked reflection on the difference between racist acts and racist environments and challenged Augustana to understand that its Lutheran mission required more than acceptance. Even in 1969, as the college responded to an inquiry about the effects of an increased enrollment of Black students by pointing to rising "resentment" among white students, it admitted that their presence had made the campus "more aware of racial problems" and that Black student activism likely precipitated the students' rights movement.[108]

Faculty and students' desire to use the religious and educational orientation of the college to serve what former president of Fisk University James R. Lawson defined as the cultivation of "self-knowledge, a drawing-out and realization of students' identities as Blacks as well as their talents as individuals" has been difficult to achieve for Augustana, as a predominantly and historically white college.[109] While Routte enjoyed individual success at Augustana by performing his Black identity in traditionally white spaces and joining the Lutheran church, Àjàlá challenged the policies and procedures of a college that was not designed for students like him. The BSU drew more attention to institutional obstacles by acting collectively on campus, using the strategies of the Black campus movement in concert with the traditions of Black churches to challenge the college's commitment to its Christian mission. The circle was indeed widening. Rather than forcing Black students and faculty to do the exhausting work of performing their Blackness in front of white audiences as Routte had done, the BSU and its allies sought to draw attention to the fact that until Black identities were woven into the fabric of the institution, its committees, studies, and policies would remain merely performative.

Notes

1. Articles about Routte and his turban were published in papers from New York City to Perth, Australia. See, for example, "Turban or Not Tur Ban," *San Antonio Light*, November 17, 1947, 1; "A Turbaned Negro," *West Australian* (Perth), November 18, 1947, 14; "Queens Negro Pastor in a Turban Gets 'White' Service in Deep South," *New York Times*, November 17, 1947, 1; "Negro Says Turban Is 'Open Sesame' for Him," *Dubuque Telegraph Herald*, November 17, 1947, 4. On the cross-burning, see Routté-Gómez, "Tale of Two Cultures," 105.

2. Kramer, "Importance," 213; Misra, "How Turbans Helped." On Routte and the turban, see also Deslippe, "Hindu in Hindoo," and Bald, "Between Hindoo and Negro." Several blogs have also recounted this story.

3. Nordmeyer, "Using Style," 4.

4. While Routte was not the first Black student to attend Augustana, he was the first to graduate with a four-year diploma. Augustana's yearbook shows that there were at least two other Black students, including one woman, in 1925. "Three Non-Caucasians Get Degrees at Augie," *Augustana Observer*, May 17, 1935; *Rockety-I* yearbook (1925).

5. Routté-Gómez, "Tale," 106. This reading of Routte's activism is influenced by Hazel Carby's assessment of performances and images of Paul Robeson in the 1920s in *Race Men*, 45–83.

6. Stewart, "Whiteness as Collective Memory," 20.

7. "A Certain Negro Congregation," *Augustana Observer*, December 1, 1902.

8. On the "Negro Question" as a Southern concern, see, for example, J. L. Larson, "Texas and Trinity College," *Augustana Observer*, December 1, 1906; "Exchange Department," *Augustana Observer*, March 1, 1908; Verner Swanson, "Exchanges," *Augustana Observer*, January 1, 1911; "Webster-Gladstone Debate," *Augustana Observer*, May 1, 1906.

9. Elda, "The Co-Ed," *Augustana Observer*, October 19, 1922; "Women's Club Play Well Done," *Augustana Observer*, May 1, 1924.

10. "Senior Sems Entertained," *Augustana Observer*, March 3, 1913; *Rockety-I* (1913), 62–68. The article did not note whether the "minstrels" wore blackface.

11. J. Frank Frysinger, "Music," *Augustana Observer*, February 1, 1919; "Music," *Augustana Observer*, December 1, 1920; Recital program; "A

Capella Choir Sings to Large Audience Tuesday," *Augustana Observer*, May 12, 1927; "Personnel of Band Chosen for Tour in Europe This Summer," *Augustana Observer*, March 15, 1928; George F. Hall, "The Augustana Concert Band Tour," *Augustana Observer*, October 4, 1928.

12. "Volunteers Hold Banquet Friday," *Augustana Observer*, February 8, 1923.

13. "Tanganyika Field Is Described by Andree," *Augustana Observer*, April 26, 1923; "Seven Augieites Are Present at Convention," *Augustana Observer*, January 17, 1924; "Hear Reports of Convention," *Augustana Observer*, January 31, 1924.

14. "Give Reports at Zion Church," *Augustana Observer*, January 31, 1924.

15. The percentage of Black residents of Rock Island grew slightly between 1910 and 1920, from 1.6 to 2.1, and in Moline, from 1.1 to 1.2; but between 1920 and 1930, both cities experienced a small drop in their Black population. US Census Bureau, Bulletin; US Census, "Composition."

16. "Organizations," *Augustana Observer*, February 1, 1921.

17. Routte's account of his early life and of his father is contradictory. In a 1926 *Observer* article he says he was born in Boston, but census data and his marriage license indicate he was born in Missouri. Several 1947 accounts describe his father as an economist at Yale. It is likely that his father was a laborer in Missouri who became a minister; it is conceivable that Routte concealed some of his own story as he negotiated his place at Augustana. Biographical information about Routte was compiled from "Jesse Routte, Colored Student at Augustana, Has Life Story of Interest," *Augustana Observer*, December 2, 1926; "Extensive Concert Tour Made During Summer by Routte," *Augustana Observer*, October 2, 1930; "Boone News," *Iowa Bystander*, October 8, 1915; "Fort Madison Notes," *Iowa Bystander*, February 9, 1917; "Boys of City Dinner Guests of Rotarians," *Rock Island Argus*, December 23, 1919; "Negro Says Turban."

18. Kramer, "Importance," 217.

19. "Jesse Routte, Colored Student," *Augustana Observer*, December 2, 1926; "Colored Student at Augustana Works Nights to Earn Way Through School," *Augustana Observer*, October 7, 1926; "Augie's Human Relations Club Lone Illinois Cosmo Organization," *Augustana Observer*, January 15, 1942; *Rockety-I* (1926–27).

20. Kramer, "Importance," 212.

21. Duncan, *Dear Church*, 2.

22. "Jesse Routte Sings at First Lutheran Church Sunday Night," *Augustana Observer*, October 6, 1927; Kramer, "Importance," 212.

23. Nordmeyer, "Using Style," 4–5. For the meaning of signifying as a cultural strategy, see Gates, *Signifying Monkey*.

24. Quoted in Kramer, "Importance," 212.

25. "Students' Union to Hear Colored Folk" and "Public Opening of New Music Building Is Well Attended," *Augustana Observer*, October 25, 1928.

26. "Jesse Routte Will Give Lecture Series on Negro Progress," *Augustana Observer*, November 22, 1928.

27. Edward Fry Bartholomew, "City Streets and the Gospel," *Augustana Observer*, December 14, 1922.

28. "Hundreds Come to Augie for Inner Missions Sessions," *Augustana Observer*, November 22, 1928.

29. "Routte Investigates Conditions in Negro Section of Chicago," *Augustana Observer*, January 17, 1929.

30. Carby, *Race Men*, 4.

31. "Jesse Routte Will Present Graduation Recitation on Sunday," *Augustana Observer*, May 2, 1929; "Jesse Routte Appears in Graduation Recital," *Augustana Observer*, May 9, 1929.

32. Dunbar, *Complete Poems*, 46; Ronda, "Work and Wait Unwearying," 864.

33. Harper, "Vashti"; Dunbar, 15. On Dunbar and dialect, see Gates, *Signifying Monkey*, 184–232, and Nash, "Realist Poetry."

34. "Routte to Appear in Many Churches," *Augustana Observer*, October 31, 1929; "Extensive Tour," *Augustana Observer*, October 2, 1930; "Jesse Routte Gives Series of Lectures on Religious Topics," *Augustana Observer*, February 19, 1931.

35. Louis Routte's "Expert Shoe Shining" at the College Barber Shop was advertised in multiple issues of the yearbook *Rockety-I* (1930–32). See also "Four One-Act Plays Will Precede Pep-Fest This Evening," *Augustana Observer*, October 28, 1932; "Class of 1934," *Rockety-I* (1935).

36. "Three Non-Caucasians Get Degrees at Augie," *Augustana Observer*, May 17, 1935; Bergendoff, letter.

37. Kramer, "Importance," 213–14.

38. John Nelson, "Highlights from the Hilltop," *Augustana Observer*, April 30, 1942; "Augie Human Relations Club." For Routte's later life, see "Black Minister Finds Challenge."

39. Routté-Gomez, "Struggle to Excel."

40. Anderson, *Black in White Space*, 15.

41. Hughes, "I, Too."

42. Chief Commander Ebenezer Obey & His International Brothers Band, "Ajala-Alhaja."

43. Àjàlá, *African Abroad*.

44. Olaoluwa, "Beyond Backpacking."

45. Àjàlá to Conrad Bergendoff, September 20, 1949, Correspondence Regarding Nigerian Student Mashood Ajala, 1949–51, box 5, HSJ.

46. Alfonso A. Narvaez, "Hunter High Students Are Given Equal Voice on Faculty Boards," *New York Times*, April 11, 1970. In his memoir Àjàlá dates his arrival in the United States to 1948, but several documents in the Johnson file note 1949 as his time of entry.

47. "Schedule Next School Party: 'Friendship Fair' Is Theme," *Augustana Observer*, March 24, 1949.

48. "Encourage Exchange of Austrian Students," *Augustana Observer*, April 1, 1949.

49. "Austrian Students Express Thanks," *Augustana Observer*, March 17, 1950; "Let's Go over the Top at the Friendship Fair," *Augustana Observer*, March 2, 1950.

50. Àjàlá indicated in a letter to Johnson that his arrival in the United States was due to "the sole effort of Augustana." Letter from Àjàlá to Johnson, August 8, 1950, Correspondence, HSJ.

51. Àjàlá, *African Abroad*, xxi.

52. "Lutherans Name Boards," *Oneonta Star*, June 7, 1963; "To Sir," letter to Johnson, no date, Correspondence, HSJ.

53. Lutrelle Palmer, "Life Begins at Augustana for African Pre-Medical Student," *Chicago Defender*, May 1950. There were likely few, if any, Mexican American students at Augustana in 1949. Almost twenty years later, there were only two. Tom Littlewood, "Illinois College Ratings in Black Scholarships," *Chicago Sun Times*, April 7, 1969, clipping in folder 8, box 15, CWS. In spite of a significant Mexican American population in the community, very few attended Augustana before the 1960s. John Cervantes, of Moline, attended briefly in the 1930s. Cervantes, *My Moline*.

54. "L.S.A. Campaign to Aid Work Abroad to Begin Sunday; List Highlights," *Augustana Observer*, March 23, 1950; "Sigma Mu Alpha, Music Students' Group, Chooses New Members," *Augustana Observer*, November 2, 1950; "Art Club Collects $134.74; Exhibit Features Modeling,"

Augustana Observer, November 11, 1949; "Society Plans Mission 'Trip' for Sunday," *Augustana Observer*, April 5, 1951.

55. "Society Plans."

56. "End Mission Week; Chapel Talks Build Interest," *Augustana Observer*, October 13, 1949.

57. Letter from Johnson to Elbert, April 12, 1951, Correspondence, HSJ.

58. Àjàlá to Johnson, n.d., and letter from Johnson to Àjàlá, October 1, 1949, Correspondence, HSJ.

59. S. E. Adeniji to Àjàlá, January 30, 1950, Correspondence, HSJ.

60. Reed to George Arbaugh, January 20, 1950, Correspondence, HSJ.

61. Johnson to Harold Smith, February 7, 1950, Correspondence, HSJ.

62. I. O. Adeniji to Àjàlá, Correspondence, HSJ.

63. R. Obayinka Àjàlá to Àjàlá, February 5, 1950, Correspondence, HSJ.

64. Johnson to A. R. Àjàlá, February 20, 1950; letter from M. A. O. Àjàlá to A. R. Àjàlá, February 21, 1950, Correspondence, HSJ.

65. M. A. Olabisi Ajala, "Africa Not an Uncultured, Dark Continent," *Augustana Observer*, March 17, 1950.

66. "Augie's Foreign Students," photograph caption, *Augustana Observer*, October 21, 1949; *Rockety-I* (1950).

67. Johnson to Nigerian Secretariat, May 3, 1950; Johnson to Jackson, June 12, 1950; Johnson to L. D. Barton, June 13, 1950; Àjàlá to Johnson, June 28, 1950, Correspondence, HSJ.

68. Àjàlá to Johnson, September 11, 1950; Àjàlá to Herbert Glynn, August 27, 1950; Johnson to Àjàlá, September 22, 1950; Johnson to Mr. Malloy, September 22, 1950; Johnson to Àjàlá, October 4, 1950, Correspondence, HSJ.

69. Àjàlá to Johnson, October 4, 1950; Johnson to Àjàlá, October 6, 1950, Correspondence, HSJ.

70. "African Student and White Doctor's Friendship Crosses Racial Bounds," *Chicago Defender* (national edition), October, 27, 1951.

71. Herbert Glynn to Guy L. Schuytema, January 31, 1951, Correspondence, HSJ.

72. "Stu-U to Borrow from F-F Funds," *Augustana Observer*, November 16, 1953.

73. Olaoluwa, "Beyond Backpacking," 6–7.

74. Lee Blackwell, "Off the Record," *Chicago Defender*, January 24,

1957; Ole Nosey, "Native African Gets 20th Century Contract for Series of Pictures," *Chicago Defender*, December 6, 1952.

75. "Bandits Stymie African Student on Bike Tour," *Los Angeles Sentinel*, July 3, 1952; Ole Nosey, "Native African." Interestingly, Àjàlá started his trip only a few months after twenty-three-year-old Che Guevara started a motorcycle journey across Latin America. He wrote a memoir of the trip in 1952, which was later published as *The Motorcycle Diaries* (Verso Books, 1993).

76. "African Actor," 4.

77. Chaplain Sorensen, "Augie Community Too Busy to Honor King," *Augustana Observer*, April 17, 1968; "Spirit of Atlanta Not at Augie," *Augustana Observer*, April 17, 1968; "United States Slowly, Surely Succumbing to Cancerous Disease of Racial Hatred," *Augustana Observer*, April 17, 1968.

78. Araiza, "Black Power."

79. The boycotts and walkouts were spearheaded by the Coordinating Council of Community Organizations. Danns, "Chicago High School Students"; Afro-American Society, "Orientation Booklet," 1969–70, Black Student Union 1969–1975, box 15, CWS.

80. On the Black campus movement at white institutions, see especially Exum, *Paradoxes of Protest*, and Williamson, "In Defense of Themselves."

81. Looney, "Is Augustana Free from Racism?," *Augustana Observer*, April 19, 1972.

82. Johnson, "Campus Division the Result of Reciprocal Racism," *Augustana Observer*, December 11, 1968.

83. Scot Ngozi-Brown argues that many historians have followed the Black Panthers in framing Us's strategies as "merely" cultural while the Black Panthers were explicitly political. Ngozi-Brown stresses that cultural nationalism included "the politics of resistance." Ngozi-Brown, "Us Organization," 164.

84. Afro-American Society, "Administration Disgusts Afro-American Society," *Augustana Observer*, October 18, 1968.

85. John W. Hullett, "Hullett Comments on AAS," *Augustana Observer*, October 30, 1968; "Afro-American Society Should Re-evaluate," *Augustana Observer*, October 30, 1968; "Greenwood's Answer: Get Over Hang-ups," *Augustana Observer*, October 30, 1968. Similar accusations of posturing were lobbed at the new leftist student organization on campus, the Youth International Party, an antiwar, anti-racist group headed by

Greenwood. "YIP Group Meets to Treat Social Ills," *Augustana Observer*, October 16, 1968.

86. "YIP Group Meets"; "Hullett Gives Police Sensitivity Lessons," *Augustana Observer*, September 24, 1970, 2.

87. See Kendi, *Black Campus Movement.*

88. Sampson, "Political Perspectives," *Augustana Observer*, September 27, 1967; Lynne Curtis, "Students Attend Conference on Institutionalized Racism," *Augustana Observer*, December 11, 1968.

89. "Demand for Black Prof Justified," *Augustana Observer*, November 6, 1968.

90. Black Power Symposium notes, Black Power Symposium: Correspondence, box 99, CWS. Powell never made it to the event due to airline travel troubles.

91. "RA Sees Thurmond Views as Generally Unacceptable," *Augustana Observer*, May 1, 1968; Anonymous note on clipping, February 4, 1969, Black Power Symposium: Correspondence, box 99, CWS; anonymous letter to Sorensen, February 4, 1969, Black Power Symposium: Correspondence, box 99, CWS.

92. Booker, "Deplorable Exegesis," 205.

93. Author Lauren Hammond-Ford points out that this lack of representation of Black theological traditions is still a problem at Augustana. See chapter 4 in this volume for more on Hammond-Ford's perspectives.

94. Richard Bush, "Symposium Subject: Black Power," *Augustana Observer*, September 19, 1968, 3.

95. Sorensen, undated memo, Black Faculty, etc., 1969–72, box 15, CWS.

96. Skyles, "Priorities," Black Faculty, etc. 1969–72, box 15, CWS.

97. Letter from Hedrick to Sorensen, September 23, 1969, Black Student Information 1969–1973, box 15, CWS. We have not found evidence that the college began such a center.

98. Hauerwas, "White Christian Liberals Resentful," *Augustana Observer*, April 23, 1970, 2–3.

99. Tisby, *Footnotes by Jemar Tisby.*

100. Swanson to Sorensen, April 24, 1969, Black Faculty, etc. 1969–72, box 15, CWS.

101. Deb Skromme, "Five Years' Constant Effort Produces," *Augustana Observer*, May 2, 1973, 10.

102. AAS, "Black Orientation 70–71," Black Student Union, 1969–1975, box 15, CWS; Memo from Tredway to Sorensen, October 14, 1970, Black Student Information, box 15, CWS.

103. Student Faculty Administration Committee Minutes, November 10, 1970, folder 1, box 6, CWS.

104. "Black Students at Augustana, 1972–73," October 6, 1972, Black Student Information, box 15, CWS.

105. Afro-American Society, "Orientation Booklet."

106. Cone, *Black Theology*.

107. "BSU Speaks Out," *Augustana Observer*, February 16, 1977.

108. "Study of the Impact of Increased Black Enrollments," survey form created by Indiana University, 1969, folder 6, box 15, CWS.

109. Lawson, "Student Participation," 28.

EMPOWERING MARGINALIZED VOICES
A Journey Toward Diversity, Equity, Inclusion and Justice

MONICA M. SMITH

I arrived at Augustana College in March 2018 as the college's first vice president for diversity, equity, and inclusion and chief diversity officer. I was impressed with Augustana's introspection and with the efforts that led to creating this cabinet-level position, including listing Diversity, Equity, Inclusion, and Justice as a pillar in the strategic plan. Much of this work showed up in the position announcement and leadership profile that drew me to Augustana, as well as in the "diversity efforts inventory," which tracked the institution's efforts to be a more diverse and inclusive place up until the time I arrived.[1] Augustana had grown the percentage of students of color from 5 percent in 2005 to 26 percent at the time of my arrival in 2018: that is tremendous and rapid growth in the number of underrepresented and often marginalized students.

While diversity is a fact supported with statistics, equity, inclusion, and justice are the products of innumerable choices by senior administrators, board members, faculty, staff, students, and alumni. Inclusion is a choice. Inclusion is a method of intentional practices as well as policies that ensure representation, engagement, and meaningful participation of underrepresented and marginalized persons in the institution. Equity is essential and evidenced by outcomes that show institutional progress toward inclusion. The processes and outcomes are a matter of social justice, one of the college's Five Faith Commitments. The college's commitment to social justice asserts that practice and policy are linked: "Augustana seeks to embody the ideals of justice, peace, civility and love in our institutional practices and relationships. To that end, Augustana seeks to develop fair and charitable policies shaping how we relate to each other, the surrounding community, and the earth."[2]

These commitments had been in place for a dozen years before I joined the institution, in an affirmation of Lutheran institutional vocation. The college had a history of responding to student needs, but institutional responses had historically been reactionary. In other words, while Augustana College had enacted policies to deter individual acts of racism, provide more opportunities for students of color, and generally lift up diversity as an institutional value, it had yet to enact *transformative* change by addressing systemic barriers. Like many liberal arts colleges in the United States, Augustana strives to provide a transformative experience for students—engaging experiences intended to affirm and challenge them. Experience resulting in personal growth and new knowledge expands their perception of the world and impacts decision-making. Still in existence, though, was the "hidden curriculum": the informal ways that schools socialize students to conform to unspoken rules and expectations.[3] In other words, at predominantly White colleges like Augustana, students were expected to assimilate to campus norms set in large part by the founders and perpetuated by the majority both in the classroom and outside it. Those who are unable or refuse to assimilate are marginalized. The hidden curriculum was a barrier to transformative change. Augustana needed someone to shepherd the college from a reactionary stance to a proactive, anti-racist one, but how does an institution move from tolerance to acceptance then ultimately to anti-racism?

Many studies of institutional change at colleges and universities have focused on responses to Black student protests of the 1960s and '70s, many of which were only partially successful. William Exum summed up this "paradox of protest" by explaining that the Black campus movement was led by mostly "utopian groups of limited power using radical tactics to achieve reformist goals in a secular, bureaucratic world that they need for individual mobility."[4] Yet the Black campus movement was less about utopian ideals than about dismantling exclusionary practices. An important element was helping campus leaders to understand that although Black students were granted access *into* the institution, they were not granted full access to resources necessary for a thriving student experience. These students were realists who understood that for Black students, predominantly White campuses reflected the same limiting social aspects as the larger society. This is a current reality on many campuses today where students and chief diversity officers are aiding institutions to recognize barriers that impede the student experience. Work in educational leadership thus stresses the "evolutionary nature" of institutions' attempts to foster anti-racist policies and the struggle to shift an institutional culture that includes both formal policies and informal relationships, those close to power and those who feel disconnected from power.[5] The Black campus movement also signaled students' recognition of their power, though limited, and their willingness to use it to influence administrators to guide campuses to more fully live into stated values and liberate themselves from oppressive systems in society, including higher education.

Having led diversity and inclusion efforts at several colleges and universities, I recognize that transformative change requires the *practice* of disrupting the status quo in order to remove barriers that stem from ineffective *policies*. I have written elsewhere that I consider myself to be a "disruptor" of the systems within which I work. First as a social worker and now as a diversity officer, I recognize that institutional processes created to help often erect more barriers, as they were meant to aid in navigating unfair systems without changing the system itself.[6] Augustana has generally responded to moments of disruption by committing itself to the free exchange of ideas, a "value neutral" policy that gained traction in higher education during the civil rights movement but that can be a barrier to the success of all students when those ideas are discriminatory.

In what follows, I take a long view of Augustana College's fitful movement toward equity, focusing on disruptive moments that exposed the hidden curriculum embedded in the "free exchange of ideas" model. Using interviews with John Hildreth (the first tenured Black professor at Augustana), Jerry Jones (a Black alumnus and the executive director of the local Martin Luther King Center), Lauren Hammond-Ford (the first tenured Black woman professor), and Dezi Primous-Gillon (a recent Black, nonbinary alum), I show how faculty, students, and community members challenged the college to justify its actions or inactions in value-laden, rather than value-neutral, ways.[7]

Many such moments led to useful, but reactionary, changes. I suggest that the college, as a church-related institution, is called to challenge the value-neutral position that is part of the hidden curriculum of higher education in order to heed the value-laden imperative to "love thy neighbor" by exposing and dismantling racist structures.

THE 1970S: "BETWEEN THE DEVIL AND THE DEEP BLUE SEA"

In 1970, John Hildreth, the first full-time, tenure-track Black faculty member, arrived on Augustana's campus. His hiring resulted from a call from the Black Student Union (BSU) and its allies to offer courses in Black history, recruit more Black students, create a Black Culture House, and hire Black faculty. But administrators at Augustana, as at other institutions, were wary of requests for separate Black spaces on campus, fearing repercussions from the Civil Rights Act of 1964 that had led to the influx of Black students. The act that barred segregation in education prohibited any space designed for a particular racial group.[8] The college may have found the request for faculty less fraught. Several Black faculty, artists, and staff arrived on campus in the late 1960s and early 1970s. Pianist Joyce Johnson, a graduate of Fisk, taught full-time in the Music Department in spring of 1966, and in 1969, opera tenor William Brown became Augustana's inaugural affiliate artist, a nonteaching position.[9] In 1971, Reed Coleman joined the Sociology Department, and Val Bush became the college's first Black admissions counselor. Michael Robinson joined the Chemistry Department in 1972; he, Coleman, and an economist from Ghana, James Ghartney, all left the college in 1973.[10]

As a tenure-track faculty member in music, Hildreth filled other roles as well. He was to advise BSU, recruit Black students (in 1970, the entering class included "8 or 9 black students," according to President Sorensen), and "teach organ lessons and a course in the religion department."[11] Hildreth credits Black student activists for calling on the college to meet their needs. At the same time, as a Black faculty member who arrived when this change in spirit was very much still in process, Hildreth experienced difficulty in meeting the expectations of Black students and White students, faculty, staff, and administrators who generally saw anti-racist efforts as something imposed on the college by external political forces rather than imperative for its mission. As a Lutheran himself, Hildreth dealt with tension between being a representative of institutional support for Black students and a personal commitment to social justice rooted in a transformative spiritual vision. He said of his attitude, then as now, "I believe in the God-given worth and dignity of every human being, and that's the way we're going to treat each other." While Hildreth recognized the effort to hire him was driven by external pressures, his own motivation was deeply intrinsic.

Today, many assume that Augustana's Lutheran affiliation was the source of resistance to progressive hiring practices. But for Hildreth and for those who advocated for his position, justice work was rooted in faith. Hildreth remembers that "a number of Chicago pastors" were "concerned about the lack of diversity and inclusion at Augustana" and advised the college to hire Black faculty. They suggested not only that Augustana help prepare Black students from underfunded inner-city high schools to be successful but also that it follow through on promises to deliberately serve Black communities. These pastors wanted to help Augustana become a place where Black Lutherans could live out vocational goals through a deeper integration of faith and justice. Hildreth grew up in a Lutheran Church Missouri Synod (LCMS) congregation in a "dirt poor" community in southern Indiana. With an upbringing similar to those students that Augustana was charged to recruit, Hildreth understood the significant influence postsecondary education can have in changing the trajectory of one's life. He considered pursuing ministry before switching to music while attending Concordia College (now University) in Milwaukee and in Fort Wayne. Before accepting the position at Augustana, Hildreth had worked at the Board of American Missions in Chicago, a ministry within the newly formed American Lutheran Church (ALC).[12] "I guess I seemed like a safe bet to them," said Hildreth, indicating both the familiar Lutheran circles and the perceived need for "a safe bet," given the prolonged "agitation" leading up to his hiring.

Hildreth's comments show tension between the faith-based imperative of justice and a more secular understanding of equality. In 1970, many White members of the extended Augustana community associated Lutheranism with conservative values while attributing Black self-determination, anti-racism, and affirmative action policies to anti-Christian forces.[13] Hildreth recalls that by the late 1960s, the college had diluted its connection to the Lutheran Church to "not much more than a 'Covenant' relationship." Secular commitment to free speech on campus gained traction in the late 1960s and early 1970s partly in response to student agitation, including the Black campus movement and Students for a Democratic Society.[14] While activism ended some administrative control, it may have caused schools to disregard social justice imperatives rooted in religious faith. When Chicago pastors called on Augustana to move toward more radical change, the administration determined that these pastors "had no authority to dictate what was going to happen at Augustana." Hildreth remembers this period as contentious. The historical ties of the college to the Lutheran Church may have proven to be more progressive than its secular stakeholders. Distancing itself from the church and subsequently deciding that Black Lutheran pastors had no authority to influence the college reveals Augustana's avoidance of race. Rather than addressing the possibility of its own anti-Black sentiments, the college seemed to conflate its distance from the church with the decreased influence of the pastors. Key to understanding this connection is the juxtaposition of a Christian commitment to faith and a social commitment to racial segregation and espoused inferiority of Black people. The notion of inferiority is encapsulated in the expectations placed upon Hildreth by the college and his experiences in the classroom.

These pressures were significant, but Hildreth stressed that his arrival was primarily due to Black students from Chicago who "knew what was going on" with respect to civil rights. They were persistently "agitating," "sitting in the President's office," and otherwise "raising hell" to pressure the administration to meet their demands. In 1969 Black students and their allies disrupted Augustana's Friendship Fair, an annual fundraising event for "the needy." The protestors distributed a statement asking "not only for the betterment of the black situation at Augustana, but also for the enlightened self-interest of the white community." In February 1972 about thirty students, nearly a third of Augustana's Black student population, staged a sit-in outside President Sorensen's office to support BSU leaders—Eric Thomas, Reggie Turner, and Joe Looney—meeting with the president to urge him to address campus racism.[15] Hildreth recalls these demands as more than policy change. The aim was to force a "spiritual change" going beyond mere tolerance of Black students and instead challenging the community to realize "the significance of the cultural differences between Blacks and whites."

Even when affirming students' demands, the college often avoided condemning racism by invoking the broad, secular value of tolerance for different viewpoints. Though deeply embedded in the American educational tradition, tolerance could also be seen as a privilege afforded those for whom racism is merely one viewpoint among many rather than a threat to one's existence. Before the 1969 Black Power Symposium, Sorensen had addressed community concerns, noting that "it is a student program and that the choice of speakers and financial support rested with the students and not with the faculty or administration."[16] According to the local paper, "the college had nothing to do with the selection of the panel . . . on Black Power."[17] The institution's position that Black activism created opportunities to introduce students at a small, church-related college to competing perspectives protected the idea of the campus as a White space, where anti-racism might be entertained as an idea but in actual practice was optional.

This was the tension into which Hildreth stepped in 1970. "What I walked into was not a good situation," he told me. In his attempt to satisfy the administration and serve Black students, he found himself "between the Devil and the deep blue sea." He recalls that some Black students "thought I was just there to shuck and jive and rap with them and get into this superficial Black stuff," when "that's not who I am." Some White students thought he was "window dressing"; they laughed when he walked into class. Being accepted as a competent Black teacher and musician seemed to be a complexity students could not initially overcome. Taking the Black body seriously required students to shift their minds and spirits to see and respect the whole person. He told me that as someone who believes in the liberal arts, he had to work to impress on students—Black and White—that "I am serious about being here." Students' belief that Black faculty's presence in the classroom is external to their "real" education and that confronting racial difference is not a project that demands intellectual rigor is an experience that I have shared. His point that "we never finish proving ourselves" resonates strongly with me, as this perceived division between intellectual and social justice work persists to this day. For Hildreth, like many Black professionals at predominantly White institutions (PWIs) including me, the reasons the college (finally) brought him to Augustana did not matter. For him, as for his White counterparts, once there he did his job with the integrity of any person who takes pride in and is serious about their work. He was not there to perform, even though the college's decision to bring him may have been performative. He refused to be a token. Like his colleagues, he was (is) a competent caring scholar who was there to educate and transform the lives of Augustana College students (Fig. 4.1).

BSU leader Joe Looney recognized the difficulty of Hildreth's position in a booklet he created in 1971 to share the "philosophy of racism" at Augustana College.[18] His thesis was that Hildreth's hiring had not disrupted institutional structures: "Augustana College has failed to assume the initiative in helping to free your Americans of

Fig. 4.1. Dr. John Hildreth with a student. Augustana College Photograph Collection, C-F02319. Courtesy of Augustana College Special Collections, Rock Island, Illinois.

both the overt and subtle components of a racist philosophy." The administration was locked in a pattern of "avoidance and denial"; it repeatedly sought to "pacify rather than cure."[19] Looney cited Keith David, a White Lutheran pastor in Chicago, who had noted, "After visiting seventeen small liberal arts colleges, I have not seen, outside of the South, a more overtly racist attitude than exists on the Augustana campus." Such charges were serious, but Looney used humor to make his case. Noting that the White student to White faculty ratio was 12:1, he calculated that all the Black students (in 1972 there were just over one hundred) had one Black faculty member who was expected to advise current students, recruit new ones, and teach in the music and religion departments. A cartoon included in Looney's booklet has a White receptionist directing an angry Black student to a worried Hildreth in the next office, saying, "See Hildreth, he's the faculty-administration-recruiter-staff-elevator operator you've been asking for." Looney decried the need of Black students to keep to themselves and to fear anything that would alienate them from the one support group that offered them a safe space. In these vulnerable, perceptive comments, one glimpses a young Black man who longs to be a part of the broader campus and yet feels forced to earn his place among a politically awakened BSU by underplaying or denying those longings. Imagine this complicated journey— balancing one's needs, desires, and rights with a PWI's avoidance and denial of these beyond the mere tolerance already "given." How does one thrive if he must constantly shrink himself?

While some might have seen Hildreth as a token or a tool of the administration, students may not have been aware of the efforts Hildreth made to call attention to addressing racism on campus as part of the college's mission. Hildreth was on the board of the Black Culture House and served on the Human Relations Committee, an early form of a diversity committee that was founded in 1971. He helped organize the 1971 Minority Cultural Symposium, which the Human Relations Committee hoped would help minority students to "hold their head high" and to know that "somebody cares and you are somebody." Organizers anticipated that White people would "leave this place with a new frame of mind and a new commitment to the struggle." The event was poorly attended, and Hildreth spoke out in the *Observer* on behalf of minority students whose frustrations went beyond the lack of an audience. He went on to recount various forms of racism that faculty and students directed at Black and Asian students on a regular basis, from comments about hygiene to uses of racial slurs. Perhaps most insulting, he noted, was that minorities "are regarded as simply invisible."[20] Such recollections are familiar. When I arrived at Augustana College in 2018, students of color expressed exasperation that events sponsored by BSU, the Office for Student Inclusion and Diversity (OSID), and the Office for International Student and Scholar Services were mostly attended by Black and other underrepresented students. The 2019 Inclusion and Belonging Survey noted persistent racist language and slurs.

Hildreth urged the campus to recognize that seeing racism as one of many perspectives available to students undermined the college's educational mission. Racism was not a mere idea, he wrote in 1971, but a sickness of the soul: "How can blacks and other minorities be expected to live, learn, achieve and work in such a situation? It is a grave injustice to subject these students to this kind of sickness. It would likewise seem to be a grave injustice to the white student who comes to a college campus with thoroughly racist notions and who is allowed to spend four years there and leave with these notions unchallenged or actually reinforced by peers, faculty and staff."[21] Hildreth had some support in addressing campus racism. The Student Action Coalition formed in the spring of 1970; it echoed BSU's call for greater effort in recruiting diverse students and faculty, including a Black coach and admissions counselor.[22] In October of 1971, the administration issued a statement that "reaffirm[ed] its . . . opposition to racism" and announced that it would create a Human Relations Committee, whose charge was to "seek means of establishing better communication and understanding between minority and majority groups on campus" and to "serve as a clearing house for charges of discrimination and racism as they might occur on campus."[23]

At a Human Relations Committee forum in December 1971, attendees wrestled with the responsibility both to investigate *acts* of racism and to combat a general *climate* of racism. Was a person racist because they committed a racist act? Could such a person change, and if so, was it the responsibility of the college to change them? Chaplain

Sorensen reminded attendees that racist acts were anti-Christian; Hildreth countered faculty fears with the reality of minority students' fear and isolation; student activist Mark Schwiebert noted that while it was difficult to "dictate morality," changes to the campus environment could "condition a new morality in time."[24] The committee created policy to investigate and punish racist acts, but it would take more work to change the climate. It can be easier for institutions to change policies than to change hearts and minds.

As I talked to Hildreth, he emphasized that changing attitudes cannot be achieved by policy alone. Racism is an evil embedded in American society and in American institutions, even faith-adjacent colleges. His diagnoses of evil structures and systems have remained razor-sharp since arriving on campus in 1970, and his frustration with the lack of racial reckoning is often raw. After Rodney King was beaten by Los Angeles police in 1992, Hildreth said this: "We keep hoping racism is going to go away . . . but reminders come along and let us know it's going backwards, not forward."[25] In 2002, following racial slurs being painted on a Black janitor's car and a themed fraternity party where unspecified costumes caused "racial tensions," Hildreth said that in his nearly thirty years on campus "he's been part of countless committees, boards, meetings and retreats devoted to tolerance, 'and yet here we are again.'"[26] This last comment stuck with me for some time. I could not help but think about the public assault and life-taking of George Floyd in May 2020. College campuses are a microcosm of society. What happens in society tends to happen on campuses. The campus is a community of people with diverse experiences, perceptions, values, expectations, and behaviors. Every four years the residents change. Intolerance, ignorance, and racial tensions may seem to remain, but in reality, they return with each incoming class.

Hildreth has stayed for fifty-three years. Why? Because "of the wonderful students and the many faculty members who stood by me and worked with me to bring about peace, respect, and equity." There were and are moments when Augustana and America have seemed to be heading backward rather than forward. But it is also true that, looking back now, "we've come a long, long way." Indeed, the college has. My hire was a significant milestone in the journey. The position is cabinet-level: reporting to the president; overseeing two student-facing offices, staff, and financial resources; and having an expectation to lead campus-wide diversity, equity, inclusion, and justice efforts. Augustana will always be an imperfect place because we are imperfect people. But many of us share a similar hopefulness and commitment "to do justice" because we know we can do better, as Hildreth said.

THE 1980S AND '90S: THE MULTICULTURAL MYSTIQUE

It is difficult to locate milestones in the quest for racial diversity, equity, inclusion, and justice at Augustana through the 1980s and '90s, even though several incidents during these decades brought national attention to racial divides on the small campus. These were the years during which current Rock Island resident and community activist Jerry Jones attended the school, and while he benefited from having BSU and its allies, he recalls a sense of alienation on campus, even as Augustana embraced diversity more publicly as an institutional asset for all students.

These decades are characterized by *multiculturalism* and *political correctness*, terms that signal the de-politicization and secularization of racial justice, making it seem more like a celebration of ethnic foods or generic open-mindedness than a substantial challenge to the cultural norms at many colleges and universities. The 1978 Supreme Court decision *University of California vs. Bakke* ended the process of reserving spaces in incoming classes for minority students. Though well-meaning, these quotas were a misapplication of affirmative action. The court ruled that the quotas were unconstitutional. This ruling led to lower numbers of Black students attending colleges and universities by the 1990s.

At the same time, schools began to recognize that diversity was a beneficial institutional value that contributed to student success. Programming, student culture groups, and, by the 1990s, general education requirements for the study of racial and ethnic diversity were integrated into undergraduate experiences. Still, institutionalizing diversity as a form of "interpersonal interaction" may have taken on what Ellen Berrey calls "instrumental purposes" as a loosely defined category of "difference" that failed to challenge structural inequalities.[27] Richard Lowy points to what he calls the "Yuppie racism" of the 1980s, where celebrations of Black culture (rap music, breakdancing) occurred alongside the dismantling of social and economic programs aimed at upward mobility. Black communities coined the term "Buppie" for young college-educated Black individuals of middle income and upwardly mobile. The appearance of similar economic status between young Blacks and Whites, combined with a new emphasis on individual success, led to a perception on the part of many Whites that racism no longer existed.[28] My own experience at a religiously affiliated PWI during these years confirms this. Race did, in fact, matter. On appearance, my parents were in an income bracket similar to that of my college friends. They each drove a Cadillac Sedan DeVille. My peers and I wore similar brands of clothing and leather shoes. My parents owned their home and had multiple streams of income. The unspoken "not like us" was evidenced in my (former) friends' distancing themselves from all of the Black students they eagerly engaged when their parents were not around.

Augustana's embrace of racial diversity as an educational asset was more reactionary than proactive, as it was likely fueled by an incident of campus racism that drew national attention and forced the college to respond. On October 19, 1979, as part of Augustana's unofficial but traditional "Little Homecoming Parade," the Beta Omega Sigma (BOS) fraternity performed a skit that portrayed Ku Klux Klan members leading a White student in blackface by ropes. Members of BSU (representing the 125 Black students at the college) took a complaint of racism before the Human Relations Committee.[29] The incident quickly drew protest from the local chapter of the NAACP (National Association for the Advancement of Colored People), whose president Phyllis Adams said that the skit reflected "ignorance of the highest order" and had belittled and angered the entire community.[30] Headlines from community papers, though, stressed the "anger," "protests," and "demands" by the NAACP and Black community, while noting that the "Augie fraternity sends 2,000 letters of apology."[31] Defenders of the act portrayed BOS members as passive, misunderstood, and befuddled. One White student discounted the act as mere play that was not representative of the campus: "I think [the skit] is just the way the BOS are. . . . I don't think there is any racial tension on the campus."

The letter of "apology" that BOS members sent to their classmates also placed responsibility on those who took offense, complete with some suggestive counteraccusations: "For the first time in the 10 years of our parade, a group has taken offense, or possibly is being pressured to take offense, over the presence of a sarcastic event depicted in our parade. To them, we would like to apologize as a group."[32] BOS presented itself as following tradition and faulted Black people and their allies for misunderstanding these traditions and rituals as inherently racist. That White students expressed opinions suggesting racial tensions did not exist on campus and that those who were offended were pressured into these feelings manifests an element of privilege found in Whiteness, that is, control of Black opinions, experiences, and feelings.

In this respect, the letter of apology was anything but apologetic. The fraternity wanted to "counter the growing misunderstanding the black community is expressing over the presence of a 'potentially' racial action by a few members of the Beta Omega Sigma fraternity." BOS members also suggested that the incident was being blown out of proportion and that "the situation" was a result of "anti-Greek group sentiment" rather than racial insult.[33] What the members and other White students did not realize was that Black students and NAACP members would have experienced this event as part of a longer history of racist acts that were part of the "cumulative impact" of being Black in America.[34] Evidence of preexisting racial polarization shows throughout the incident and the subsequent communications about it. The community newspapers' headlines and BOS's refusal to validate Black voices, intellect, and experiences are indeed evidence of racial polarization. Not knowing that the skit was indeed harmful and likely not an isolated incident was evidence of racial polarization. Attempts to minimize Black voices, invalidate their anger, and misinterpret their reasons for filing a complaint with the Human Relations Committee are evidence of racial polarization.

The Human Relations Committee deliberated for hours before affirming that the BOS fraternity skit "constituted an overt racist act in violation of stated college policy" and required the members to meet with Black students.[35] While the local NAACP had demanded the suspension of the fraternity or individual students, the college opted for a solution that fit more closely with the educational goals of the college, where the "exchange of ideas" took precedence.[36] Yet the burden of this learning tool was placed on Black students who were *required* to educate Whites while BOS received probation. Perhaps well-meaning, the college's response was punitive to the Black students who were offended and educational for the White students who initiated the offense.

Rock Island's city council passed a resolution supporting this disciplinary action."[37] The sole dissenter was James Davis, the city's first Black mayor, who said he simply did not understand what the fraternity's probation meant well enough to agree or disagree with it. Local NAACP chapter president Phyllis Adams, who had asked the city council to take a stand, publicly criticized its resolution and called for a rally near the college to protest the disciplinary action, while White council member Robert Maurus, who had been a member of BOS when he attended Augustana, compared the "stupid prank" to campus panty raids in the 1950s.[38] The Chicago region of the ALC's Illinois Synod denounced the act and called on Augustana's Board of Trustees to likewise repudiate an action that was "racist, demonic, and immoral."[39] Rev. Julius C. Hope, NAACP national director for religious affairs, condemned the skit and wondered in an interview whether "all those college students were [just] playing."[40] The resurgence of White nationalism at this time prompted Adams to compare Rock Island to Greensboro, North Carolina, where five people were shot to death during an anti-Klan protest just a few weeks after the skit. In a cruel twist, one of the five was Bill Sampson, a White Augustana graduate, Yale-educated divinity student, and member of the Communist Workers Party, who had been active in students' and civil rights actions on campus in the late 1960s.[41] A number of students wished this local-turned-national attention would just go away. "I can't believe it is being blown up like this," said one fraternity member. "It was just an innocent stunt not meant to be racist at all."[42]

Incidents of racial harm were becoming more common on campuses nationwide in the mid-1980s.[43] Such incidents were only the most overt attempts to preserve "white public space" on campuses through means that were not always so high profile. Helán Page and R. Brooke Thomas argue that these spaces are maintained in part by the "symbolic resources" that White professionals have access to.

Administrators and educators at PWIs like Augustana could control and monitor campus concerns through educational and policy choices that seemed to address the problem of racism at the individual level without scrutinizing the systems that gave them these powers.[44] Augustana began to turn to cultural diversity as a learning tool, encouraging students to "reach out to those different than themselves."[45] In this respect, multiculturalism at Augustana invested in "celebrating, affirming, or respecting diversity" in forms that, in privileging White people's comfort and student success over the uncomfortable work of disruption, were "cosmetic rather than transformational."[46]

Embracing diversity as a mildly educational celebration of "culture" that did not require challenging exclusive practices or structures may have contributed to the alienation of Black and Brown people. Jerry Jones, the current executive director of the Martin Luther King, Jr. Community Center in Rock Island, characterized his relationship with his alma mater as "rocky." Jones traveled to Augustana from his suburban Chicago home in 1986, intending to go to law school after graduating. He took the Law School Admission Test his senior year but then became involved in a community service project that changed his vocation. He decided to stay in the Quad Cities after graduating with a psychology degree in 1991, working in the area with troubled youth until he came, in 1998, to Rock Island's Martin Luther King Center, a community center located in Rock Island's West End, to serve as a youth program coordinator before being promoted to executive director in 2001, a position he still held at the time of my interview with him.

Jones experienced classroom environments that were not attuned to the presence of Black students. While Jones did not mention some of the forms of racism mentioned by other Black students of his era, such as biased grading and teachers refusing to answer their questions, he found that assumptions about race were still prevalent. In a 1995 *Observer* article, the reporter led with a story of a White male mocking King's "I Have a Dream" speech during a video shown in class.[47] Jones also experienced "several insidious microaggressions," including "the time in a sociology class [where we were] talking about differences. Someone with supreme confidence and passion raised their hand to say that Black people are superior on the athletic field because they have extra muscles in their legs. . . . They said that *with complete belief that it was true*," Jones told me, still astounded. Jones even conjectures now that if he had been more mature or aware of racial injustices while attending Augustana, he probably would have transferred.

Black students in the 1960s and '70s had fought to expose campus racism, but many in the 1980s and '90s seemed content to leave institutional transformation up to administrators. They focused on earning their degrees and moving on.[48] While Jones stayed in Rock Island, he did not maintain a connection to Augustana. As he explained to me, "I wouldn't say that I turned my back [on Augustana after graduating], but I didn't view Augustana as . . . a resource for me, professionally or personally. I still have friends [from Augustana] and some of the professors [had an influence on me], but I didn't view Augustana as something that [was] going to have any [continued] influence on my life. It's in the rearview mirror."[49] Jones's experience seems to have been all too common for Black students during this era who entered PWIs hoping for affirmation and equitable treatment but found that attending an institution where even services and policies meant to help them created a sense of shame and separation.[50]

When organizing the fiftieth anniversary of the founding of BSU for homecoming weekend of 2018, I met more than one Black alumnus of the college who had lived in the Quad Cities for decades and had never stepped foot back on campus. They suggested to me that their alma mater had ceased to offer them anything of substance. Until they were invited to come back for the special BSU celebration, they had never thought to participate in "homecoming," presumably because the place never became home. As Jones now works closely with residents in Rock Island, he notices that many consider Augustana's campus to be not merely "a bubble" (as those on campus frequently call it) but something closer to "an impenetrable fortress." Even today, then, a campus that has worked to enact its social justice mission lives with the ongoing effects of its reputation as "public White space," maintained by admissions requirements, campus security, and other institutional policies.

Over time Augustana included formal ways of learning about difference: adding African American literature to the curriculum, adding Black faculty and staff. A combination of student persistence and institutional responses led to these progress points. Jones says that the professors "were probably the most positive welcoming force," mentioning his English professor Paul Olsen, who taught African American literature, Marsha Smith in sociology, religion instructors, and others who "just opened my mind . . . and broadened my worldview." Associate Dean of Students Carol Brown was hired in 1982 to provide special support services for minority and nontraditional students, a position that was an early precursor to the one I now hold. She was responsible for arranging a better-maintained and more centrally located Black Culture House in the 1980s. She introduced Jones to the Illinois poet laureate Gwendolyn Brooks, who did readings on campus multiple times in the 1970s and '80s. She gave Jones advice that he has never forgotten—to write, rewrite, and rewrite. But Brown's husband, Marcellus, the concert band director, did not get tenure, which was a huge loss to the Black student population. Said Jones, "She and he were our resource and our voice on that level. We were really upset about losing [them]." Upon leaving the college in 1990, Brown noted the importance of diversity programming, which started with a small grant. "We miss the mark when we don't consider this an important issue," she warned.[51] While it is difficult to know what went into the decision not to award tenure, it reinforces Hildreth's experience in that institutional barriers to success were at least as high for faculty as for students, and the college lost a Black woman administrator as a result.

While campus multiculturalism was often framed in terms of greater tolerance for difference on the part of White students, enough cannot be said about co-curricular spaces and events and the salience of cultural enclaves to Black identity and success at Augustana College. Many culture groups were created between 1979 and 1995: the Majestic Gents, Ladies of Vital Essence, the Lighthouse, the Asian Student Organization, the Alliance of Islamic Awareness, the International Club, and Global Affect. Jones thinks that his experiences growing up in suburban Chicago helped him negotiate White spaces on campus. His deepest sense of belonging, though, came through the Majestic Gents and BSU, where he served as president, as well as through intramural sports and his work as an admissions ambassador. Safe spaces included the snack bar, where Black students would sit together, hang out, and sometimes brainstorm a "common agenda to make change on campus." He hung out in the Black Culture House at the top of the wooden steps now called the Olin stairs. The house itself was almost hidden in the woods, which Jones suggested may have been, even if unintentionally, a way to signal who belonged.

When I asked Jones about the perceived problem of Black and Brown people separating themselves, he said, "I want people to be able to understand the significance of the cultural enclaves and what they do for a student in their formative years." They are necessary—then and now. "I don't have to worry about [microaggressions] when I enter the Black Student Union or Black Culture House with all the folks who have a shared experience. [There and with them,] I'm not on guard. And I can grow when I am not on guard. When I am on guard, there is no room for growth." Cultural enclaves are safe, affirming and empowering. They are a necessity for thriving student experiences at PWIs. In these spaces there is no need to assimilate to a hidden curriculum. There is freedom to grow.

At least some of the lack of comfort and belonging that Jones felt in White spaces taught him "a level of autonomy." Much of what is now called the hidden curriculum simply forced Jones to find his own "informal learning environment." He read Richard Wright, James Baldwin, and other Black authors on his own, sometimes passing books and ideas back and forth among Black classmates. Jones concluded that both the "collegial" and "adversarial" relationship with Augustana "has shaped who I am now and who I can be." He said he is grateful for that experience. Yet "I still have friends that have very hard feelings about Augustana," and he admitted that it has not been until the "last ten years or so that I've been drawn closer to Augustana," after assuming that he would leave it in the rearview mirror. His daughter, well known in the community for a mural, *Black Pride*, that she painted in downtown Rock Island, enrolled at Augustana as a first-year student in the fall of 2023.[52] Said her father, "I think Augustana [will offer her] a better opportunity to help her grow . . . and maybe she'll find her tribe." Hearing this, I wondered if Jones was somehow acknowledging Augustana's progress. Certainly there have been many incremental changes that have resulted in an improved campus environment and student experience.

If BOS in blackface dragged Augustana into national culture wars on the eve of the 1980s, nationally polarizing events a decade later led to difficult conversations on campus among students, faculty, and Black community leaders. "Those dudes had an incredibly different experience than I had," said Jerry Jones, talking about students who came immediately after him and needed to reckon with the aftermath of the Rodney King beating and O. J. Simpson trial. On March 3, 1991, Rodney King, an unarmed Black man, was brutally beaten by four Los Angeles police officers. On April 29, 1992, the officers were acquitted by an almost all-White jury. Anger over racism and police brutality led to uprisings in south Los Angeles, leaving more than sixty people dead. "I would say that the pot was simmering [when I was on campus] and then was boiling [for] students that came after me," said Jones.

National media once again called attention to the different ways that Black and White Augustana students experienced racially charged incidents, as a famous photograph of starkly different reactions to the O. J. Simpson trial's conclusion so clearly suggests. *Quad-City Times* photographer Larry Fisher arrived on campus a half hour before the Simpson verdict was announced on October 3, 1995. He positioned himself beneath a mounted television in the game room and captured the reactions of the students who had gathered. *Newsweek* republished the photo over two pages a week later (Fig. 4.2).[53] The photograph captures the evident surprise and elation in the faces and raised hands of the Black students gathered, while White students show consternation, confusion, and concern. Not only are the reactions by the two groups diametrically opposed: intermixed and standing shoulder to shoulder, White and Black Augustana students seem nonetheless to be living in different worlds.

Responses to the photo also demonstrated differences. Some dismissed it as unrepresentative of Augustana while others looked more deeply at systemic inequity. In an opinion piece in the *Observer* following *Newsweek*'s publication of the photograph, one White male student cheekily wrote, "Well, Augustana finally got its 15 minutes of fame and what is it for? . . . the quality liberal arts education received by all students? . . . the caliber of faculty and staff? Oh no, Augie gets

Fig. 4.2. Augustana students react to O. J. Simpson verdict, 1995. Photograph by Larry Fisher. Copyright *Quad-City Times*. Reprinted with permission.

it's [*sic*] best press thanks to the O. J. Simpson trial . . . [N]ow the whole country has caught a glimpse of exactly how tacky the game room is."[54] Other students and faculty recognized the trial as a moment of potential reckoning for the campus. Student Azeem Ahmed noted, "All across the nation, and yes, even on the campus of Augustana College, students were divided along racial lines concerning their reactions to the verdict. Instead of addressing the Simpson verdict and the students' reactions, the *Observer* . . . [hid] behind . . . a lame slogan."[55] BSU organized an emergency meeting and a "teach-in"; a few days later, three hundred Quad Cities residents gathered on Augustana's football field for a "Race against Racism" event sponsored by Ladies of Vital Essence, Majestic Gents, and Sigma Pi Delta. There, Larry Ware, a Black Baptist minister from Davenport, Iowa, used words that echoed those of Hildreth when, in 1971, he had defined racism as a sickness: "Racism is a sin . . . It is an evil—it's a cancerous blight on this nation." Despite this condemnation, some students interpreted the event through the purely positive lens of multiculturalism, returning to the familiar script that seeking common ground is more productive than disruption.[56]

Throughout the 1980s and '90s, there was a good deal of bubble bursting on Augustana's campus. It is one thing to burst bubbles and another to build bridges, however.[57] While the local chapter of the NAACP directly confronted the college in 1979–80, there is little evidence that Augustana sought out opportunities to understand the perspectives and experiences of its neighbors. According to Jerry Jones, this made the campus more fortress than bubble, not because of its geographic incursions into the community, but because of a propensity to wall itself off from the broader concerns of minoritized people. That would change—slowly and surely—in the twenty-first century when leaders such as President Steven Bahls; student activist Dezi Primous-Gillon; the first Black tenured woman, Lauren Hammond-Ford; and I, the inaugural vice president for diversity, equity, and inclusion, would work with many other students and faculty to educate students not only for, but also within, a diverse and changing world. Indeed, Augustana's campus was becoming a reflection of this world.

THE 2000S: "SOME FOLKS ARE GLAD TO KNOW THAT I'M HERE"

In the spring of 2002, students and faculty again contended with racist acts on campus. A "blackface" fraternity party, racial epithets scrawled on a custodian's car, and a faculty member's reference to a group of Black students sitting together as the "colored section" roused the anger of students and faculty who called out structural racism. The administration condemned these acts as unacceptable, which showed a positional change on the part of the college: no longer minimizing behaviors but taking a stand against them. Faculty challenged their colleagues to do better. A letter to the campus community from faculty stated that it was "not enough to say that such acts have no place in a community of learning . . . Such acts have no place anywhere."[58] Nina Abney, a queer Black artist whose work deals with politics, race, and representation, graduated from Augustana in 2004. In a 2015 *Vanity Fair* interview, she identified herself as one of the group of

Black students that the faculty member had targeted. Like Jerry Jones, Abney suggested that feeling ostracized led to political awakening. The interview noted that a "campus-wide walkout protesting a lack of black faculty members [was] a turning point for her as an artist interested in tackling political themes."[59] For some students and faculty, then, the 2000s marked a shift to understanding racist incidents as not just unfortunate outcomes of free speech but as part of a pervasive structure of inequality.

Reactions to events in 2002 affirmed that addressing racism must go beyond institutional apologies that condemn racist acts to become more open to critique and systemic change.[60] In order for the language of diversity to keep its critical edge, it is important not only to celebrate diversity at an institution but also to ask the harder question of "what diversity can and does do."[61] In this final section, I consider how the college has institutionalized its values through my position and other actions and how our social justice mission requires us to confront more authentically what diversity *does* in our community. Students cannot thrive without commitments to equity and inclusion. Diversity without practices of inclusion and equity does not confront racism, nor does it progress toward necessary institutional change. Transformation happens when inclusive practices are embedded in institutional functions. Equity is a practice and outcome.

Steven Bahls strengthened the institutional commitment to build bridges to and within the community after his appointment as college president in 2003. Greg Aguilar, a founding member of the Greater Quad Cities Hispanic Chamber of Commerce, served as the director of the Office of Multicultural Services from 2010 to 2013, and Dr. Christopher Whitt, a member of the Political Science Department from 2007 to 2018 and current vice chancellor for diversity, equity, and inclusion at the University of Denver, founded Augustana's Center for Inclusive Leadership and Equity in 2016. A leader in local NAACP chapters, he also helped to start the Quad Cities Empowerment Network and hosted a podcast with local change agents that focused on "groups of people who are marginalized politically and socially, and the people working to provide change for those communities."[62] Whitt fostered conversations between campus and community, helping to turn the conversation on campus from accommodating racial difference to confronting systems of White privilege through a series of campus summits open to the public.

Indeed, my interview with Dezi Primous-Gillon affirmed that student voices are but one critical element that attends to the change in culture or ethos that college communities like Augustana so deeply need. Primous-Gillon, a Black nonbinary alum, graduated from Augustana with religion and sociology majors in 2016, having participated in Interfaith Understanding, BSU, AugiEquality (an organization for LGBTQ+ students and allies), and a residential community partnered with a local Lutheran church. After graduation they went on to study Black liberation theology, earning an MDiv degree at Union Theological Seminary in New York. Since then, they have worked with youth as a community organizer, with LGBTQ+ folks in the criminal justice system, as a service provider for those seeking abortions, and in serving those with accessibility needs at a Chicago mosque/masjid.

At Augustana, Primous-Gillon thought that the machinery of institutional change was too slow to get out ahead of persistent, violent forms of racism. The murder of unarmed Black teenagers—particularly Michael Brown on August 9, 2014, in Ferguson, Missouri—had Primous-Gillon coming back to campus for their junior year feeling, together with a close Black community and White allies, that they needed one another to work through the collective trauma. They were "feeling like the administration wasn't doing enough. It felt like—when we were having conversations with the administration, on our own or [with] one or two people—it didn't feel like our voices were being heard. It felt like we were sort of like [told,] 'Thank you for sharing your concerns,' you know, like everyone has valid concerns . . . I remember feeling really frustrated." Primous-Gillon clarified that what Augustana did not do is what mattered most—to explain *why* racist acts are "extremely hurtful" and to give a "history of why [they are so hurtful], you know?"

Later that year, Primous-Gillon organized a campus "die-in" to protest the deaths of unarmed Black people as well as a separate demonstration against white supremacy in which both Black and White students took part. These impactful but provocative acts left Primous-Gillon and others "feeling like half the school, like, hated us." They joined other BIPOC (Black, Indigenous, and People of Color) leaders and White allies in making a list of demands for the administration, ranging from making the campus aware of its own racism to stopping the use of "multiculturalism" as a marketing strategy to creating conversation between Public Safety (which had recently begun carrying guns) and Black students (who expressed feeling unsafe because of this) to adding Yik Yak to the Augustana internet firewall. Most if not all of these demands have now been met. As students had in 1969, Primous-Gillon was asking for change in Augustana's ethos, culture, spirit. Recalled Primous-Gillon, "We were asking for a deeper appreciation for students like us and the community around us, and it felt like people weren't necessarily seeing that."

Dr. Lauren Hammond-Ford, who, from 2014 to 2023, taught Latin American history and Africana studies with a focus on the Black diaspora, suggests that valuing diversity is a spiritual as well as institutional change. She hoped that Augustana's small size would allow her to have more influence on students: "at big colleges there can be a lot of red tape, and it can be more difficult to be impactful with all of those students." She surveyed the campus and community closely when interviewing for the position in 2016. She was pleased to find there were communities of color near campus, including the vibrant and historically significant Floreciente neighborhood. She talked with Black faculty member Christopher Whitt, who let her know that she "would be okay." At Augustana she developed courses on women in Latin American history and Afro-Latinx history and culture and created the first Augustana course to focus solely on the experiences of Black women. She served as BSU's advisor and worked closely with 2012 Augustana graduate and the inaugural director of the Office of Student Inclusion and Diversity, Michael Rogers, to lead students on a trip to various important sites in the historical struggle for Black civil rights in the United States. Hammond-Ford mentioned feeling that supportive faculty "invested in me from the beginning and wanted me to be successful." When, in 2022, Hammond-Ford became the first Black woman to earn tenure in the college's 163-year history, it was a troubling honor: "I am definitely proud of myself, but I don't think that I thought I would be the first anything in 2023."[63]

Like Hildreth, Hammond-Ford felt the strain of working at Augustana as a member of a Black community in which social justice work is inseparable from practicing Christianity. She struggled to "spiritually refuel" herself on campus because she felt that her faith "is often something that remains hidden." She noted that faculty who identify as Christians do not always feel "welcomed or embraced" on a campus that is church-identified but is not centered on the "radically liberatory faith practice" that she has experienced in the Black church. "Black church is not just where you go for Black church," she said; "it's where you go for Black history." This history has included church as "a place for you to be seen and to be respected in a world where many people disrespected or overlooked you. . . . Black church has been a place for the humanization of Black folk for centuries." Hammond-Ford taught a class on Black history through her church, where she was able to center faith as a force in history in ways that are not as welcome in a college classroom.[64]

Because Augustana has, for the last few decades at least, based its progressive politics on secular liberalism rather than creating space for faith-based liberation, faculty, students, and staff who do center faith find it "hard to put down roots" on campus. Hammond-Ford has worked to mentor students from those traditions, letting them know they can safely talk about faith with her. At the same time, she notes that her presence at Augustana is reassuring to the Black community. They are "glad to know I am here," she said.[65] As Black students and clergy suggested in the 1960s, Black faculty are critical to the college not simply because they outwardly represent diversity but because they challenge the college to grapple with the limitations of its academic version of how and where social change occurs. While senior administrators sometimes assume that bridges are built from campus to community in that direction, Hammond-Ford's status as an ambassador of the Black faith tradition is a reminder that in order to be truly inclusive, the college cannot embrace a purely secular story of progress. Faith—as an empathetic, relational, and even ecstatic counterpoint to the rational, institutional, and legal powers that have privileged some and oppressed others—has long been a necessary and productively disruptive force in the world and, as this volume shows, on campus.

Much racial justice work at Augustana was done by mere handfuls of students without Augustana's official sanction. By contrast, recent events such as the Vigil for Lives Lost, held on Augustana's football field after a summer of racial reckoning following George Floyd's murder in 2020 and attracting over four hundred students, were officially sanctioned by the institution (through my and other offices) and have thus brought marginalized voices into the center (Fig. 4.3). Support for BIPOC students now overlaps with and contributes to support for communities including LGBTQ+ and international students. The PACE (Preparation, Awareness, Community, and Engagement) Multicultural Mentorship Program is a yearlong program for first-year students of color to promote students' sense of belonging and retention by developing strong relationships within the cohort. Over the last six years, participation in PACE has increased exponentially, and PACE student retention has reached parity with nonminority students at the college. Participants note the positive impact the program has had on their development, sense of belonging, and success at the college. These are catalytic spaces for underrepresented students.

Fig. 4.3. Students at Vigil for Lives Lost, Augustana College, 2020. Courtesy of Augustana College Communication and Marketing.

Since I came to Augustana as the inaugural vice president for diversity, equity, and inclusion in 2018, we have further institutionalized Augustana's commitment to diversity, equity, inclusion, and justice in a myriad of ways, including hiring a director of disability services, marking the fiftieth anniversary of the Black Power Symposium with guest speaker Yusef Salaam (a member of the wrongly convicted Central Park Five now known as the Exonerated Five), establishing a Presidential Racial Justice and Equity Fund, hosting racial healing sessions together with members of the broader community, and requiring the presence of a designated and trained equity guide on all faculty and administrative searches. As noted earlier, the commitment to justice is one reason I was interested in the position. Augustana's journey was written into the leadership prospectus. Portions were on the college website and in local newspapers. During my interviews, faculty, staff, and students openly discussed challenges that persisted. The commitment to change and to focus on justice was clear, so I focused my work there. Augustana was ready to do the work of transformation. Like Hildreth, I engaged with many faculty members, staff, and students who partnered, collaborated, and supported the vision for diversity, equity, inclusion, and justice.

By 2018, the social ethos around diversity had shifted. According to reports as early as 2010, college-age students were indicating they wanted diversity in their college experience. Researchers from the Higher Education Research Institute noted students' strong desire for campuses with racial, ethnic, socioeconomic, and cultural diversity.[66] The American Council on Education's Board of Directors authored and published a brief highlighting the educational benefits of exposure to different perspectives and experiences.[67] Furthermore, the Association of American Colleges and Universities included intercultural knowledge and competence and global learning in its VALUE rubrics. The rubrics are intended to guide colleges' and universities' assessment and discussion of student learning. The National Association of Colleges and Employers created a diversity statement and added equity and inclusion to its list of competencies for career-ready graduates.[68] The explicit support by these professional organizations aided in making the case for transformative changes to curriculum and co-curricular supports like career services, student development, and social activities on campus.

Among the reasons students are drawn to Augustana are diversity and a commitment to justice. Neither is taboo on campus any longer. Multiple sources have reported that college-age students want to be on campuses that focus on justice; they believe justice brings about change, and they want to be involved in justice work.[69] Students are seeking justice for others and themselves and wanting to contribute to the world beyond Augustana College, and they recognize the college as a place that offers opportunities for each. Following the public assault and murder of George Floyd, many colleges and universities across the nation issued diversity statements and created justice initiatives. Augustana College leaned into its existing justice mission. Campus and community-engaged conversations led by me, Jason Mahn (religion), Michael Rogers (then director of OSID), and alumnus Jack Cullen grappled with what we witnessed and shared our own experiences with racialized injustice. Students grappled with issues of race on campus, shared their experiences, and challenged their own and one another's assumptions about race and justice in American society. The president's cabinet spent weeks reading and discussing Nikole Hannah-Jones's *The 1619 Project*. These dialogic processes drew from our participation in the Institute for Truth, Racial Healing & Transformation and served to increase awareness, enhance knowledge, and deepen our relationships with one another. As a result, the college received the Higher Education Excellence in Diversity Award from *INSIGHT into Diversity* magazine (now called *Insight into Academia*) five times between 2019 and 2024. These are just a few instances of the college actualizing its commitment to justice. The Presidential Racial Justice and Equity Fund is an outcome of these processes and continues to show our commitment to justice by funding student engagement in justice and equity work.

Investing in the thriving of others involves decentering the campus in ways that open it up to those who have been historically excluded. The Augustana Prison Education Program, spearheaded by faculty member Dr. Sharon Varallo, launched in the fall of 2021 as a partnership among Augustana College, the Illinois Department of Corrections, and the East Moline Correctional Center eight miles up the Mississippi River. Varallo described the program as an imperative to "live out the mission *to go to places of deep need*. The goal is to build a bridge that is authentically an Augustana bridge, one that is true to our mission and calling as a college."[70] The program started with ten degree-seeking students; in May 2024, David Staples walked across the stage to receive his diploma, becoming the first graduate of the program.[71]

The dual pandemics of COVID-19 and widespread racial violence that spanned 2020 provided the opportunity for Augustana to address more explicitly issues of race, disparate treatment, racialized bias, discrimination, and violence—specifically on and toward Black and Brown people. In 2021, as part of the larger "Know Justice Know Peace" initiative, the college engaged about five hundred students, employees, community members, and alumni in conversations about race. On-campus sessions for students and employees sustained open and vulnerable conversations. Two alumni from Augustana—one Black and one White—agreed to host similar racial healing circles for alumni, and all of us were surprised at the number of alumni who attended and the gratitude they expressed. Commenting on Augustana as a PWI, one older alumna stated that she was finally given a chance to participate in discussions of the political movements of the 1960s. The college invited predominantly White, predominantly Black, and multiracial churches in the Quad Cities area to a series of related conversations that used the *1619* podcast to unpack the history of race in America and the resultant systemic inequalities that continue to produce racial ignorance, intolerance, and violence. Community engagement also included training for local and regional law enforcement and public safety officials on strategies for building trust within Black and Brown communities; it acknowledged the inherent tensions between the police and those policed, whether based on perceptions or realities. These community collaborations prompted the college's Office of Diversity, Equity, and Inclusion to announce an intention to "dismantl[e] racism and other hierarchies of human value throughout the Augustana College community and across the Quad Cities region; to bring people to the table and commit to staying at the table doing the work of reconciling our differences and committing to teach and model this for others." While the work is institutional, it does not stop at the boundaries of campus.

Augustana College lives out its Lutheran-ness and commitment to social justice through intentional efforts at inclusion and community engagement for the purpose of addressing current social ills. These social ills are rooted in the discriminatory and exclusionary past of our nation, communities, and social institutions—including higher education. We must address contemporary social issues by understanding the deep history of racism and other systemic injustices that have shaped our sense of place. Justice involves creating policies and practices that produce equitable access to opportunities, power, social goods, and services. Institutions must proactively promote these policies in order to eliminate disparities, whether on campus, in the community, or in the nation. Thus, our commitment to social justice demands that we confront current issues that arise from historical sins. This account has rehearsed—or rather confessed—to these sins let the wind of truth-telling carry us forward. I know that Augustana faculty, students, administrators, and community partners will continue to do this work with courage, hope, and a deep hunger to become communities of peace and justice. Onward together.

Notes

1. Augustana College, "The Search"; Augustana College Office of the President, "Diversity Efforts Inventory." As a scholar-practitioner in inclusion and belonging, I view language as a tool of consciousness. I have capitalized all racialized identity terms (i.e., Black, White, Brown, People of Color) in order to emphasize these as socially constructed racial categories, to ensure equity in language, and to challenge White default norms. Terms like "DEI" often become jargonized, depersonalized, or misrepresented in public discourse. By naming each word, I resist the impulse to rush past complexity. I center the human and institutional work required in each area, avoiding the shorthand that allows critics to dismiss or oversimplify these efforts, instead affirming the distinct value and transformative potential of each term.

2. See the "Five Faith Commitments" at the end of this volume's foreword.

3. The term *hidden curriculum* was coined by Philip W. Jackson in *Life in Classrooms.*

4. Exum, *Paradoxes of Protest*, 177.

5. Carr, "Transforming."

6. See Monica Smith, "Making Diversity Matter."

7. A thank-you to Jane Simonsen for conducting the interview with Lauren Hammond-Ford, to Jason Mahn for conducting some of the archival research, and to both for helping to bring together earlier drafts of this essay.

8. Sorensen had a copy of the American Council on Education's special report from April 8, 1969, "Black Studies and Civil Rights," folder 8, box 15, Black Faculty, etc., CWS.

9. "Hardesty Comments on AAS Demands," *Augustana Observer*, October 30, 1968; "Affiliate Artist Stirs Audience," *Augustana Observer*, September 25, 1968, 1. Johnson was on a break from what would be a lengthy career at Spelman College, where she played the organ as King's body lay in state at the college. She was in Illinois while working on her doctorate in piano at Northwestern. She was the first Black woman to do so. Brown's presence at Augustana was the result of a national program to link artists to colleges as ambassadors for the arts. Brown went on to teach at the University of North Florida and was the star of the opera *Frederick Douglass* at its world premiere in 1985. Johnson, "Recollections."

10. Black Faculty Status memo, October 10, 1973, folder 8, box 15, Black Faculty, etc., CWS.

11. C. W. Sorensen, "B-10d Report of President Statements—Racism," Black Student Information, 1969–1973, box 15, CWS; John Hildreth, interview with author, July 29, 2021. All comments by Hildreth not attributed to other sources come from this interview.

12. Augustana was, since this time, a member of a parallel denomination called the Lutheran Church in America (LCA), which was formed in 1962 when the Augustana Synod merged with three other Lutheran bodies. Twenty-five years later, the LCA and ALC (but not the more conservative LCMS church of Hildreth's childhood) merged to form the Evangelical Lutheran Church in America.

13. Sociologist of religion Robert P. Jones argues that if you wanted to recruit for a white supremacy group on a Sunday morning, you would have better luck hanging out in the church parking lot of any random White evangelical, mainline Protestant, or Catholic church than nearly anywhere else in the country. Jones, *White Too Long*.

14. Felber, "Integration or Separation?"

15. "Blacks 'Crash' Augie Fair," *Rock Island Argus*, Monday, April 28, 1969; "Black Student Union Protests," *Augustana Observer*, February 9, 1972, 3.

16. Illinois Synod's Racial Reconciliation Fund made a $1,500 contribution, becoming the largest supporter of the symposium. "Augie Students Pleased."

17. "Sorensen Criticizes Wallace Protestors," *Augustana Observer*, October 30, 1968; "Sorensen Affirms Student Program" and "A Student Responsibility," *Rock Island Argus*, February 1, 1969.

18. Joseph Efferus Looney, "The Philosophy of Racism: Augustana College," 1971, Black Student Information, box 15, CWS.

19. Looney, "Philosophy of Racism."

20. Hildreth, "Hildreth Berates Apathetic Attitude," *Augustana Observer*, March 25, 1971.

21. Hildreth, "Hildreth Berates."

22. "Statement to the Press," April 14, 1970, Student Rights, 1970–73, box 100, CWS.

23. Sorensen to John Teleen, "Notes Regarding Statement on Racism," October 28, 1971, Human Relations Committee, January–August 1971, box 50, CWS; Human Rights Committee memo, November 30, 1971, Human Relations Committee, January–August 1971, box 50, CWS; Faculty Health Committee to Nominations and Rules Committee, Human Relations Committee, January–August 1971, box 50, CWS.

24. Transcript, Human Relations Committee hearing, December 7, 1971, and Faculty Health Committee to Nominations and Rules, Human Relations Committee, January–August 1971, box 50, CWS.

25. "Black Culture House Serves as Vent for Frustration," *Augustana Observer*, May 8, 1992.

26. "Augie Walks Out on Racism," *Dispatch/Rock Island Argus*, May 7, 2007.

27. Berrey, "Why Diversity," 575, 577.

28. Lowy, "Yuppie Racism."

29. "Augie Blacks Protest Fraternity KKK Skit," *Rock Island Argus*, October 23, 1979; "Black Students Denounce Skit," *Quad-City Times*, October 23, 1979.

30. "Fraternity Skit Angers NAACP," *Quad-City Times*, October 24, 1979.

31. "NAACP: Suspend Augie Students" and "NAACP Demands Suspension of Fraternity at Augie," *Quad-City Times*, October, 26, 1979; "NAACP President Seeks Suspension of Fraternity," *Rock Island Argus*, October 25, 1979; "NAACP Rally Saturday to Protest Fraternity Skit,"

Rock Island Argus, November 6, 1979; "Augie Fraternities Fear Repercussions from Skit" and "Augie Fraternities Feel the Heat," *Quad-City Times*, October 25, 1979.

32. "Fraternity Skit Angers NAACP," *Quad-City Times*, October 24, 1979.

33. "Augie Fraternity Sends 2,000 Letters of Apology," *Rock Island Argus*, October 24, 1979.

34. Feagin et al. argue that Black students' experience of racism on White campuses in the 1980s and '90s was shaped by "collective memory" of violence and racism. *Agony of Education*, 23.

35. "Augustana Fraternity Gets 1-Year Probation," *Quad-City Times*, November 4, 1979.

36. "Rights Protected in Frat Penalty," *Daily Dispatch*, November 8, 1979.

37. "Council Backs Frat Discipline; David Lone Dissenter," *Daily Dispatch*, November 6, 1979.

38. "Davis, NAACP Upset by Stand," *Quad-City Times*, November 6, 1979. Clearly, Maurus did not see panty raids as sexist acts.

39. "Augustana Responds."

40. "NAACP Questions Attitudes," *Quad-City Times*, November 18, 1979.

41. "Public Forum Slated Today to Air Augie Frat March Gripes," *Daily Dispatch*, November 10, 1979.

42. "Augie Fraternity Sends."

43. Feagin et al., *Agony of Education*, 60–61.

44. Page and Thomas, "White Public Space," 111.

45. Kathy Atkins, "Student Efforts Can Resolve Divisions in Campus Community," *Augustana Observer*, November 12, 1980.

46. Case and Ngo, "Do We Have to Call It That?," 218.

47. Leigh Ann Johnson, "Diversity Offered at Augustana Through Campus Organizations," *Augustana Observer*, February 3, 1995.

48. This desire to get a degree and move on might be attributed to what scholars have called "neoliberal multiculturalism," or a "soft" acceptance of diversity in the interest of individual success rather than systemic change. Case and Ngo, "Do We Have to Call It That?"

49. Jerry Jones, interview with author, April 12, 2023. Subsequent comments from Jones are from this interview.

50. Feagin et al., *Agony of Education*, 115–34.

51. "Brown to Direct Minority Affairs," *Augustana Observer* January 12, 1983; Roberta Sweeper, "Dean Carol Brown Moves On," *Augustana Observer*, May 3, 1990.

52. The mural is based on a painting that won the district's Congressional Art Competition in 2021 and was displayed in the US Capitol. Brooks, "High School Student's Nationally-Recognized Artwork."

53. Jan Touney, "Journalist Leaves Four-Decade Legacy in Pictures," *Quad-City Times*, May 11, 2014; "Times Photo Joins D.C. O. J. Simpson Exhibit," *Quad-City Times*, October 1, 2010.

54. Neil Mardis, "Newsweek Missed Out on the Real Scoop at Augustana," *Augustana Observer*, October 20, 1995.

55. Azeem Ahmed, "O.J. Simpson Slogan Reflects Poor Judgment," *Augustana Observer*, October 13, 1995.

56. "Teach-in Focuses on Fundamental Problems," *Augustana Observer*, May 8, 1992; "Runners Strive to Outpace Racism," *Augustana Observer*, May 8, 1992.

57. See Eboo Patel's remarks at an interfaith understanding gathering for the colleges and universities affiliated with the Evangelical Lutheran Church in America, which was hosted by Augustana College in 2014. Patel, "What It Means."

58. Ali Harrison, "Don't Let Racist Attitudes Ruin Augustana," *Augustana Observer*, May 3, 2002.

59. McVey, "Nina Chanel Abney."

60. Melamed, "Spirit of Neoliberalism," 20.

61. Ahmed, *On Being Included*, 1.

62. Christopher Whitt, *Margins* podcast, https://www.npr.org/podcasts/525417635/margins.

63. Kayla Palliser, "History Professor's Tenure Makes Augustana History," *Augustana Observer*, March 24, 2023.

64. Lauren Hammond-Ford, interview with Jane Simonsen, March 8, 2023.

65. Lauren Hammond-Ford, interview.

66. Pryor et al., *American Freshman*.

67. American Council on Education, "On the Importance of Diversity."

68. National Association of Colleges and Employers, "What Is Career Readiness?," https://www.naceweb.org/career-readiness/competencies/career-readiness-defined/.

69. "Why Student Activists Care About Social Justice," Bestcolleges .com, November 18, 2021; Jessica Bryant, "Students Believe Supporting Social Justice Drives Change," Bestcolleges.com, January 20, 2022; Chris Burt, "More than 70% of College Students Motivated by Social Justice," University Business, August 2, 2021.

70. Smith, "Just Communities," 12.

71. For more on the Augustana Prison Education Program and a photograph of Staples, see chapter 8.

5 CONTESTED COUNTERSPACES: *Creating Latinos/x Unidos at a Midwestern College*

CHRISTOPHER STRUNK AND
LIZANDRA GOMEZ-RAMIREZ

Even as its student body has become more diverse in recent decades, Augustana College's history as a predominantly white institution (PWI) continues to shape how students of color belong both on and off campus. In this chapter, we document the history of Latinos/x Unidos (LU), a student group founded in 1992. We draw on interviews with former and current students to show how LU has become a space of belonging at the college for generations of students with Latin American heritage. Latinx students have often encountered discrimination and barriers to full participation in campus life, but LU has represented a counterspace that offers opportunities for students to connect with others who share similar experiences and to develop a deeper appreciation for family and community traditions. At the same time, LU has also been a contested space that reveals important debates at Augustana College around tradition, political activism, ethnicity, race, gender identity, and relationships with local communities. Our chapter argues that student organizations like LU have played a major role in transforming Augustana College and creating a community that better reflects students from underrepresented backgrounds.

On January 16, 1994, Casa Latina opened as Augustana College's first Hispanic culture house (Fig. 5.1). The location of Casa Latina on 7th Avenue in Rock Island, the campus's main street, symbolized the newly visible position of Latinx students at the college.[1] While only a small number of students from Latin America and domestic Latinx communities attended Augustana before the 1980s, this had begun slowly to change by 1994. Two years earlier, a small group of students founded Latinos Unidos (LU) as part of an effort to create a space where Latinx and Latin American students could feel comfortable on an overwhelmingly white campus. In the years since, LU has pushed Augustana to develop a more inclusive curriculum, expand its connections to Quad Cities communities, and transform its identity as a white institution to which students of color must adapt. More than thirty years after its founding, LU continues to embody the college's struggles over diversity, equity, inclusion, and belonging.

Our chapter is a collaboration between Christopher Strunk, a geography professor and current co-advisor of Latinx Unidos, and Lizandra Gomez-Ramirez, a former vice president of LU who graduated in 2017. Lizandra's experiences as a Mexican American native of Rock Island and an Augustana graduate provide a unique perspective on the position of Latinx students and Augustana College's role in the Quad Cities. Lizandra's narratives, which draw on her experiences in LU and Rock Island, are included throughout the chapter to reflect her position as an insider and now alumna observer in many of these debates. These contributions are styled in italics.

Fig. 5.1. Group photo of members of Latinos Unidos in front of the Casa Latina sign, 1999. Augustana College Latinx Unidos Records. Courtesy of Augustana College Special Collections, Rock Island, Illinois.

When I agreed to be a part of this project, I didn't realize how emotional it would be for me. When I graduated from Augustana, I was ready to leave. I wanted to forget my experience at Augustana, as if Augustana was not a microcosm of the world and I could escape the political reality of 2017. This project has helped me reflect on my time at Augustana and realize how much I have grown and how Latinx Unidos was the safe space that I needed during that time. Latinx Unidos was one of the best parts of Augustana for me; it was a place of community for the good times and bad times.

This project also comes with a lot of responsibility. I majored in anthropology, which raises the question of who am I to tell the story of Latinx Unidos and how do I do it justice. I studied cultural anthropology, where historically an outsider, usually white, would go to an "exotic" place in the world and study a different culture. Eventually, scholars realized that they were participating in colonizing behavior by categorizing and studying non-European peoples as "others." Since then, the field of anthropology has been more cognizant of this tendency and is asking questions like, Whose culture is being studied? Who is doing the studying, or what are the power dynamics between the people being studied and the person doing the studying?

I am a cishet, female Latina who was born in the United States. From this project, I have learned that Latinx Unidos was founded out of love, for our people, for our culture, and for the world that we live in. It was founded so that Latinx students on campus could have a safe space and so that they could share their culture with other students. And Latinx Unidos continues because of that love. Each transformation of Latinx Unidos is a representation of the student class behind it and is curated with love to meet their needs.

Higher education research shows that students from underrepresented backgrounds often experience isolation, alienation, and marginalization at PWIs.[2] Latinx enrollment at US colleges and universities has doubled since 2000, but Latinx young people are still less likely to attend college than are other ethnic groups in the United States. In 2021, only 32 percent of Latinx 18- to 24-year-olds were enrolled at least part-time in college, compared with 37 percent of young white people and 58 percent of young Asians. Furthermore, while 45 percent of white 25- to 29-year-olds have a bachelor's degree or more, only

23 percent of Latinx 25- to 29-year-olds do.[3] More than 40 percent of Latinx students attend community colleges, and Latinx students at four-year institutions have only a 51 percent graduation rate, 12 points lower than white students.[4]

Latinx students have described feeling uncomfortable at PWIs not only because they can experience discrimination and microaggressions in classrooms but also because PWIs tend to lack faculty, staff, and other students who understand their experiences.[5] Latinx students are also more likely to encounter what education researchers have called the "hidden curriculum," or unwritten rules about college that can make students question whether they belong in college and can create barriers to participation in campus activities.[6] However, research has also shown that participating in cultural organizations on campus can help students to "feel less alone, experience a sense of belonging, reflect on shared experiences, and generally participate in a familiar cultural environment."[7] Latino and Chicano student organizations have been an important presence on US university and college campuses since the 1960s, when groups like the United Mexican American Students demanded greater access to higher education and programs that focused on the experiences of Latinx students.[8] The 1990s, when Latinos Unidos was founded at Augustana, also saw an increase in student organizing around cultural diversity on college campuses, and LU quickly became part of a larger ecosystem of Latino student organizations in the Midwest and eventually formed collaborations with similar student groups in the Quad Cities and beyond.

The history of LU also reflects some of the broader tensions between Augustana and the Quad Cities community. While the college was founded in the 1860s to serve Swedish immigrants, it has often had a complicated relationship with immigrants and refugees in Rock Island and elsewhere in the Quad Cities. Most local first- and second-generation immigrants attend Black Hawk College, a local community college in northwestern Illinois, in part because Augustana is seen as an elite, inaccessible institution for local residents. As Augustana began to recruit non-white students from the Quad Cities and beyond, the presence of non-white students has forced the college to develop new programs for historically underrepresented students and to reimagine itself as an institution that again serves the immigrant community. Lizandra's history as a Rock Island resident who was initially hesitant about Augustana is reflective of the college's efforts to attract a more diverse study body.

I did not plan to go to Augustana. The ironic part is that I grew up really close to campus, and my family and I always walked our dog through the Swanie Slough, even before it was called the Swanie Slough. Swanie, a former pastor at Augustana, was a part of my congregation, and when he died, I thought it was perfect that they named the slough after him. I was familiar with the physical campus, but I did not envision myself attending the school. Each fall, I would watch the college kids move in, and each spring I would watch them leave. I loved/love the Augustana campus during the summer because the college kids are gone and it feels like I have the campus all to myself. I went to Longfellow Elementary School in Rock Island, and my class was very diverse. I remember that in the sixth grade some Augie students came to our school and taught us Spanish. It was a weird experience because most of the college students that came were white, and they came to a diverse elementary school to teach Spanish. There was another time where I participated in an after-school activity: a school bus took us to Augustana, and we got to hang out with the Majestic Gents (a Black fraternity) and the women's version of them. That was an empowering experience because I got to imagine and really envision myself going to college. I got to see that college was a place for me, not just rich white people.

Augustana has been branching out and becoming more active in the Quad Cities. The feeling I got as a child is that Augustana is a place that you have to be invited to, and if you did get an invitation, it was a big deal. Augustana is in the community, but it is not for the community. Augustana was not on my radar for colleges. When I was in high school, Black Hawk was free for the top 10 percent of the class. I was in the top 10 percent of my class, so I planned to go to Black Hawk and transfer out. I applied to Augustana because my mother encouraged me to do so and to see if I got any scholarship money. I received a generous scholarship, and that is why I picked Augustana.

Though the college has made progress in attracting and retaining historically underrepresented students, the college continued to see white, upper- and middle-class students as the norm and expected non-white students to adapt. However, the efforts of Latinx students at Augustana College created a "counterspace" on campus that affirms the cultural identities of marginalized groups and challenges stereotypes held by the dominant culture.[9] The history of LU illustrates the key role that students have played in Augustana's efforts to become a more diverse and inclusive campus—as well as the tensions that continue to exist around these transformations—by affirming and strengthening the different racial, ethnic, and cultural identities of Augustana students.

Student clubs often provide a physical space on campus (such as Casa Latina or the Black Culture House at Augustana College) where historically underrepresented students do not have to navigate exclusionary institutions or microaggressions. These spaces can serve as a place to relax, to connect with students from similar ethnic, racial, or geographic backgrounds, and to build alliances across racial and ethnic differences, most notably as students of color have called for policy changes by the college around diversity, equity, and inclusion (DEI) initiatives. We argue that understanding the transformation of Augustana College over its history requires both an account of administrative decisions as well as the influence of students over policies and campus culture. Our chapter raises crucial questions about whether the college is currently meeting the demands of an increasingly diverse student body and how Augustana can continue to improve its efforts to be a more inclusive and diverse institution.

LU has come to be an important part of campus over the last thirty years, particularly in conversations around DEI, but there are few records about the organization's history or Latinx student experiences at Augustana College. In response, we decided to build a Latinx student archive at Augustana. To supplement our research in the library's Special Collections and our review of *Augustana Observer* articles, we also conducted oral history interviews with ten current and former LU members, who were key participants in the organization in the early 1990s, about their experiences on campus and the activities of LU over its thirty-year history. We also conducted interviews with several former staff members involved in DEI initiatives at Augustana. As part of the archive, transcriptions of these oral histories and other materials from LU's history will be cataloged in Special Collections for future researchers.

FOUNDING LATINOS UNIDOS

There were fewer than fifty Latinx students enrolled at Augustana when Sandra Cantu arrived on campus in the fall of 1993. Latinx students at the time were aware that they were not typical Augustana College students. For most of Augustana's history, the vast majority of the college's student body was white. In 1990, when the founders of LU started taking classes in Rock Island, Latinx or Hispanic students represented only 1.4 percent of Augustana students, and students of color barely made up 6 percent of the student body. Augustana had only recently begun recruiting in the city of Chicago and announced that it was welcoming the largest incoming Latino class in the college's history that fall. Sandra recalled thinking, "that's it, that's all? . . . There [weren't] many people that looked like me."

As the number of Latinx students at Augustana slowly increased during the 1990s, students developed informal social networks among their classmates with similar experiences and identities. Anna and Jose Castro, who met at Augustana and were later married, grew up less than a mile from campus in the west end of Moline (now known as the Floreciente neighborhood). Even though both had strong local connections, Anna and Jose were drawn to other Latinx students when they arrived on campus in the early 1990s. Jose remembered "just looking for someone who had the same background as me, even though they weren't from the Quad Cities. I was always looking for that sense of community . . . We kind of all tended to hang out together."

Even with these informal social networks, Latinx students described feeling isolated on campus and in classrooms. Consuelo Martinez, one of the founders of LU, noted that many Latinx students at the time were first-generation college students and struggled to navigate an entirely new social system: "Their parents didn't know how to help them, support them, didn't understand what it feels like to be [on] a campus with predominantly white students . . . that don't share the same struggles." Latinx students who attended Augustana in the 1990s described their parents as broadly supportive of their decision but unable to provide the same assistance that their classmates from middle- and upper-class families received. Sandra recalled that her parents did not come with her to visit Augustana's campus, even though the family lived in the Quad Cities, because her parents did not attend college and "felt that they really couldn't help me here." Instead, prospective Latinx students often visited campus on their own or with a high school teacher. Javier Perez, one of LU's first presidents, was dropped off on campus his first day in 1993 with only a handshake from his father, who had no experience navigating higher education in the United States.[10]

Latinx students also described feeling excluded when their roommates received care packages, an initiative the college used to organize among Augustana families. This was another example of the so-called hidden curriculum that excluded Latinx students and families from full belonging on Augustana's campus, as Consuelo recalled: "I never got care packages; I didn't even know about care packages until I came home and I saw the letters unopened from Augustana. It was the care package for the first quarter your kid is there, Christmas, Thanksgiving, different things like that. I never got a care package. My friends all got care packages because people read their letters. My parents were illiterate; they couldn't even read in Spanish, so how were they going to read in English? So those kinds of things were really hard."

As part of a small group of non-white students on campus in the early 1990s, Latinx students also experienced microaggressions in their dorms and classrooms. Consuelo, for instance, recalled being asked by a friend if she "ate beans every day" because of her Mexican heritage. Others described being frustrated by classes that ignored Latinx experiences and asked exam questions about their experiences as either a white or Black student, invalidating their experience as Mexican Americans.[11] These microaggressions took a toll on students. During interviews, students from the early 1990s recalled the names of multiple Latinx classmates that did not graduate from Augustana because they did not receive enough support from the college.

In this isolating environment, socializing with other Latinx, Black, and international students offered comfort and ultimately the inspiration for creating a Latinx counterspace on campus. In 1992, a small group of Mexican American students began to discuss forming a group like the Black Student Union (BSU), a much older Augustana student organization that was founded in the late 1960s. Students initially considered creating a sorority for Latina students, again modeled on Black student organizations like the Majestic Gents fraternity. As Consuelo described, the impetus for these conversations came "from hanging out so much with the Black Student Union and the group. We realized we needed to be around other people that were from the United States, from the area, first generation, homesick, sick for our culture, homesick for our families." By intentionally modeling LU on the experiences of other historically underrepresented students at Augustana, Latinx student leaders created a foundation for a student organization that would eventually participate in conversations around the place of students of color on campus.

Students of color at Augustana, particularly Black students, have a long history of advocating to make campus a more inclusive space. In 1968, Black students formed the Afro-American Society (predecessor to BSU) and pushed Augustana's administration to hire a full-time Black faculty member as well as Black counseling and admissions staff to improve recruitment and support for Black students. Four years later, BSU students held a sit-in at the president's office to demand a written statement condemning racism and concrete steps that the administration would take to address racist actions on campus. And, in the first of many such demands by students, BSU called on the faculty to develop a curriculum that focused more on Black history and culture.[12] Chapters 3 and 4 in this volume cover the activism of Black students in more detail.

Once Consuelo Martinez, Christina Torres, Julio Valdez, and other student leaders decided to form Latinos Unidos, they received institutional support from BSU leaders, the Student Government Association, and John Pollitz, a librarian who served as the group's first advisor. Help also came from community organizations, which provided furniture and decorations for Casa Latina, as well as from the families of local students. Sandra recalled that her parents hosted many early LU meetings at their house in the Quad Cities: "[Students] would come over, they would have dinner at our house, they would stay the night. There's a couple times where people even stayed for a couple of weeks . . . because Latina moms are like that." Assistance from local families was a critical part of a support system for Latinx students who had little experience with higher education. After the club's second year, LU students hosted a Mother's Day event "so parents could come and see what we had done and be proud of us."[13] For early student leaders like Consuelo, LU was a group that "filled a void for all of us."

Within the context of a PWI that did not reflect the lived experiences of Latinx students, LU represented a comfortable, welcoming space that validated and affirmed Latinx identities and challenged dominant representations of the Latinx community. Both goals are embodied in Casa Latina, which served as the primary representation of Latinx culture and students on campus. Sandra Cantu described the importance of having a physical space, located in a highly visible spot along 7th Avenue, for Latinx students: "And I think all of us were just so happy that we were able to show them this piece of Augustana that we all had because we had, through Latinos Unidos, chipped in a piece for us at Augie; this little Augustana was us. This was where we belonged." On a campus where Latinx and other students of color were often invisible, Casa Latina was a physical marker of Latinx presence at Augustana and in the Quad Cities community. Students invited Rosa Granado-Mohr, a local Mexican American artist, to paint a seventeen-by-eight-foot mural that included Mexican cultural and religious symbols such as Our Lady of Guadalupe and scenes from Latinx communities in the United States, most notably Hero Street USA, the neighborhood of a group of Mexican American military veterans in nearby Silvis (Fig. 5.2).[14] Having a physical space on campus apart from classrooms and dorms allowed Latinx students to connect with others from similar backgrounds and to build relationships with Mexican American community organizations like Ballet Folklórico and veterans from Hero Street, both of which were invited to give presentations on campus in the 1990s.

Augustana initially provided support and resources for the new student club, but the lack of an institutional structure to promote DEI meant that LU student leaders were also given the responsibility for representing Latinx students and cultures to the majority-white student body on campus. As Consuelo recalled, "Most of us didn't want there to be a rite of passage; we just wanted to have an organization where people can go; and initially it was to just find other people like

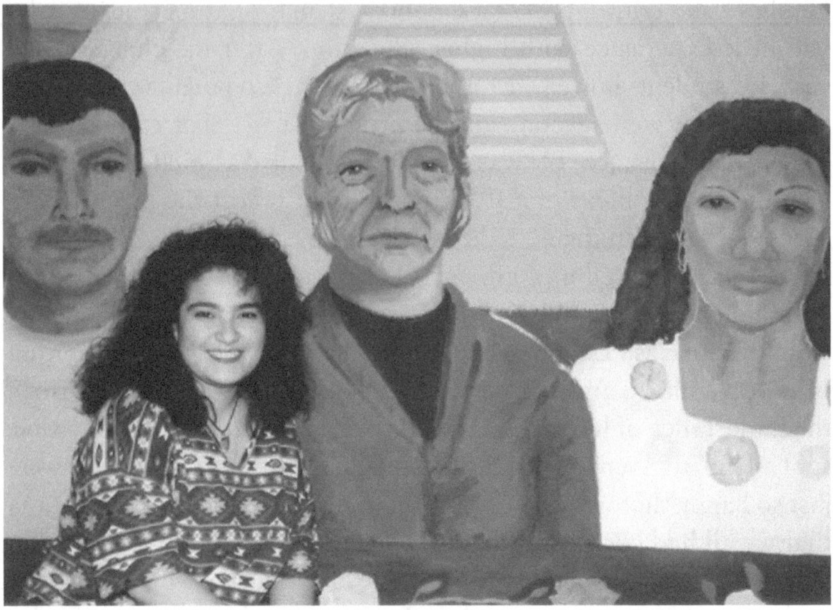

Fig. 5.2. Consuelo Martinez in front of Casa Latina mural. Augustana College Latinx Unidos Records. Courtesy of Augustana College Special Collections, Rock Island, Illinois.

us, and then the university really wanted us to have a little bit more of a cultural reason to exist, and that's when we started incorporating teaching others about our culture and be[ing] representatives of our culture, our traditions." While students quickly embraced their new role as Latinx ambassadors by hosting educational events and recruiting Latinx high school students, it would take much longer to transform Augustana's institutions so that they began to reflect the college's increasing diversity.

A PLACE TO BELONG

While the organization's mission, activities, and even its name have changed over the last thirty years, the goals of LU student leaders have remained broadly consistent. In 1999, LU stated that the organization's purpose was to "encourage a support network and comfortable environment . . . for our members" and "provide our members with a cultural identity." Stephanie Carreno, LU's president during the

2021–22 academic year, similarly described the mission of LU as ensuring that "Latinx students and people who support Latino culture feel that they have a secure place on campus, where they're able to have fun . . . and also let them know that they belong at a predominantly white institution." Much like early LU leaders in the 1990s, current Latinx students emphasize the importance of creating a sense of belonging on a campus that, while it has become more diverse in many ways, continues to privilege white, middle- and upper-class experiences over those of students of color. In this context, LU has sought to make the experiences of Latinx and other students of color more visible and valued at Augustana.

Despite the broad agreement on LU's mission, there has always been a struggle over the social and political nature of the student club. As Consuelo recalled, "Those were issues we had to figure out because most of us that started the organization came from low-income homes, and the other ones that didn't, they didn't see some things as important. So there had to be a balance so that we still had a united front because some people didn't feel the need to find out more about their culture or be big brothers or big sisters and be role models for the future generation because they didn't feel like they had needed it and they were okay." The diversity of Latinx students at Augustana, both in terms of their life experiences and their needs in college, has meant that LU has had to work to create a variety of spaces where students can feel comfortable. While many students have joined the club to socialize and connect with people from similar backgrounds, LU has also represented a space where students could explore their identity and politics.

By 2016, the number of Latinx students enrolled at Augustana had increased from only 49 in 1993 to 250. While Latinx students were a much more visible presence on campus, representing almost 10 percent of the student body that year, recent graduates described feeling alienated at times because of racial and class differences with the upper-middle-class white students who continue to make up the largest group on campus. In an interview, Lizandra described LU as a crucial part of her Augustana experience in part because she was not able to connect with many of her white classmates: "I think it's because we're coming from different places; again a lot of the people . . . had money and were from the [Chicago] suburbs, and I just wasn't [able] to connect with that, so then I ended up at LU."

Several recent LU leaders similarly argued that Latinx students' belonging on campus often depends on their high school experiences, noting that Latinx students from mostly white suburbs outside Chicago are more likely to make a relatively easy transition to Augustana while students with less experience in predominantly white environments have more difficulty. Cindy Morales, a former LU president who graduated in 2017, described having "culture shock" at Augustana after her experiences attending high school in the city of Chicago: "For a lot of the suburban kids, except for large Hispanic suburbs, you're used to being in an all-white classroom; you might already be used to toning down certain things. But we had students who, you know, who never been in a classroom with so many white people. All of a sudden they were thrown in there, and, you know, they were told that they acted 'ghetto.'" Cindy's reflection on the microaggressions she and other Latinx students experienced at Augustana demonstrates how student identities that diverged from what was seen as the typical Augustana student—white, upper- and middle-class young people from suburban environments—continued to be marginalized despite increasing demographic diversity at the college.

Latinx students in the 1990s recalled that most students of color at Augustana came from the city of Chicago, where the college focused its early recruitment of "minority students." As the Latinx student population grew, so too did its diversity. Whereas Latinx students from diversifying but still largely white suburbs could fit in, students from urban settings continued to feel alienated and could be perceived as coming from a different, even dangerous, "ghetto" environment that contrasted with the predominantly white space of Augustana. At the same time, even Latinx students who adapted to Augustana were not always able to be their full selves around their classmates. At LU's twenty-fifth anniversary, Kristen Glass Perez, who served as an assistant chaplain at Augustana from 2012 to 2017, shared a story about when she first met her husband, Javier, who graduated from Augustana in 1997. When Kristen later learned that Javier's best friend from Augustana did not know that he spoke Spanish, Javier replied that there was no reason for him to speak Spanish at Augustana, an indication of the extent to which Latinx identities were not seen to belong and not acknowledged in the 1990s.

The marginal position of Latinx students on Augustana's campus has shaped how LU has interacted with the rest of campus. While early LU leaders focused primarily on constructing a space where Latinx students could belong, they were also given the responsibility of teaching non-Latinx students about Mexican American and Latin American traditions. LU students have continued to serve as ambassadors for the college by hosting cultural events and helping to recruit incoming students. LU leaders have also encouraged members to develop networks outside the student club. When he served as LU president in the mid-1990s, Javier required all members to be a part of other student groups so that they learned how to navigate different contexts, a crucial part of life on a predominantly white campus.[15]

Even if they had previous experience in a predominantly white high school, Latinx students arriving on a rapidly diversifying campus in the 2010s found few institutional support systems for students of color. The college had recently begun to develop DEI programming in the Office of Diversity Services in 2010 when Greg Aguilar, who grew up in East Moline's Mexican American community, was hired as the office's director. At the time, Greg was the only staff member, and the office lacked stability, having had three directors in the previous four years. In his first year, Greg recalled that most non-white students had student jobs in the cafeteria, not in admissions or the alumni office, because campus offices hired workers through informal social connections with mostly white student groups. Moreover, prospective Latinx students and parents continued not to feel fully welcomed on campus. Kristen Glass Perez recalled that Javier would attend the college-organized visit days with her to serve as a volunteer translator for families that spoke Spanish. The lack of support for students of color resulted in an alarmingly low retention rate of 52 percent in the early 2010s for these students, but this improved as Latinx and other students of color found new opportunities.[16]

By 2021, Latinx students represented 12.4 percent of Augustana's student body, and offices across campus had begun hiring more Spanish speakers and Latinx staff members, although the college's faculty still has only a handful of Latin American and Latinx professors. For many students, LU continued to be a place where they could be themselves and connect with others who had similar experiences. Domingo Dominguez, a former LU president who graduated in 2016 and uses they/them pronouns, recalled their relief in finding other students with similar cultural backgrounds despite having attended a predominantly white high school: "I was like, 'Where are my people?' I want to find my folks. And I always felt like I was searching for my folks. Wherever I went, from high school to college. And so when I was introduced to LU, I was just enamored by the idea of being a part of a group that also shares my same culture." Many LU leaders described this shared sense of culture as one of the primary reasons they chose to participate in the student organization. Nick Teng, a former LU president who graduated in 2022, said that the organization "reminds [students] of home and emphasizes that family feeling that you get when you go to the meetings, because you not only identify with whatever your interests are and that you do have a shared culture, even if, obviously, there's many different cultures within what is Latino, but there's a lot of shared aspects in there as well, that we relate on a lot." For students, cultural events organized by LU have been important points of connection with their identity as Mexican, Mexican American, or Latino/a/x young people.

Some students, like Lizandra, described having limited experiences with important Mexican holidays like Día de los Muertos (Day of the Dead) and La Fiesta de la Virgen de Guadalupe (Our Lady of Guadalupe festival) prior to attending Augustana. LU has a long history of inviting Mexican and Mexican American communities in the Quad Cities to campus for cultural events, and Lizandra described in an interview how they helped her make connections with her heritage in new ways:

> Up until Augustana I didn't really celebrate Día de los Muertos, and my grandparents are dead, and my mom didn't really celebrate it because I don't think her mom really celebrated it. And I do know once a year my dad would pull out my grandpa's photo and my grandma's photo, and he would light a candle all night, and that was it . . . We'd have Alma, who was one of the staff at Augustana . . . She'd come in her traditional clothing and set up

the altar and explain the different parts of the altar. That was just beautiful, and I think that event was done really well because you have the presentation and the explanation, so it's not just like, "here's some skull candy and we celebrate the dead."

While most of the club's activities focus on student life on Augustana's campus, LU has also sought to improve Latinx student belonging by making connections off campus with the local Mexican American community. The Quad Cities has been home to a significant Mexican and Mexican American community for more than one hundred years after early Mexican immigrants were recruited to work in rail yards in Silvis and Bettendorf in the wake of the Mexican Revolution. In the first half of the twentieth century, Mexican and Mexican American residents were largely concentrated in substandard informal housing located at rail yards or in flood-prone sites along the Mississippi River in Iowa.[17] As second- and third-generation Mexican Americans began to settle across the Quad Cities, they developed a variety of cultural, political, and educational institutions. Perhaps the most visible representation of the local Mexican American community has been folkloric dance groups like Ballet Folklórico, which LU has invited to Casa Latina and to perform on campus many times since the 1990s.[18]

Ballet Folklórico continues to have an important presence at Augustana's Our Lady of Guadalupe festival, which LU hosts annually in December to celebrate the most important religious holiday in Mexico (Fig. 5.3). Greg Aguilar helped to organize the first public celebration of Our Lady of Guadalupe at Augustana in 2011 in part because many Mexican and Mexican American community members could not travel to Mexico for the festivities. Kristen Glass Perez recalled that hosting a major event for the Mexican American community, which has routinely filled the large auditorium in Centennial and now Wallenberg Hall every December, had a transformative effect on the campus. Not only did the festival provide a space for local folkloric and music groups to perform, but it also made Latinx students more visible and inserted their experiences in campus life during the important holiday festivities around Christmas at Augustana.

Particularly in its early years as a student club, LU's community outreach revolved around efforts to encourage Latinx youth to attend

Fig. 5.3. Tribute to Our Lady of Guadalupe event flyer, 2016. Augustana College Latinx Unidos Records. Courtesy of Augustana College Special Collections, Rock Island, Illinois.

Augustana. LU students hosted shadow days for children involved in the Ballet Folklórico and regularly visited local high schools such as Moline, Rock Island, United Township, and Alleman. In 1995, LU invited the Cultural Awareness group at United Township to Casa Latina for "pizza and pop."[19] LU students often participated in a mentoring and tutoring program at nearby Erickson Elementary School and volunteered at the Boys and Girls Clubs in Moline's Floreciente neighborhood. While Erickson Elementary was shuttered in 2019, students from LU continue to volunteer at Palomares Social Justice Center, a nonprofit organization started by Mexican American residents in Floreciente and former LU advisor Dr. Araceli Masterson-Algar, which helps to organize neighborhood cleanup activities and a Celebra Floreciente (Celebrate Floreciente) event each year.

As students like Sandra Cantu and Jose Castro graduated from Augustana and began teaching Spanish at United Township High School and Moline High School, respectively, they hosted LU there and encouraged their own students to attend Augustana, as Cantu explained in an interview. LU also developed connections with Latinx student organizations at Black Hawk (ALAS) and at Knox College in Galesburg, Illinois (Lo Nuestro). In the late 1990s, LU was part of the Tri-College Coalition with Latinx students at Monmouth and Knox Colleges and hosted a coalition meeting at Augustana in February 2001. LU also regularly sent students to the national United States Hispanic Leadership Conference during the 1990s.[20]

Many of LU's traditions focus on Mexican and Mexican American cultural heritage because most students in the student group have had, and continue to have, Mexican roots. This has begun to slowly change, however, in recent years. Greg Aguilar recalled that when he first arrived at Augustana in 2010, most Latinx students had similar cultural experiences because they were Mexican and had immigrant parents. As more students from non-Mexican backgrounds enrolled at the college, he remembered thinking, "we just now are seeing the layers of what is diversity just in the Latino community."[21] LU leaders have also increasingly acknowledged that not all Latinx and Latin American students are represented by events like Día de los Muertos. Cindy, whose parents are from Guatemala, was one of several students who helped to push for an embrace of other Latinx and Latin American identities. She remembered LU during her time as a student as "mostly Mexican centered. When I first started, I think the only non-Mexican people was me and then someone from Ecuador. Everyone else was Mexican, Mexican American, and they didn't really care to learn about anything."

For Cindy, the exclusive focus on Mexican holidays reflected a bigger problem with LU. The student group lacked both knowledge and interest in histories from other parts of Latin America that were a critical component of her identity, and thus LU was unable to create an inclusive identity for non-Mexican Latinx students: "Learning about what happened to my family, and then having it kind of dismissed, just made it kind of more aggravating because it was very Mexican centered. But basically, all of Central America went through a type of civil war. You guys don't talk about, or you guys don't even know about it." As a Venezuelan international student in the 1990s and now a Spanish professor at Augustana, América Colmenares has a unique historical perspective on Latinx and Latin American identities in LU. While the student group has gotten more inclusive in recent years, América also described how non-Mexican students have sometimes felt excluded in LU: "When you have people from all of Latin America, there is a balance, but when you have a dominant group, then sometimes you don't feel as included as you should be."

In response to these concerns, LU leaders began to organize different events like Noche Caribeña (Caribbean Night) and a series of cooking classes where members from countries across Latin America prepared food and taught their classmates about a different cuisine in the region. Much like the group's founding, LU's efforts to acknowledge multiple Latinx and Latin American identities have been shaped by connections with other student groups on campus. Cindy remembered that "our senior year, we made it a point to have LU and BSU meetings together, because there are black Latinos, [but] that wasn't really something that was talked about much. So, we made it a point to have meetings together every now and then, to talk about that sort of thing." The increasing recognition of the intersectionality of LU members has contributed to further transformations of the student club's identity and goals in recent years.

A CONTESTED SPACE

Beyond providing a space for students to learn and teach about Latinx and Latin American cultural heritage, LU leaders have increasingly pushed the organization to become a political space where Latinx students can challenge their marginal position on campus. LU has a long history of working for institutional change, often in collaboration with other students of color on campus. In the late 1990s, for instance, student leaders from Latinos Unidos, the Black Student Union, and the Asian Student Organization regularly met with administrators to discuss their concerns as part of the Augustana Multicultural Affairs Network (1997) and the Multicultural Coalition (1999). Students of color were also consulted on the development of a campus-wide strategic plan as part of the Multicultural Programming Board. In 2000, LU leaders in the Multicultural Coalition expressed concerns in a meeting with the dean about anti-Black racism and discrimination against Spanish speakers in classrooms and called for changes in Augustana's curriculum so that courses would emphasize multicultural issues to a greater extent.[22] In recent years, student leaders from LU and other groups met with the college's General Education Committee to demand that the faculty address issues of power and privilege in required courses on domestic and global diversity. These conversations, along with related calls for greater institutional support for students of color, helped convince the college to implement new guidelines for diversity course requirements and to create an Office of Diversity, Equity, and Inclusion led by a new vice president at the college.

Over the last decade, LU leaders have become more likely to speak out about political issues in the United States and Latin America. In September 2015, LU leaders worked with campus ministries to organize a vigil on the one-year anniversary of the horrific disappearance and murder of forty-three students in Ayotzinapa, Mexico (Fig. 5.4). Kristen Glass Perez recalled the vigil as part of a broader effort to build a "solidarity culture" on campus: "The first week of classes of my first year as chaplain was the week of the mass shooting at the Sikh

Fig. 5.4. Ayotzinapa vigil, 2017. Photograph by Kristen Glass Perez. Reprinted with permission of the photographer.

Temple of Wisconsin in August of 2012. I then worked with student groups to plan and respond to community tragedies. That marked a distinct new moment in my own work, as this type of community vigil became routine throughout a host of different social and political contexts. This includes the Ayotzinapa vigil and several others. I think that LU served an important role in helping to shift various student organizations into this type of advocacy."

The 2016 election stands out as a particularly important catalyst for the group's new political identity because it made issues of racism and equity on campus much more visible. In the fall of 2016, a group of College Republicans drew messages across campus supporting then-candidate Donald Trump's anti-immigrant stance on the US-Mexico border wall and derogatory comments about Mexicans. Latinx students, many of whom have immigrant family members from Mexico, saw messages calling for the United States to "build a wall" as a threat to their right to be at Augustana and led a protest on campus. The college's decision to create "free speech" zones on campus that limited chalking to specific areas did little to satisfy students and resurfaced existing tensions between formal and informal policies for students of color. As students experienced growing concern that the new Trump administration would deport so-called Dreamers, or young people with tenuous legal status as recipients of Deferred Action for Childhood Arrivals (DACA), the college was reluctant to openly support undocumented students. Behind the scenes, however, the college expressed support for undocumented students, and campus leaders like Kristen Glass Perez were able to use emergency grant funds to support student DACA renewals.

The protests and demands for a stronger institutional response against anti-Latinx racism made the organization more relevant for many students even as it created tensions. Again, LU students drew inspiration from BSU, particularly recent Black Lives Matter protests on campus and the much older BSU demand for concrete actions to address racist actions on campus in the early 1970s. Though Nick Teng enrolled at Augustana after the 2016 election, learning about the protests from older LU members "made me realize the importance of having a group like that on campus," he said, "because when those times do come, you have that support system." While the 2016 election brought LU closer together, Nick described how LU simultaneously became isolated from the rest of campus and struggled to recover from those events: "We've changed to try and open up to more people and actually go out ourselves and recruit, and be actively educating versus isolating ourselves and kind of keeping things within our own group. I think there's been a pretty positive change. And our numbers have been growing every year, and the group's doing very well. So I think that's a testament to the change in mentality for sure." National political events brought many of the underlying tensions at Augustana to the forefront and reinforced student perceptions of the overwhelming whiteness of campus, but they also may ultimately lead to LU being a more visible and welcoming organization on campus.

The increased emphasis on DEI among LU student leaders reflects the changing nature of Latinx identity at Augustana. Beginning in 2015, LU leaders discussed changing the organization's name from Latinos Unidos to Latinx Unidos to be more welcoming to gender-nonconforming students. Domingo, who supported the name change, recalled that "especially within my four years, we were a very fluid group in terms of what we wanted to stand for. And so that always shifted with the group, and I feel like we went in a more inclusive direction, as the younger folks started taking over." As LU members and Latinx students at the college discussed the student group's name, the sometimes-acrimonious debate focused on inclusivity, the role of language, and tradition. For some, these yearlong discussions helped to clarify LU's role in creating an inclusive environment on campus. Lizandra, for instance, remembered discussions during this time as helping her understand that "there were members of LU who were LGBTQ+, and I was like, oh my gosh, I hadn't thought about that, having this identity; our culture is not accepting of that."

Other students, and even some alumni, opposed the name change, arguing that the organization had always been Latinos Unidos and that students should honor this tradition. As Cindy recalled, those older students

> didn't want to change the name. I think they took it very personally as, like, an attack that we wanted to change the name. Because we were pretty much saying, yes, we want to change it to Latinx . . .

> because we want it to be known from the get-go that we were inclusive, regardless of genders, stuff like that, and that we're going that direction. And so, basically, some of the upperclassmen were like, well, we've always included everyone, no one's ever felt not included. I was like, well, you can't say that. You don't know. And then someone said that, you know, LU is basically a Hispanic group. It's not a LGBTQ group.

Opponents of the name change were, as Lizandra described, largely "hung up on the language part and 'this is how we've always done it.'" Calls for "tradition" to guide the identity and name of the student group failed to dissuade members from pushing for changes. Domingo responded by noting that "language is fluid. I remember that being an explanation . . . It's ever changing, right? We're always coming up with new words." LU leaders in the mid-2010s insisted that the name of the student group, like Latinx identity more generally, is not fixed and can evolve in response to the needs of members.[23] At one point, some older LU members and alumni suggested that Latinx students concerned about gender and sexual identity should create a separate group. Domingo is still hurt by the debate, which they interpreted as "trying to separate the queer LU members from the straight ones . . . Yeah, the reactions really shook me, I think still shake me to this day. And, yeah, I'm honestly still very proud of the folks that presented and that really stood up for what they believed because at the end, the shift happened, whether the upperclassmen liked it or not."

There continues to be debate among LU members over the student organization's name even after it was formally changed to Latinx Unidos in 2017, and the college has attempted to strengthen connections between Latinx and LGBTQ+ advocacy on campus through two recent LGTBQ+ coordinator hires who had strong links to local Latinx communities. Lizandra, who was part of the executive board that supported LU's name change, recalls being "appalled" at the acrimonious nature of the debate and the hurt feelings it produced among past and current members. At the same time, she reflected, LU is a "microcosm" of broader Latino/a/x culture in the United States and the sometimes divisive debates over identity and language in that community. In other words, debates over belonging among Augustana students cannot be separated from national conversations over Latin American heritage and identities in the United States. Stephanie recalled hearing that some Latinx students "don't join LU because it's the term 'Latinx' instead of 'Latinos' . . . because I guess politics, and gendered language." She also noted that, despite the name change, "There's still so many white students who call us 'Latinos Unidos'; they don't acknowledge 'Latinx,' and so if we were to change it, again, to 'Latine,' it's going to be the same thing . . . It kind of sucks that we have to cater to the white audience at the school in terms of our name, but I think just keeping it the way that it is right now, and hopefully as the years come, people are gonna start calling us by our actual name."

Ultimately, the debate over LU's name reflects both the increasing recognition of the diversity of the Latinx community on college campuses and in the United States generally, as well as tensions over the language used to represent intersectional identities. While the debate was and continues to be a point of conflict for some members, it is also part of LU's goal, addressed in sometimes halting ways over more than thirty years, to create an inclusive space for Latinx students on a predominantly white campus. By resisting suggestions to marginalize LGTBQ+ members of the Latinx community, LU student leaders prioritized support for an inclusive identity that must also necessarily acknowledge the fault lines within the broader Latino/a/x community.

Previous accounts of Augustana's history have been told primarily from the perspective of past presidents.[24] As a result, these histories tend to focus on the role of the administration in transforming the institution. In contrast, this chapter explored how students have also played a part in developing an alternative vision for the college and helping to create social and policy change on campus. We argued that Latinx Unidos represents a counterspace for students of color whose experiences were not—and are not yet fully—reflected in the college's institutional structure. This counterspace is both a physical and a symbolic space that allows Latinx students to express themselves on a campus that is still predominantly white, to challenge dominant representations of Latin American and Latinx communities through cultural events and community connections, and to propose concrete changes in how the college functions.

By looking back at the history of student clubs like LU, we can begin to assess the impact of Augustana's legacy as a historically white institution that has often been an exclusionary space for students of color. Latinx student leaders created LU in 1992 because their experiences and identities were not reflected in the institutional structure at Augustana, and LU continues to serve a similar need for many students today. At the same time, Latinx students and LU have helped to transform institutional structures and cultures at Augustana. Examining this history, therefore, can allow us to assess the pace of change at the college. Over the last thirty years, Latinx students have become a much more visible presence on campus and now represent more than 12 percent of the student body. LU has helped to create campus traditions that recognize and promote Latin American and Latinx culture, including annual Día de los Muertos and Fiesta de la Virgen de Guadalupe events on campus, and has been part of broader advocacy efforts to strengthen institutional support for students of color and DEI initiatives.

The role that students have played in transforming Augustana College has often been hidden from the rest of campus, but projects like this one can help to recover this history and build institutional memory for future student leaders. A 2002 letter from the outgoing LU president to the next president, a common occurrence in the 1990s and 2000s among LU leaders, laments the traditions "that we have let go" and encourages future leaders to return to hosting an appreciation dinner and visit days for local high school students.[25] In this spirit, Lizandra recommends that *current and future LU members realize the impact they have on the college and in the community. LU used to be very involved in the community and area schools. As college students, they can inspire the younger generations by being present and visible. It is a lot of responsibility to represent your culture and to teach others about it, but it is a way to build connection and understand each other. Augustana is becoming more diverse, as is the world, and the way to build community is to understand each other. LU can facilitate that by showing Augustana and the surrounding community who they are and what they stand for with the activities that they facilitate.* This chapter reflects both the lasting contributions that Latinx students have already made to the college and the broader community as well as a foundation for future advocacy efforts to make thc college respond more effectively to the needs of its students.

Notes

1. A note about terminology: People of Latin American descent in the United States use a variety of terms to describe themselves. In this chapter, we primarily use the term *Latinx* to refer to students and parents from Mexican or Latin American backgrounds in order to reflect the decision of Augustana student leaders in LU to adopt a gender-inclusive name for the club in 2016. While the term *Latinx* is used on many college campuses like Augustana, *Latino*, *Latina*, and *Hispanic* are much more widespread in the United States (Noe-Bustamente et al., "About One-in-Four"), and many of our participants also used these terms to describe themselves. We use these other terms when describing LU at specific historical moments.

2. Flores and Garcia, "Latina *testimonios*"; Sánchez-Connally, "Latinx First Generation"; Von Robertson et al., "Racism and the Experiences." Predominantly white institution, or PWI, refers to colleges and universities where the majority of the student population is white. Scholars have also argued that PWIs have norms, values, and practices that privilege white students and can create less-welcoming environments for students of color (Cerezo and Chang, "Latina/o Achievement"). Bonilla-Silva and Peoples have argued that most colleges and universities in the United States should be understood as historically white institutions, or HWIs, because their history, curriculum, physical environment, climate, and symbols and traditions "embody and reproduce whiteness and white supremacy" ("Historically White Colleges," 1491).

3. Mora, "Hispanic Enrollment Reaches New Highs."

4. Excelencia in Education, "Ensuring America's Future," https://www.edexcelencia.org.

5. Gonzalez et al., "They Say They Value Diversity"; Yosso et al., "Critical Race Theory."

6. Keels, *Campus Counterspaces.*

7. Gonzalez et al., "They Say They Value Diversity," 69; Museus et al., "Impact of Culturally Engaging Campus Environments"; Lucero et al., "Reforzando las Redes."

8. O'Donnell, "Chicanas/os Begin"; López, "USC El Centro Chicano"; Vaughan, "History of LALS at UIC."

9. Keels, *Campus Counterspaces*, 2.

10. Kristen Glass Perez, interview with authors.

11. Sandra Cantu and Anna Castro, interview with authors.

12. Bluemle, "Augustana and the Civil Rights Movement."

13. Consuelo Martinez, interview with authors.

14. Moira Kinnally, "Casa Latina Opens with Hispanic Traditions," *Augustana Observer*, January 21, 1994; Tony Pena, "Latinos Unidos Celebrates Hispanic Culture," *Augustana Observer*, October 21, 1994.

15. Glass Perez, "Tribute."

16. Greg Aguilar, interview with authors.

17. Terronez, "Iowa History Month."

18. Latinos Unidos meeting minutes, 1996, box 2, LUR.

19. Latinos Unidos meeting minutes, 1995, box 2, LUR.

20. Tri-College Coalition Organizational Directory, 2001, box 2, LUR; Laura Martens, "Latinos Unidos Raises Funds," *Augustana Observer*, October 1, 1999.

21. Aguilar, interview.

22. Latinx Unidos meeting notes, 2000, box 2, LUR.

23. Holguín Mendoza et al., "Too Latinx."

24. Tredway, *Coming of Age*; Bergendoff, *Profession of Faith.*

25. Latinx Unidos President Letter, 2022, box 2, LUR.

QUEERING THE LANDSCAPE
Radical Hospitality at the "Good Life" College

ROBERT BURKE

Bluffs in the landscape remind us that we live atop the crust of an earth that is both distinct and dynamic. As vestiges of a fluid past, their sodden valleys and scarped walls can augur both refuge and restriction. In the years since Augustana College found repose among the limestone shoulders of the upper Mississippi River, it too has morphed to prepare distinct generations of dynamic students for lives of purpose and transformation.

Given the scope of history, our senses cannot be trusted to determine which elements of our physical or cultural landscapes are fixed and which are fluid. Imagine the ravine around which Augustana's campus has gradually wrapped. Regarded by students as "Lake Bergendoff" in the 1940s, the valley comprised little more than a "mysterious jungle off to the right, where few ever ventured." Now an iconic centerpiece, the Slough—once a much drier bed that quadrupled in surface area as recently as 1990—may be easily mistaken for a natural, permanent fixture; the path that runs along its western edge was laid in the 1960s.[1] Even with knowledge of these recent alterations, we may be inclined to consider such changes in terms of "progress" toward some venerable goal, such as "beautification." Indeed, the cultural landscape of the campus is much like the physical one. Its relationship with its Lutheran roots has evolved through a series of synodical mergers, realignments, and reinterpretations of what Lutheranism tells us we can do and what we can be.

The landscape that I came to know as a student in the late 2010s initially did strike me as rooted in something sacred that I did not yet understand and yet was open enough for me to feel at home as a queer person. My arrival was unanticipated: I applied to the college on a whim and decided to attend almost as capriciously. When I finally visited the campus, something about its ravines and resolves spoke to me. Within a day, I went from never having set foot in Augustana's valley to declaring my commitment to the college by ringing a gong on Zion Hill.

I was not sure I had made the right decision. My choice was so impulsive that my mother wondered if her seventeen-year-old percussionist just wanted to ring the gong. I did know that I felt at ease at Augustana: intrigued, welcomed, even relaxed. Everyone on campus that weekend was happy to see me, showing me around, answering my questions, and more than anything else, modeling what it meant to be an Augustana student. They were curious about the world around them, and they seemed to enjoy flexibility, openness, and empowerment here.

When I reflected on this moment with Dr. Tom Bengston, an openly gay, retired professor of mathematics, he raised an eyebrow. "How does a high school student whose [gay] identity is important to them decide that this is an okay and a good place to be? That was not a question that I knew all the answers to." My identity was important to me, but even as an alumnus, I could not put my finger on why I thought Augustana was an open enough place for me to be. "That's going to be hard to do," he warned.[2] As a teenager heading to college on the heels of *Obergefell v. Hodges* and other societal markers of "progress" on gender equity, I was not thinking too much about being L, G, B, T, or Q at any of my college choices.[3] I did not consult the Campus Pride Index. I did not look for gay-straight alliances or queer resource centers. Perhaps ignorantly, I figured that as long as I steered clear of places with socially conservative reputations, I would be fine. As I wrote upon graduation from Augustana, "I trusted my instincts that this would be a good place for me to grow, and it was."[4]

Bengston attended Augustana, too. Matriculating in the fall of 1971, he did not come out to himself until a few years after college. Several of his friends did the same, including some who maintained their "straightness" despite sexual activity that may have suggested otherwise. "I don't know how you can compartmentalize things so much, but you know . . . there wasn't YouTube videos to check out. It wasn't a question you had to confront every day. The assumption everybody had was that you weren't [gay], and nobody would ask you." Astounded by the change in attitudes since the 1960s, Bengston began tearing up. "I get the impression [that] for students, it's really just not an issue anymore. It's just not."[5]

My own perception that my sexuality need not be a factor in determining which institution would best challenge and inspire me as I openly explored my intellectual curiosities exposes a privilege afforded to my generation that Bengston's fought for. Whether future students will feel the same privilege I did is not guaranteed, and indeed, the cultural climate of the United States has since challenged political notions of linear progress. But at the time I arrived at Augustana in the fall of 2016, the queer landscape appeared to be in acceptable shape, much like the Slough in the center of campus.

In my time at Augustana, both the physical landscape and the landscape of inclusion saw dramatic changes. Many of these changes were prompted at least in part by crisis. The Slough saw a substantial reengineering and "beautification" following the collapse of a pipe that ran beneath it. As for the students, staff, and faculty, their long-standing efforts as watchdog activists accelerated following a national political awakening over fall break of 2016, when Donald Trump was first elected president. During this period of uncertainty, I managed to find community and purpose at Augustana. The connections I made and the ideas I encountered blended into a supportive backdrop for living into who I was and what I hoped to accomplish. It was a welcoming, nurturing, and challenging home that served me well.

Not coincidentally, college leaders have long posited that Augustana should be a place of refuge and hospitality. If you ask Pastor Richard Priggie, who served as the college's chaplain from 1999 to 2020, this worldview is a hallmark of the college. The Augsburg Confession (a theological assertion of beliefs created by Lutheran leaders in 1530), he reminds me, is at the root of not merely the college's Latin name but also its identity:

> Why would you choose the name Augustana, after a statement of faith? Other institutions are named after individuals—even Luther College is named after Luther himself—or places. . . . But no: our founders wanted to emphasize something—they were clear why

> they were doing this. They wanted to emphasize the conciliatory, welcoming, hospitable; [being] open to change and welcoming of diversity—I'd like to say that that's in our DNA as Lutherans. When we're really being authentic Lutherans, we're not building walls, but we're opening doors and windows and welcoming and being willing to learn from one another what it means to be human under God.[6]

Priggie's assessment emphasizes the dynamic sensibilities necessary to live up to our aspirations. Our name and our mission call us to check on our neighbors, identify injustice, and correct the landscape appropriately.

In this essay, I uncover how the queer aspects of this distinct and dynamic landscape have developed, highlighting some of the most reconstructive sections of its history. I focus especially on moments of friction and faulting: seasons in which the cultural landscape was called into question or reformed. Who led in these moments, and what did they accomplish? Which narratives worked against them, and when did new ones emerge? How have these events transformed the college's identity, and why should we study them?

To answer these questions, I began, roughly, with the Stonewall uprising and ended with the present moment. I assembled a history of queerness at Augustana that I cannot call complete but that I can certainly call a first attempt to piece together the answers to the questions I have posed. Using newspaper articles; interviews with alumni, faculty, and staff; my own experiences as a queer student; and other archival materials, I begin a conversation about a community that has long existed in the shadows and only within the last half century has come to shine its light.

AN IMAGE TO MAINTAIN

Prior to Western industrialization, homosexuality was less of an identity and more of a practice. Urbanity introduced vast potential for forming voluntary communities, and by the end of the nineteenth century, most large cities on both continents had areas known to homosexually inclined individuals. Queer life still flew under the radar, and little was documented. But queer migration to these dingier corners of cities grew through much of the twentieth century. As they proliferated, so did social and political discrimination. Underground, the masses organized and began to identify together. "Being gay" meant associating with shared politics, and coming out was inherently political. In the 1960s and 1970s, the assimilationist homophile movement gave way to direct political action and spontaneous protests—most sparklingly, those at the Stonewall Inn. Thus began a new era of collective coming out that rapidly changed the landscape.[7]

Students across the country began questioning social norms and restrictive policies that defined their cultural landscape. According to former Augustana President Thomas Tredway in *Coming of Age: A History of Augustana College, 1935–1975*, the 1960s "were not the more tranquil days of the Eisenhower era, when grey flannel suits and buttoned-down minds supposedly prevailed in society and on campus."[8] Augustana's staid interpretation of Lutheranism began to feel outdated; frustrated, students began taking aim at strict social codes.

College leadership feared liberalization would threaten Augustana's reputation, which had recently risen. President C. W. Sorensen, who arrived in 1962, became notorious for "prohibiting changes that were sought not only by students but by members of Augustana's Student Affairs Office and supported by many faculty."[9] He was especially likely to veto demands stemming from liberation movements: antiwar protests, civil rights, student rights, and the sexual revolution. The fight against co-ed housing became emblematic of Sorensen's managerial tactics. Although students had convinced President Conrad Bergendoff to permit co-ed dining in 1958 (albeit limited to two meals per week), women were still subject to a curfew when Sorensen arrived.[10] Quarterly open houses were the only sanctioned co-ed dorm visits.[11] In a national wave of colleges instituting co-ed visitation policies, Augustana students demanded freedom from such restrictions, yet Sorensen and the Board of Directors decided in 1964 to allow only limited co-ed visitation. Even after a hall's residents voted in favor of it by the requisite two-thirds majority, a host of other regulations were still in effect: notably, the "open door" provision, requiring that "there must be nothing blocking a clear view of all parts of the room from the doorway," which was to remain open during heterosexual visits.[12]

Sorensen thought anything more liberal than these stringent codes of conduct would be perceived as a permissive value judgment that would damage the "institutional character" of the college. Of concern was the image of Augustana held by prospective students and faculty and "persons interested in providing financial support for the college."[13] Sorensen embraced this narrative through the end of his presidency in 1975. By that time, he had repeatedly denied proposals to liberalize housing from students, faculty committees, task forces, and Student Affairs staff (including the dean of students)—even when the Board approved.[14] In this regard, Augustana had become an island: according to a 1972 report by the Student Personnel Committee, 70 percent of the nation's colleges and universities offered not just closed-door visitation but also co-ed housing.[15]

While staff were busy inspecting doors in Augustana's dorms, nonheterosexual relationships and activities may have been carried on subversively behind the closed ones. Heteropatriarchal norms still defined Augustana culture, and homosexuality was not policed. This began to change following the 1969 Stonewall uprising, when Augustana found itself navigating the inevitable: students and faculty alike began leaving their closets en masse. The administration was unprepared for this shift, and the most contentious and conspicuous outing in the college's history made its way to Founders Hall in 1972. That summer, a student's mother discovered correspondence from Lane Bateman, a theater instructor, addressed to her son. The letters contained proof of a relationship between the two, who had been living together in Rock Island. She alerted the dean of men, James Ribbeck, who looped in Dean of Students Tredway, President Sorensen, and Director of Information Services Frank Telleen.[16] While these men had received an anonymous tip about the relationship earlier, they did not address it, since the claim was unsubstantiated.[17]

Ribbeck held that the major concern was that Bateman's lover was a student: "A private college has its rules and these can be more explicit than the law. Such a situation is inappropriate in this day and age and inconsistent with the character and image Augustana tries to maintain." But *Observer* editor Linda Gesling questioned Ribbeck's defense: "Teachers dating students, while not encouraged, is certainly not frowned on. And in the past, school action when a married teacher has been having an affair with a student has not followed a set policy."[18] Indeed, a policy barring relationships between faculty and current students was still decades away, and affairs between male faculty and women students were not unheard of at Augustana.

Sorensen, though, was particularly adamant that a "homosexual" should not be on the faculty.[19] He sent Tredway to break the news. According to Bateman:

> Dean Tredway, in a kind, direct, and honest manner, explained things to me. There was no cat-and-mouse: "Is there anything you'd like to tell me?" I much appreciated his honesty. He told me that as things stood, I probably would not be rehired. He told me that if the President had his choice, he'd prefer I left immediately . . . Even though the tone was polite and the word "fire" was never used, the plan was clear: We cannot fire you now because you're protected by contract, BUT when we are free to not re-hire you, we will indeed not. We will not because of your private life, of which we cannot approve.[20]

Offered a full year's pay, Bateman took the deal and left at the end of the fall quarter. To him, the ignorance and fear surrounding gay people paralleled that which drove the Inquisition, Salem witch trials, and McCarthy hearings. He knew that putting up a fight might endanger those he cared about, such as other closeted faculty.[21] "The vanguard is inspiring to study, but hell to be part of," he wrote to the *Observer.*[22]

Following Bateman's departure, Ribbeck reversed his claim that the primary concern was the student-faculty aspect. When pressed, he admitted that the same-sex relationship *was* a factor, drawing a hierarchy of student-faculty relationships. Unmarried faculty dating students was all right; heterosexual affairs, if discreet, were allowable. A relationship was "definitely questionable" if either teacher or student were married, but "highest on the list" was if the two were of the same sex. Ribbeck's personal views may have been different. However, the prevailing societal narrative held a power he felt he could not ignore in his professional capacity. He "felt strongly that [homosexuality] should be regarded in view of admissions and support from alumni and the community," and he would have continued pushing for Bateman's dismissal if he had stayed.[23]

Consequently, Sorensen got what he wanted without ever having to deal directly with Bateman. He even resisted speaking with Gesling: Tredway's office evidently declined a request for an interview, stating, "academically, Bateman is great!" and opining that the president must answer to the "matter of morals" himself.[24] Sorensen made the extent of his prejudice clear: "I felt concern for the personal difficulty the man was in—sorrow and regret. Being homosexual is incompatible with the 'good life' Augustana tries to uphold. Bateman perceived his own [incompatibility] with the school and decided to leave. If I knew a prospective teacher were a homosexual I would not hire him."[25] In claiming that Bateman simply "perceived his own incompatibility" and left, Sorensen avoided confronting the bigotry of his perspective, even as this perspective came to define the institution's position. As Tredway later affirmed, "Augustana confronted issues such as homosexuality, if not by policy developed ahead of a crisis, by a sort of de facto action which upon being taken implied an institutional stance."[26]

Perhaps Sorensen believed that the campus community would support Bateman's departure. Bateman himself, though, felt that most did not:

> Homosexuals are not horrible, wicked, filthy creatures who must be rooted out of their hiding places and destroyed. Thank God most people realize that. Many of my students now know that I am gay. They have gone out of their way to be kind and understanding. Many have been irate that I am being forced to leave. In fact, no one on this campus has said an unkind thing to me. Yet I am still forced to leave. Dean Tredway apologizes. My department head is sorry to see me go. My fellow theater teacher is sorry to see me go. My students are sorry to see me go. Who then wants me to go? The President.[27]

Some of Bateman's colleagues and particularly students were hit with a sense of "blind rage" when learning of the news. Letters from students in support of their soon-to-be-departed professor appeared in the *Observer* for weeks. "I think he's one of the greatest men I've ever met," said John Sundine, who wrote a two-page guest editorial singing Bateman's praises. "We don't give a *damn* if he's a homosexual. All we know is that nothing will ever be the same without him."[28] "The point is that Augustana College is taking action against an individual solely on the basis of his private life," wrote student Teresa Lee Harris. "All of Lane's marvelous attributes were wisps or shadows compared to the blinding horror of his homosexuality. It is THAT which was acted upon, and unjustly so. It is this type of terrible injustice, this sort of narrow ignorance, which is to blame for depriving Augustana students of enjoying the presence and tutelage of Mr. Lane Bateman, and which, more importantly, deprives homosexuals here and elsewhere of the feelings of dignity and self-worth deserved by every human being."[29] Harris was not alone in feeling that the college was letting its students down. "The ideals of your generation are quickly dying, when someone can be asked to leave his job because he is a homosexual," wrote sophomore Cherrie Kolben. "I fail to see how you are aiding me in my education by doing away with one of the finest teachers of the speech department, from whom I have learned so much . . . I (one among *many* others) am deeply sorry Lane is leaving here, and yet am glad, knowing that he will go on to much greater success than he would have ever been allowed here at Augustana—the 'good life' college!"[30]

The students' disapproval suggests that their Augustana education was leading them to a conclusion much different from the president's about what constituted the "good life." By prioritizing the pocketbooks of outsiders while failing to weigh the perspectives of the campus community, Sorensen's actions made the college more of a follower than a leader—a position that students who loved and cared for the college countered fiercely and from which future administrators would in fact distance themselves.[31] In forcing Bateman out of the closet, administration inadvertently surfaced a counternarrative of support for queer individuals.

Bateman went on to receive his PhD from Southern Illinois University. There, he wrote a triad of plays, the "Proud Plays," partially inspired by his experience of being outed and ousted at Augustana. Dramatizing what it is like being forced to live a lie in order to survive, his play *Lying in State* won an award at the American College Theater Festival, with "the highest possible number of points in regional judging." It received attention from LGBTQ+ newspaper *The Advocate* in January of 1974 and toured the country soon after. The tour included a performance at nearby Monmouth College.[32]

It is difficult to know how Bateman's career would have played out had he been allowed to stay at Augustana. He was arrested in 1992 on charges of producing and distributing child pornography while teaching at Philips Exeter Academy in New Hampshire.[33] While there is no evidence that such acts occurred at Augustana, the reporting makes clear that the administration regarded homosexuality itself as problematic. Likewise, administrative inaction on other student-faculty affairs does not indicate that Sorensen's "good life" included protecting students from potential abuses of power in either heterosexual or same-gender relationships. In fact, when a formal policy barring "amorous relationships" between employees of the college and students was contemplated by faculty committees in 1993, many faculty (especially men), students, and even administrators objected, wondering where the line would be drawn, whether adults needed policies controlling their private relationships, and why existing rules regarding harassment were not sufficient.[34] "The thing got absolutely nowhere—I don't think we even tried to bring it to a vote," recalls faculty member Dr. Taddy Kalas, who had worked on the proposal. "And we certainly didn't bring it back anytime soon after that—the whole thing was just too discouraging." A version of the policy eventually was passed and remains in effect today.[35]

SHINING A LIGHT ON HATE

Sorensen never clearly articulated the "good life" narrative. He defined it circularly by the things it was not, constructing an intimidating barrier for posterity to navigate. Sorensen reached retirement age in 1975, and Dean Tredway was named his replacement.[36] Many students, faculty, staff, and administrators hoped that the new president, an alumnus who taught in the History Department, would provide a chance to define the "good life" differently from his predecessor. Tredway's more inclusive leadership style was immediately welcomed and would prove to be a boon to student activism in the coming decades.[37]

Deans of Tredway's choosing would also soon arrive. In 1981, Ribbeck was replaced by Jack Hullett as dean of Student Services.[38] Hullett also came from the faculty ranks, and his methods clearly departed from those of his predecessor. The tension on Zion Hill dissipated with this transition, as Hullett planned "to utilize a different, and possibly looser style of administration."[39] According to Dr. Deb VanSpeybroeck, an alumna who had become head of the Student Counseling Service earlier that year, "you could breathe more; you could speak your mind more," after the transition.[40]

It was in this landscape that feminist efforts began to germinate. While the Committee on the Status of Women had been active on and off since 1972, several of its members in 1979 organized the "Feminist Forum," a weekly gathering intended for education and discussion on a variety of feminist topics.[41] These fora included readings from feminist scholars, screenings of short films, visits from women running for office, discussions of women's issues on campus, and debates about the role of women in the church.[42] In regular attendance at the Fem Forum were members of an unofficial club of student feminists and lesbians. Known as the "Rad Fems," the group reserved a table in the College Center over lunch with a small RAD FEMS table placard. Member Linnea Stenson explained the sardonic origin of the group's name: "Augustana is a conservative community . . . *Any* kind of admitted feminism is going to be seen as radical here."[43]

Indeed, feminism seemed deviant to the broader campus community. The *Observer*'s annual lampoon editions mocked feminist views. The 1984 edition is full of these: one article accuses Dean Betsey Brodahl, chided as historically "serving no purpose whatsoever," of operating a prostitution ring on behalf of the college. Another laments the antiwar movement and threatens the "faggot [pacifists]" behind it.[44] While facetious, these articles offer glimpses into the fears and prejudices Stenson described. But to feminists, organizing and engaging with each other was overdue and quite fruitful. At first, the group of women coordinating the Fem Forum intended to talk only about issues. "I think there was no sense of going any further," says Dr. Marsha Smith, a professor emerita of sociology who became a leader of this group shortly after arriving in 1982. "There really wasn't any support—ever."[45] Yet the group continued to influence the intellectual landscape of the college for decades. Smith and her counterparts persuaded a skeptical administration in 1984 to approve what would become the Women, Gender, and Sexuality Studies Program. Beginning as a concentration, it was one of the first such programs among the twenty-nine colleges and universities then related to the Evangelical Lutheran Church in America (ELCA).[46]

Perhaps the most enduring and transformative outcomes of the feminist wave were college-sponsored, organized communities for gay and lesbian students. In 1982–1983, the Student Counseling Service advertised support groups for gay women and men; these were coordinated by VanSpeybroeck and counselor Bill Johnson.[47] Many of the Rad Fems participated in the women's group. Don Faust ('85) was a member of the men's group: "I remember how paranoid I was each meeting time as I walked to the side door, sure that one of my [Delta Omega Nu] fraternity brothers would confront me as to my business, and I'd have to try to lie my way out. No one ever did, however. At the time, I said I was 'bi,' which meant I was still half 'normal.' After a year or so, I realized there was nothing 'bi' about me! . . . But the group was monumental in helping me come to grips with my budding sexuality." Johnson, a straight man, later took the group out to Club 506 in Davenport, the city's sole gay bar. "I was terrified to go in there. But it's also where I first saw and met many others 'like myself,' and it was very liberating," said Faust.[48]

The men's group had lost steam by Faust's graduation, but a new informal group began meeting in the fall of 1986 "to discuss problems associated with being gay or lesbian, and to offer support in dealing with those problems."[49] In 1987, they approached VanSpeybroeck about formalizing their organization. As a former student of Hullett, who was rather open-minded to begin with, VanSpeybroeck remembers having a relatively easy time convincing him to support the idea. Tredway proved convincible, too.[50] The students gained the stamp of approval in February 1988.[51]

VanSpeybroeck, who became the first advisor of the organization, felt the group's establishment was an important milestone. It represented a turning point in that the college welcomed gays and lesbians rather than rooting them out. For the *Observer*, she wrote, "I commend the [Student Personnel] committee for acknowledging the need to have a group whose purpose is to support our gay and lesbian students through educational programming, providing peer support and friendship, and creating a place where grievances may be expressed in a confidential setting. I am most grateful to the students, faculty, and administrators who have taken an active, positive interest in this issue. This decision reflects a growing acceptance and appreciation of diversity within our campus community, which deepens my pride in this institution and its citizens."[52]

The students named the group "Lighthouse," and it soon began shining. "Lighthouse members bravely resist the tendency to pretend that they do not exist," according to an undated pamphlet. "We come together at a common place—the Lighthouse. You no longer have to be a lonely ship in the ocean." One early member described the group this way: "At least for one hour every week, I can shed the burdensome fear that I carry with me everywhere else, and just be *myself*" (Fig. 6.1).[53]

Similar organizations at other colleges and universities formed in the late 1960s and early 1970s. Many of these groups facilitated social interaction, affirmative support in coming out, friendship and community building, and even partner-seeking. These became campus

Fig. 6.1. Lighthouse members holding a banner for the Augustana College homecoming parade. Photograph by Chuck McMahon. *Augustana Observer*, October 26, 1990. Courtesy of Augustana College Special Collections, Rock Island, Illinois.

fixtures in the 1980s—a period in which harassment and violence against queer people rose nationally. But unlike Lighthouse, which was incubated within a comparatively hospitable administration, many of these groups had political, antiestablishment origins. The national Gay Liberation Front became a model for groups wishing to build coalitions to remake their campuses and society. Sorensen had put his foot down against other types of liberation movements on campus, perhaps contributing to a delay in Lighthouse's formation. But by the late 1970s, most nonheterosexual campus activists had moved toward an assimilationist approach, borrowing tactics such as public demonstrations and visibility, but with aims of awareness, tolerance, and inclusion in all aspects of life.[54]

This approach largely characterizes Lighthouse's activism. Unconcerned with how welcome their efforts were, the group brought sharp attention throughout the 1990s to injustices that the "very conservative and homophobic campus" had not reckoned with previously. The small-but-mighty fleet held events such as "Gay Awareness Day," participated in Homecoming and Cultural Diversity Week, and produced a newsletter known as *The Beacon*.[55] Members of the group were "pleasantly surprised" by the initial lack of negative attention.[56] Their activities did not always take place without contempt, however, and incidents of hate, ignorance, and exclusion—especially toward members of the group—rose during the same period. National narratives against queer people had become hostile, setting up clashes with the increasing number of queer students living out loud. But organized students such as the Rad Fems and those in Lighthouse became quite successful in calling attention to the injustices of acts that may have otherwise been viewed as unremarkable and routine.

Lighthouse's sphere of influence quickly enveloped Founders Hall, where Evelyn Campbell replaced Hullett as dean of students in fall 1991. A string of hate incidents that began during Homecoming tested the new dean's willingness to combat injustice and hate on campus. Lighthouse members attended a college-sponsored dance aboard a Mississippi riverboat and garnered Campbell's support when faced with harassment in the months that followed.[57] In response to the slashing of a banner Lighthouse had hung from the campus bell tower, Campbell and the Student Services staff penned a letter to the *Observer* denouncing the incident. Perhaps the first official statement addressing homophobic violence, the letter did more than simply state disapproval. Student Services seemed to take responsibility for the tenacious cultural forces behind it: "Individuals and groups develop histories which are not easily shaken. . . . Christians are not proud of the Crusades which began in Europe or the witch trials that were conducted in America. Both were past events which continue to have the power to turn people away from the Christian God. Similarly, as Christians view the Crusades, Student Services is not proud of the lack of respect which was shown to the members of Lighthouse this weekend. We cannot [undo] the history of this campus, but we would like to help change the future."[58]

Campbell and her cosignatories' desire to foster inclusion and protection was a turning point. They implicitly acknowledged not only that the college had been exclusionary and disrespectful but also, for the first time, that such hateful acts were manifestations of a harmful worldview that college officials had a hand in maintaining: *We cannot undo the history of this campus, but we would like to help change the future.* This is a remarkable statement. Student Services expressed a desire to reshape the landscape it had helped construct. It took an interest in joining the activist students who had gotten in their boats and set sail without hesitation against a forceful current, knowing the Lighthouse they had constructed would guide them.

Henceforth administrators and faculty saw education, protection, and nourishment as a matter of procedure. Lighthouse leaned into these assimilationist approaches, gaining seats at tables rather than overturning them. Graduation-induced turnover, though, is a perennial problem for student groups.[59] After some ebbs and flows, new leadership jump-started the organization in 1997 under the name Augustana Gay/Straight Alliance (AGSA), which was intended to better reflect its approach and activities. These included educational seminars for the campus community and starting the "Safe Zone" project on campus, still active today. Over ninety members of the Augustana faculty and staff displayed Safe Zone signs in their offices in 2001–2002. The original symbol meant that the person displaying it was "willing to discuss issues of sexuality and will not judge or discriminate against students based on sexuality or any other minority status."[60]

Rallies and demonstrations also became valuable tools. In the spring of 2004, sophomore Theresa Lawrence and junior Erin Bertram organized a Rally Against Hate in response to the delivery of "an anonymous note reading 'AIDS cures fags' to a homosexual student" and a reported sexual assault. The protest drew eighty to ninety supporters, including Pastor Priggie and President Steven Bahls, who had arrived the previous year. Another demonstration in the fall of 2005 drew media, an even larger crowd, and a more robust institutional response (Fig. 6.2).[61] The crowd of about two hundred students, faculty, administrators, clergy, and leaders of local organizations turned out in support of sophomore Travis Sabran and several other queer students who organized the rally after being targeted by hateful messages and intimidation. AGSA, which had a new, luminary alias, PRISM, had its triangular rainbow mailbox vandalized a month prior. Bahls applauded Dean Campbell's efforts to "identify the cowardly and

Fig. 6.2. "Say No to Hate" rally, October 4, 2005. Photograph by Larry Fisher. Copyright *Quad-City Times*. Reprinted with permission.

immature perpetrators of these acts and to take all appropriate actions to stop these incidents."[62] As hateful messages kept appearing, Campbell redoubled her efforts: she began moving possible offenders from dorms in hopes they would come forward or the behavior would dissipate. Administration also confronted Sabran's accoster (who had told him, "All fags should die") and arranged for the two to have coffee. "I'm really proud of the school . . . I don't feel unsafe," Sabran later told the *Observer*. "I think it's fantastic. I really love it here."[63] In 2006, PRISM organized another demonstration—this time, before hate had another chance to infiltrate the campus. Sponsored by faculty members, the group quickly ran through eight hundred T-shirts reading, "Gay? Fine by me," which were worn by over a quarter of the campus community on September 15, 2006 (Fig. 6.3).[64]

BUILDING UP THE NEIGHBORHOOD

Echoes of Campbell's 1991 "Crusades" letter rang louder across campus as students continued to garner administrative support to stamp out hate and bigotry. In spite of the letter's references to Christianity,

Fig. 6.3. "Gay? Fine by Me" event sponsored by Augustana College PRISM, 2006. Photograph by Kevin E. Schmidt. Copyright *Quad-City Times*. Reprinted with permission.

a substantive Christian case for or against homosexuality had not yet been debated by the church-related college. This may be surprising, given the stereotypical view of Christians as closed-minded and Sorensen's fierce opposition to homosexuality in the early 1970s, but even Sorensen provided no Christian (or even ethical) argument against it. His defense rested on money and optics.

Institutional decisions such as removing the chapel requirement in the 1960s and reducing the number of pastors and Lutherans serving on the Board may lead some to assume that Augustana's acceptance of LGBTQ+ people followed the conventional narrative of secular enlightenment.[65] But according to Priggie, Augustana's path was very different. In his meetings with new faculty, "Priggie makes it abundantly clear that Augustana is welcoming not *despite* the fact that we are Lutheran, but *because* of it."[66] Predecessors to the ELCA (formed in 1988) may have been more conservative, yet many of the policies that shaped the institutional response to the hate incidents of the 2000s were supported if not created by the faith community on campus. In 1970, the national body of Augustana's controlling church, then the Lutheran Church in America, adopted a statement titled "Sex, Marriage, and Family" that expressed the church's opposition to discrimination against gay people. *Observer* editor Gesling had pointedly included the entire statement as a preface to her editorial on Bateman's dismissal, reminding readers that according to church teachings, bigotry had no place at a Lutheran college.[67]

Campbell's letter seems to have finally forced the issue to the fore. Anonymous antagonists laid out a violent distaste for homosexuality, citing moral and Christian defenses. The threatening nature of the comments prompted *Observer* editors to respond, imploring those who lacked the self-confidence to sign their names to do so.[68] In January of 1992, Paul Jensen, an assistant professor of philosophy, did so, begging faculty, administration, Campus Ministries, and counseling staff to produce and debate a "valid moral argument" to defend homosexuality; his letter prompted a spate of responses.[69] On April 27, Campus Ministries sponsored a well-intentioned faculty panel, moderated by Campbell, to discuss sexual orientation. The goal, according to Rev. Richard Swanson, the dean of Campus Ministries, was to "speak and listen about a subject that's controversial," but Jensen, a panelist, saw a platform. According to the *Observer*, "Dialogue quickly turned to debate . . . as several audience members disagreed with one panelist's stance on homosexuality."[70] Jensen seems to have dominated the panel, but protestors were not the usual suspects: instead of attending, Lighthouse's members penned a letter to the *Observer* questioning the need to justify their existence: "Questions of morality and tolerance are not up for debate from our perspective."[71]

Swanson and the faculty later registered consensus with Lighthouse's view. In spring of 1993, Swanson and the Women's Studies Program submitted a proposal to the Human Relations Committee that added "sexual orientation" to the identities against which the college would not discriminate. The fact that this policy was developed from above differs from what was happening at other Midwestern institutions, where documented instances of bias were scant and pushes for policy protections came from students.[72] Possibly the first of its kind among the twenty-nine colleges and universities in the ELCA, the resolution was adopted by the Faculty Senate without dissent. Tom Bengston recalls that the policy was a catalyst for him to come out to his colleagues: "At the faculty meeting . . . nobody dissented. Maybe that's just because the liberal left was just too effective in browbeating people. I don't really think that was the case, but nobody was willing to go on record saying no."[73]

The policy became a formidable tool. President Tredway cited the policy when he publicly condemned a professor's classroom ban on a 1998 rainbow ribbon campaign for gay and lesbian awareness. Tredway's campus email, published in the *Observer*, stated that "Augustana's position is that all people are certainly entitled to express their views on questions such as those raised in the current rainbow ribbon campaign by wearing ribbons wherever they wish on campus, including all classrooms, and that no one may, implicitly or explicitly, forbid them from doing so."[74]

Spiritual advocacy only swelled in the new millennium, and it was more than just Lutherans doing it. The college's Catholic ministries and Religion Department joined the cause in 2001, hosting a series of workshops sponsored by AGSA titled "What, if anything, does the

Bible say about sexual orientation?" Spearheaded by Sister Marilyn Ring, a member of the Benedictines who served as Augustana's associate chaplain and coordinator of Catholic ministries between 1995 and 2012, the goal was "to offer support to people who have been maligned, mistreated, or have suffered abuse at the hands of others, even on this campus."[75] In doing so, Ring and her counterparts set an interfaith model for making the college a healing power, regardless of who did harm in the first place.

President Steve Bahls's arrival in 2003 provided further spiritual and intellectual reassurance to LGBTQ+ students that they were welcome at Augustana. While the Tredway decades set a new tone and created space for assimilationist activists to make meaningful, lasting change, demands to achieve greater diversity had grown louder. Bahls's agenda prioritized these aspirations. Investing in diversity was a means to achieving multiple goals, including recruitment, and Bahls wasted no time getting to work.[76] The Five Faith Commitments, reproduced in the foreword to this volume, became a cornerstone of Bahls's inclusion efforts. The commitments include welcoming persons of all genders and sexual orientations, working to maintain diversity, acting against injustice and intolerance, and working to "embody the ideals of justice, peace, civility, and love in our institutional practices and relationships." Assembling existing practice and aspirations, the Five Faith Commitments were approved in the spring of 2005 and became foundational to the college's identity in the twenty-first century.[77]

Before they were even approved, ideas in the Five Faith Commitments had filtered into policy. The college's January 2005 strategic plan, Authentically Augustana, reflected the newly defined "church-relatedness" of the college while clarifying its goals of diversity and inclusion.[78] Bahls extended health care benefits to employees' partners regardless of gender beginning in 2004.[79] In February of that year, it became the first ELCA college designated a Reconciling in Christ (RIC) institution. Awarded by Lutherans Concerned (now ReconcilingWorks), the designation signals the college's commitment to "the acceptance, full participation, and liberation of all sexual orientations, gender identities, and gender expressions within the Lutheran Church."[80] Becoming RIC required the faculty to approve an Affirmation of Welcome, a statement that reminds the community that as people of God, they are to be healers. It passed so easily that it was not reported on for nearly two months—not uncommon among Augustana's pioneering breakthroughs among ELCA institutions.[81] At the time of writing, Augustana remains one of only two ELCA institutions with this designation at the campus level, with Augsburg University in Minneapolis joining in 2009.[82]

By 2012, Augustana had become such a leader among the twenty-six ELCA colleges and universities that it unknowingly became the first to permit same-gender weddings and ceremonies on its campus.[83] Until that point, nobody had asked and nobody knew if same-gender ceremonies could be held in Ascension Chapel, but gay and lesbian alumni had been asking to use it. The ELCA permitted ceremonies "so long as the local congregation consents" in 2009. Bishop Gary Wollersheim of the Northern Illinois Synod determined that, for Augustana, it was up to President Bahls to consent. When Pastor Priggie and Associate Pastor Kristen Glass Perez requested that Bahls authorize the ceremonies, he did. In a campus-wide memo, Bahls wrote, "When I came to Augustana 10 years ago, I wanted to give meaning to our existing assurance to students and staff that they would not be discriminated against based on their sexual orientation. To me, it is about integrity. If we say we do not discriminate, our policies and practices should honestly reflect it."[84] Though Bahls's decision came at a time when Illinois provided only civil unions for same-gender couples, neighboring Iowa approved same-sex marriage in 2009, and the chapel became available for Augustana students, alumni, and staff to affirm unions regardless of gender.

Priggie felt that the decision was overwhelmingly popular. "We see support not only within the student body but also within our alumni," he said. "I mean, we're way above 90% and probably almost 100%."[85] Priggie did not share his statistical methods, but Bahls confirmed that his numbers were not far off. "That was probably the biggest surprise . . . how this has been overwhelmingly accepted—not unanimously, but for every negative comment, I received a dozen that were positive." Bahls personally called each critic to discuss his decision, which garnered national attention.[86]

GENDER IDENTITY AND FLUIDITY

As progressive as Augustana was in some areas, those identifying as transgender or nonbinary were still largely invisible in the early 2010s—much like the experience of gay and lesbian students and staff in the early 1970s. This too began to change. Led by calls from trans and nonbinary students, the Gay-Straight Alliance (GSA, successor to PRISM) began to push more forcefully for gender-neutral accommodations. Approaching Dean Campbell in 2014, the organization proposed changes to policies and practices, including records of a student's official gender. "You have to put yourself in one of those two gender boxes, and right off the bat that is very nerve-racking. There are people who don't assign themselves with a single gender. They are going to college, and it's really scary to walk into that situation and not know if you are going to be supported," said agender first-year student Allen Serafini.[87] One transgender student recalled teasing from faculty and staff after requesting that they use a name different from the one listed in the college's systems. "It brought up a bunch of personal issues that are the reasons why I go by that name, and I shouldn't have to disclose them every time I use my ID," said Evan.[88]

After the new year, faculty passed a general resolution supporting gender-inclusive initiatives. Echoing many of the calls from students, the final resolution read, "We, the faculty, support college policies, infrastructures, and processes that make our campus more inclusive to people of all genders. As college officials make decisions about future projects and programs, we request that they will be mindful of matters such as including the option to use a chosen name for official purposes, use of gendered pronouns, access to gender neutral housing both on campus and in off campus programs, and access to gender neutral restrooms." First-year student Audrey Johnson was happy to see the support. "Augustana, like many colleges, has ignored transgender students on an administrative level, and I sincerely hope that can change during my four years here, and I intend to try and usher that change," Johnson said. "I came to Augie for a liberal arts education, to become a better person, and I want to feel safe and comfortable on campus as I get my degree, and I want every other student to feel the same."[89]

That summer, the college administration jolted into motion. In August 2015, Registrar Liesl Fowler implemented a new software-based student support platform that made the burdensome process of changing one's name as easy as logging in and clicking through a few menus.[90] Around the same time, GSA changed its name to the "Gender and Sexuality Alliance."[91] Gender-neutral restrooms were another priority for student activists and their supporters. "Not only can they help transgender students, it can be very helpful for people with disabilities, families with small children, and people who don't want to wait in line for the bathroom," said Jason Carey of the GSA. Much like gay and lesbian activism under Sorensen, though, the students' efforts were met with a dulled but still pertinent concern among apprehensive administrators for the costs of reform in a time of statewide financial uncertainty for higher education. Students garnered some support from Dean Campbell, who made the decision to install fourteen facilities, but the *Observer* questioned their small number and inconvenient locations. While the answers were largely logistical (the first restrooms installed were those that were already single-occupant facilities), this did little to address equitable access to facilities.[92] The college finally began converting several binary, multi-user facilities to be genderless in 2022, just ahead of a state law giving explicit permission for such facilities.[93]

Gender-inclusive housing policies have seen several spurts and stops. Like restrooms, this is at least in part due to physical limitations. Co-ed halls were slowly introduced beginning in 1984, with major expansions in 1987 and 1992, each time on a wing-by-wing or floor-by-floor basis.[94] Swanson Commons, built in 2006, features suite-style rooms for underclassmen complete with private bathrooms, which enabled mixed-gender floors. The last remaining women's building, Andreen Hall, was converted to co-ed in 2009 as a logistical solution to overcrowding.[95] First split by floor, Andreen was further integrated in the fall of 2016 when the college began to house both men and women on floors with two communal bathrooms.

As predicted by the Student Personnel Committee in its first proposal for co-ed housing in 1972, shared arrangements were instantly welcomed by residents and administrators.[96] Still, these options represent the assumption that gender exists on a binary and that housing should be split as such, which may be uncomfortable if not invalidating for students. While seniors have long had access to off-campus housing, housing for trans and nonbinary folks on campus was handled on a case-by-case basis. Junior transitional living areas (TLAs) were fairly accommodating: by the time I was a junior in 2018, signing up to live in a mixed-gender TLA was as easy as sending an email, but first-year students and sophomores still lacked a gender-neutral environment. This changed in fall 2022. Spearheaded by Michelle Mason, the assistant director of residential life, the college began offering gender-neutral living for underclassmen in residential halls. The option proved so popular that Mason's office scrapped original plans to use a low-capacity floor. Even with space for over fifty individuals, the space still had a waiting list.[97] It expanded for the 2023–2024 school year.

RADICAL HOSPITALITY AT THE "GOOD LIFE" COLLEGE

As the college transformed from a place where some happened to be queer to a refuge that was truly hospitable, perceptions remained that a sense of queer community was struggling to develop. Neal Shipley ('13) recalls this environment: "Queer community for me was sitting on my friend's bed and watching *Nip/Tuck* together." Eco House, he notes, a former TLA with an environmentalist focus, served as a home base for a "kind of queer" community, and GSA was active, but these forms of community did not appeal to all. This echoes one reporter's critique of the scene from two decades prior: "There are no outlets of any kind for gays or lesbians on this campus, other than Lighthouse (and this is more of an "inlet" than an "outlet")."[98]

Dating for queer students was also problematic. "It was all about 'straight passing' on campus. If you wanted to date, you couldn't be too faggy, and I was probably the gayest person on campus," said Shipley. "Many students just stayed closeted—some until after college." Having arrived three years after Shipley graduated, I began nodding during our conversation, recognizing his descriptions. Administrators and faculty, he noted, were plenty liberal (in some instances more so than students)—more nodding—he adored Sister Marilyn Ring and Pastor Priggie, who had run an annual "Heartways Retreat" for alternative spiritual reflection—more nodding. The college was increasingly doing almost everything right, so what was the problem with us?

One factor may be the "mainstreaming" of LGBTQ+ issues and culture. While queer populations once clandestinely sought community and partners, acceptance of queers by mainstream society has led to a degree of assimilation, sometimes supported even by the community itself.[99] I have noted throughout this chapter that Lighthouse (and its successors) indeed embraced a "seat at the table" approach. As a result, throughout my years at Augustana, a growing proportion of my friends were, in fact, queer, but I never conceived of those circles as "queer community"—just "community," since we never felt ostracized enough to mandate herding (though this is only a personal perception). Geosocial apps and other virtual communities in use on campus, which do not replicate all dimensions of in-person community, may also paradoxically dampen any feelings of queer connectedness.[100] Lastly, as Shipley alludes to, there may simply be a desire within small queer populations to "lay low," especially in an already small institution where everybody knows your name. This magnifying-glass effect ironically leads to queer invisibility on campus, which may in part be helped by the establishment of a queer cultural house, which is being discussed.[101] At the same time, a distaste for the "incestuous" pool associated with small communities is found among some Quad Cities residents *outside* Augustana.[102]

Hope for the future, though, comes from many places. It comes from the many advocates named in this chapter, many of whom were women. It comes from appointing a cabinet-level diversity officer in 2018. It comes from the 2021 hiring of the first LGBT+ coordinator and the creation of a campus-wide LGBT+ committee. It also comes in the form of a very vocal student body, which is demanding more of a say in social policy, programs, and procedures that better reflect who they are and cater to their specific needs as people.

With respect to the last half century, it seems there is something about Augustana that implores community members to ensure it remains true to its mission. In the handful of moments where higher-ups instinctually tried to put brakes on reform (often alluding to an interest in keeping the lights on),[103] activists familiar with the transformative power of the college have won by emphatically framing decisions about the future as questions of hospitality. The culture of the college invites this historical criticism, and as a result, today's inhabitants enjoy a landscape that has blossomed with openness to diversification and change.

Despite their occasional hesitancy, administrators have often acted proactively. Upon his retirement in 2003, President Tredway told *Augustana Magazine*, "One of my deepest convictions is that leadership is a matter of working together with other people and listening to them. Many, many times, by getting a sense of what the faculty, administrative leaders and trustees wanted, we've made better decisions than if I had done what I thought we ought to do from the beginning."[104] Augustana's caretakers have occasionally made headlines for this approach, humbly and pragmatically choosing paths cleared by vocal students and their advocates that outsiders judged as "radical" and even extreme. Like the Rad Fems of the 1980s, decision-makers often have not viewed their actions as such. Yet by the other meaning of "radical," relating to the foundation of something, Augustana has been quite radical as far as the modern ELCA is concerned. Inclusion has been justified as consistent with our rehabilitated theological roots, which call on institutions of Lutheran higher education to remain open to others and "to serve the neighbor so that all may flourish."[105]

Being radically hospitable stood out in the late 1980s and early 1990s, and it stands out now (in the mid-2020s). However, it is important to remember that landscape modifications can be undone—perhaps more handily than when they were made in the first place. The second, more decisive election of Donald Trump is only one example. The feeble illusion of some national one-way march toward eternal human rights has shattered. In the absence of radical, value-driven inclusion, we will continue losing to blatant, fear-driven measures of extreme repression and discrimination. Such measures are quickly moving from the fringe to the floor—and winning—in statehouses across the nation and at the federal level. It is wrong to assume that Augustana, the State of Illinois, and the ELCA will be permanently immune from this national culture. Our history shows us as much: bigotry and other acts of hate have not necessarily followed such a clear, linear pattern. It is just as important as ever that Augustana remains a radical lighthouse of hope for the world.

In light of this reality, it is my hope that readers continue building up their neighborhoods. I came to Augustana having never attended a full church service, and the fact that it was a Lutheran college almost did not register until I arrived. Yet much like Dr. Kiki Kosnick of the Women, Gender, and Sexuality Studies Program, I was pleasantly surprised and grateful that it was.[106] It was in Kosnick's class where I learned to identify my loose convictions as a very Lutheran feeling: a calling to uncover truth and foster justice in the world around me. It is a power and responsibility I will carry with me for the rest of my life.

It is easy to take for granted the space that Augustana's queer family has carved for itself. Such refuges do not build or maintain themselves: as in the past, we must constantly reevaluate how mission meets the needs of today's neighbors. The institutional absorption of some activist functions may be a net positive, but advocates must still keep watch. Our predecessors did not wait; in many cases, they could not afford to. It is up to us to ensure that we continue paddling against even the fiercest of currents so that we are not swept away by adversarial waters. There will be times when we will feel we are rowing harder than we should have to. But as we engage in this work with credit to and in hand with those who have fought for so long and so hard to be heard, we will undoubtedly leave this place we call home a more hospitable refuge for all who are lucky enough to know it.[107]

Notes

1. Brolander, *Historical Survey* (1992), 21–22, 90–91; Richard Swanson, quoted in Elizabeth SanFilippo, "The Old Amphitheater and More Slough Lore," *Augustana Observer*, December 12, 2003; Dick Hansen, "Fraternity Row," *Augustana Observer*, April 17, 1946.
2. Thomas Bengston, interview with author, April 26, 2022.
3. *Obergefell v. Hodges* is a landmark Supreme Court case decided in 2015 that outlawed state bans on same-gender marriages.
4. "Robert Burke."
5. Bengston, interview.
6. Richard Priggie, interview with author, June 22, 2022.
7. Dilley, *Gay Liberation to Campus Assimilation*; Foucault, *History of Sexuality*, 43; Myrdahl, "Sexuality and the City," 48–52; Rubin, "Thinking Sex."

8. Tredway, *Coming of Age*, 263–64.

9. Tredway, *Coming of Age*, 245; see Ross Paulson, "Chapter Twelve: [A Final Summary, 1962–1975]," April 25, 2001, "Chapter Twelve," box 46, RPP.

10. "Co-Ed Dining Set as Policy for Coming Year," *Augustana Observer*, March 10, 1958.

11. Kathy Cairns, "Committee Considers Co-Ed Housing," *Augustana Observer*, April 18, 1984.

12. Tredway, *Coming of Age*, 242–43.

13. Memo from C. W. Sorensen to James Ribbeck and attachment "A Statement for Reference in Clarifying College Policy," November 10, 1969, folder 2, box 41, CWS.

14. Tredway, *Coming of Age*, 243.

15. Student Personnel Committee, "Co-Ed Housing Proposal," January 15, 1972, folder "Sorensen Project, Student Rights, 1968–1974," box 4, RPP. Co-ed housing had also become overwhelmingly popular among at least twelve of Augustana's peer institutions as well as nationally, which the Student Personnel Committee cited in developing its initial proposal.

16. Tredway, *Coming of Age*, 192; Linda Gesling, "Bateman Leaves," *Augustana Observer*, November 8, 1972. Telleen's position changed after his retirement in 1986, but his duties were like those of staff specializing in public relations and communications today. Denise Osburn, "Telleen Retires as Information Director," *Augustana Observer*, March 19, 1986.

17. Gesling, "Bateman Leaves"; Theresa L. Harris, "Harris Comments on Editorial," *Augustana Observer*, December 6, 1972.

18. Gesling, "Bateman Leaves"; Linda Gesling, "OBServations," *Augustana Observer*, November 8, 1972.

19. Use of the terms *homosexual* and *homo* has fallen over time. While their usage in this era was commonplace, both terms, and especially the latter, have been weaponized as insults. Given this connotation, many queer people remain uncomfortable when others use them, and style guides generally recommend against their use. It may be advisable to use another term such as *lesbian*, *gay*, or *gay person*, depending on the context.

20. Larry Lane Bateman, "In the Editor's Mailbox," *Augustana Observer*, November 8, 1972.

21. Indeed, Bengston recalls having at least one instructor in the early 1970s who came out later in life, after leaving Augustana (Bengston,

interview). With Sorensen making an example out of Bateman, we can speculate as to why.

22. Bateman, "In the Editor's Mailbox."

23. Gesling, "Bateman Leaves."

24. Memo, November 6, 1972, folder 1, box 42, CWS. Typed on a small scrap of green paper, this memo was evidently passed between Sorensen's and Tredway's secretaries.

25. Gesling, "Bateman Leaves."

26. Tredway, *Coming of Age*, 192.

27. Bateman, "In the Editor's Mailbox."

28. John P. Sundine, editorial, *Augustana Observer*, November 8, 1972 (emphasis in original).

29. Harris, "Harris Comments on Editorial."

30. Cherrie Kolben, "Question Good Life," *Augustana Observer*, December 6, 1972 (emphasis in original).

31. Sorensen alluded to the outsized voice of external parties when vetoing the co-ed housing proposal earlier that year. In a memo about that case, he cited conversations with "numerous persons who have some relation to the College, including alumni, donors, parents of prospective students, and citizens of the community. At a conference in Washington, D.C., I also had an opportunity to discuss this subject with representatives of perhaps a dozen other colleges, from almost as many states." The memo was eventually sent in copy to all members of the faculty. Memo from C. W. Sorensen to James Ribbeck, April 5, 1972; Memo from C. W. Sorensen to members of the faculty, April 18, 1972, folder 2, box 7, AFC.

32. Bunny Husted, "Bateman Debuts 'Proud Plays' at SIU," *Augustana Observer*, December 12, 1973. Bateman's lover went with him to Southern Illinois University at the end of Augustana's fall quarter. He wrote the *Observer* on occasion, evidently to boast of Bateman's initial successes and share his disdain for the college's leadership. His first letter, in 1973, humorously informed the fictional "Good Life Committee" that the college had a meditation room named after a man rumored to be gay (Peter Pehrson, letter to editor, *Augustana Observer*, April 18, 1973). Bengston happened to attend the Monmouth production with a former resident advisor of his, Scott Johnson. According to Bengston, the play begins with naked actors jumping out of bed. He recalls the rest of the play being humorous, taking shots at Sorensen (Bengston, interview).

33. N. Y. Times News Service, "Ex-Augie Instructor Charged in Porno Case," *Moline Dispatch*, August 4, 1992. Bateman was sentenced to five years in prison in 1993 and died in 2013. "Teacher Gets 5 Years in Child-Pornography Case," *New York Times*, January 14, 1993; Certificate of death, State of Idaho, 2013, https://ancestors.familysearch.org/en/L6L2-NHZ/larry-lane-bateman-1941-2013.

34. Tony Macaluso, "Committees Discuss Faculty-Student Relations," *Augustana Observer*, December 18, 1992; "Biases Inherent Part of System," *Augustana Observer*, January 15, 1993; Julie Wilde, "Faculty Debates Dating Policy," *Augustana Observer*, March 26, 1991; Greg Stolze, "Do They Think We're Stupid?," *Augustana Observer*, March 26, 1993. See Marcy Geighes, "Sexual Harassment Misinterpreted by Students," *Augustana Observer*, March 15, 1989.

35. Taddy Kalas, personal communication with author, June 13, 2023; Augustana College Office of Human Resources, "Section II: The Augustana Workplace."

36. Peers had noted that Sorensen became very absent-minded in his final years at the helm (Paulson, "Chapter Twelve"). Until 1977, the constitution of Augustana College stipulated that the president's tenure shall automatically terminate following the academic year in which the president reaches sixty-eight years of age. "Proposed Revisions to Charter of College [and] College Constitution," 1977, folder 3, box 8, JTT.

37. "A Decision Well Made," *Augustana Observer*, October 1, 1975.

38. "Ribbeck Resigns from Deanship," *Augustana Observer*, April 15, 1981. It is unclear whether Ribbeck's departure was hinted at earlier, as was the case with Dean Harry S. B. Johnson's upon Sorensen's arrival. In both cases, each was replaced by someone perceived to be more suitable for the social and intellectual climate of the era. (Tredway, *Coming of Age*, 232–33). The department was also renamed "Student Services," formerly Student Affairs, to reduce the perception that its role was to intrude into the lives of students. Sandy Schuman, "Hullet[t] Assumes Deanship," *Augustana Observer*, September 23, 1981.

39. Schuman, "Hullet[t] Assumes Deanship."

40. Deborah VanSpeybroeck, interview with author, April 12, 2022; Kathy Atkins, "Student Counseling Service," *Augustana Observer*, April 23, 1981.

41. Dana Shugar, "Committee on the Status of Women Reactivates!," *Augustana Observer*, January 13, 1982; Stephanie Johnston, "What ARE

They Trying to Do? Or, Feminism at Augustana," *Augustana Observer*, February 10, 1982. The committee had previously developed policy statements on matters relating to equity in salaries, fringe benefits, health programs, hiring and promotional procedures, affirmative action, and education on the women's movement. Committee on the Status of Women, Policy Statement.

42. "Feminist Forum," *Augustana Observer*, January 16, 1980; "Women in the Church," *Augustana Observer*, February 13, 1980; "Learner at Fem Forum," *Augustana Observer*, October 1, 1980; "Fem Forum Film," *Augustana Observer*, February 12, 1981; "Fem Forum on Security," *Augustana Observer*, March 25, 1981. These are only a small sampling of topics.

43. Johnston, "What ARE They Trying to Do?"

44. "Betsey's Brothel, an 'Undercover' Cash Scheme: Augustana's Board Probes Red Light District," *Augustana Observer*, April 5, 1984; "Nuke the Bastards," *Augustana Observer*, April 5, 1984.

45. Marsha Y. Smith, interview with author, April 28, 2022. Smith was the first woman in her department to receive tenure and serve as chair. She was also the first woman chair of the Social Sciences Division, and the first woman to chair the Faculty Welfare Committee, an important decision-making body established in 1971 that set policy pertaining to faculty salary, rank, and tenure. Tredway, *Coming of Age*, 180.

46. Smith, interview.

47. "SCS Support Group," *Augustana Observer*, October 13, 1982; "Support Group, Advertisement," *Augustana Observer*, October 3, 1984.

48. Faust, "Augie Gay History," email to Special Collections librarian Jamie Nelson and the Gay-Straight Alliance, October 21, 2001, in the Lighthouse, vertical file, Special Collections, Augustana College, Rock Island, Illinois.

49. Faust, "Augie Gay History"; "Breaking Stereotypes: Coming Out at Augustana," in *Rockety-I*, 1991, 124–25.

50. VanSpeybroeck, interview.

51. Eric Bottom, "One Foot out of the Closet," *Augustana Observer*, May 3, 1990.

52. Deborah VanSpeybroeck, letter to editor, *Augustana Observer*, March 16, 1988.

53. "Lighthouse: Augustana's Lesbian and Gay Organization," undated (emphasis in original), Lighthouse, vertical file, Special Collections, Augustana College, Rock Island, Illinois.

54. Dilley, *Gay Liberation*, 3–10, 235–36.

55. *The Beacon: Lighthouse's News Monthly*, April 1991, Lighthouse, vertical file, Special Collections, Augustana College, Rock Island, Illinois. Only one issue may have been produced.

56. "Breaking Stereotypes," 125.

57. Melanie C. King, "Student Suffers Harassment in Erickson," *Augustana Observer*, January 24, 1992; Sean Stu Firmiss, "Gay Bashing Is Out, Growing Up Is In," letter to editor, *Augustana Observer*, October 18, 1991.

58. Evelyn Campbell and Student Services staff, "Dean Chastises Vandals," *Augustana Observer*, October 18, 1991.

59. Dilley, *Gay Liberation*, 5.

60. Adam Malak, "Lighthouse Takes on New Name," *Augustana Observer*, October 10, 1997; Megan Panther, "Alliance Stays Active with 'Safe Zone' Project," *Augustana Observer*, February 1, 2002.

61. Abernathy, "Statement."

62. Abernathy, "Statement."

63. Stephanie De Pasquale, "Students Band Together," *Augustana Observer*, October 7, 2005; Jon Maxson, "Gay-Bashing Angers Campus," *Augustana Observer*, October 7, 2005; Tory Brecht, "Anti-Gay Activity Elicits Backlash," *Quad-City Times*, October 1, 2005; Tory Brecht, "Students Protest Hate at Augustana," *Quad-City Times*, October 5, 2005; "Augustana Combats Hate as a Community," *Quad-City Times*, October 12, 2005.

64. Thomas Geyer, "Students Fight Hate Before It Starts," *Quad-City Times*, September 15, 2006; "Students, Faculty Join to Promote Tolerance," *Augustana Observer*, September 22, 2006.

65. Tredway, *Coming of Age*, 265–66; Jason Mahn, personal communication with author, June 5, 2023.

66. Kosnick and Varallo, "Conciliatory and Queer."

67. "Proceedings of the Fifth Biennial Convention of the Lutheran Church in America," July 2, 1970, quoted in Gesling, "OBServations."

68. "Editor's response," *Augustana Observer*, December 13, 1991. Two anonymous letters published in the same issue may have prompted the response ("Simple Solutions"; "A Moral 'Pep Talk.'")

69. Paul Jensen, "No Valid Moral Argument Has Yet Been Produced to Defend Homosexuality," letter to editor, *Augustana Observer*, January 17, 1992. Signed letters to the editor on this issue submitted to the *Observer* between December 13, 1991, and February 1992 included Steven

R. Strack, "Theological Argument Crumbles," December 20, 1991; Erika Engelhardt, "Homosexuality Not a Choice," January 17, 1992; Mary K. Oettinger, "Insults Stem from Insecurities and Dullness," January 17, 1992; O. F. Diaz-Duque, "Attack on Challenger," January 24, 1992; Paul Chung, "Attack Avoids the Issue," January 31, 1992; Elizabeth Falconer, Tamara Felden, Therese Gay, Lars Scott, and Kim Vivian, "Jensen Letter Counter to the Purpose of Higher Education," February 21, 1992; Lon J. Wehrle, "Discrimination Lingers On," February 21, 1992; Morten Lund, "Jensen Argument Illogical," February 21, 1992; Mary K. Oettinger, "Moral Justification and Other Grand Dilemmas," February 28, 1992; Eric Knepper, "Learn to Be Productive," February 28, 1992.

70. Julie Wilde, "Faculty Panel to Discuss Issue of Sexual Orientation," *Augustana Observer*, April 10, 1992; M. Beverly, "Panelists Debate Sexual Orientation," *Augustana Observer*, May 8, 1992.

71. M. Acuff, Arne Brage, and Derek Johnson, "Morality Debates Pale in Comparison to More Pressing Issues," letter to editor, *Augustana Observer*, April 24, 1992.

72. Dilley, *Gay Liberation*, 181, 235.

73. Faculty Senate minutes, April 15, 1993, folder 3, box 16, JTT; Bengston, interview.

74. Erin Borsdorf, "Difficult to Be Different Today," *Augustana Observer*, October 23, 1998; John T. Tredway, email memo, October 14, 1998, republished in *Augustana Observer*, October 23, 1998.

75. Michelle Pavek, "AGSA Promotes Education on Sexual Orientation Issue," *Augustana Observer*, March 23, 2001.

76. Jason Busch, "Presidential Search Ends with Elect Bahls," *Augustana Observer*, March 21, 2003; Jon Maxson, "President Bahls Settles In at Augie," *Augustana Observer*, September 19, 2003; Stephanie De Pasquale, "Students React to Bahls Inauguration," *Augustana Observer*, October 17, 2002.

77. Priggie, interview; Augustana College Office of the President, "The Five Faith Commitments of Augustana College."

78. Augustana College Board of Trustees, "Authentically Augustana."

79. De Pasquale, "Students Band Together"; Abernathy, "Statement." Several articles reference health care for partners as beginning in 2004, but Human Resources could not provide an exact date. See Dooley, "Augustana College Welcomes"; Baker, "Illinois' Augustana College."

80. Priggie, interview; "Our Mission," Reconciling Works. Five Lutheran seminaries and fifty campus ministry organizations (independent

of the parent institution) have also established RIC affiliations. Thonvold, "RIC Seminaries."

81. Tom Foss, "Augustana Rallies Against Hate," *Augustana Observer*, April 2, 2004.

82. Augsburg University, "Reconciling in Christ Statement."

83. Priggie, interview.

84. Steven C. Bahls, email memo to campus, November 26, 2012, referenced in Dooley, "Augustana Welcomes."

85. Priggie, interview.

86. Rubin, "Lutheran College Opens the Door."

87. Erik Gustafson, "GSA Proposes Transgender Accommodations on Campus," *Augustana Observer*, September 18, 2014.

88. Rachel Reiter, "Campus Considers Gender Neutral Options," *Augustana Observer*, April 16, 2015.

89. "New Resolution to Promote Gender Inclusiveness," *Augustana Observer*, March 27, 2015, https://augustanaobserver.com/12025/news/new-resolution-to-promote-gender-inclusiveness/.

90. Marlen Gomez, "College Approves ID Name Change," *Augustana Observer*, October 1, 2015.

91. Name change inferred from reporting before and after; no date or announcement could be located.

92. Reiter, "Campus Considers"; Daniel Williams, "College to Install Gender-Neutral Bathrooms on Campus," *Augustana Observer*, October 8, 2015; "Editorial: Campus Policy Needs More," *Augustana Observer*, March 17, 2016.

93. Michelle Mason, personal communication with author, October 15, 2022; Daisy Moran, interview with author, October 12, 2022. Legislation passed by the Illinois General Assembly and signed by Governor J. B. Pritzker in 2019 required all single-occupant restrooms in the state to be labeled as gender neutral beginning January 1, 2020, effectively enshrining Augustana's stance into state law. The law still did not require single-user facilities to exist.

94. Tredway, *Coming of Age*, 243; Cairns, "Committee Considers Co-Ed Housing"; Jill Standard, "Co-Ed Housing: Students Respond to New Survey," *Augustana Observer*, December 19, 1984; Becky J. Kempton, "Seminary Dorm Goes Co-Ed," *Augustana Observer*, March 18, 1987; Josh Fenton, "Co-Ed Housing on the Rise," *Augustana Observer*, February 28, 1992.

95. Rhiannan Wiles, "Dormitory Update: Former All-Female Andreen Reimagined," *Augustana Observer*, December 16, 2010.

96. Student Personnel Committee, "Co-Ed Housing Proposal."

97. Mason, personal communication with author.

98. Neal Shipley, interview with author, August 21, 2022; Eric Bottom, "Lighthouse Steps Forward—But Are We Still in the Dark?," *Augustana Observer*, May 3, 1990.

99. Drushel, "Evolution"; Harris, *Rise and Fall.*

100. Miles, "Sex in the Digital City;" Drushel, "Evolution."

101. Moran, interview.

102. Robert Burke, "LGBTQC."

103. Notable examples of the latter can be found in the early 1970s, as discussed in the chapter, but even Bahls braced for a firestorm when quietly approving same-gender unions in 2012, indicating that he might have gone so far as to reject such a request a decade prior due to predicted swarms of angry alumni (Rubin, "Lutheran College Opens the Door").

104. "Reflecting on Thomas Tredway's 39 Years at Augustana."

105. Jodock et al., *Rooted and Open.*

106. Kosnick, "What Does It Mean?"; Kosnick and Varallo, "Conciliatory and Queer."

107. Special thanks to Dr. Kiki Kosnick for kindly suggesting that I contribute to this book. I am immensely thankful for the opportunity to have produced this chapter on behalf of my community. Dr. Tom Bengston '75, Dr. Taddy Kalas, Daisy Moran, Michelle Mason, Dr. Marsha Smith, Pastor Richard Priggie '74, Neal Shipley '13, and Dr. Deb VanSpeybroeck '74 each contributed a wealth of their time and insight along with the editor of this book. Thank you to Harrison Phillis '19 and Micaela Terronez '15 for exposing me to the potentialities of Special Collections and to Cristina Rios for fact-checking Human Resources policies. I also want to distinctly acknowledge every student who has written for the *Observer* and the *Rockety-I* in their time at Augustana and the Special Collections staff that has worked over the years to digitize the library's archives, as without their curiosity and vigilant recordkeeping, we would have a much narrower window into the world that I have been lucky to explore so thoroughly. Lastly, the biggest thanks go to the students, faculty, and staff that lived loudly and proudly and gave me something to write about. This essay would not be half as informative without any of these people.

7 TOWARD A PEDAGOGY OF ACCOMPANIMENT
Transformative Community, Spiritual Formation, and Augustana's Useable Past

MARK SAFSTROM

The interpretation of history benefits from diverse perspectives and changing contexts. What one generation takes for granted or loses from its heritage, a later one may recover. Newcomers and sojourners embrace the values and traditions of communities that their current members may have discounted, even doing so in ways that their founders could not have anticipated. This can be a refreshing and often essential process.

In 1934, the African American preacher Martin King Sr. visited Berlin for a conference of the World Baptist Alliance. While there, he was so moved by the story of the sixteenth-century Protestant reformer Martin Luther that he was inspired to adopt "Luther" as his middle name as well as that of his young son. He also could not help but note the startling rise of Nazism then animating the country. At a time when even the clergy of the Lutheran Church in Germany was mostly silent on the human rights abuses of the Third Reich, there is inherent symbolism in this African American preacher returning home bearing Luther's name and then leading marches in Atlanta to protest voting rights abuses. Though he was not Lutheran, the work of King and his family stands as a vital reinterpretation of the legacy of the Reformation. This work also bore implications for reimagining education.

In 1956, Martin Luther King Jr. delivered a speech to Alpha Phi Alpha, the oldest intercollegiate fraternity founded by African Americans. In the address, "The Birth of a New Age," King articulates a vision for reforming collegiate education and civic engagement that sparkles with a deep appreciation for Christian theological understandings of work and community, and it rivals the best of Martin

Luther's own explanations of education for vocation. King's audience was gathered to celebrate the fiftieth anniversary of their fraternity, yet he challenged them to see how their engagement in the Montgomery bus boycott and the campaign to end segregation was an essential outgrowth of their educational philosophy. Work is not just work. Education is not just education. Both must be done right. King explained, "We need more people who are competent in all areas and always remember that the important thing is to do a good job. No matter what it is. Whatever you are doing consider it as something having cosmic significance, as it is a part of the uplifting of humanity. No matter what it is, no matter how small you think it is, do it right."[1] Furthermore, he locates his vision for the new age not in an abstract ideology but in authentic human relationships, which he calls the "beloved community."[2] Modern science and engineering had ushered in a "jet age"; however, it was not technology that would save humanity. Rather, what mattered was whether humanity could draw from its moral and spiritual values to forge genuine community. He told his listeners, "Through our scientific means we have made of the world a neighborhood and now the challenge confronts us through our moral and spiritual means to make of it a brotherhood. We must live together, we are not independent, we are interdependent."[3]

The three thematic sketches in this chapter illustrate how Augustana College has drawn from its particular faith tradition to create an educational community in which all students can develop as whole persons in "mind, spirit and body."[4] I assert that a coherent understanding of the "third path" in higher education that Augustana has charted for itself, between sectarian and non-sectarian models, depends on its spiritual heritage for its vibrancy and structural integrity.[5]

Augustana's Lutheran educational philosophy has received ample scholarly treatment over the past two decades, but the conversation among staff and students about faith has paradoxically become decentered, existing more often in optional, marginal spaces than in plenary gatherings. Bemusing anecdotes abound. One student of mine earnestly asked one day, unprompted, "Did Augustana used to be a religious school?" Prospective students are sure to visit the new pool on their campus tour, but seldom are they shown our beautiful chapel. After touring Augustana not long ago, some friends confessed to me with some regret that their daughter had chosen Boston College over Augustana because of, in the student's words, its "opportunities for developing her spiritual life." References to faith are buried on the Augustana website and often are absent from promotional brochures. Such omissions imply an assumption that faith is not a value proposition of the school but rather a market liability. During the writing of this chapter, workers completed grinding off the stone cross from the facade of Sorensen Hall as part of an otherwise much-needed facelift—whether the cross itself was an eyesore remains questionable (Fig. 7.1). It is possible for students to go through the entire admissions process, and faculty to go through the hiring process, without having more than a vague conversation about what role faith plays here, if any.

While the college has spent great effort to articulate how the Lutheran faith informs its educational philosophy (e.g., "Five Faith Commitments" and *Rooted and Open*, discussed below), there often remains a disconnect between our educational philosophy and our

Fig. 7.1. Removing cross from Sorensen Hall, October 20, 2022. Photograph by Mark Safstrom.

practice. The trends that decenter the Christian markers of the school implicitly run counter to the overall effort to present faith as the core from which the institution's values emanate. Can it be that the neoliberal market pressures and demographic changes facing higher education have prompted a felt need to hide Augustana's lamp a little too far under the bushel basket?[6]

With this question in mind, the chapter problematizes the assumption that Augustana's heritage is one monolithic identity or set of (theological) values and principles that can simply be updated for the (secular) needs of the present, or decentered or rejected if found not relevant enough to market realities or societal trends. Instead, the examples below illustrate how the development of the college has been the result of negotiating and renegotiating Augustana's educational priorities in relationship to the needs of the community it has served. Christian theological questions have been intrinsic and indispensable to these discussions. As Augustana is a religious-educational community, its leaders have regarded its theological heritage as a *norma normans*, or a "norming norm." The school has adapted and thrived by continually returning to and measuring itself against scripture, Lutheran history, and the lived example of Christ. This has at times in the school's history been a conservative or sentimental impulse, to be sure, but equally if not more often also a radical and progressive one, as is borne out below and in several of the other chapters in this book (notably those by Robert Burke and Monica M. Smith).

When a secular educational institution is asked to point to its values, it may be able to point to a broad humanistic tradition, but likely it would have difficulty speaking with anything near the specificity that a school like Augustana can. The defining asset of the religious-educational college is that when asked which values motivate its activities and the relationships it hopes to foster between teachers and students, it does have something specific to measure itself against. If there is a basis for claiming that an Augustana education is relational, holistic, and transformational in nature, it is because its educational ethos emerged as an attempt by educators to articulate, mirror, and emulate the relational nurture of God, especially as manifested in the life and ministry of Christ. Furthermore, the aspirations for inclusivity and diversity that have been increasingly pressing since the 1960s have found resonance in the Lutheran tradition's sensitivity to the nature of faith as paradox. Augustana has developed an educational ethos that is expansive enough and bold enough to claim that all areas of human inquiry are welcome, whether secular or sacred, and to welcome students and faculty with a variety of postures toward religious faith to this conversation. This is a project that secular educational institutions would not even attempt, and which sectarian religious schools are seldom comfortable enough to imagine.

The following sections outline three examples of how Augustana's history and identity can provide a useable past in serving students today. The first explains the important work that the college community has done in the past three decades to define our particular inclusive expression of Lutheran education. Important aspects of the identity of the Augustana Lutheran Synod came to serve as a basis for ecumenical and then interfaith dialogue and understanding. The second section then identifies how Augustana educators can creatively reclaim aspects of the school's immigrant story to understand how the school helped students bilocate and move between multiple identities. An oft-quoted description of Augustana's ethnic and church-related identity is that the college inherently "lives with a hyphen," and this relationship between church and school, as well as ethnic enclave and mainstream society, has continually been negotiated across different generations.[7] I make the case that this Swedish immigrant school did not rapidly become Americanized, and how the school gradually evolved has something to teach us about the intersectional needs of today's first-generation, immigrant, international, and minority students. The third example reimagines the concept of *in loco parentis* in order to pivot to a pedagogy of accompaniment. Whereas nineteenth-century educational institutions understood their legal role "in place of a parent" in terms that later generations came to see as disciplinarian, hierarchical, and often paternalistic, I argue that reframing this role as *in loco comitis*—"in the place of a companion"—naturally recasts the role of educators as one of accompaniment and even friendship, finding resonance with the Lutheran theology of accompaniment. Historical and contemporary voices from the college's history are consulted throughout to highlight aspects of continuity in the Augustana ethos, particularly with regard to formational relationships among faculty, staff, and students.[8]

AN INCLUSIVE EXPRESSION OF LUTHERAN HIGHER EDUCATION

At first glance, the casual visitor to Augustana's campus may not find a discernible difference between this college and a secular one. When the church affiliation is mentioned, it often comes with an awkward qualifier that Augustana is "not *that kind* of Christian college," whatever *that kind* means. The need for a positive definition for this relationship has become more acute over the past several decades, as the number of Lutheran students and faculty has declined. Eboo Patel, a prominent advocate for interfaith understanding, is emphatic in saying that we need to be grounded in particular religious identities if we are to build bridges between them. He offers the following typology of religious identity responses to diversity:

> Faith can be a bubble of isolation, a barrier of division, a bomb of destruction, or a bridge of cooperation. A fifth response—the final "b"—is blasé. Faith can be something we neither care too much about nor think too much of. Barriers and bombs—the fundamentalist response—are actively destructive in a diverse democracy. Bubbles are extremely hard to build and maintain. . . . Blasé seems to be the order of the day, and the question then is how do you help shift the tide from blasé to bridge? I think the answer lies in the metaphor. A bridge goes from here to there and has to be made of something, preferably something solid. Without a strong anchor "here," you can't bridge to "there."[9]

The history of Augustana College offers many such examples of efforts to translate a specific Lutheran identity and its faith commitments into ecumenical and interreligious relationships and community. To this end, in 2004, the college formulated its Five Faith Commitments, distilling from its Lutheran heritage an educational philosophy that can be generally useful to all students, religious or otherwise, in developing a sense of wholeness and purpose, while at the same time allowing some students to go deep in their spiritual formation. This section provides some historical background for these conversations about identity and highlights ways in which a pluralistic, humanistic education emanates from the college's "Lutheran expression of the Christian faith."[10]

In a profound way, it all begins with a name. The choice of "Augustana" for the Lutheran Synod (1860–1962), which founded the college, identified the Augsburg Confession as a rallying cry to gather like-minded Lutherans into a common mission. Originally written in 1530, the "confessio Augustana" was intended by its primary author, Philip Melanchthon, to be a unifying resource, which Protestants could use to sort out differences with the Catholic pope following the Reformation. It should be acknowledged that the confession was often used historically to reinforce boundaries between denominations and discourage theological heterodoxy. For instance, early aspirations for the Augustana Synod to be a big tent for all Swedish Lutherans had stalled by the 1870s, particularly over splintering debates about Christian praxis and theology.[11] Conformity to the Augsburg Confession became a litmus test for compatibility with the synod.[12]

Theological divisions among the Scandinavian Lutherans in the United States had cooled by the 1890s, gradually giving way to intra-Lutheran dialogues and later the ecumenical movement of the early twentieth century. The conciliatory emphasis of the Augsburg Confession was resurrected by Augustana leaders like college president Conrad Bergendoff (1935–62), who was an active participant in the ecumenical movement.[13] This was manifested in negotiations that eventually unified several ethnic Lutheran denominations, culminating in the church merger of the Augustana Synod with several other synods to form the Lutheran Church in America in 1962. A second merger in 1988 built the Evangelical Lutheran Church in America (ELCA), which is the current denominational affiliation of Augustana College. Despite this meandering path, church historian Maria Erling sees strong grounds for identifying the Augustana Synod as having become an "ecumenical pioneer" by the turn of the twentieth century. "Understood first as the foundation for separation from other Lutherans and a defense against the broader danger of American religious freedom," she explains, "Augustana's confessionalism in later years served as the basis for its efforts toward American Lutheran unity."[14]

These mergers effectively integrated the Swedish Lutherans with their co-religionists who were Danes, Finns, Germans, Icelanders, and "Americans"—and even with some of the Norwegians with whom they had parted ways back in 1870. While such a multiethnic Lutheran synod had proved impossible in the nineteenth century, the rapid language transition from Swedish to English between the 1920s and 1940s facilitated a process of Americanization, bringing the marginal Lutheran groups closer to the mainstream white Protestant culture.[15] The colleges of these synods were now also associated, and this broader denomination expanded the recruitment base for Augustana College's student body. The GI Bill after the Second World War served as a catalyst for diversifying the student body as many non-Lutheran students sought a general education.[16] The college's first century marked a gradual transition from an ethnic, confessional college and seminary into a more accessible educational institution sponsored by the Lutheran tradition. As former president and historian Thomas Tredway explains, the touchstone in leaders' negotiations was having a confident understanding of who they were as Lutherans, with their confessional documents as the common ground for relating their own faith to that of others.[17] In other words, the basis for reaching out to other Christian denominations, and later other religious faiths, was essentially "I need to know who I am so that I can know how to relate to you."

The demographic and social changes that were apparent by the 1960s prompted conversations among faculty about how to serve a more diverse student body yet still articulate the Christian traditions of the school. In his inaugural address in 1962, President C. W. Sorensen spoke to concerns at the time regarding the role of a religious college: "I recognize on this campus, a forthright concern with the total human heritage. . . . The curriculum of almost every college, public and private, includes work in this field. At Augustana, however, and at similar colleges, many people recognize a distinctive place given to the heritage in religion, in particular the Christian tradition. I believe this is no intrusion of irrelevant material. Strands labelled religion are interwoven in the entire tapestry of the human story. These strands cannot be removed without damage to the fabric."[18]

Four years earlier, in 1958, Bergendoff had solicited input in applying for a Lilly Foundation grant to strengthen religion and values in private colleges, namely to aid colleges in taking "full advantage of their freedom to deal explicitly with religion and values." In response, dean of students and professor of history Betsey Brodahl explained that students and faculty were missing the opportunity to engage in meaningful conversations about values due to a fear of the college being regarded as an "indoctrination institution." This had resulted in a loss of a "sense of mission in the classroom."[19] Brodahl then noted that one of the limitations in religious instruction was pedagogical. She explained that the historical survey was the main method used in the Christianity department, as well as in her own classes. "Covering the material becomes an end, a good, a value, in itself . . . We doggedly plod through the events but miss the substance. 'There is so much shifting of the dishes for the fewness of the food.'"[20] In effect, the Augustana curriculum was missing opportunities for deeper conversations about what the content meant for the students personally. Rather than seeing the demographic changes facing the college as a crisis or a reason to abandon the school's Lutheran mission, Brodahl saw these changes as an opportunity for faculty to renew their engagement with students concerning values. However, a clearer understanding of those values would be essential. (Jason A. Mahn's chapter in this book returns to Brodahl's concern, relating it to the contemporary challenge of neoliberal culture to liberal arts education.)

Thomas Tredway explains that such views were indicative of conversations among faculty and administrators during the 1960s and '70s. These conversations identified Christian humanism as a touchpoint for understanding the goals of a religious college in an increasingly pluralistic American society. In this way faculty could continue to facilitate important existential and spiritual conversations with students without conceding to relativism, while also trusting that the students would need "to figure these matters out for themselves."[21] According to Tredway, this was not a secular academic forum but rather a pluralistic forum sponsored by a specific Christian faith tradition: "At moments in the college's history . . . Augustana faculty and administrators spoke explicitly of the Christian humanism that had inspired their forebears and that moved them as well. At other times this commitment was implicit, not so publicly discussed. But whether it was spelled out or simply implied, to have continued to seek the meaning of one's life in these two places, Christianity and humanism, gave the college and its people a sense of their location in the vast uncertainty and relativism that increasingly characterized twentieth century society and thought."[22] Nevertheless, such ambitious conversations were often uneasy as the faculty felt pressures from conservative religious voices who pushed for doctrinal clarity and from voices assuming that society was moving toward secularity and religious colleges toward obsolescence. To both pressures, Augustana chose a different response and path. As Tredway writes,

> Even in the twenty-first century we are surely aware that some of our devout countrymen do not think that Christianity and humanism should have much to do with each other. They see them as ultimately irreconcilable. With the third century Christian thinker Tertullian they ask, certain beforehand that "Nothing!" is the answer, "What hath Athens to do with Jerusalem?" . . . The Augustana people we have been dealing with did not think that they had all the wrinkles ironed out of these religion-culture problems. . . . But they found all fields of university study worthy of examination, even when these seemed at times to be in contradiction, with each other or with religious assumptions.[23]

The project to define the nature of Lutheran higher education only increased in complexity in the twenty-first century. In 2002, the final year of the Tredway presidency, the college received a two-million-dollar Lilly Grant to establish a program on vocation in the Lutheran tradition.[24] The grant began in summer 2003 along with the presidency of Steven Bahls. The initiatives started at this time included the Center for Vocational Reflection, the first iteration of what would become CORE (Careers, Opportunities, Research, Exploration), and elevated vocation as a central value of a Lutheran education. Conversations about Lutheran identity led the Board of Trustees, chaired by Brenda Barnes, to commission guiding documents to clarify this relationship. A "campus ministry committee," composed of eight staff members, eight students, and the campus pastors, informed a draft document about how Augustana "expresses its values as a church-related college," a topic that the whole campus community was invited to discuss throughout the academic year 2004–5.[25] One of the questions was how the college can understand its Lutheran mission when only a minority of students and staff bear that identity. Yet the responses of Augustana community members indicated that the Lutheran identity of the college lay deeper than nominal membership.[26] The resulting Five

Faith Commitments document was adopted by the Board of Trustees in May 2005.

The Five Faith Commitments consciously drew from the priorities of the historical Augustana Synod, including "encouragement of personal piety," a "commitment to higher education," a "practice of servant leadership," the "pursuit of ecumenism," and an "engagement in world missions."[27] This heritage from the synod was translated into "five commitments" that the college makes today to continue this faith-based mission: to offer "every student the opportunity to develop a life-shaping spirituality"; to encourage the "campus community to wrestle with ways in which faith and reason challenge and enrich each other"; to affirm that "work and career . . . are aspects of an understanding of vocation, which the Lutheran tradition in higher education helps illuminate"; to celebrate "God's regard for the worth of all persons"; and to develop a "campus community which seeks justice, loves kindness and acts with love and humility."[28] In 2015 a task force further refined and reordered the language of these commitments to read more succinctly as "interfaith engagement," "social justice," "spiritual exploration," "reasoned examination of faith," and "vocational discernment."[29]

Some of this work can be seen as either broadening or deepening understanding of Lutheran identity, and at times these impulses may be working at cross purposes. The temptation to make this language sound less religious is apparent in the vocabulary changes between 2004 and 2019 (such as the systematic removal of the words *Christian* and *faith*). However debatable such a strategy may be, these changes were well intentioned as a means of creating a welcoming environment for all students and staff. The Five Faith Commitments articulate that the college "welcomes faculty and staff, regardless of creed, who will advance our mission, and the college celebrates the diverse contributions they make to our mission."[30] The number of board members required to be Lutheran has been decreased several times, and since 2019, even the president of the college is no longer required to be a Lutheran but is expected instead to "have a demonstrated commitment to Lutheran higher education."[31] This can work only when there is some consensus on what "Lutheran higher education" is and a way to assess commitment to it and realization of its potential. If such community conversations are regularized in the form of annual events and practices, then Lutheran educational heritage can serve as a touchstone and resource for an educational experience that is rooted in Christian humanism, ecumenism, and interfaith engagement. Community members can be invited to engage with Lutheran higher education on their own terms, whether from the experience of their own Christian faith, other religious traditions, or another point of philosophical resonance with the school's mission.

For this to succeed will depend on some minimal amount of curricular programming being central to the student experience. The only place in the Augustana curriculum that presently does this is the Reasoned Examination of Faith (REF) course that students usually take as sophomores. This course takes its name from one of the Faith Commitments and builds upon the earlier "Christian Traditions" courses. Interfaith engagement has been increasingly emphasized as a starting point for engaging Augustana students in discussions about religious values and diversity, following conversations throughout the network of ELCA colleges and universities.[32] The pedagogical approach of studying the Christian faith through an interfaith framework is based on research indicating that such an approach increases students' interest in deep existential questions, in contrast to studying one religious tradition in isolation.[33] As devised, REF courses are comparative in scope and taught by Islamic and Buddhist faculty, for instance. Though ecumenical, the courses include time and space for the students to reflect on and write about their personal vocational discernment and growth, as well as how the material covered relates to their own values and beliefs. It is by sponsoring interfaith engagement and fostering interreligious community that Lutheran theology is able to inform a conversation about how religious faith relates to campus conversations regarding diversity, equity, and inclusion. This is what can make Augustana's community-building efforts truly distinctive from those of secular institutions, by *leaning into* spiritual formation and making it part of life in a diverse community, rather than avoiding spirituality altogether.

In advance of the most recent presidential search, changes to the college's constitution in 2019 clarified that the college community has a calling, both as an institution and as individual members. Whereas the president previously had been charged with promoting the "Christian life" and "Christian purpose" of the college, revisions were explicit that what this means is explained in two documents, the "Five Faith Commitments" and *Rooted and Open*, in a statement endorsed by the ECLA in 2018 as articulating the "common calling" of affiliated institutions. These documents provide the basis for defining the "higher educational values of the ELCA," which the president of the college is expected to firmly commit to advancing, including to "actively affirm and nurture" the relationship with the network of ELCA colleges and universities. Similarly, the Lutheran language of vocation was introduced to the governing documents, as it is the charge of the college collectively to help students "discern their life's calling" as well as "communal callings."[34]

Because these aspects of the Lutheran educational tradition have been codified in institutional documents, the responsibility for ensuring that this discernment happens rests on every single staff member. An institution cannot be "Lutheran" if only a minority of its members are engaged in actualizing this program. It requires meaningful conversations with incoming staff members to build a shared culture around these goals. The revised constitution explicitly welcomes the diverse gifts that "faculty and staff from all religious traditions and non-religious traditions" can bring.[35] For this to be successful there ought to be some dependable programming where faculty, administrators, and staff are invited to consider and talk about how they might personally advance the church-related mission of the college. In practical terms this is defined by each staff member individually. This discernment might range from a reflection on one's own faith to a philosophical resonance with the ethos of the school that animates one's work, relationships, and pedagogy. Vocational discernment will need to be infused throughout the life of the college, in both curricular and co-curricular activities. While there are numerous ways this need could be addressed, the following sections identify two concepts, both retrieved from the college's past, that can inform those conversations. These are intended to revive some essential aspects of the immigrant story and to reclaim what it means for the college to stand "in the place of a parent" in the lives of students.

BUILDING A SCHOOL FOR TWO HOMELANDS

As an immigrant institution at its founding, Augustana needed to ask hard questions about how to help students transition between social locations as well as how cultural, religious, and educational values were to inform that movement. This is a key distinction from other nineteenth-century American colleges that were not founded by immigrant groups and therefore did not need to ask the same questions or set the same educational goals. The liminality of the immigrant community is on full display in its hymnals, for example. *Hemlandssånger* ("Homeland Songs," 1891) was one of the early hymnals of the Augustana Lutheran Synod that founded Augustana College and Theological Seminary in 1860. As a tribute to its cultural significance, the Augustana Heritage Association (1998–2012), composed mainly of graduates of the seminary, republished selections from that hymnal in a songbook in 2000 for use at their biennial gatherings, called *Songs of Two Homelands*. The concept of "homeland" for any immigrant group is profound and involves compounded meanings for an ethnic-religious group like Swedish Lutherans.

Immigrants are inherently aware of the fact that they occupy a liminal space between cultures and societies. There is also a duality in being situated between an earthly homeland and a heavenly one, and a sense of alienation and longing is native to either location. The "homeland" referred to in such songs is both the old one that was left behind with sorrow and the new homeland that is being entered with difficulty. This can be a blurred reference to Sweden, the United States, or heaven. The name of the hymnal thus points to one of the main functions of an immigrant denomination or school, which is to facilitate movement from one space to another, as well as movement back and forth. In the history of Augustana College, this liminality and movement is key to understanding what its early generations of educators were aspiring to accomplish.

As the immigrants sought to adapt to life in their new homeland, it was apparent that they would need schools to assist them with everything from ministerial and vocational training to larger questions of fostering an intergenerational community identity. The period from the 1860s through the 1890s has been famously described as a "college mania" for the Scandinavian immigrants in the United States, as scores of colleges were founded, most of them short-lived, along a range of confessional and ethnic lines.[36] As Emmet Eklund explains, while the founding generation of the Augustana Synod agreed that education was essential, "there was no agreement as to what must be taught in order to maintain its identity."[37] There was disagreement about almost every aspect: what the educational philosophy would be, where the schools would be located, and how they would be financially supported. Furthermore, fully three-quarters of these Swedish American academies, colleges, and seminaries would go out of business by the end of the Great Depression, the result of limited resources, waning demand, increased competition, or migrating constituencies.[38]

Augustana's journey to becoming a stable institution took two decades, beginning with a joint attempt by Norwegians and Swedes to establish a Scandinavian professorship at the Illinois State University in Springfield in 1855.[39] These two immigrant ethnic groups with (almost) mutually intelligible languages had pooled their resources to support pastoral training for their congregations, as they each still lacked a critical mass to support their independent ventures. On June 5, 1860, the thirty-six Swedish congregations and thirteen Norwegian congregations met to establish their own new denomination, the Scandinavian Evangelical Lutheran Augustana Synod. They also established Augustana College and Theological Seminary at that same meeting, initially located in Chicago following founder Esbjörn's preference for an urban location.[40] An alternative vision favored by the second president, Tufve Nilsson Hasselquist, resulted in a brief experiment in 1863 to support the school financially by embedding it in an ethnic agricultural colony in Paxton, Illinois, which did not meet with the hoped-for success.[41]

By 1870, the rising tide of immigration from both Norway and Sweden had changed midwestern demographics, enough that the Norwegians withdrew and formed their own Norwegian Augustana Synod that year. They had begun the year prior to establish their own school, which became what is today Augustana University in Sioux Falls, South Dakota.[42] The promise of Rock Island led the Swedish remnant of Augustana College to relocate to land near the Mississippi River in 1875. The brick and stone buildings they erected on that campus speak a story of having arrived, of permanence and monumentality. Yet the last century and a half has witnessed numerous examples of how, in response to changing demographic, cultural, and financial realities, Augustana has continued to negotiate its identity while also demonstrating clear lines of continuity in its mission.

By the mid-nineteenth century, the Scandinavian countries had developed a variety of school forms available for emulation and adaptation by the immigrants to America. Augustana resulted from an ongoing effort to combine these different, and sometimes competing, educational ideals. These included preparatory education for university for the children of the elite, the *gymnasium*, as well as the universities at Uppsala (1477) and Lund (1666).[43] Augustana's founders included graduates of both universities, and they brought this experience with them as they started their own schools.[44] Yet many immigrants who studied at Augustana were from the lower classes, and as such the gymnasium-to-university pathway would not have been open to them in Sweden. What is more, educated Swedish visitors to Swedish American schools like Augustana had mixed reviews of the quality and level of the education they observed, not knowing quite how to compare it with the typical school forms offered in Sweden; they often referred to the immigrants' colleges as *läroverk* or *högreläroverk* (secondary schools) rather than *universitet*.[45] Yet by the 1890s, there were plenty of visiting dignitaries who praised the synod's colleges as a valid form of higher education, and some visitors even referred to Augustana as "America's Uppsala."[46]

Although Augustana's founders had experienced the European university model, they were keen to follow trends set by American colleges, such as embracing the classic liberal arts. Bergendoff traces the influence of four American colleges in particular: Beloit College, Knox College, Capital University, and Gettysburg College.[47] Historian Philip J. Anderson explains that while the founders of the synod's schools were "mindful of the Swedish university tradition," by the 1870s they were inspired *instead* to emulate the liberal arts tradition. For instance, Hasselquist praised Knox College as "a complete American college," and during his presidency Augustana began offering a baccalaureate degree on a liberal arts model in 1877.[48] What is clear is that the Swedish immigrants were not simply importing a preexisting school form but were indeed adapting available models of all kinds to meet their needs. This was not the same kind of education that one received at Uppsala.[49] Conversely, Augustana graduate and later founder of Bethany College, C. A. Swenson, on his visit to Sweden in 1890, quipped that the rigid, theoretical education that students were receiving at universities in Sweden did not seem sufficient preparation for employment in the real world.[50]

It was not until well after the Swedish American community had become established that the connection between Augustana and universities in Sweden was renewed and deepened. This happened particularly through the initiatives of Professor and Dean Jules Mauritzson (1901–1930) and President Gustav Andreen (1901–1935) (Figs. 7.2, 7.3). Both men spent significant time studying at Scandinavian universities, including Uppsala, Lund, and Copenhagen, to prepare for their posts at Augustana and to cultivate academic relationships with these institutions.[51] Bergendoff's contacts with the archbishop Nathan Söderblom, made during the archbishop's visit to Augustana in 1923, blossomed into an extended research visit in Sweden and participation in the international ecumenical movement, spearheaded by Söderblom.[52]

Fig. 7.2. Professor Jules Mauritzson. Augustana College Photograph Collection, C-D00283. Courtesy of Augustana College Special Collections, Rock Island, Illinois.

Fig. 7.3. President Gustav Andreen at the dedication of the Augustana seminary buildings, November 6, 1923. Augustana College Photograph Collection, C-S01754. Courtesy of Augustana College Special Collections, Rock Island, Illinois.

The inspiration for the specifically *Lutheran* character of the schools came from the educational models with which the immigrants had the most direct contact in Sweden, namely the training schools for preachers and colporteurs, such as the Fjellstedt School, Ahlberg School, and Johannelund School of Theology. The leaders of all three schools played an important role in recruiting pastors for the synod and were associated with the internal revival wing of the Church of Sweden, the Evangelical Homeland Foundation (Evangeliska Fosterlands-Stiftelsen, or EFS).[53] These schools trained missionaries and lay preachers and had a broader socioeconomic reach than the universities. G. Everett Arden also notes that it was through figures like Peter Fjellstedt and Peter Wieselgren in the EFS that pastor O. C. T. Andrén was successful in his fundraising efforts when he was sent to Sweden in 1860 to secure funding for the synod, college, and seminary.[54] By contrast, there was little initial support from the Church of Sweden itself.[55]

Behind these preachers' schools were many other Lutheran educational endeavors, often with pronounced charitable goals. Since the seventeenth century, Lutheran reform movements had sought to increase accessibility to education, including for the children of the poor, such as at August Herrmann Francke's Foundations in Halle, Germany, founded in 1696.[56] In the nineteenth century this benevolent educational impulse found expression in the ministries of the EFS and the Augustana Synod, exemplified in the numerous children's and old-age homes and aid organizations for immigrants and sailors that were established. This charitable impulse was also mirrored in the so-called Deaconess movement, which began at Kaiserswerth, Germany, in the 1850s and quickly spread to Scandinavia.[57] Deaconess schools trained nurses, operated hospitals, and served as an outlet for women, most between girlhood and marriage, to engage in idealistic public service. The legacy of these institutes came to be seen in the preponderance of hospitals and nursing schools founded by Swedes across the United States, especially within the Augustana Synod.[58] For instance, Olof Olsson, while a professor in the seminary, led the campaign to establish a Deaconess institute and hospital in Chicago, which bore its first fruits in 1884 as Augustana Hospital, with other national Deaconess ministries following.[59]

Perhaps the most radically egalitarian educational model was that of the *folkehøjskole* ("folk high school," or "people's college"). Founded by the Pietist clergyman N. F. S. Grundtvig in 1844 in Denmark, this school type was intended to give the whole nation access to a general cultural enrichment, especially the lower classes. John Mark Nielsen explains Grundtvig's mission as providing "further education for the children of farmers and peasants in a residential environment that nurtured love for life and learning in a Christian context" and nurturing "the personal qualities necessary in solving the problems of an evolving society." The pedagogy was a radical departure from the norm, as it was based on interactive relationships between students and teachers.[60] On the folk high school in its pure form, Richard Solberg explains that Grundtvig "regarded education as an instrument for developing enlightened, cultured, and sensitive human beings, rather than the means of assuring a livelihood."[61] Contrary to the rising emphasis on the practical and vocational in both secondary and higher education, the folk high school sought instead to introduce students to great ideas and personalities in history and literature and thereby to awaken both mind and spirit. Rather than books and recitations, these schools made extensive use of the lecture as a means of instruction. They set no examinations, established no grades, awarded no diplomas. Their openness to both men and women and their focus on adult education anticipated the future."[62] In many ways, the "Christian humanism" that Tredway identifies as obtaining at Augustana in the later twentieth century is traceable to influences like Grundtvig.

Danish immigrants were the most active in attempts to transplant this school form to the United States. Though most attempts in a pure form were short-lived, the impact of the folk high school movement is apparent in the broader Scandinavian American educational experiment and beyond.[63] The combination most common among Swedish immigrants was to pair a residential preparatory academy with a liberal arts college and seminary.[64] This was partly by necessity, since the immigrants' schools needed to accommodate students with insufficient preparation for college, including those seeking seminary studies. Augustana received a revised constitution in 1870, which outlined a tripartite structure: a preparatory academy, college, and seminary.[65] Preparatory studies filled the gap between the limited education that immigrants and their children had received but were required to begin college and seminary programs. Intrinsic to this idea was that education should be accessible to all, an ethos far more indicative of the folk high schools and the preachers' schools than of the European university.[66]

In forming their own independent immigrant denomination and school, the founders of Augustana were building for the short and long terms. They knew they needed to adapt and assimilate but did not want this assimilation to come at the expense of values and traditions they wished to maintain and even contribute to their new country. They had already seen how quickly the younger generation could assimilate to parts of American life and culture. Arden explains that this realization had begun by 1860: "it was generally acknowledged that an eventual Americanization was both inevitable and wholesome, for the children of the immigrants, reared in an American environment. . . . In the meantime, however, the church must be concerned with the fathers and mothers whose formative years had been spent in the old homeland. Thus, the process of Americanization must be given time and patience."[67]

Even so, tensions arose regarding the speed and degree of assimilation, evident for example in the conflict between Hasselquist's advocacy for and Esbjörn's resistance to rapid Americanization.[68] A school that accommodated different speeds of assimilation would allow the immigrants and their children to determine whether, how, and to what degree they wished to adapt to American ways, as well as give them a space from which to speak in broader discussions of American civic life. As Emmet Eklund writes, "Preparing the youth of Augustana for its role in the new land became a chief concern. . . . They have sought to make their students and graduates better citizens in the wider community of the world."[69]

An immigrant school allowed them space to bilocate between two cultures indefinitely and transition from one social location to a new one. By choosing this third way, the immigrants could "enter more or less consciously into a creative relationship with the surrounding culture or cultures, so that communication is established without loss of identity. This response may involve an equally strong determination to retain the faith, but it also involves sufficient creativity and flexibility to withstand the pressures of the larger community."[70] At the dedication of the campus at Rock Island in 1875, Hasselquist noted that "our Swedish national character contains elements which should not be thrown away—they are needed in that blending of various national characteristics that are represented in this country and from which a future rich and strong national character may evolve, if the Gospel be permitted to make its cleansing and sanctifying influence felt. In this spiritual work Augustana is now to share."[71]

In summary, Augustana was a hybrid of different, and sometimes competing, educational ideals, the product of choices and debates that was never complete. Augustana as a "Swedish Lutheran" college was not a monolithic identity. From the beginning, the school was influenced by models from the homeland and affected by the general pressures of societal change in the United States. As much as Augustana naturally compared itself with elite universities and sought professionalization and respectability for its students, it was a school with a different purpose. Providing a practical education to immigrants of limited means and their children was central and reflected egalitarian Lutheran missional impulses and benevolence work. A common theme throughout the many changes of the past century and a half was that the school's primary mission was to form students spiritually for service to their community.

In the twenty-first century, as immigrants and the children of immigrants from places other than Northern Europe have increasingly become part of these shifting demographics, the college's useable past as an "immigrant institution" can provide a framework for focusing its goals today. As Augustana had once helped immigrants to transition, or bilocate, between an old homeland and a new one, an expanded understanding of this vocation could inform how the college can function as today's students transition between a variety of cultural contexts. Initiatives to support first-generation college students and their parents with immigrant backgrounds may be the most directly analogous.[72]

However, as English professor Umme Al-wazedi points out, it is often international students "who seem to feel that tug of the homeland more so than the second or third generation students whose parents are immigrants."[73] Addressing the needs of international students prompted the development of programming for Muslim students, including designating worship spaces on campus and forging connections with the Islamic Center of the Quad Cities. As Augustana continues to recruit increased numbers of international students, the "two homelands" concept can give shape and meaning to the liminal experience of those students, as well as foster meaningful cultural exchange with domestic students.

Former history professor Lauren Hammond-Ford noted how the school's role in navigating between homelands is even applicable to the experience of domestic students of color: "As a professor who is a woman of color, one of the things that I try to do is help all students understand and navigate terrains or worlds of greater and lesser privilege . . . [A]n individual student's 'homeland' will vary from student to student and even from situation to situation. Within that, I try to teach students to advocate for themselves and for others. In this, I think about the Biblical idea of love in which love is self-sacrificing and also covers."[74] In this view, the role of faculty becomes one of advocacy.

Yet the simple fact that Augustana has an immigrant past does not automatically translate to living into its potential for facilitating this bilocation and movement for students of all backgrounds. As the number of non-white students has grown over several decades, Augustana has come to terms with the ways the institution reflects the assumptions and expectations of the dominant American culture, rather than that of the ethnic minority. Lauren Hammond-Ford and Jane Simonsen investigate in their chapter of this book several examples of how Black students and faculty created space for themselves at this predominantly white institution. Christopher Strunk and Lizandra Gomez-Ramirez further identify Augustana as a "contested space," recounting how Latinx students have often encountered discrimination and exclusion from full participation in campus life. These students and their organizations made counterspaces where students could connect with others who shared similar experiences. In their words, the activism of non-white students "forced the college to develop new programs for historically underrepresented students and to reimagine itself as an institution that again serves the immigrant community." I would add to this that while much of this recent work at Augustana was reactive, developing a sense of pedagogy that leans into the "two homelands" identity can do so proactively. This would entail pivoting from a strictly immigrant narrative to a framework for general application, in which the campus community sees its work as part of facilitating such movement between social locations for all of its constituent groups.

IN LOCO COMITIS—THE PROFESSOR AS COMPANION

If Augustana is to continue to be the kind of school that provides a formational education, this will depend on how the community nurtures quality relationships among faculty, staff, and students. As highlighted in the sections above, Augustana educators in the past articulated different iterations of such a vision for how the school would help students move between social locations. This section seeks to explain the relational ethos that makes this movement and transformation possible, as well as how it is grounded in Lutheran theology.[75] Voices from multiple Augustana educators of the past are called upon to present a picture of this relationship that ranges from parental concern to advocacy and friendship.

One of the fundamental shifts in higher education during the 1960s was the reevaluation of the role of college educators as functioning *in loco parentis*, or "in the place of parents." In the nineteenth century, surely there were teachers who aspired to be sources of nurture. However, a prominent dimension of *in loco parentis* was its legal function of supervising and disciplining students in their moral decision-making by monitoring dress, sexual relationships, and perceived social vices. Changes in societal expectations by the mid-twentieth century had eroded the acceptability of this kind of personal intrusion in students' lives. Furthermore, curtailing "immoral" viewpoints came to be seen as infringement of freedom of speech. In 1961 *Dixon v. Alabama* marked the beginning of the end of a philosophy that expected colleges to police the moral choices of their students. At Lutheran colleges across the country, especially Midwestern schools, students pushed against all manner of restrictions on visiting hours, social dancing, and women smoking. Richard Solberg described a "concerted drive to eliminate all requirements" at Lutheran colleges through "demonstrations, marches, placards, sit-ins, and direct appeals to the president of the college or the board of trustees," and he notes that mandatory chapel attendance and all-college convocations too became "casualties" in this drive.[76]

Such pressures bubbled over at Augustana College in April 1963 in a confrontation between students and the dean of students, Harry Johnson. The students were protesting being "locked out" of the College Union as punishment for a prank—after some of them had piled all the furniture into one room of the union building. Tredway writes that this episode was a breaking point for Dean Johnson, who had "had enough of a career spent trying to control Augustana's men," and he therefore stepped out of the role of dean in favor of teaching. The new dean of men, James Ribbeck, who started in 1964, as well as the dean of women, Betsey Brodahl, spent the next few years reassessing the role of the college in how it related to students. In a meeting with the Board of Directors in January 1965, Ribbeck explained that instead of serving as a disciplinarian, he viewed "his principle responsibility as being that of a counselor."[77] Brodahl went further, calling into question the premise of her role as dean, asking "what business of hers is the student's personal life, what she does, where she goes, and how she looks, and with whom she goes . . . [T]here is a rebellion in the present student generation against existing structures and forms." Tredway concludes that Brodahl "understood that the college's role *in loco parentis* was the matter that would be in question in the coming years."[78]

Two decades later, Brodahl explained the change in student expectations not as a forfeiture of responsibility on the part of the college but rather as a shift in the location of that responsibility: "This doesn't mean . . . that college administrators have lowered their expectations of students; rather, students have greater responsibilities. The freer a society is, the more is required of everyone."[79] Brodahl's role as dean by the 1980s no longer involved monitoring curfews, mandatory chapel attendance, or truancy, but instead she oversaw the development of things like an "Augustana Student Code of Conduct," which students themselves adjudicated through a Student Judiciary.[80] Such changes reflected trends in American higher education toward reducing the hierarchy between students and staff and shifting responsibility onto the students for promoting good conduct.

Yet it is far from the case that the college's historical role as "parent" was ever limited to discipline or regulating morality. The more profound meaning of *in loco parentis* is reflected in the quality of professor-student relationships. Much can be learned about the values of an institution by looking at which professors the community celebrates and why. Across the history of the college, there has been a tradition of professors who saw the mentoring of students as central to their vocation. In all eras, excellent and kindhearted teachers have won the admiration of students. Augustana has had no shortage of such celebrity teachers, and sampling the stories of these figures reveals something about the character of the school.

Edward Fry Bartholomew was a professor of philosophy and English from 1888 to 1932, known for articulating clear ideas about how Christian humanism is connected to a life of purpose and service

(Fig. 7.4). Asked in 1946 by E. E. Ryden, editor of the *Lutheran Companion*, to reflect on his career upon reaching his hundredth birthday, Bartholomew responded with lyrical reflections on teaching, interwoven with references to Tennyson's "Ulysses," Wordsworth's "A Psalm of Life," and Christ's parable of the vineyard workers from Matthew 20: "We are here, not by chance, but for a purpose in the scheme of the world's ongoing. . . . We are here because we are needed. The words of the Master, 'Why stand ye here idle? Go ye also into the vineyard,' apply to all of us as they did to those to whom they were spoken."[81] Education should cultivate a sense of purpose and lead to action. Echoing Ulysses' ambition to do what is useful and what is good, and Wordsworth's charge to "be up and doing," Bartholomew distilled the answer in Christian terms as spreading the "gospel of love," noting, "We are here to help make love the ruling principle among the nations of the globe."[82]

Once asked about his teaching philosophy by an interviewer, Bartholomew responded that a teacher must look at things from the

Fig. 7.4. Portrait of Professor Edward Fry Bartholomew by Karl Tolpo, 1948. Augustana College Photograph Collection, C-D00202. Courtesy of Augustana College Special Collections, Rock Island, Illinois.

students' point of view. The convention at Augustana had previously been to elevate the teacher's desk on a platform in the classroom: "The idea was that the teachers should sit high up and overlook the students on a lower level." Bartholomew explained, "There is no such platform in my room. . . . I want to be on the same level as that of the students, so I refused to have my desk elevated. Students resent superiority on the part of the instructor." The reporter concluded that "Dr. Bartholomew had the modern idea of teaching, which is rapidly coming into vogue everywhere, even when he first came to Augustana back in 1888."[83] The reporter's assessment suggests that Bartholomew succeeded to some degree in leveling the classroom hierarchy.

By the 1930s, Bartholomew expressed concern about the dilution of the college experience. It was the "excessive machinery of education" that had "smothered its true spirit." Going to college had become a matter of course instead of a purposeful decision to undergo a regimen of study. To preserve a liberal arts education that could facilitate vocational discernment, the school would need to resist negative societal trends that would reduce education to something transactional. Instead of "going to college because Johnny goes" or "the folks want me to," Bartholomew argued that "purpose should dominate all pursuits."[84] In a homily at Bartholomew's funeral service, Bergendoff indicated how Bartholomew's teaching philosophy pointed to that deeper purpose:

> Literature is a mirror of life. What we seek in the mirror reflects what we are seeing in life. Dr. Bartholomew found the mirror fascinating, but what is more, he found it meaningful. Year after year he introduced his students to the characters created by the English and American writers. He studied with them the rule of writing and led them into their first attempts at literary criticism. But it was not as a philologist that they remember him. . . . What remains after the years have passed is his conviction that all this play of thought and emotion which fills the volumes of literature is not a passing show, a fleeting act on the stage of shifting scenes of history. It is part of a great plan, an unfolding drama of more than cosmic proportions. Back of plot and persona dramatis is the great Creator, the shaper of human history who is himself a Maker of more than lines.[85]

Teaching a subject such as literature, or any subject, has its potentially greatest value to the extent that it connects students with a sense of their purpose or divine calling.

Another teacher acclaimed for her ability to befriend and relate to students was Dorothy Parkander, a professor of literature from the 1950s through the mid-1990s. While she accumulated many honors that elevated women's status on campus, her focus was on teaching.[86] Her belief in the "sacredness" of each student guided her rigorous academic expectations. In the 1960s, as Augustana sought to define and refine its identity, selected faculty were asked to deliver papers exploring what it meant to be a teacher in a Christian or church-related college. Parkander's essay explored the dual ideological identity of Augustana and similar colleges.[87] At such schools, there exists a tension between the identity of faith, which is sacred and God-centered, and that of humanistic culture, which is secular and anthropocentric. In the field of literature, she explained, there can be a tension between the vision of the writer and the vision of the Christian believer. What, Parkander asked, is the teacher's responsibility both to the purposes of the college and to her students as they grapple with these competing visions?

Like Bartholomew, Parkander urged students to look at literature not simply as an academic discipline but as a guide to their own lives. Yet she diverged from Bartholomew in how she explained why it mattered, resisting the idea that the sacred simply undergirded or subsumed the secular. The first responsibility of the teacher of literature, she felt, was "to bring the student to the poet so that what the poet has to say may be heard with understanding." The students' minds and spirits can be opened to the variety of perspectives that literature offers as the teacher helps students listen to each writer's unique voice and limited perspective. Thus the tension between secular and sacred is best addressed "not by interference, trespass, or domination, but by *inclusion*."[88] Believing that all reality is the province of God, a Christian teacher may overly sacralize the subjects being studied. Parkander cautions that much of literature bears no immediate reflection of God's grand cosmic design and should not be forced to do so. The teaching of literature should open rather than close possibilities of interpretation. She understood that such an inclusive vision could leave students disoriented by dismantling traditional certainties. As she said of her own faith journey, "I respect the tradition [Augustana Synod] from which I came, but I can no longer live within its confines."[89] Literature helped her to recognize those confines and to enlarge rather than abandon her faith. For Parkander, the Christian professor was called to model a form of parenting that worked, not to correct students' errors or to resolve their perplexities, but to free them to grow into their authentic selves (Fig. 7.5).

As administrators reassessed the college's role in managing student life on campus, the emphasis shifted from discipline to counseling. One challenge after the Second World War was expanding enrollment, which made the school larger and less of an automatic community. Betsey Brodahl lamented that it was not possible to know every student as before and that students did not all share the same campus experiences. She noted that there were "fewer occasions to be involved in each other's lives."[90] Hiring professional counselors would be essential, but Brodahl hoped that mentoring would not be completely outsourced. Instead, Augustana teachers would need to

Fig. 7.5. Professor Dorothy Parkander teaching an English class in Cable Hall, Old Main, circa 1980s. Augustana College Photograph Collection, C-F02254. Courtesy of Augustana College Special Collections, Rock Island, Illinois.

continue considering their relationships with students as opportunities for mentorship, even "outside the classroom or outside their subject matter." She explained, "The fact that a teacher sees a student regularly in class in a normal relationship, hears him recite, reads his paper—all this gives the teacher a special advantage in knowing the student. Teachers don't realize that most contacts a counsellor has with students are contrived or unnatural. I don't suggest that every teacher has to be a counsellor but I believe the better teachers will be. It is also my belief that most teachers are dissatisfied with their own teaching and want to deal with values."[91] The advising model that Augustana has since come to adopt, and which Brodahl's comments anticipated, is described sometimes as "intrusive advising,"[92] and it rests on an expectation that all faculty are advisors in some regard.

As Augustana's mission explicitly names "the body" as part of its concern, in addition to mind and spirit, it is essential to take seriously the ways that embodied existence and physical performance factor in student experience. While sports might be seen as a distraction from the academic program, yet "necessary" to recruitment, such a view misses entirely how life transforming athletics can be for students. The tension between athletics and academics goes back to the beginning of intercollegiate sports.

In 1905, as concern about athletics and safety swept across American college campuses, the Augustana Synod voted to abolish football, baseball, and basketball at all of its schools out of safety concerns. Bergendoff relates that after the board denied a 1906 petition by 157 Augustana College students to bring back basketball, the students "reacted violently." Students marched in protest to the homes of certain faculty and board members and followed two board members onto a train at the Rock Island station and publicly accosted them. The incident became known as the "October 23rd disturbance." After students from both Augustana and Gustavus Adolphus College petitioned the synod for several years and "nearly all" of the Augustana faculty voted in favor, basketball and baseball were finally restored in 1910. Football returned in 1917.[93] This episode, although sensational, symbolizes the disconnect that still often exists for students between the expectations of their professors and those of their coaches, as well as musical ensemble directors, employers, or family members. In this instance it is notable that it was faculty who supported the reinstatement of these sports in the 1910s, indicating an early advocacy for a holistic view of the Augustana student experience.

For those student-athletes who form deep relationships with coaching staff, the legacy can literally last a lifetime. As the faculty mentor for the baseball team a while back, I arranged an oral history project in which four leaders from the Augustana baseball team interviewed a ninety-four-year-old alumnus, Richie Erickson. Erickson had been a second baseman and team captain and graduated with the class of 1951. All of us on the video call found it quite moving to hear Erickson explain just how much he loved his coach, Lenny Kallis, whom he referred to as a "second father" (Fig. 7.6) What he remembered most about his time at Augustana seventy-two years later was how his

Fig. 7.6. Coach Lenny Kallis, *left*, with Richie Erickson. Augustana *Rockety-I* yearbook, 1951. Courtesy of Augustana College Special Collections, Rock Island, Illinois.

coach took him under his wing and even invited him to his home for Sunday dinner.[94] That spoke powerfully to all of us about the primacy of mentoring grounded in purposeful friendship.

Alumni have similarly fond remembrances of Anne Greve Lund, the first director of women's athletics, who organized banquets and socials, was famously down-to-earth, and was called "Anne" by "her girls" at a time when no one would have dreamed of calling professors by their first names (Fig. 7.7).[95] The legendary Augustana coaches and professors all seemed to have shared meals with their students, taken an interest in their personal lives, valued the things that the students valued, and challenged and shaped their students' worldview or faith. The centrality of table fellowship in many of these accounts attests to the importance of a culture of faculty and staff sharing meals and opening their homes to students. It also raises the question of how willing we are today to continue to create such a community, particularly as fewer faculty live close to the college and potentially spend less time on campus. (See Sarah Lashley's chapter on trends of Augustana's relationship with its Rock Island neighborhood.)

Fig. 7.7. Augustana Girls' Athletic Association. Anne Greve (Lund), front row, fourth from left. Augustana *Rockety-I* yearbook, 1934. Courtesy of Augustana College Special Collections, Rock Island, Illinois.

One faculty member who bridged the athletics-academics divide was longtime track and cross-country coach and professor of English, Paul Olsen, who retired in 2018 after fifty-two years. This dual role afforded him a vantage point for comparing the role of teacher and of coach. When asked in an interview about whether these roles conflicted with one another, Olsen responded that "good teachers coach and good coaches teach" and that neither should be limited to "disseminating" or "motivating," respectively.[96] Asked to account for the disproportionately high number of All-American student-athletes that Augustana has seen over the years, Olsen said this depended on faculty support: "[T]here's no hope without an administration, without a faculty, that understands that kids care about their academics *and*—I mean there's room for two, or three or four, important things in your life. We've had great kids sing in the Augustana choir, *and* be an All-American pole vaulter, *and* be a straight A student in physics, because you can do it all."[97]

Olsen noted that advising students includes discussing and modeling for them how to balance their competing callings, as well as to be present in the moment and present to the people in their midst.[98] As Olsen explained,

> There's room for more than one "number one" in your life. . . . I look back at 104 squads of indoor/outdoor track and cross-country, and every guy is a number one. And there's room for that. But that does encourage, teach, demand a kind of discipline, a kind of self-awareness. . . . And then we start to weigh things like, *this* is most important, but it's up against *this* that's most immediate. . . . We hosted the conference meet, and our third best half-miler skipped it. He just wasn't at the meet, and he would have been a sure placer. . . . I asked him afterwards, "Come on, you didn't tell anybody, you just didn't show up?" He said, "There was an anti-war march. I had to be there." I disciplined him by scolding him in front of the team, but years later I patted him on the back, and I said, "You made this incredibly hard choice." I know he wanted to run. But he was having teammates, classmates looking at their draft numbers, a little bit frightened when they were number 10 or number 1. And he was looking at his friend that

> got drafted, [who] wrote him a letter telling him what it was like to learn how to shoot an M16. It's more important than a track meet. And for him, it was also more immediate. Because I [had] asked him that, I said, "Well you could have marched tomorrow." "No, the march was today."[99]

Olsen concluded by explaining that good mentoring depends on awareness of the value systems that the students come from, as well as the value system that they come to, namely the college's. Helping students make difficult choices as they negotiate conflicts in their callings depends on coaches and professors alike having meaningful conversations with those students about how their values inform the choices that will lead to a holistic sense of self in relation to community.

Over the last twenty years, Augustana College has leaned heavily into the language of Lutheran vocation, or calling, to develop a series of initiatives to help students navigate and understand how all the pieces of their lives work together to support their personal, academic, and professional success.[100] This includes an advising approach that is integrative and draws on a circle of people in the lives of students in the curricular and co-curricular realms to help them succeed and reflect before, during, and after degree completion. The circle includes coaches, work-study supervisors, residence hall directors, and student organization advisors, in addition to faculty.

Former Augustana chaplain Kristen Glass Perez explained this model in theological terms as one of "accompaniment."[101] As reflected in Augustana's advising culture, accompaniment is "a collective network of support that journeys with students amid and alongside their questions about life. It does not try to replicate the *in loco parentis* model of the past, nor does it attempt to ignore the very real issues that are present in the lives of students including questions of identity, meaning, impact, and purpose. In this model, the college matches the support for students in the ways the *students* experience the college, which are holistic and embedded throughout the curricular and co-curricular realms."[102] Following national trends, the college added resources to support student needs such as food insecurity and short-term emergency grant funding.[103] Including these initiatives recognizes the complexities of student life and acknowledges that academic success is never free from the tangible realities and pressures faced by students and their families.[104]

In the wake of the interruptions of the coronavirus pandemic that began in 2020, Augustana continued to craft academic community in a constellation of digital, in-person, and hybrid formats. As that crisis eased, returning to a "normal" and mostly residential campus was of paramount concern. Yet, even before the pandemic, the nature of a residential college community had fundamentally changed in the twenty-first century. In the nineteenth century, when students went away to college, they had to communicate with their family at home through letters. Parents entrusted their children to the protection and nurture of the college, which meant months of separation and minimal communication. The on-campus residential experience was truly immersive. In the digital era, by contrast, staff and faculty must compete with an "age of distraction" in order to create a mentoring community. Professor of music and faculty-in-residence Michelle Crouch reflected on these challenges:

> [W]e still provide food and shelter, protect our students from harm, and seek to actively develop the minds and affections of students toward the good, the true, and the beautiful, preparing them for responsibility and engaged citizenship. But, our students—even our international students—in contrast to their earlier counterparts are much less disconnected from both their parents and the rest of the world. That is to say, our job as educators is more difficult, because we are seeking to do those same things in the midst of a highly mobile, digitally connected world, where distraction is normalized and the priority of learning and developing one's intellectual, interpersonal, and intrapersonal potential has very strong competitors.
>
> . . . [W]e must reckon with distraction more energetically than we do, not complaining about it, but working to counter it in various creative ways. . . . I think students need more help to think that through, and to be encouraged in the virtue of self-control. It used to be assumed that the cultivation of virtue was essential to both the parental and the educational project, and although that has not been disproven it has gone somewhat out of fashion to emphasize. "You do you" isn't going to yield the same results.[105]

As Augustana originally helped immigrant students navigate between two homelands, the challenge today is to identify how the college community can assist students in bilocating between the digital and embodied worlds, between home life and campus life, and for international students, between long-distance relationships with their homelands and the friendships and cultural exchanges they came to Augustana to experience. To successfully facilitate these movements, Augustana faculty and staff will need to continue asking existential and spiritual questions about how communal values can offset and avoid the perils inherent in a hyper-individualized, relativized, and distracted society.

This sampling of voices from Augustana's past and present points to a rich and complex conversation about what it can mean for a school to stand "in place of a parent." It also is an unresolved conversation that requires the active engagement of today's faculty and staff to carry forward. While the 1960s saw the shedding of certain aspects of *in loco parentis*, Augustana faculty did not completely abandon a parental responsibility to befriend and mentor students. On a curricular level, the college "came of age" in the late twentieth century as faculty articulated an ethos for how conversations with students about values could continue to take place within the framework of the school's Lutheran theology and Christian humanism. The examples of teachers and coaches above give testament to a markedly pastoral dimension to Augustana's teaching philosophy and community culture of standing with students "in the place of a companion"—*in loco comitis*.[106] A companion is a friend, a fellow traveler, and "one who breaks bread with another."[107]

For Augustana to continue being a formational and transformational community for all students will necessarily depend on inviting colleagues into this heritage, as well as gathering a staff diverse enough to be able to relate to a diversified student body. As a residential college community grounded in a specific theological heritage, Augustana is well situated to offer students not merely mentorship opportunities—which most of its competitors also advertise[108]—but a truly "radical approach" that views these transformational relationships between students and staff as opportunities for spiritual formation.[109] While market pressures seem to be dictating what colleges should teach and that teaching should be guided by student demand alone, Augustana can and should articulate a compelling case that a Lutheran education, grounded in a theology of accompaniment, is worth a four-year investment.

A CREATIVE RETRIEVAL

Despite the wide range of influences, and even tensions, evident in the history of Augustana College, the foregoing sections speak to a high degree of continuity in its educational philosophy and community values. In articulating and revising its Lutheran mission and priorities, the school developed its particular sense of Christian humanism, giving students opportunities to relate the head to the heart and hands. In choosing a kind of school, the founders of the college prioritized an educational ethos based in egalitarianism and access and promoted civic responsibility by steering students toward service and community engagement. This ethos has also involved engaging meaningfully in ecumenism and interreligious community. In prioritizing a pedagogy of accompaniment, key professors and staff created meaningful mentorship relationships with students that embodied in community the very values that they hoped to teach. Augustana people across history have articulated a desire for a school that can facilitate the movement of students between social locations and toward their life's callings.

The creative retrieval that this chapter advocates is a recommitment to the spiritual development of students and staff, not as something that the college simply hopes will happen as a bonus, but as the very source of the college's values. Lutheran higher education principles cannot exist only in abstraction, or in well-crafted institutional documents; these principles will wither if the roots are not watered, namely, the faith from which they sprang. As the college reimagines its commitments to the purposes of an Augustana education and to transformational engagement with students, the school will do well to draw on its history and reclaim the two concepts outlined herein. The first to reclaim is the immigrant story, by pivoting from a specific immigrant experience to a general understanding of how the college helps today's students bilocate and move between social locations. The second to reclaim is the core meaning of *in loco parentis* by pivoting to *in loco comitis* and embracing the Lutheran theology of accompaniment.

Augustana has an enviable position in the landscape of higher education in that it is a college that knows what kind of school it is, has a clearly articulated identity, and possesses deep resources in its educational and faith tradition from which to draw. The challenge ahead may be less to avoid the persistent temptation to minimize the central role that faith has played in this development and more *to actually lean into this identity.* The college's educational and relational ethos has emanated out of a perennial engagement with a productive dialog among Christianity, the humanistic disciplines, and the ever-changing broader culture. To neglect the cultivation on campus of an inclusive and vibrant Lutheran expression of the Christian faith that engages at least a core of students and staff would be to render the college's broader higher educational goals incoherent and to fail to replenish the source of these values. It would also make the college indistinguishable from its secular competitors. Augustana's Lutheran educational heritage cannot help the college fulfill its mission if the faith at the center of it is viewed as a liability instead of as an asset. It should be central in the college's strategic plan. This heritage has consistently provided the theoretical structure and inspiration for the transformational education that Augustana has offered to its students. And for countless faculty and staff across the decades, this mission was also anchored and animated by a faith in a God whose steadfast love and faithfulness endures for all generations.[110]

Notes

1. King, "Birth of a New Age."
2. King, "Birth of a New Age."
3. King, "Birth of a New Age."
4. The current mission statement of the college: "Augustana College, deeply rooted in the liberal arts and sciences and an inclusive expression of Lutheran higher education, is committed to offering a challenging education that develops the qualities of mind, spirit and body necessary for students to discern their life's calling of leadership and service in a diverse and changing world." Augustana College, "Mission, Purpose, and Goals."
5. This chapter draws from Darrell Jodock's typologies in "The Third Path."
6. Cf. Matthew 5:13–16.

7. Roald Tweet, quoted in *On and Beyond the Mississippi*, 1.

8. The author is indebted to several colleagues who enriched this essay by offering valuable edits or answering queries, including Umme Al-wazedi, Ann Boaden, Michelle Crouch, David Crowe, Kristen Glass Perez, Lauren Hammond-Ford, and Megan Havard Rockwell, as well as students Erik Bergren and Linnea Tabaka.

9. Patel, "What It Means," 21.

10. "Five Faith Commitments."

11. Karl Olsson notes that Lutheran leaders in the 1870s like Tufve Nilsson Hasselquist viewed adherence to the confessions as the only way to unite the low-church Rosenian Pietists with more orthodox Lutherans. Olsson, *By One Spirit*, 103–5, 194–95.

12. The infamous "Galesburg Rule" of 1875 enforced that "Lutheran pulpits were for Lutheran ministers only, and Lutheran altars for Lutheran communicants only." For the development of the Galesburg Rule, see Granquist, *Lutherans in America*, 181.

13. Tredway, *Conrad Bergendoff*, 175, 199.

14. Erling, "What's in a Name?," 118.

15. It is worth pointing out that Lutherans have never had a firm place in "mainline Protestantism" in America, due in large part to the ethnic associations of their churches.

16. Bluemle, "GI Bill."

17. Tredway, *Conrad Bergendoff*, 199.

18. Sorensen, Inaugural Address, November 17, 1962, 3, folder 1, box 95, CWS.

19. Betsey Brodahl to Conrad Bergendoff, October 1, 1958, 1, Lilly Faculty Seminar: Faith and Values 1959–1962, box 44, AAR. The Lilly Foundation is a philanthropic organization founded in 1937. Its gift-giving is driven by "two potentially contrasting convictions: that tradition is an important resource and that fundamental rethinking often is necessary to respond effectively to new challenges and circumstances." "Our Philosophy."

20. Brodahl, letter.

21. Tredway, *Coming of Age*, 337.

22. Tredway, *Coming of Age*, 334.

23. Tredway, *Coming of Age*, 337.

24. "150 Years."

25. Bahls to Faculty, "Discussion of the draft of Five Faith Commitments," October 18, 2004, electronic correspondence, in the "Five Faith

Commitments" vertical file, Augustana College Special Collections, Rock Island, Illinois.

26. Seventy percent of faculty responded in 2005 that the Lutheran identity of the college was "important," yet around the same time, only 54 percent of faculty "felt they were knowledgeable about the Lutheran expression of higher education." Bahls, "The Five Faith Commitments: Proactively Expressing the College's Roots with Today's Students, September 15, 2006," 2, 7, in the "Five Faith Commitments" vertical file.

27. "Appendix One" (2004), 3, in the "Five Faith Commitments" vertical file. These original five priorities notably echo the four characteristics of the synod outlined by Herbert Chilstrom, which included "personal piety, dignified worship, social consciousness, and global awareness." Chilstrom, "What Was/Is Augustana?," 3–10.

28. "Draft (September 27, 2004): Five Faith Commitments of Augustana College," 1, in the "Five Faith Commitments" vertical file.

29. On April 1, 2015, the "Five Faith Commitments Task Force" members were listed as Anne Bergren, Ann Boaden, Lendol Calder, Michel Clark, David Crowe, Anne Earel, Mike Egan, Grey Giovanine, Kristen Glass Perez, Tamar Grimm, Tom Hanson, Jason Mahn, Richard Priggie, and Sam Slouch. Sam Slouch to First Year Students, Sophomores, Juniors, Seniors, Faculty, "Essay Contest: Augustana's Five Faith Commitments," April 1, 2015, electronic correspondence, in the "Five Faith Commitments" vertical file.

30. "Five Faith Commitments: Introduction."

31. Bahls, "Beyond Labels."

32. Patel, "What It Means," 117–32.

33. Rockenbach et al., *Navigating Pluralism*, 11.

34. Richard Priggie, correspondence with the author, May 7, 2019. This summary is based on Priggie's explanation of what was "added" by the constitutional changes.

35. Bahls, "Beyond Labels."

36. Anderson, "Swedish-American 'College Mania,'" 26–27.

37. Eklund, "Faith and Education," 75.

38. Anderson, "Swedish-American 'College Mania,'" 30.

39. The immediate predecessor to Augustana College was the theological department of the Illinois State University. It began as a college preparatory academy serving the Northern Illinois Synod, with which Lars Paul Esbjörn, like many Swedish and Norwegian Lutherans, had affiliated. The

school moved to Springfield in 1852, and a Scandinavian professorship was established in 1855, funded by the Norwegian and Swedish churches of the synod. Esbjörn was a principal fundraiser for this effort and was called to fill the professorship in 1858. Bergendoff, *Profession of Faith*, 10–11.

40. Augustana College was essentially Esbjörn himself, as his Scandinavian professorship became the nucleus of the new school. Bergendoff, *Profession of Faith*, 16.

41. Erling, "Augustana's Theological Tradition," 70–71.

42. Olson, *Augustana Lutheran Church*, 12.

43. Bernhard Erling notes that the *gymnasium* provided a model for Augustana College in its early days, in addition to the Swedish universities. Erling, "Augustana's Theological Tradition," 69. Esbjörn was educated in the Swedish gymnasium, thereafter studying at Uppsala University, which culminated in his ordination to ministry in 1832. Bergendoff, *Profession of Faith*, 4.

44. Eklund, "Lutheran Higher Education," 268.

45. Barton, "Swedish Visitors' Views," 29–30.

46. Barton, "Swedish Visitors' Views," 31–32.

47. Bergendoff, *Profession of Faith*, 5–7, 10, 12.

48. Anderson, "Swedish-American 'College Mania,'" 31.

49. This is apparent in one visitor's bemused comment in 1901 that the reverence and enthusiasm for teaching ancient languages at Augustana seemed dated and lacked a counterpart back in Sweden. His example was an Augustana professor who had taught his students to sing "A Mighty Fortress" in ancient Greek! Waldenström, *Nya Färder*, 269.

50. Barton, "Swedish Visitors' Views," 37.

51. The Augustana library became an official agent for the Royal Library in Stockholm, Sweden's national library. Blanck, introduction, x–xii.

52. Bergendoff's dissertation on the Swedish reformer, Olavus Petri, benefited from Söderblom's tutelage, and it anchored Bergendoff in a thorough understanding of the Church of Sweden's history and identity and its relation to Augustana. Arden, *Augustana Heritage*, 290. See also Erling and Granquist, *Augustana Story*, 244–45.

53. Bredin, "Ahlborg and America," 159–67; Arden, *Augustana Heritage*, 7, 9.

54. Arden, *Augustana Heritage*, 41–42.

55. Arden, *Augustana Heritage*, 2, 29.

56. Solberg, *Lutheran Higher Education*, 20, 28; Bergendoff, *Profession of Faith*, 5.

57. One of Esbjörn's contacts was the Lutheran pastor William A. Passavant in Pittsburgh, who had established Deaconess ministries modeled after Kaiserswerth and including an orphanage and hospital. Bergendoff, *Profession of Faith*, 6.

58. Chilstrom, "What Was/Is Augustana?," 7.

59. Olson, *Augustana Lutheran Church*, 89; Deaconess Community—ELCA, https://deaconesscommunity.org.

60. Nielsen, "Tracing Threads," 38–39.

61. Solberg, *Lutheran Higher Education*, 251.

62. Solberg, *Lutheran Higher Education*, 253.

63. The Augustana school that most explicitly drew inspiration from the folk high school model was Gustavus Adolphus College when it was founded in 1862 as St. Ansgar's Academy. Erling and Granquist, *Augustana Story*, 80. The American elderhostel movement was directly inspired by Grundtvig's philosophy. Nielsen, "Tracing Threads," 40–41.

64. Solberg, *Lutheran Higher Education*, 253.

65. Bergendoff, *Profession of Faith*, 42.

66. Characteristic of this diverse inheritance with Swedish educational models is the fact that Augustana has sought out partnerships with a variety of institutions in Sweden, including exchanges with universities like Uppsala as well as with the Grebbestad Folkhögskola, at which Augustana ran a popular summer school between 1982 and 2008.

67. Arden, *Augustana Heritage*, 48–49.

68. Arden, *Augustana Heritage*, 49.

69. Eklund, "Faith and Education," 85.

70. Eklund, "Faith and Education," 73.

71. Olson, *Augustana Lutheran Church*, 59.

72. Augustana currently has a separate First Year Inquiry 101 PACE course for multicultural students. The two sections are taught by two professors of color who are also immigrants. They bring immigrants' perspectives to the class and ensure that the connection between the Lutheran ideal and the changing world is made.

73. Umme Al-wazedi, correspondence with the author, August 22, 2022.

74. Lauren Hammond-Ford, correspondence with the author, August 21, 2022.

75. For more on this, see Mahn, "Educating Whole Persons."

76. Solberg, *Lutheran Higher Education*, 328.

77. Tredway, *Coming of Age*, 233.

78. Tredway, *Coming of Age*, 233.

79. Trudy Ring, "33 Years Later, She Still Likes the Job," *Moline Daily Dispatch*, December 28, 1980.

80. Tredway, *Coming of Age*, 233.

81. Bartholomew, "Centenarian Answers," 12–13.

82. Bartholomew, "Centenarian Answers," 13.

83. "Dr. Bartholomew Attains 80th Year: Pays Tribute to Present Student Generation Here," *Augustana Observer*, March 24, 1926.

84. "'Students Now Seek to Be Entertained,' States Dr. E. F. Bartholomew as 89th Birthday Nears," *Augustana Observer*, March 21, 1935.

85. Bergendoff, "Our Lofty Destiny," 1.

86. Parkander was notably the occupant of the first fully endowed academic chair and the college's first recipient of the CASE Illinois Professor of the Year Award.

87. Parkander. "Lilly Foundation Paper," Lilly Foundation Seminar: Faith and Values, box 44, AAR.

88. Parkander, "Lilly Foundation Paper." Italics in original.

89. Ann Boaden, correspondence with the author, August 12, 2022.

90. Irene Shearer, "Dean Proud of Augustana College," *Moline Daily Dispatch*, March 9, 1980, in the Betsey Brodahl vertical file.

91. Brodahl, letter, 1–2.

92. "Holistic and Intrusive Advising."

93. Bergendoff, *Profession of Faith*, 128–30, 151.

94. Richie Erickson, interview with Harrison Boushele, Alec McGinnis, Alex Simon, Zachary Vrbancic, Mark Safstrom, and Kai Swanson, March 2023, OHC.

95. Boaden, *Light and Leaven*, 228–32.

96. Paul Olsen, interview, September 14, 2010, OHC.

97. Ekberg, "Half a Century."

98. Ekberg, "Half a Century."

99. Ekberg, "Half a Century."

100. The approach includes a defined first-year experience, specific programs for first-generation college students and parents, and the CORE Center that integrates advising, career development, and research; see Augustana College, "Advising."

101. The theology of accompaniment is part of the ELCA Global Mission framework; see Schock, "Accompaniment," 29–32.

102. Kristen Glass Perez, correspondence with the author, August 20, 2022.

103. Examples include establishing the Campus Cupboard in 2017 to address student food insecurity; the M25 Student Emergency Grant fund established in 2015 by a donor who named the initiative based on Matthew 25: 35–45; and the Hameetman emergency loan fund established by a donor in 1976. "M25 Provides Emergency Assistance for Students," *Augustana Observer*, September 8, 2016; Michael Nolan, "Hameetman Bequests $30,000," *Augustana Observer*, January 4, 1976.

104. Glass Perez, correspondence.

105. Michelle Crouch, correspondence with the author, June 29, 2022.

106. Thanks to classics colleagues Kirsten Day and Mischa Hooker for proposing this term.

107. Campus chaplain Melinda Pupillo's morning devotion on "breaking bread" outlined these meanings of companionship as also being the hallmarks of fostering authentic community among colleagues. Pupillo, Morning Devotion.

108. A cursory survey of college advertising reveals there is nothing particularly distinctive about offering mentorship opportunities, as exemplified by Eastern Iowa Community Colleges: "You deserve more. It's that simple. At Eastern Iowa Community Colleges (EICC) you get more support, more mentorship, and more opportunities. It's why we're the #1 choice of area high school graduates. No matter what you choose to pursue after graduation—a short-term certificate, a career-ready diploma, or a two-year associate's degree—you can expect the same high quality education delivered by instructors who truly care." Eastern Iowa Community Colleges, "Get More."

109. The Augustana Board of Trustees' "Strategic Competency" report identified one of its goals as "A mentor for each student: A radical approach and commitment to mentoring that includes a stakeholder orientation toward ensuring that each student makes a deep connection with a member of the Augustana community [faculty member, administrator, staff, coach, etc.] that constitutes a mentor/mentee relationship."

110. Cf. Psalm 100. Notably the psalm was read at Thomas Tredway's campus memorial service on April 28, 2022, by Provost Wendy Hilton-Morrow.

8 THE VALUE(S) OF LUTHERAN LIBERAL ARTS IN A NEOLIBERAL AGE

JASON A. MAHN

In the fall of 1958, Betsey Brodahl, the legendary professor of history and dean of women at Augustana College, wrote a letter to President Conrad Bergendoff about participating in a new Lilly Foundation initiative. The initiative was "to help private colleges and universities take full advantage of their freedom to deal explicitly with religion and values."[1] Conceding that Augustana was not currently taking full advantage of this freedom, Brodahl mused about why this was the case: "Surely it is not lack of personnel or money. I will venture the answer that it is partly in shying away from being an indoctrination institution we have lost the sense of mission in the classroom and partly that neither student nor faculty knows just how to move toward the other where values are concerned."[2] Brodahl thus suggests that a gap between institutional mission and classroom pedagogy makes the two difficult to connect when it comes to thinking about values, and harder still to help shape those values (Fig. 8.1).

It seems that, by 1958, Augustana had decided that it was not, and should not be, an "indoctrination institution." Rather, students and faculty alike were and should be *freed from* any illiberal imposition of a person's (or the college's) values onto another. The challenge of the Lilly initiative was to move from a negative sense of freedom (freedom *from*) to a positive sense (freedom *for*). How was Augustana to take full advantage of its freedom as a Lutheran liberal arts college "to deal explicitly with"—and even help foster—spiritual formation, moral reflection, and religious commitments?[3]

Faculty at Augustana were not alone in experiencing tremendous shifts in thinking about the mission of the school, their role as educators, and whether these could or should include inculcating values.

Fig. 8.1. Dean of Students Betsey Brodahl meeting with a student, circa 1970s. Augustana College Photograph Collection, C-F05374. Courtesy of Augustana College Special Collections, Rock Island, Illinois.

According to William F. May, the predominant model of US higher education shifted from the liberal arts college to the positivist university in the 1950s, a shift perceptible even *within* liberal arts colleges. The prior liberal arts model had thought of intelligence *aesthetically*; to become learned was to have one's tastes and appreciations broaden, to come to value a wider range of subjects and points of view. Faculty thought of teaching as a calling or vocation rather than (only) a career, and they hoped for the same discovery of a calling in their graduates. According to May, "On the whole the consensus which the liberal arts college presupposed fostered a sense of vocation which embraced more than the graduate's job. The ideal of well-roundedness correlated with a vocation that included additional responsibilities as a spouse, parent, citizen, and participant in voluntary communities. Liberally educated graduates would reflect a *pleroma* of shared values that let them play out a variety of social roles within the setting of the common good." In all of this, "the college largely relied on a consensus on ends and goals that shaped its life."[4] It was that shared goal, or at least a lively debate about it, that Brodahl found missing in the work of Augustana faculty and students in 1958.

Augustana College has remained a Lutheran liberal arts college. Like the twenty-five other colleges and universities of the Evangelical Lutheran Church in America (ECLA) as well as hundreds of other church-related liberal arts institutions, it has been able to resist, at least in part, the economic and cultural shift that William May recounted in 2001, that Betsey Brodahl worried about in 1958, and that largely occurred in the intervening decades. We have become neither a university nor a secular college with only "historic" ties to a church. Instead, we articulate shared institutional values and even name them "faith commitments."[5] One faith commitment—to the "reasoned examination of faith"—brings together the objective reason and the so-called subjective faith that positivism otherwise splits asunder. Another faith commitment is to "vocational discernment"—the discernment of one's place within and contributions to the common good—and both the mission statement and purpose of the college now include language of being educated for vocation and calling.

Still, the concerns that Brodahl articulated in 1958 have not *simply* or *easily* been answered. Rather, only through a host of initiatives—the Lilly Faculty Seminar in the late 1950s, the curricular and calendar revisions of the late 1960s, participation in critical retrievals of Lutheran identity by Lutheran-affiliated colleges in 1990s, the development of the Center for Vocational Reflection in the early 2000s—has Augustana been able to resist the national trend toward becoming a value-neutral university, hold on to its institutional vocation, creatively retrieve the "liberal arts," articulate its Lutheran identity, and commit to educate for vocation. I think the most important, and perhaps most difficult, work is ahead of us.

In this chapter, I situate Augustana's unfolding understanding of and pride in itself as a Lutheran liberal arts college next to the precipitous rise of neoliberalism, a default worldview that relegates deliberation about values, goods, and final ends to market forces and consumer choices. Together alongside other institutions belonging to the Network of ELCA Colleges and Universities (NECU) and the Network for Vocation in Undergraduate Education (NetVUE), Augustana has over the past fifty years come to articulate its primary goal and purpose in terms of education *for* vocation, that is, education as *for* service to the neighbor and *for* the flourishing of the common good. This understanding of education is an answer and corrective to more consumerist and careerist (or "neoliberal") models of education. And yet—or maybe *and so*—education for vocation may also harbor the marks of the neoliberal culture it is meant to get out from under.

Neoliberal commodification of education and the concerted effort to reassert education's chief value and proper end occurred together, beginning after World War II, increasing in speed in the 1980s and '90s, and reaching an apex during the financial crisis of 2008. Given the simultaneity of these movements and how they inevitably inflect one another, this chapter asks: How does a Lutheran liberal arts school make a case for the moral value of education, with its purpose in terms of communal and ecological well-being and the restoration of democratic processes, in a neoliberal order bent on reducing moral values to monetary value, students to consumers, and the curriculum to a giant menu from which individuals choose what they will? Given this volume's attention to the full inclusion of marginalized perspectives (and bodies) within higher education, this chapter also asks: Which approach gets us closer to diversity, equity, inclusion, and justice—the freedom of individuals to choose their own paths, or the creative reformulation of a liberal arts tradition that has been, and still seems to many, elitist and exclusive? I suggest that, although Augustana's liberal arts continually risks becoming what William Deresiewicz names the neoliberal arts, the deep history of Lutheran and liberal arts ideals at Augustana continue to shape educators and students to value and work for the flourishing of all, including those for whom flourishing seems like a luxury.

THE *AD HOC* MAKING OF A LIBERAL ARTS COLLEGE

Augustana's mission speaks of being "deeply rooted in the liberal arts and sciences." Augustana is nationally ranked among *U.S. News and World Report*'s liberal arts colleges (in 2025, Augustana was ranked one hundredth).[6] As one recent graduate rightly observed, "the professors and administration take great pride in Augie being a liberal arts school."[7] And yet, unlike some secular liberal arts institutions that value "a free life of the mind," Augustana has always been practical in orientation. Most church-related liberal arts colleges are similar. They have a number of preprofessional and even professional degree programs because, since their founding, they have linked liberal arts study to practical work and service through the professions.[8] Is this tradition—sometimes called "liberal-arts-plus"—already a falling away from an original and purer form of the liberal arts?

The narrowest definition of liberal arts goes back to the medieval era, when the seven liberal arts were composed of the *trivium* (grammar, logic, and rhetoric) and the *quadrivium* (arithmetic, geometry, astronomy, and music). These are distinguished from the "servile arts," which included the trades, agriculture, commerce, and other tasks not befitting of free citizens. From *this* beginning, then, the liberal arts were a privileged affair available to those who had others voluntarily or involuntarily doing servile arts on their behalf so that they could enjoy a "free life of the mind." So long as we define *liberal* in opposition to the *servile* or *practical*, then Augustana and other so-called tier II liberal arts colleges already risk crossing over from liberal to "vocational" education.[9]

But *that* starting place of the liberal arts does not seem to be *ours*. Throughout its history, church-related higher education has been about character formation and practical service above and beyond the liberal-free paradigm. Soon after Augustana was founded in 1860 as a school to train ministers and teachers serving Swedish American communities, the college added programs in stenography, bookkeeping, and secretarial skills; by the 1880s there was a commercial department as well as a conservatory of music.[10] Then as well as now, "practical" programs proved to be the more popular. By 1910, 688 students had graduated from the commercial department while only 468 had graduated from the general college.[11] One could even make the case that, rather than falling away from a "pure" liberal arts school, Augustana rather belatedly became one and did so precisely because the line between "academic" and "practical" training became increasingly blurred.

Augustana College catalogs from the early 1950s mention liberal arts only twice. The first is under the section listing faculty serving the "College of Liberal Arts" or the School of Music, the "Summer School," or the "School of Swedish." The second is a description of "Life on Campus," presumably geared toward prospective students, identifying a "campus of an American college of liberal arts" that—with its picturesque grounds and intimate residential life—forms a "unique closely knit community." Other references to organization within Augustana are simply to "the College," fiscally and organizationally distinguished from Augustana Seminary since 1946. In 1952, the college had four divisions (humanities, religion and philosophy, social studies, and sciences). Each student passed from two years in a "junior college" devoted to general education to the "senior college," where "the emphasis is placed upon concentration in the department or division chosen by the student." Students were instructed to choose their "major interest" by the end of their second year. They could choose among departmental majors, divisional majors, a rather loosely defined "area major," and "functional majors," which students might consider if they were "preparing for a certain career or for later professional study"—what also got glossed as "a life of work."[12]

The 1952 catalog lists functional majors including accounting, business administration, Christian ministry, Christian service, predentistry, pre-engineering, graduate study (with a note to resist "overspecializing"), journalism, law, medicine, medical technology, minister of music, secretarial training, social work, speech rehabilitation, teaching, and an American studies major (for international students in the "Summer School"). While most of these would have been housed within the "College of Liberal Arts," the categories seem capacious. More operational is the line between divisional or departmental majors and functional majors offered to those pursuing "a life of work." Students attracted to the latter were explicitly warned that "departmental majors and divisional majors will frequently serve equally well in preparation for a life of work even though they do not refer specifically to vocation."[13]

It was not until 1953–54 that the four-year curriculum was described as a liberal arts education. The catalog's introductory statement, called "The Spirit of Augustana," began with the claim that "Augustana is a four year liberal arts college"—a designation that would need to hold the academic and practical together. There is evidence that the popularity of the latter continued to threaten core subjects. That catalog includes the warning not to overlook the vocational importance of majors that are not explicitly named "functional." Curiously, the introductory statement goes on to claim that "Augustana's most prized achievement" is its "record of its graduates in all professions and occupations." However, it immediately clarifies that such success marks not only "high technical accomplishment" but also "lives made full and happy."[14] It would seem that explicitly naming the institution as a liberal arts college correlated with, and perhaps was a response to, the rising value of practical career training. If I am interpreting these fairly, then institutional self-descriptions from the mid-1950s reveal a subtle strategy: Augustana could have continued to contrast its college of liberal arts with practical programs and functional majors and to encourage pragmatic postwar students not to overlook the importance of core subjects and liberal studies. Instead, it included every discipline, from the "purest" to the most pragmatic, within what it came to call a single liberal arts college.

This strategy of valuing liberal arts by making it inclusive of all subjects continued through the 1950s. By the end of the decade, the "functional majors" (also called preprofessional studies) were listed under the major departments that began to house them. Journalism became an option under English, accounting under economics, surveying under geology, and mechanical drawing under mathematics. Throughout the 1950s, preprofessional studies that had been offered in addition to, and clearly secondarily to, core departmental and divisional majors were listed as emphases within departments. Along with centering the functional majors, and presumably because of it, the college increasingly emphasized its entire collegiate identity as a liberal arts institution.

If we stand back and examine Augustana's first one hundred years (1860–1960), the contours of this plot line stand in even greater relief. Augustana went from originally offering *a program in liberal arts and sciences* to forming a *college of liberal arts*, in which departmental and functional majors were clearly distinguished. Whatever else we can say about the shifting uses and denotations of "liberal arts," this story cannot be simplified into a "fall" story from so-called pure liberal arts to the sins of mission drift. Rather, Augustana came to describe itself as a liberal arts college precisely when, and perhaps because, so many preprofessional and career-oriented tracks were put side by side with the "traditional liberal arts."

REVISIONIST RETRIEVALS OF LUTHERANISM

In 1946, Augustana Theological Seminary, which resided on top of "Zion Hill," legally and fiscally separated from Augustana College down below. In 1962, the year C. W. Sorensen became president of Augustana, the national Augustana Evangelical Lutheran Church merged with other Lutheran bodies to become the American Lutheran Church. Four seminaries previously serving the smaller denominations merged, and until 1967, the Augustana campus in Rock Island was one of two locations for the newly formed Lutheran School of Theology.[15] Before the mid-1960s, then, Augustana was a Christian college and a college of the church—you could look up at the seminary on the hill for evidence. Afterwards, it became a church-related college, and the hyphen could be read as either connecting or disconnecting the collegiate and ecclesial institutions.[16]

This shifting relationship between college and church occurred alongside the new understanding of Augustana as a liberal arts college, traced above. By the end of the 1950s, the catalog cover page described the institution as "A Four-Year Liberal Arts Co-educational Church Related College."[17] That verbose description does not do justice to the way the four descriptors interfaced. *Liberal arts* and *church related* emerged as primary descriptors during the same period, and each named a college that was not "of" or "owned by" the church but that still (as of 1966) had the mission "to teach youth the way of life, determined by the revelation of Jesus Christ in the Word and the

Church."[18] We have seen that Augustana came to think of itself as a liberal arts college in an *ad hoc* way and by stretching that term to include all the practical educational tracks that were originally to the side. How does the *Lutheran* in Lutheran liberal arts contribute to or forestall this consolidation?

It is common to hear Lutheran accounts of vocation that emphasize its democratization. Before Martin Luther and the sixteenth-century Lutheran Reformation, the story goes, only nuns, monks, and priests had "vocations"; indeed, they alone were "the religious." Luther and company leveled this spiritual-material hierarchy between the ordained and the laity. Because they understood all people—saints and sinners, princes and peasants—to need God's unmerited grace, no one and no one's work were more "godly" or entailed a "higher calling" than the others. When Lutheran colleges emphasize this vocational democratization, they often include a variety of practical, work-oriented programs within the central purpose and mission of the school. All of that is needed and good. Still, we should not forget that, while Lutheran understandings of vocation are as capacious as understandings of the liberal arts, they do have limits, and the term becomes vacuous when those limits are ignored. We should also note that understanding Lutheran higher education *for* vocation was also the product of revisionist history and creative retrieval—one that was not conducted in earnest until the 1980s and '90s. Looking again at the history of vocation appropriately complicates the story we tell about Lutheran liberal arts.

Martin Luther described the paradoxical "freedom of a Christian" in a 1520 theological tract by that name. Luther opens that work with this antinomy: "A Christian is a perfectly free lord of all, subject to none/A Christian is a perfectly dutiful servant of all, subject to all."[19] Whereas some accounts of liberal arts pit the freedom of the leisure class against the bondage of servile work, Luther, with his characteristic proclivity for paradox, understands servanthood to all as the natural, inevitable outcome of having been freed by Christ to be lord of all.

Within this theological framework, one is freed from the consuming anxiety and despair that ensue when having to make oneself worthwhile, valuable, lovable, or—in the reformers' favored term—justified before God. Because God through Christ unconditionally loves each creature as she is, limited and sinful though she may be, and thus justifies her "by grace through faith," she is set free from the fearful and anxious striving toward merit that otherwise imprisons her. *Freedom from* this self-enclosure naturally redoubles as *freedom for* gracious attention to, love, and service of neighbors. The underlying logic, which is also a fundamental Christian worldview, is that humans are created for community and fully flourish only in relation to the whole. The self-defeating attempt to justify one's individual worth and existence—to be self-standing—alienates us from relationships with God and neighbor. Freed from that self-imposed bondage, a person freely promotes, participates in, and profits from the health of the whole. In this worldview, salvation (from *salus*, or "health") can never characterize an individual alone—a claim that can be made by a public health professor as readily as a Christian theologian. An ecologist might add that salvation is not for humanity alone. Salvation must be of whole communities, which Wendell Berry describes as all the human and nonhuman creatures who inhabit a place, plus the place itself.[20]

This theological journey into the sixteenth century suggests that *Lutheran* liberal arts education has a unique understanding of that from which the free arts free us, and to what end. In contrast to the "liberal free" model of a small, elite community that is free to enjoy a life of the mind, the Lutheran liberal arts model asserts that, because God frees individuals from preoccupation with individual merit and worth, we are free to serve others in body, mind, and spirit, with gratitude, and for the flourishing of whole communities. At its best, the liberal arts at Lutheran colleges become training grounds for living out the liberation procured by God in service to neighbor and neighborhood.

Yet it is easy to forget that retrieving Lutheran accounts of vocation as a, if not *the*, primary characteristic of Lutheran higher education was itself the product of creative retrieval. It was not until the 1980s, when Augustana began experiencing a rapid decline in the number of students from Lutheran churches (together with a decline in all students) that the school began to question what it meant to be a Lutheran college.[21] It could no longer assume that *Lutheran* named a place where Lutheran students went to be educated by Lutheran faculty. That decline and the conversations it sparked continued for more than a decade until President Thomas Tredway called for an articulation of an institutional Lutheran identity toward the end of his presidency and President Steven Bahls renewed the call at the beginning of his. The result was the 2004 articulation of the Five Faith Commitments of Augustana College. "Vocational discernment," beside the other four commitments, thus became a way to talk about what it means to be Lutheran as an institution or to live out the school's "Lutheran roots" in contemporary ways.

Thus, the school's commitment to educate for vocation—for lives of service to the neighbor and for the flourishing of whole neighborhoods—may have shaped Augustana's purpose from the start, but it has only been over the past several decades that we have re-narrated our past in these ways. In fact, language in Augustana's current mission statement about students "discern[ing] life's *calling* of leadership and *service* in a diverse and changing world" was not added until the mission and constitution were revised in 2019, occasioned by an upcoming presidential search and worries that the pool of applicants would be prohibitively small if the incoming president needed to be a member of the Lutheran Church or a church with official ecumenical ties to it.[22]

Forgetting this history of the retrieval of vocation as a leitmotif for Lutheran higher education tempts us into thinking that we can and should simply and directly live out our tradition or mission. Instead, faithfulness to a tradition that is always reforming itself requires our own continual reinterpretation and re-rooting of the traditions in light of present realities. There is another danger endemic to narrating the history of education-for-vocation within Lutheran liberal arts, one that is important for how we consider callings in relation to careers and careers in relation to our prevailing economic order. It is easy to see how recounting Luther's democratization of vocation could and often does sanction any and all work as entailing legitimate callings. Post-Reformation Christendom saw almost any job or task—brewing beer or changing diapers as well as governing nation-states or presiding over Mass—as a calling from God because it serves a neighbor in need. Following Augustana's broadened understanding of the liberal arts in the 1950s and '60s, the language of vocation retrieved in the 1980s and '90s validated understandings of college as practical training for a career. Yet in the college's anxiety to recognize the legitimacy of practical majors within Lutheran liberal arts, it is easy to forget Luther's key distinction in the thicker account I have offered above.

That distinction is between work that is done out of a desperate quest for worth and merit and work done from a sense of freedom and for the good of whole communities and the landscapes that sustain them. Luther certainly democratizes vocation in terms of the kind of work (paid and unpaid) that potentially serves the neighbor and neighborhood. But the democratization is not boundless or automatic; any and all work should not get christened. Rather, designating vocation as work *that leads to communal flourishing* should discount some careers (and maybe some majors that lead to those careers) that turn on competitiveness among neighbors and that diminish communal, ecological flourishing.

Augustana educators in recent history have been split between those who endorse any and every new major as naturally and easily contributing to the Lutheran liberal arts, and those who traffic in stories of mission drift and a fall from our liberal arts center and thereby object to new majors or programs largely because they are new. Needed is sustained deliberation about the ends and purposes of Lutheran liberal arts. Educators must prudently distinguish between education programs and work that leads to a shared good life and those that produce an individual life of acquiring goods. Making such distinctions is incredibly difficult in a neoliberal culture that largely gives up deliberations and negotiations about final ends in exchange for the right of individuals to choose based on their own interests.

HIGHER EDUCATION'S (NEO)LIBERAL ARTS?

I have tried to suggest that assessing whether my own college is a liberal arts institution—or just *how* liberal arts we are—according to the percentage of students who choose a traditional liberal arts major versus those who pursue more "vocational" paths is a nonstarter, not least because the Reformation tradition does not pit the freedom of some against the necessary service (or servility) of others. At the same time, just because Augustana has had an expansive understanding of how neighbors and neighborhoods can be served through paid and unpaid work does not mean that any and every major or career should be counted among the Lutheran liberal arts. Between stories of a fall from the "pure liberal arts" and origin stories about unlimited meaningful and purposeful careers stands careful discernment and judgment concerning what Lutheran liberal arts should include—and should not. In other words, we should assess the strength of our Lutheran liberal arts according to whether, and to what degree, our students are freed for careful, creative work that leads to the flourishing of the whole and themselves as integral parts thereof. In the language of the Network of ELCA Colleges and Universities, we must assess whether and how our graduates come into a place where they are "called and empowered—to serve the neighbor—so that all may flourish."[23]

Making such judgments is difficult enough. But it gets exponentially more difficult because, beginning in the 1970s and continuing through today, any attempt to educate for vocation and for the flourishing of the common good exists within a neoliberal order that relegates the value and purpose of education and work to individual return on individual investment. Neoliberalism is notoriously difficult to define. In terms of economics, the theory was first proposed in 1938 by Friedrich Hayek and others. It took hold in the popular imagination in the early 1970s, after some conservative politicians and economists sought to end forty years of New Deal government spending, public works, and social support systems. Neoliberalism's chief markers include the deregulation of the market and its expansion into an open flow of capital between countries, the deregulation of the financial industry, and unfettered finance. It leads to the outsourcing and offshoring of jobs to low-wage countries and to an outsized role for speculative finance and to under-investment in the real economy. All of this privatizes and commoditizes the commons, or what were once shareable, public goods and services.

Neoliberalism as an economic theory became a political agenda with Ronald Reagan and Margaret Thatcher in the 1980s and the "market triumphalism" of that time.[24] The subsequent wave of democratic leaders, President Bill Clinton in the United States and Prime Minister Tony Blair in England, did not so much overturn this new political-economic order as make it more palatable through their own version of "market-friendly liberalism." Social welfare and other supports were extended to those who needed help "at no fault of their own." And yet, as that oft-invoked phrase suggests, the extension of opportunities to the disadvantaged was also increasingly coupled with calls for individual accountability and responsibility. Whereas during the three decades following the New Deal, Americans considered social welfare in terms of what we owed one another as members of a shared whole, by the end of the century it became a debate about whether the poor were undeserving or deserving.[25]

Such economic, political, and cultural trends—the privatization of what were once public, shareable goods; the confinement of social support systems to individuals "responsiblized" for deserving it; and the reframing of the public or common good in terms of the sum of the self-interests of individuals—became the primary, unquestioned worldview of both political parties and almost all citizens ("consumers") in the late twentieth and early twenty-first centuries. Together they have influenced the place and role of higher education in the United States.[26] And while public investment in public institutions often does not directly affect independent colleges such as my own,[27] the broad change in public perceptions about college certainly does. According to political philosopher Michael Sandel, "One of the casualties of [neoliberalism's] triumph may be the loss of broad public support for higher education. Once widely seen as an engine of opportunity, the university has become, at least for some, a symbol of credentialist privilege and meritocratic hubris."[28]

The role of campus leadership also changes. Neoliberalism's reliance on individuals to decide their own ends—and the Market to decide, without deliberation, our "shared" end—corresponds to the idea that leaders are called to achieve the common good almost exclusively by maximizing consumer welfare and economic growth. Leaders (of colleges, as well as governments) thus become *technocrats*; they apply efficient means to bring about the necessary (market-driven) ends but deliberate less and less about what is good for the whole. For their part, professors are also urged to focus on the efficiency of processes and procedures in their interactions with students. Many of us now tend to maximize efficiency while we "deliver" education and students "consume" course material (often without digesting it). We market education as an investment with financial returns and then value those parts of the curriculum that garner the most student-consumers or produce the highest incomes. Obviously, these trends change the way we make institutional decisions. Deliberation about institutional mission and how to live out our collective calling "to serve the neighbor, so that all may flourish" gives way to conversation-stopping invocations of economic necessity, followed by presentations from consultants about the most efficient, affordable measures needed to enroll and retain students.

As a covenantal model of community gives way to a contractual one, the way we value and why we value diversity, inclusion, and belonging can also flatten. Throughout the neoliberal era, globalization and the openness of markets often became the primary vehicle for, and proof of, society's openness to "difference." The high point of this shift was 1989, with the downfall of the Soviet Union, after which Americans began to equate civil liberties with global capitalism.[29] The Clinton administration's political rhetoric from the 1990s further linked the neoliberalization of markets with the multiculturalism and the liberalization of individual rights—a trend that continued through 2016, although backlash against it also then appeared.[30] Because the economic-political-cultural ideology of neoliberalism essentially fuses market deregulation with democracy and economic freedoms with civil freedoms, substantial accounts of justice also morph into broad appreciation for cultural differences, but with little sense of common cause, purpose, or a community to which diverse people belong.

In this slow and steady slide toward neoliberalism as the prevailing, unquestioned order of the day, the *practical* education that Augustana has associated with deep, vocational responsibility for the common good can be quickly reduced to personal betterment. What was a problem for Martin Luther—the endless individual striving for personal merit and recognition—has become the largely unquestioned measure of value, freedom, and success. When work that should enable a flourishing commons is mistaken for an end in itself, education becomes transactional, that which one does/buys in order to get what one wants/earns. The difficulty is thus also an irony: by offering practical programs ideally leading to paid work—and whole lives—that serve the common good, Augustana invariably plays into a dominant understanding that undercuts its deepest mission and purpose. Taken to the extreme, the more than 100 majors and programs of study and

150 student groups come to be understood not as various formative ways of becoming servant-leaders of and full participants in concrete communities but rather as consumer goods that are selected with the price of admission and then leveraged for personal success. Admittedly, such success, and a measure of upward mobility, is invaluable to first-generation and other underrepresented students who lift themselves and their families out of generational poverty, develop social capital, and move in from the margins through their college education. Still, higher education does a disservice to marginalized students when it offers career training to all yet reserves meaning and purpose for the privileged. Under neoliberalism, commitments to inclusion can look little different from the inclusivity of a shopping mall, which welcomes every consumer.

Through his own version of a fall story, William Deresiewicz condemns liberal arts institutions for almost entirely capitulating to the "neoliberal arts"—a phrase he coins to name and condemn how liberal arts colleges have "sold out."[31] Anthropologists Carolyn Hough and Adam Kaul take up the term *neoliberal arts* while questioning it, expressing their own ambivalence. Identifying with "faculty who wish to resist reframing the value of an education in terms of capitalist exchange-values," they note that such resistance is never straightforward or simple. Unilateral resistance to the "neoliberal corporatism" of higher education would only land us in "a romantic ideal of the liberal arts," one trumpeting the "free life of the mind." More difficult and needed than single solutions and "oppositional politics" is the commitment to "work on cultivating and fostering non-capitalist relations and new subjective orientations right now, where we already are."[32]

Kaul, who teaches at Augustana, estimates that our institution has done better than most in resisting market forces that pressure institutions to sell liberal arts by way of career choice and earning potential. Still, since the financial crisis of 2008, there has been increasing pressure among the social sciences and humanities to justify their value by serving preprofessional programs that make our students "career ready." Kaul notes that his Introduction to Anthropology class has never been in higher demand but that today's students enroll either to get the general education requirement "out of the way" or to tick off prerequisites for other majors, most notably, Augustana's

"MCAT-oriented" premed major.[33] He feels called to step in front of career-bound, pragmatic, professionalizing students in order "to disrupt the rest of their learning, to attempt to reorient their thinking about cultural differences, inequalities, the human condition, and so on."[34] This is an important example of cultivating non-capitalist relations in the classroom, which he and Hough lift up as a way forward. Valuing transformative learning and teaching the (non-exchangeable) value of that learning may just "find a symbiotic space, ambivalent, contingent and nuanced, between neoliberal corporatism and a romantic ideal of the liberal arts."[35]

In the following sections, I turn to two moments in Augustana's history during the ascendancy of the neoliberal age that exemplify the possibility and difficulty of negotiating spaces between romanticizing the liberal arts and crassly marketing them. The first period, which occurred during the ascendancy of neoliberalism, exhibits a positive example of serious deliberation about the aims and goals of a Lutheran liberal arts education and thereby of resisting commodification, accreditation, and other outside pressures to define who we are and what we do. The second negotiation (by first-year students) occurred around the time of the financial crisis of 2008, which is something of neoliberalism's apex. This second example shows just how difficult it is to see and explore any understanding of higher education except as personal return on individual investment. My hope is that rooting present realities in this history will help us locate the kind of generative, symbiotic spaces needed to form students to serve for others' flourishing, as well as flourish themselves.

ENDS AND MEANS, MISSION AND CURRICULUM (1960S–'80S)

It is not surprising, given the *ad hoc* creation/retrieval of Augustana as a liberal arts college throughout its first hundred years followed by rapid changes in how the college considered and lived out its relationship with the church, that faculty in the 1960s felt pressed to clarify what it meant for Augustana to be a Lutheran liberal arts institution. Such deliberations were occasioned by ongoing discussions over revisions to the curriculum and academic calendar. According to Thomas

Tredway, the 1960s and '70s were "spent in an almost continuous faculty debate about which academic calendar would best fit the curriculum." By a sixty-six to forty-two vote in 1967, the faculty voted to move from a traditional semester system to the quarter (later called "trimester") system, which went into effect in 1969 and lasted almost fifty years.[36] (That the 1960s and early '70s were a time of upheaval on most college campuses for reasons very different from curricular realignment is something to which we will return.)

According to Clarence Woodrow Sorensen (Augustana president, 1962–75), the 1967 curricular change was almost entirely centered around concerns about recruitment in a competitive market. He explained that "it became of growing importance that the calendar also meet the needs of the expanding number of special programs and co- and extra-curricular activities that the college was offering in response to the rising expectations of students and the increasing pressure from outside agencies, accrediting bodies, and competing institutions."[37] Regardless of how they were *occasioned*, however, the curriculum and calendar revisions in the 1960s were clearly *driven* by reflections on the central aims, purposes, and institutional vocation of an Augustana education. Arguments about how many general education requirements there should be, the number of major programs, how many electives students should be given, and so forth were framed by broad deliberation about the central purposes of Lutheran liberal arts.

Similarly, in January of 1966, roughly a year after the Augustana Project for Calendar and Curricular Review was underway, the faculty issued a statement that clarified and underscored what Augustana was for. Called "Faculty Opinion on the Aims and Objectives of Augustana College: A Report on Faculty Discussions," the document conveyed agreement across departments about the "central purposes of the College as a Christian, liberal arts institution" before detailing what it meant to be a Christian and liberal arts college, articulating what we now call learning outcomes, and noting (in a penultimate paragraph) the need for "awakening students to social and political problems." (That paragraph manages not to mention racism, civil rights, or war, much less the Selma to Montgomery marches, the assassination of Malcolm X, or the United States' entrance into the Vietnam War, all of which occurred in the months before the faculty report was issued.)[38]

In the document, faculty admitted that Augustana's "traditional role" with its "heavy emphasis on the liberal arts" was "in contrast with present trends in the educational picture." Still, a number of faculty thought "that the kind of education offered at Augustana is *more valuable* to persons and society than in an earlier era because society has an *increasing need* for liberally educated [people]" (my emphasis). This assertion was likely based on the faculty's understanding of the purpose of liberal arts at a Christian institution. The authors appreciated that the college is ecumenical (freed from denominational homogeneity) in its spirit and its selection of non-Lutheran faculty and students. This freedom from "externally imposed restrictions" enabled it—in keeping with the Lutheran tradition's twofold sense of freedom—to be "free to accomplish the purposes incorporated into its constitutions" as well as to live out its institutional commitment "to teach youth the way of life, determined by the revelation of Jesus Christ in the Word and the Church." While the Christianity department (renamed the religion department in 1960) presumably was charged with instruction in religion, the faculty as a whole remained "concerned that a significant Christian witness be given in the College community" so that each student "will be able to think deeply about a faith he can make his own."[39]

A section called "Augustana as a Liberal Arts College" then reaffirmed the primary goal of an Augustana education in terms of liberating the mind. It defined liberation *from* "prejudice, shabbiness, and shallowness" not as liberation from tradition and traditional ways of knowing but rather as the freedom to enter into classical, critical education more fully: "to seek inspiration and guidance from the enduring elements in the human tradition." Freedom from ignorance and indoctrination thus redoubles as the free, committed pursuit of truth, which should be carefully discriminated from error—"a search which is an essential commitment for free men."

Turning from the overarching goal of liberating minds to the "subject matter of the liberal arts," the faculty in 1966 alluded to an ongoing debate about the relation between traditional subjects within liberal arts and more "practical" courses and programs. The document's allusions to the "certain subjects" central to the liberal arts and the "reasonable number" of "practical courses" not incompatible with it perhaps indicate a failure to define clearly what it means to be a liberal arts school and what is and is not included in that designation. Faculty seemed keenly aware that students were "severely pressed to meet graduation requirements in a few programs because of increasing demands within the undergraduate curriculum to meet professional standards." Exactly because of this, however, a number of faculty "expressed a firmly held conviction that our traditional emphases should not be compromised to accommodate professional requirements." Whether it be the incorporation of preprofessional majors or accommodation to professional standards, Augustana faculty were clear that those needed to "serve the purposes of the college," and not the other way around. Indeed, references to a *reasonable* number of *practical* courses, *properly* related and *adequately* taught, and so serving the *purpose* of liberal arts *well*, suggest that evoked here is a kind of *phroenesis*, or practical reason, which can be employed only when chief purposes or final ends have been established.

Ironically, this ongoing commitment to the central purposes of Lutheran liberal arts may have led, in part, to the almost immediate reconsideration of whether the 1969 change to trimesters, which ostensibly issued from the above concerns, helped alleviate those concerns or exacerbated them. A year into trimesters, many Augustana faculty were convinced of the latter. A "Report of the Evaluation Study Committee," dated April 20, 1970, concludes that the "educational experience" under trimesters was not meeting expectations. While the curricular and calendar change was meant to lead to more depth and reflection in both teaching and student learning, many felt the opposite was true: "There seems to be a general feeling that the gain in variety and breadth [accompanying the change to trimesters] has come at the expense of depth."[40] A year later (March 1971), a more extensive "Evaluation of the Augustana Quarter System" confirmed that the majority (60 percent) of faculty and students thought the ten-week term asked students and faculty to take or teach too many courses at once, robbing them of the freedom to pursue curiosities, preventing them from absorbing their learning, and so obscuring their flourishing. This was not just grumbling about a new system. In 1975, the North Central review team (a regional accrediting agency) raised concerns about the proliferation of curricular offerings. There was by then an amazing "breadth and variety" of majors, preprofessional programs, courses, coordinated degree programs, and academic concentrations at Augustana, but could the center hold? The agency raised questions about coherence and pleaded with Augustana to help restore "its potential to foster the shared values and knowledge that bind us together as a society."[41]

In 1978, President Tredway wondered whether that summons might not warrant a reconsideration of what kind of college Augustana wanted to be: "Institutionally we must decide if we want to go a 'pure' liberal arts route or continue the strategy of the last decade of trusting the general education requirements to meet liberal arts goals and allowing a proliferation of majors in deference to faculty interests. An alternative is to meet the central questions head on. Faculty and administration must come to some agreement on objectives and then devise programs from them."[42] He offered a third option that would keep with a "liberal arts plus" model of education, one that syncs up with Lutheran higher education's emphasis on education for vocation. Could a more substantial articulation of this third option also include our calling to educate for justice, to understand the common good and civil rights as integrally linked? Could we have considered—or might we now consider—the healing of human and ecological communities as an integral part of our institutional and individual callings?

Tredway, writing in 1978, thought that Augustana had walked an easier and more dangerous path by letting faculty teach what they wanted and allowing students to pursue what they wanted, each "trusting" (or rather hoping—against the evidence) that many individuals pursuing their own interests would somehow lead to overarching good. That is essentially a neoliberal faith, which Tredway wanted to reverse. He urged them to begin (again!) with the aims and purposes of Augustana as a Lutheran liberal arts school and let new programs, curricular changes, and other means follow from those ends.

In 1985, history professor Ross Paulson renewed this plea to put the ends of education before the means to achieve them. He endorsed an *ad hoc* committee's case to switch back to semesters and acknowledged the significant budget constraints the college faced. (Student population had declined 10 percent over the prior five years.) But his major call was for discussions about what Augustana was ultimately for and to let cost-saving measures follow from that. He was quite clear and emphatic on this point:

> Remorseless "cost-benefit-analysis" that looks only at numbers (quantity) without regard for priorities or essential value commitments (quality) can, over time, transform an educational institution piecemeal and change its essential character. But if the primary mission of the college is clarified . . . then questions of efficiency of operation can be made in ways which undergird rather than undermine the liberal arts. Efficiencies of operation are important only to the extent that they represent a redeployment of scarce resources to support and extend the liberal arts mission of the college.[43]

Paulson here underscores the importance of efficiency and solvency but only insofar as each serves the mission of the school. He called on his colleagues to clarify the mission and deliberate about priorities. There is little indication that they heeded his summons.

When Augustana underwent its next major revision of the calendar and curriculum in 2016–18, the size of majors with outside accrediting agencies, together with the need to become more efficient and thus save money in how we "deliver" an Augustana education, largely decided the footprint of general education requirements, the calendar year, and more. By then, those who proposed new majors and programs made their cases primarily based on how many students they stood to bring into the school; secondary (and sometimes nominal) was the effort to show the programs' compatibility with the liberal arts, rather broadly defined. Some will say that this was unavoidable because we live in an age where monetary and quantifiable value drives and eclipses talk of higher purposes. While that description is true, documents and deliberations from the 1960s through the 1980s show that pressures toward commodifying, credentialing, and other "present trends in the education picture" were no less clear to faculty then, faculty who *nonetheless* made a strong case for liberal education as *more valuable* (when properly, qualitatively valued) than a less mission-driven institution that perpetually "pivots" to offer "just-in-time" learning opportunities "responsive" to market forces.

FIRST-YEAR SEMINAR VS. EDMONDSON (1990S THROUGH THE GREAT RECESSION)

In 1997, Mark Edmondson, a literature professor at the University of Virginia, wrote a piece for *Harper's Magazine* titled "On the Uses of a Liberal Education: As Lite Entertainment for Bored College Students." In 2004, Augustana republished Edmondson's essay in *Liberal Arts Through the AGES*, Augustana's liberal studies first-year reader. Between 2006 and 2011, students read Edmondson's piece, did some modest research in the college's archives, and then responded in their own short essays.[44]

The date of Edmondson's publication (1997) was a high point of neoliberal culture in the United States, especially as that culture blended laissez-faire economics with liberal politics, both advanced through the internet revolution.[45] The same blending of economic and political liberalization showed up in American universities. There, in Edmondson's words, "left-liberal politics have collided with the ethos of consumerism."[46] Given this collision, education had become entertainment, the teacher a performer, and the student a passive consumer. He wrote that "university culture, like American culture writ large, is, to put it crudely, ever more devoted to consumption and entertainment, to the using up of goods and images." This "cool consumer worldview" turns students into passive consumers of education who play a particular part—that of "calmly self-interested though never greedy [people who are] attuned to the conventions, and ironic." They may volunteer at a soup kitchen from time to time (and then put it on their résumé), but they are devoid of passion and allergic to deep critique, including a critique of anything new ("a new need, a new product, a new show, a new style, a new generation"), and especially a critique of capitalism and consumer culture itself.[47]

Recall that the North Central review team noted a problem of proliferating courses at Augustana in 1975. Two decades later, Edmondson noted how the marketization of education put pressure on all liberal arts colleges to relax requirements and multiply options. Edmondson admits that "there are some good reasons for introducing more choice into curricula," but, he says, it also "jibes with a tendency to serve—and not to challenge—the students." He notices too that students can "shop" for classes for multiple weeks and drop the ones they do not like; they can withdraw from a course that they would otherwise fail with only an "innocuous 'W' on their transcripts." There is also a "widening elective leeway" that enables students to avoid professors or programs that they do not like, which incentivizes professors and programs not to become unlikeable and thus disposable. Choices and options are good, but their multiplication can undercut opportunity to learn commitment, grit, and even life lessons about how and when to fail. According to Edmondson: "A happy consumer is, by definition, one with multiple options, one who can always have what he [or she] wants. And since a course is something the students and their parents have bought and paid for, why can't they do with it pretty much as they please?"[48]

Edmondson also reflects on "multiculturalism" and "political correctness"—those key ciphers for 1990s progressivist university politics. He notes that within the consumerist environment, the celebration of racial and cultural differences slips into a chic appreciation for only those particular differences that university faculty and students find most attractive and least challenging.[49] Edmondson likewise notes of "political correctness" that "raising the standard of civility and tolerance in the university has been . . . a very good thing" but observes that "the movement for urbane tolerance has devolved into an imperative against critical reaction." According to Edmondson, appreciating everyone while criticizing nothing has become all too easy and comfortable within higher education. Or again: being tolerant of others and open to diverse points of view has become yet another component of the university's cool consumerist worldview.[50]

Beginning in 2006, Augustana first-year students were asked to respond to Edmondson's essay, practicing one of various writerly responses and using some modest research into Augustana's historical archives in the process. Approximately a third of the students agreed with Edmondson; about a third countered his critique, and about a third gave a more nuanced (or ambiguous) response. A number of students concurred that what they called social life (Edmondson's "lite entertainment") had, by 2006–2011, become more predominant and divorced from academics compared with earlier eras in Augustana's history. Most students, however, regarded this as a good thing, many arguing that the holistic education vaunted by the school depended on robust extracurricular offerings. Many students compared admissions materials from their era with those sent by the school in earlier decades, concluding that, yes, the photos are glossier now and the marketing of Augustana more aggressive, but, they added, Augustana has always "sold" what it has to offer. (One student noted that in the early twentieth century, Augustana boasted of "a new $60,000 gymnasium, [the] finest college gym in Illinois."[51])

Whether they understood themselves as agreeing or disagreeing with Edmondson, many students confirmed his understanding of the curriculum and classroom as marketplaces, where professors and departments competed for student enrollment numbers and students browsed for educational items. Wrote one student: "I know many students who do not know what they want to do with their education yet, and are taking advantage of the Liberal Arts education to test all the waters" and "explore all their options." A number of students concurred that liberal arts encourages exploration, which is more dignified than mere self-interested shopping. Others were clear that shopping for the right major leading to the right career and chosen lifestyle is exactly the point: "Students need a good education in today's society to get a job after graduation in their specific field. Therefore, they think about what style of education they are receiving and if it is a good fit for them." One student claimed that the 1960s actually entailed more conformity, as every student expressed school spirit around homecoming. In 2011, they went on, students are rather "passionate about whatever they please and go in their own direction." Notice here the way students take personal exploration and the choosing of their own individual paths (according to "whatever they please") as evidence against Edmondson's charge that college has become a mass-marketed, consumer-friendly good. I think that it is closer to supporting evidence.

Some students critiqued their college for not marketing its "outstanding pre-med or business program" as much as "the new lacrosse field or the brand new dormitory." Others defended Augustana, which is "still sold based on educational purposes rather than for entertainment." Such critics and defenders essentially agreed that academics, rather than movie theaters and workout facilities, *should* be marketed.

Edmondson thinks the danger is almost the reverse. When education has become a product worth choosing, and the liberal arts a giant menu from which students order what they want, we essentially lose their nonquantifiable value.

A number of student responses suggested that, for them, the increased competition among and consumerism within colleges went hand in hand with women's liberation and/or racial justice and was thus justified, if not "progressive," in and of itself. One male student understood the amount of money being spent on nice dorm rooms to be the result of full female inclusion at Augustana. A second student admitted that, in 2011, Augustana was more focused on entertainment than in decades past. But compared with 1902, when Swedish was the only culture club, there were only two female sports, and morning prayer was mandatory, today "Augustana promotes cultural diversity"—presumably by offering an array of optional experiences that appeal to students of different backgrounds. A third student claimed that Augustana College admissions materials not only sold the school but also promoted diversity and inclusion: "In [2011] brochures, color is used very effectively and diversity is the bas[is] of all the pictures. Augustana prides itself on diversity and makes it clear with all the diverse groups of people used in [its] brochures."[52]

These neoliberal assumptions—the almost exclusive value of individual interests, education as a host of opportunities from which the student chooses, and the subtle association of consumer choice and open markets with civil rights and just communities—are strewn throughout the first-year papers written in 2006 and 2011. If anything of tone or substance changes when comparing responses before and after the financial crisis of 2008, it is the resignation with which the 2011 cohort wrote of the necessity of having to play by market rules when advertising Augustana, running it, or being a student within it. One football player admitted that many students went to college to have fun rather than to learn. Still, Augustana and other colleges should get them there by whatever means necessary—otherwise, the United States would "fall behind other world powers in creating innovative technologies." One student incisively analyzed the recent turn to emphasizing YOU (the prospective student) in admissions materials, focusing on ten promises that Augie can make for YOU!, as well as on

Augie Choice, a program that promises to take each student wherever she or he wants to go. All this confirms Edmondson's observations about a commoditized education that maximizes options and opportunities for each student-consumer. Still, the student replied, "we live in an ever changing society and anyone who isn't willing to change will not survive in the world." And then, as if the financial solvency of Augustana were a final end needing no further justification: "Schools are just doing what is best for them by attracting the most students with entertainment and excitement."

These assumptions that self-interest ("just doing what is best for them") is self-justifying and that staying financially solvent is a—if not the—final goal of liberal arts institutions were rather common among students who came of age during the financial recession and anxiously entered college in its prolonged wake. Some assumed that success spoke largely for itself. One student countered what she took to be Edmondson's charge that "all students are shallow" by referencing recent data about the record number of applications Augustana had received, which showed that the marketing techniques were working—"students want what Augustana has to offer."

This equation of financial necessity with high purpose characterized even some of the most thoughtful critiques of consumerism and its effect on higher education. One 2011 first-year student mounted a fairly incisive critique of Augustana recruitment materials, including the YOU rhetoric, which "plays up the authenticity claim." She also noticed how the footprint of the new multimillion-dollar student center would take literal space from the library and mental space from academics. Still, she says, all this is necessary, and therefore good. Marketing materials "want the consumer to feel as though they have choices and options at this school," while the new Center for Student Life will "add a dimension to the Augustana experience that will serve as an enticing addition for prospective students."[53] Her conclusion is a strange mixture of warning and resignation: "Whether for better or worse, advertising will continue to evolve and college marketing strategies will continue to adjust along with it." Her final sentence marks the stakes of such resignation: "If [or, one assumes, *when*] the current trends in college and university advertising continue, we could lose any academic merit altogether, replaced by the promise of an unforgettable college experience."

My analyses of how students responded to Edmondson's piece do not comment on the often high quality of writing and thinking with which they responded to a difficult prompt, one that asked them essentially to examine the water in which they were presently swimming (and had been swimming since they first enrolled in a high school Advanced Placement course or received an Augustana admissions Frisbee through the mail). My analyses rather try to show just how immersed both students and educators had become in neoliberal assumptions by the 2000s and just how difficult it is to critically examine those assumptions without also presupposing them. Whereas faculty from the late 1960s were able to see the dawn of the neoliberal arts and resist it by speaking of the value and purpose of an education that could not be reduced to individual return on investment, student responses from the 2000s largely show how pervasive, internalized, and normalized neoliberalism had become.

And how about all of us—faculty, administration, the board of trustees, and students—more than a decade later, in this twilight of the neoliberal era? Are we, to use President Tredway's language from forty-five years ago, able to carve a path between the "pure" liberal arts and simple trust that general education requirements will meet liberal arts goals while attractive majors proliferate? That narrow third path "meet[s] the central questions" about the value and purpose of liberal arts "head on"[54] Are we, to use the more recent anthropological language, able to create symbiotic spaces "between neoliberal corporatism and a romantic ideal of the liberal arts"[55]—spaces of non-capitalist relations and deep deliberation about our collective purpose? And finally, what are we to make of the fact that 1960s professors arguing for renewed commitment to Lutheran liberal arts said far too little about social justice, racial healing, and environmental restoration as part of the "purposes and goals of Augustana," while turn-of-the-century students, however schooled by market forces, do explicitly write about the values of diversity and equity? Has neoliberalism, in fact, done better than Lutheran liberal arts at including those once excluded from higher education?

THE LAST AND NEXT FIFTEEN YEARS

A full answer to these questions depends on a perspective available sometime in the future. I conclude this chapter by indicating some recent opportunities, partially missed and partially met, for renewing the Lutheran liberal arts at Augustana, especially as we seek equity and justice for all.

At the 2022 national NetVUE conference, Eddie Glaude Jr., the distinguished scholar of African American studies, pleaded with the audience: "We have got to argue."[56] In other words, said Glaude, those of us in higher education have to disagree and then keep deliberating—even across political and racial lines—about what the liberal arts are for, and for whom.

Over the past fifteen years, Augustana faculty and administrators have indeed argued about Lutheran liberal arts, sometimes deliberatively and productively. One example is when we deliberated about whether to add a bachelor of science in engineering (BSE) to the curriculum, which would be Augustana's first professional degree program. Over a chain of long email exchanges spanning three days in May 2020, while trying to wrap up the most unprecedented semester in college history (having taught online while "sheltering in place" after the onset of COVID-19), faculty debated with deep concern about what liberal arts on this campus meant, whether the general education curriculum was synonymous with it, whether disciplinary expertise meant certain departments should teach certain requirements, and whether the footprint of any single major should be allowed to grow (based on professional standards or outside accrediting bodies) while general education and the chance to encounter other disciplines shrinks.

After a back and forth about a number of these issues, one business professor evoked the competitiveness of Augustana in a tight industry market as sufficient reason to pass the BSE proposal: "Augustana is currently in a highly competitive environment, and the environment will only become more competitive with the upcoming demographic cliff. . . . [From] a strategic point of view, the last place Augustana wants to be in five years . . . is a laggard when it comes to adopting engineering. . . . The engineering program could provide Augustana with a competitive advantage in these uncertain times."[57] Other faculty, however, did not allow the financial necessity of offering a BSE to have the final word. Rather, they continued to discuss and debate the role of disciplinary expertise, the merits of general education, the balance between traditional liberal arts and (pre)professional majors at Augustana, and much more. At the end of this exchange, the BSE proposal passed. At least as important as that outcome, however, was the ability and willingness for professors to deeply disagree and continue to deliberate about the value and purpose of Lutheran liberal arts, even and especially when financial necessity and the assumed inevitability of such programs were invoked.

By contrast, robust deliberation about the value and purpose of Augustana was largely missing two years later, when a "Working Group on Achieving a Sustainable Student-to-Faculty Ratio" submitted its findings to Provost Wendy Hilton Morrow on May 2, 2022.[58] Faced with serious budgetary restraints, the board of trustees had charged the college (through the provost's office) to return to an economically sustainable student-to-faculty ratio, after that ratio had declined from nearly 12:1 in 2016–17 to 11:1 in 2020–21, due in part to declining student enrollments. A small faculty "affinity group" interested in renewing shared governance raised a number of concerns about the seventeen "levers" that the working group had brainstormed—levers that, if pulled, promised to raise the faculty-to-student ratio by eliminating the need for the equivalent of eighteen full-time professors.[59] These concerns included the fact that the working group charged with brainstorming and vetting the seventeen levers was appointed by the provost, whereas the establishment of financial exigency and any response to it should be from an elected faculty governance body or another committee elected by the faculty, according to the American Association of University Professors.[60]

Members of the working group charged with brainstorming cost-saving levers had carried out their charge in careful and conscientious ways; they both gathered and distributed quantitative and qualitative feedback from the whole faculty on the "curricular levers" and "non-curricular levers" they drew up. The central problem, as I see it, was the missed opportunity to think about educational goals and then—and only then—to consider how to reallocate shrinking budgets to best meet those goals, as Ross Paulson urged his colleagues to do in 1985 in the face of an earlier demographic cliff and budget shortfall.[61] Instead, the working group nonjudgmentally brainstormed levers according to their cost-saving value (i.e., positions that could be cut) and then electronically surveyed the faculty as to whether pulling each lever should be explored further.

Faculty gave quantitative feedback (ranking their preferences on a five-point scale) and qualitative comments, and the working group faithfully tabulated, graphed, and summarized the responses. But the survey could only capture self-interested votes, not collective wisdom about the character and purpose of an Augustana education. Not surprisingly, given the structure of this process and lack of deliberation about ends, levers that garnered the highest votes were the ones that affected courses with the fewest professors to teach and those hardest to staff—namely, the second of a two-semester first-year inquiry sequence, an advising seminar for first-year students, senior inquiry, and the immersive January term. When Augustana pulls these or other levers, it will not be because we deliberated and decided that these components of our Lutheran liberal arts curriculum were less essential for fulfilling our purpose but because they are the least painful to cut, recruit the fewest students, or affect the fewest professors. The whole technocratic metaphor of objectively devising *levers*, collecting survey data about them, and later *pulling them*—letting market forces decide which positions are redundant—is a failure on our part to take moral responsibility for deciding what and whose work is essential to the aims and purpose of an Augustana education, and what (and whom) Augustana's mission can do without.[62]

Understandably, no one cheerfully discusses such difficult topics. Not doing so does not save jobs, however. It simply relies on market forces (the classes and departments that most students want to be in and most faculty want to teach in) to decide—so that we do not have to—what an Augustana education should be and do.

If deliberation about the liberal arts has been mixed in recent years, have today's faculty and administration deliberated more robustly about education-for-vocation, that chief marker of our Lutheran identity? Over the past fifteen years, our institution has run faculty development programs around our institutional vocation, including ALE (Augustana as Lutheran Education) and, more recently, New Faculty

Flourishing. We have updated our Five Faith Commitments and created a Presidential Center for Faith and Learning, the mission of which is to "lift up and live out" those commitments, including the commitment to vocational discernment. We have shepherded three major grant projects sponsored by NetVUE, the first of which brought together faculty and co-curricular leaders to structure vocational discernment among students, the second of which supported critical reflections on Augustana's institutional vocation and culminated in the book you are reading, and a third of which is presently connecting career preparation for business administration students with vocational reflection in the wider liberal arts curriculum. Despite all these programs and initiatives, I still do not know how to answer the question of whether Augustana has deliberated well and often about its Lutheran institutional calling to educate for vocation.

The difficulty seems to stem from two ideas associated with vocation, both of which fail to capture Luther's understanding of vocation as retrieved by Lutheran colleges and universities. First, it is common and easy to associate vocation with career and thus to assume that vocational reflection and discernment happens primarily among "undecided" students in order to get them to decide on a career and major. Vocational reflection within Augustana's CORE offices (Career, Opportunities, Research, and Exploration) has sometimes sounded like it is a precursor to career readiness, a sort of remedial help for less ambitious students or those with commitment issues. When vocational reflection is linked to choice of career (and that with choice of major), we forfeit all the countervailing Lutheran understandings of vocation explored above. One's calling ceases to be that through which one contributes to the flourishing of democracies and ecosystems, having been freed from the anxious demand to secure oneself, earn one's keep, and become self-sufficient. In the hands of anxious parents, anxious students, or anxious educators, a calling instead can mean employability and entrance into a desirable "lifestyle" as efficiently as possible, regardless of whether the career takes away from—rather than contributes to—the good of the whole.[63]

Over the past fifteen years, a number of policies and procedures and a change in the ways that we talk about them have accelerated the trend toward linking vocation with career and career with major choice and associating general education and liberal arts with unwanted requirements to be gotten out of the way. We have instituted a four-year graduation guarantee, the conditions of which depend on declaring a major early and not switching majors afterwards, thereby disincentivizing ongoing vocational reflection. We have structured prospective student visit days around intended major interests and multiplied the scholarships that departments award (again, conditioned on the student staying in that major), reserving presentations about liberal learning and vocational exploration to a few "undecided" students. We have redistributed scarce academic resources to newer programs that attract the most students and have even taken the high income potential of graduates in some majors as evidence of the discipline's value.[64]

At the same time, recent innovative programs such as ALIVE (Augustana Leaders in Vocational Exploration) have forestalled such trends, making Lutheran understandings of vocation more central to the college and to lifelong learning.[65] Currently, twelve to twenty-four sophomore ALIVE fellows are selected annually to live beside one another in residence halls, participate in a weekend retreat and weekly conversations about the gifts with which they serve others, and lead a "Pizza with Purpose" speaker series and other events for fellow students. Unlike vocational exploration sessions that help students get on track, ALIVE fellows from the first three cohorts have expressed gratitude for the time and space to slow down, to questions themselves and the path that they are on (often one that was assigned to them by parents, especially in the case of international students), and to imagine communal flourishing. ALIVE and its robust vocational reflection has become central to the sophomore experience and should prove invaluable within a new strategic plan that doubles down on community engagement, high-impact experiences, and the college's commitment to service of neighbors and neighborhoods.

Another problematic association with vocation creates something of an opposing ditch—a ditch that also trips up institutional callings to diversity, equity, and inclusion. Finding one's vocation still seems to be a privileged affair for many. Linked with personal meaning, fulfillment, and a transcendent sense of purpose, vocation can sound like a luxury—something offered to white, upper-middle-class students of yesterday but hardly available for the average student today. Here, vocation is associated with the liberal arts, that with a "free life of the mind," and is distinguished from the realities and necessities of the real world. First-generation and domestic students of color, who aim to survive college and obtain a measure of upward mobility, and international students, who often come to the United States to pursue careers in health care, engineering, or computer programming, can think of vocation (if they think of it at all) as something for "traditional" (white, comparably affluent) students. Educators concerned with access and retention of historically marginalized students often find Augustana's commitment to "offering a challenging education that develops the qualities of mind, spirit and body necessary for students to discern their life's calling of leadership and service" to be incongruous with, if not tone-deaf to, more pressing needs.[66]

There is truth to this. It is not always clear that Lutheran liberal arts institutions have done better than less mission-driven institutions at bringing about more equity in terms of access to and success within higher education. In *The End of College: Religion and the Transformation of Higher Education in the 20th Century*, Robert Wilson-Black notes that the mid-century movement we explored at the start of this chapter—that from liberal arts focused on character formation to the positivist university focused on "the scientific/practical/useful"—also entails some real benefits, namely, "from having an elite constituency to democratization."[67] In the college's history recounted above, we have seen that in the late 1960s, when Augustana faculty discussed at length the "central purposes of the College as a Christian, liberal arts institution," they failed to directly address racism, civil rights, the Vietnam War, and other issues related to social justice. Augustana recruited many more international and domestic students of color at the same time that it multiplied majors and became more careerist and transactional; indeed, students from the early 2000s understood the array of options as evidence of Augustana's inclusion and equity. As Robert Burke's chapter in this volume also indicates, too often invocations of final ends and purposes—of "the 'good life' that Augustana tries to uphold"—exclude rather than include lives that would otherwise contribute to communal flourishing.[68]

The question becomes whether the democratization of access to Lutheran liberal arts institutions can be achieved while also hanging onto—or even strengthening—a shared understanding of the purpose and values of those institutions. Are Lutheran liberal arts colleges and other historically white institutions able to become places of belonging for underrepresented and marginalized groups while remaining liberal arts colleges? Or is the liberalization of education only or best achieved by forfeiting talk of shared values and the common good, allowing each student to determine what is best for him/her/them and simply offering an array of majors and programs that attract the largest and most diverse set of students?

There are some signs of hope that a renewal of Lutheran liberal arts and the democratization of access to higher education can go hand in hand. At our institution, the most important example comes from the Augustana Prison Education Program (APEP), launched in 2021. Executive director Sharon Varallo decided early and wisely that the curriculum offered within the East Moline Correctional Center should be an Augustana liberal arts curriculum—despite pressure to make education more practical or "vocational" (in the sense of training for a trade) in order to give incarcerated students what they most need.

Varallo found inspiration and guidance from the Bard Prison Initiative (BPI), formerly codirected by Daniel Karpowitz, who writes this about liberal arts among marginalized students: "When it comes to education, the liberal arts are the first to be disparaged—especially, it is crucial to emphasize—for students who are poor, ethnically diverse, and, of course, incarcerated. Is this a function of sound policy and prudent concern for their long-term welfare? Or is it a function of bias against both liberal learning and the poor, shared by popular elected officials and many elite liberals?"[69] Karpowitz finds the second explanation too often to be true. He argues that the underserved deserve the full scope of a liberating, intellectually rich, and also practical college education. He thus argues that "there is too much emphasis in policy on 'training,' on [vocational-technical] education for poor people generally and especially on education for people in and exiting prison." Instead, he writes, "BPI has attempted to break down the facile boundaries between 'vocational' and 'liberal arts' education. We do this by cultivating students' deepest and broadest intellectual and creative capacities through diverse and rigorous liberal arts learning, while also creating smart, innovative approaches to more focused career training."[70]

Augustana is doing the same. APEP is presently serving its fourth cohort of incarcerated students, who take at least six "perspectives" (the cornerstone of our general education system); a second language; classes in quantitative reasoning, global diversity, and domestic diversity; a "reasoned examination of faith" course; and other key components of liberal learning as they also make progress in one of two majors: communication studies or American studies. One member of APEP's first class, David Staples, was released after serving twenty-nine years for a crime he did not commit, and then he finished his bachelor of arts on Augustana's main campus, majoring in psychology (Fig. 8.2). He recently began a graduate program in clinical psychology, following his calling to become a counselor serving those stuck within the carceral system.[71] The liberal, liberating arts have freed him and countless other students past and present for the flourishing of the common good.

As I write this, Augustana is also implementing a new strategic plan that may invite or require us to return to the central purposes of Lutheran liberal arts and include social and ecological justice among them. One of three central goals is to "connect with community partners,"

Fig. 8.2. David Staples at graduation, May 2024.
Photograph by Jason Smith. Contributed by David Staples.

"enhance neighborhoods around campus," and become an "engaged presence in the region."[72] That might entail revitalizing "college hill" to be more student-friendly and minimizing the blight that prospective families notice on their first trip into our rust-belt city. In this case, the goal would encompass a means for better attaining an unnamed true goal—the admission and retention of more students. On the other hand, we might interpret this call to work in and with the neighborhood according to Martin Luther's definition of vocation as a capable response to the neighbor for the flourishing of the neighborhood. In other words, we will live out the strategic plan in order to be relevant and attractive within the tight sector of higher education, or we will do so as members of the Rock Island community and the Upper Mississippi River watershed, and in order to contribute to the flourishing of those communities, which are racially and biologically diverse. In the words of Christine Jeske, the choice is between markets and meritocracy, on the one side, and membership and mutuality, on the other.[73]

Another pillar of the strategic plan—to prioritize engaged learning—charges us to "transform general education."[74] Because general education requirements constitute the liberal arts for many, and because most "gen ed revisions" entail *reducing* the number of required courses outside a student's major, some faculty in the arts and humanities are appropriately worried. To truly and qualitatively transform general education will require that we decide which particular learning outcomes, particular classes, and perhaps even particular foundational texts lead to broad liberal learning and to the flourishing of whole communities. Roosevelt Montás, former director of the Center for the Core Curriculum at Columbia University, argues that deliberating over and deciding on shared texts within the core curriculum is, in fact, a primary way to clarify "the values that inform curricular choices" *and* to include diverse perspectives both within those deliberating and in the canon deliberated about. Montás admits that decisions about a core curriculum—"weighted toward the past and therefore toward 'dead white males'"—and efforts toward diversity, equity, and inclusion rarely overlap, and often conflict. At Columbia University, however, "debates about exclusion, hegemony, and representation are an inherent aspect of the Core Curriculum. They are integral to, rather than a distraction from, the liberal education that the Core delivers." And so, according to Montás, "those of us who believe in the value of liberal education based on the study of important texts from the past—a core curriculum—must be prepared to explain our choices, defend them, and, when they don't stand up to scrutiny, revise them."[75] In other words (specifically Glaude's words), we are going to have to argue.

Regardless of whether Augustana follows Columbia and the Teagle Foundation in choosing a core curriculum as the primary means toward renewing the liberal arts, we should hear and heed Montás's broader twofold claim and calling. That claim is, first, that "in this time of fundamental change, perhaps our greatest need is for clarity and conviction about the values and purposes of higher education"; and, second, that "making liberal education available and accessible to all students is the most important contribution that higher education can make to [addressing social inequity]."[76]

Despite recent positive signs such as APEP, and regardless of how we decide to implement a new strategic plan, the question of whether diversity, equity, and inclusion work runs alongside or against any renewal of the liberal arts is a question that will only be answered in the next fifteen years. We will answer it, in this twilight of the neoliberal era, by focusing again on what and whom an Augustana education is for, as President Tredway pleaded with his faculty to do some forty-five years ago, at neoliberalism's dawn. Or, we will answer the question by *not* asking it, by *not* deliberating about values and purpose, convinced that staying financially solvent by any means necessary is the greatest gift we can offer the world.

Many progressivist understandings of diversity, equity, and inclusion tell a story of the "closed-ness," or exclusivity, of the past versus the openness, or inclusivity, of the present and future. I have tried to complicate that narrative to the degree that most of our implicit associations with openness rest on the neoliberal-consumerist relegation of any aims and purposes to individual preferences. Renewal of the common good—including social justice for humans and ecological wholeness and health for all creatures—depends on deliberating about, and then questing fiercely after, the final aims and goals of Lutheran liberal arts.

Notes

1. Letter from Betsey Brodahl to Conrad Bergendoff, October 1, 1958, Lilly Faculty Seminar: Faith and Values 1959–1962, box 44, AAR.

2. Brodahl, letter.

3. Brodahl, letter. For more on this historical moment in Augustana's history and the vocation of mentorship for college educators, see Mark Safstrom's chapter in the present volume.

4. May, "Professors," 244–53.

5. Augustana College Office of the President, "Five Faith Commitments" (2015).

6. Augustana College, Rankings and Recognition.

7. Meyer, "What's a Liberal Arts College Anyway?"

8. Schwehn, "The Value of Evoking Vocation," 17–25.

9. Ferrall, *Liberal Arts*, 186. According to the study reported by Ferrall, 18.6 percent of all graduates in 1986-87 majored in a "vocational" program; in 2007-2008, it climbed to 39.2 percent.

10. Hough and Kaul, "Symbiosis or Entrepreneurialism?," 118.

11. Hough and Kaul, "Symbiosis or Entrepreneurialism?," 118.

12. Augustana Bulletin, 1952.

13. Augustana Bulletin, 1952.

14. Augustana 94th Year: Record 1953–54, Announce 1954–55, Augustana College Special Collections, Rock Island, Illinois.

15. See Tredway, *Coming of Age*, 269–72; Lutheran School of Theology at Chicago, "History."

16. *On and Beyond the Mississippi*, 4. For further discussion, see Saftrom's chapter in the present volume.

17. Language depicting our "church relatedness" begins with the publication of the 1956–57 catalog. Earlier, the school was described as "church-owned," and later (in 1962), the catalog would add the hyphen between "church" and "related."

18. "Faculty Opinion on the Aims and Objectives of Augustana College: A Report on Faculty Discussions," January, 1966, box 1, AAR.

19. Luther, *Treatise on Christian Freedom*, 344.

20. Wendell Berry has used this definition of community as inclusive of the place itself throughout his writings, and again most recently in *The Need to Be Whole*, 241.

21. Ross E. Paulson references a 10 percent decline in student population spanning 1980–1985. Paulson, "Change and Structure in Liberal Arts Education," January 1985, Research, 1930–2001 and undated, box 34, RPP.

22. Augustana College, "Mission, Purpose and Goals."

23. Jodock et al., *Rooted and Open.*

24. Sandel, *Tyranny of Merit*, 62.

25. Sandel, *Tyranny of Merit*, 64–66.

26. Some of that influence is direct. Ronald Reagan ran for governor in 1966 and then for reelection in 1970 on the promise of dismantling California's free public college system. Schwarz, "Origin of Student Debt."

27. Public support for students attending Augustana is significant. When Illinois's Monetary Assistance Program (MAP) was put in limbo during state budget disputes in 2015–16, the college needed to draw on reserves to supplement student financial aid packages. See "College Explores MAP grant," *Augustana Observer*, February 7, 2016.

28. Sandel, *Tyranny of Merit*, 100.

29. Gerstle, *Rise and Fall of the Neoliberal Order*, 141–49.

30. Sandel, *Tyranny of Merit*, 26–27.

31. Deresiewicz, "Neoliberal Arts."

32. Hough and Kaul, "Symbiosis or Entrepreneurialism?," 107, 123.

33. Kaul, "Critical Pedagogies of Hope," 27–40.

34. Kaul, "Critical Pedagogies."

35. Hough and Kaul, "Symbiosis or Entrepreneurialism?," 123.

36. Tredway, *Coming of Age*, 208, 211.

37. Tredway, *Coming of Age*, 209–211.

38. "Faculty Opinion." The fact that calendar and curricular reform was Augustana's focus throughout the 1960s says much about its position within wider American culture. In the words of one alumnus who participated in a Racial Healing Circle in 2020–21: "The 1960s didn't make it onto Augustana's campus." Author's personal notes, Racial Healing Circles.

39. "Faculty Opinion."

40. Report of the Evaluation Study Committee, April 20, 1970, 2–3, as cited by Paulson, "Change and Structure."

41. Paulson, "Change and Structure," 12–13, 7.

42. Paulson, "Change and Structure," 10.

43. Paulson, "Change and Structure," 18–19.

44. "LSFY student essays" from Liberal Studies First Year (LSFY) classes by Gillette, Hare, and Leech (2006–2010), box 24, AET. Because these professors shared a common prompt, I treat their students as a group, distinguishing papers written before or after the financial fallout of 2008.

45. Gerstle, *Rise and Fall*, 161–70.

46. Edmondson, "On the Uses of Liberal Education," 44.

47. Edmondson, "On the Uses," 36–38.

48. Edmondson, "On the Uses," 40.

49. Compare Eboo Patel's repeated mantra, which is also the title of one of his books: *Diversity Is Not Just the Differences You Like.*

50. Edmondson, "On the Uses," 43.

51. "LSFY student essays."

52. See Monica M. Smith's analysis of Black students' demands in chapter 4.

53. The student is quoting an opinion piece in *Augustana Observer*, September 29, 2011.

54. Report of the Evaluation Study Committee, in Paulson, "Change and Structure," 10.

55. Hough and Kaul, "Symbiosis or Entrepreneurialism?," 123.

56. Glaude, "Keynote Address."

57. Author email correspondence with anonymous source, May 12, 2020.

58. Crouch et al., Report from the Working Group, 3.

59. The affinity group prepared a motion and case study for faculty review in May 2022. The motion was "to call on faculty, Academic Affairs, the Presidential Cabinet, and the Board of Trustees to restore a collective sense of shared governance at Augustana."

60. American Association of University Professors, "Role of the Faculty"; American Association of University Professors, "Recommended Institutional Regulations."

61. Paulson, "Change and Structure."

62. I am working from a broadly Aristotelian or teleological virtue ethic, where the *telos*, or proper end of an activity or tradition, provides norms for ethical reflection and action. Sandel essentially agrees with Eddie Glaude Jr: We have got to argue about what and for whom education (and democracy) is for.

63. Karma, "'Meritocracy Trap,' Explained."

64. In 2023 a faculty member supported a case for needing to expand the "footprint" of a major by citing that graduates from that program often earned $100,000 annually right out of college.

65. Presidential Center for Faith and Learning, "Augustana Leaders in Vocational Exploration."

66. Augustana College, "Mission, Purpose, and Goals."

67. Wilson-Black, *End of College*, 42–43.

68. See chapter 6 in this volume.

69. Karpowitz, *College in Prison*, 18.

70. Karpowitz, *College in Prison*, 18, 19.

71. Campbell and Barr, "From Wrongfully Convicted," *Augustana Observer*, May 6, 2023.

72. Augustana College, "Bold and Boundless."

73. Jeske, "Overturning for the Common Good."

74. Augustana College, "Bold and Boundless."

75. Montás, *Rescuing Socrates*, 214.

76. Montás, *Rescuing Socrates*, 225.

EPILOGUE

ANDREA KATHRYN TALENTINO

Joan Didion said, "We tell ourselves stories in order to live."[1] In a complex and often inexplicable world, stories give comfort and provide direction and purpose as we make sense of the world around us. As a result, our stories reflect both our best and worst impulses. They contain prejudice and hope, fear and promise, assurance and uncertainty. Indeed, they are fed by contraries, for as poet William Blake said, "Without contraries there is no progression. Attraction and repulsion, reason and energy, love and hate, are necessary to human existence."[2] By imposing this "narrative line upon disparate images," we make sense of what we experience in a way that is most meaningful to us but that tends to be least discordant with our own preferences and needs.[3] In this twin reality we confront our fears and aspirations, sometimes one and the same, in ways that force us to reflect on where we have been as well as where we might go. As this book shows, our stories exist at every level, from the national to the personal, and they change over time because we even tell ourselves stories about our stories. As our lived experience changes, so too does the sense we make of it.

As my predecessor in the office of president, Steven Bahls, notes in the foreword, the story of Augustana College is enriched precisely by highlighting where it has been less than heroic. The stories of exclusion, marginalization, and even outright prejudice are as essential to its history as are stories that laud the institution. The shared knowledge of where the college community has not served its mission well reinforces what I think is a hallmark of Augustana today—the commitment to mission that every employee brings to their work. As part of that commitment to mission, faculty and staff are not afraid of learning what has been done poorly in the past. Indeed, they welcome those stories so that they can redirect outcomes for the future. I have never known a campus where the commitment to serving students well has been so prominent among all employees and where there has been so much openness to learning both what has been done well and what has not.

One of the most important parts of Augustana's story, and one of the key factors that drew me to the institution, is the Lutheran commitment to "serve thy neighbor." While that seems simple on its face, the chapters in this volume show us the many ways in which neighborliness and serving can be principles that guide assistance to others even as they are narrowly defined so as to benefit some but not all. The concept of a boundary is a particularly important one, not only for the ways in which the idea entwines with possession and dispossession, but also because it expresses how the college defines itself today in the midst of Rock Island. It is now fully an American institution, not an immigrant one, yet Rock Island remains a sanctuary for immigrants from many continents. The college's perspective has changed over time, but the tension between abstract and community-based ideals continues, and the responsibility incumbent on the college community to understand how we will be perceived across cultural differences is greater than ever. Navigating a boundary to be both porous and meaningful, so that students recognize our campus and yet also see it as part of the larger community, is a challenge we have not yet fully figured out.

The stories that make up the current saga convey much knowledge, and this knowledge contains a kind of weight that is measured on a scale of responsibility and accountability. To take the knowledge from the preceding stories along on the journey into the next decades means accepting the worthwhile burden of envisioning a new and stronger institution, ready to meet those challenges of which we are aware, as well as those we cannot yet see. Most important for me is to continue Augustana's commitment to education with a purpose: producing impactful citizens who can contribute to the common good. That commitment has sometimes blinded our own, and other institutions, to errors and marginalization on campus, which means that we must all be mindful going forward for how we treat our own community as well as others.

In reading the contributions in this volume, I cannot help but wonder how a task such as this might have been approached by Augustana leaders a few decades ago. How would the tumult of the 1960s or the rise of neoliberalism in the 1990s affect their saga? In the vein of Sarah Lashley's essay, to what extent did those who participated in the outmigration from Rock Island in the 1970s and since consider what broader trends they were contributing to? I hope that these pages have assisted us, will continue to assist us, in being honest and open about the potential and prejudices of our stories. The story of Latinos/x Unidos, which provided space for the marginalized even while opening new points of friction, is a good example. That story underscores the most important point of a saga—creating space for conversation and debate.

As we look forward into Augustana's next decade, its stories will be shaped by our strategic direction and our commitment to focus on three things—engaged learning, which seeks to modernize our essential liberal arts foundation in creative ways; student support, which is and always has been essential in ensuring success but has sometimes been observed more in the breach, as the stories here suggest; and community partnership, which envisions direct partnership with Rock Island and an understanding that the campus is a part of this community, not an island removed from it. These three directions provide pathways for exciting initiatives that showcase why the liberal arts remain so essential for success in today's fluid world of work. They also remind us that truly seeing people and places and recognizing their strengths and potential should be a hallmark of the institution. Blake's focus on contraries warns us that efforts to include can also exclude. A commitment to Swedish heritage and to community as we understand it at any moment in time, for example, can lead us to overlook or dismiss points of commonality in the midst of difference and variation.

We have been fortunate that some groups, such as Latinos/x Unidos and the Black Student Union, have insisted on being seen and heard and have enriched the campus in the process. As the college becomes increasingly diverse with both domestic and international students, it should also be accountable for reconsidering and reassessing traditions in light of new perspectives arriving on campus. Already this is happening slowly. We celebrate the Sankta Lucia festival every December, and we also now have a Step Team that performs at our spring festival. How much more can our story still change as we incorporate students from across the United States and, indeed, the world?

To answer that question well we must recognize evolution as a strength. There is messiness in change, to be sure; stories need to evolve. That is not to suggest that Augustana's existing stories are bad, though this volume certainly shows some limitations, but it does mean that continued change is important. Further, this volume *helps* us grow—by chronicling what we have been, it also shows us who we can be. Ken Saro-Wiwa, an Ogoni activist, knew well the power of words to catalyze change. Saro-Wiwa had served in the Nigerian government but resigned to focus full time on his fiction and playwriting because he believed that his greatest ability to propel change came through his writing. Saro-Wiwa said, "The writer cannot be a mere storyteller; he cannot be a mere teacher; he cannot merely x-ray society's weaknesses, its ills, its perils. He or she must be actively involved shaping its present and its future."[4]

Augustana College seeks to answer Saro-Wiwa's call. Although the institution is not a writer in the true sense, the stories in this volume reveal how it has created stories that shape the past and so defined pathways to the future. This is a propitious moment for this volume to be published, because for Augustana, as for many institutions, examination of the past helps inform new strategic directions. As we move forward, we do so with some essential principles at the top of mind. First, being a good neighbor starts at home. We cannot connect well with the community around us if we are not first connecting, and including, all the members of our immediate community. Second, the pursuit of vocation is transformative and has defined the Augustana experience for 163 years. Students learn who they are and what they can be during their college years, and we need to preserve and extend that experience to all. And finally, action and reflection should be equal parts of our focus. As we move forward, we must continue to reflect on our strengths and our weaknesses and let this reflection inform our actions.

Ken Saro-Wiwa ultimately devoted his writing full time to advancing the Ogoni cause, until he was hanged by the government for his activism in 1995. But his story does not end there. He reminds us that the value of writing is to help us shape what comes next. To do that well we must look behind in order to look forward and embrace all the ways in which we have failed our aspirations. That is the gift that this book gives us. In doing so we can advance our understanding of liberal arts institutions in ways that reinforce mission and purpose and improve our ability to help all to live our commitments to service and neighbor.

Notes

1. Didion, "White Album," 11.
2. Blake, *Marriage of Heaven and Hell.*
3. Didion, "White Album," 11.
4. Saro-Wiwa, "Trying Times."

BIBLIOGRAPHY

CONTRIBUTORS

INDEX

BIBLIOGRAPHY

Newspapers

The Augustana Observer (Rock Island, Illinois)
The Chicago Defender (Chicago, Illinois)
The Iowa Bystander (Des Moines, Iowa)
The Moline Daily Dispatch (Moline, Illinois)
The New York Times (New York, New York)
The Quad-City Times (Davenport, Iowa)
The Rock Island Argus (Rock Island, Illinois)

Manuscript Collections

Augustana College Special Collections, Rock Island, Illinois

AAR	MSS 42, Augustana College Office of Academic Affairs Records
AET	MSS 240, Academic Essays and Theses
AFC	MSS 243, Augustana Faculty and Committees Records
CWS	MSS 6, Clarence Woodrow Sorensen Papers
HSJ	MSS 166, Harry S. B. Johnson Papers
JTT	MSS 7, John Thomas Tredway Papers
LUR	MSS 409, Latinx Unidos Records
OHC	MSS 91, Oral History Collection
RPP	MSS 144, Ross Paulson Papers

Primary Sources

Abernathy, Jeff, on behalf of Steven C. Bahls. "Statement of President Steve Bahls Regarding Recent Homophobic Incidents at Augustana College," October 4, 2005. Faculty advisor binder, 2004–2009 and undated, box 1, MSS 362, Augustana PRISM Alliance Records. Special Collections, Augustana College, Rock Island, Illinois.

"African Actor Ordered Deported, Attempts Suicide." *Jet Magazine*, June 11, 1953.

American Association of University Professors. "Recommended Institutional Regulations on Academic Freedom and Tenure." Reports and Publications. 2023 revision. https://www.aaup.org/report/recommended-institutional-regulations-academic-freedom-and-tenure.

American Association of University Professors. "The Role of the Faculty in Conditions of Financial Exigency." Reports and Publications. July 2013. https://www.aaup.org/report/role-faculty-conditions-financial-exigency.

American Indian Chicago Conference. *Declaration of Indian Purpose: The Voice of the American Indian*. Proceedings of the American Indian Chicago Conference. University of Chicago, 1961. https://files.eric.ed.gov/fulltext/ED030518.pdf.

Armstrong, Perry. *The Black Hawk War*. H. W. Rokker, 1887.

Association of American Universities. "Tax-Exempt Status of Universities and Colleges." October 2, 2022. https://www.aau.edu/key-issues/tax-exempt-status-universities-and-colleges.

"Augie Students Pleased with 'Symposium' Results." *Illinois Lutheran*, February–March 1969.

Augsburg University. "American Indian Full Tuition Recognition Program." Accessed November 6, 2024. https://www.augsburg.edu/american-indian-recognition/.

Augsburg University. "Reconciling in Christ Statement." Accessed November 24, 2024. https://www.augsburg.edu/multicultural-life/programs/lgbtqia/reconciling-christ-statement/.

Augustana Bulletin, 1952. Augustana College. Augustana College Special Collections, Rock Island, Illinois.

Augustana College. "Advising." Accessed August 22, 2022. https://www.augustana.edu/academics/advising.

Augustana College. "Bold and Boundless: Augustana's Strategic Plan (2024–2029)." https://www.augustana.edu/about-us/president/strategicplan.

Augustana College. "Mission, Purpose, and Goals." Accessed March 9, 2024. https://www.augustana.edu/about-us/mission.

Augustana College. "Rankings and Recognition." Accessed March 1, 2024, https://www.augustana.edu/about-us/rankings.

Augustana College. "The Search for a Vice President of Diversity, Equity, and Inclusion." October 3, 2018. www.augustana.edu/files/2017-10/VP_Diversity_Search_Oct3.pdf.

Augustana College. "Upper Mississippi Center." Accessed May 30, 2023. https://www.augustana.edu/academics/core/upper-mississippi-center.

Augustana College and BLDD Architects and Sasaki Associates. "Campus Assessment and Capital Priorities." 2005.

Augustana College Board of Directors. "Record of Proceedings of the Board of Directors XXXV," January 16, 1873. Box 4, MSS 242, Augustana College Board of Trustees Records. Augustana College Special Collections, Rock Island, Illinois.

Augustana College Board of Trustees. "Authentically Augustana: A Strategic Plan for a Premier Liberal Arts College." January 2005. https://www.augustana.edu/files/2017-03/strategicplan.pdf.

Augustana College Board of Trustees. "Strategic Competency." Undated handout. Augustana College Special Collections, Rock Island, Illinois.

Augustana College Catalog 2008. "Academic Policies: Fall Connection."

Augustana College Office of Human Resources. "Section II: The Augustana Workplace." In *All Employee Handbook*. Accessed October 29, 2022. https://www.augustana.edu/about-us/offices/hr/handbook/section2-workplace.

Augustana College Office of the President. "Diversity Efforts Inventory." Accessed May 3, 2023. https://www.augustana.edu/about-us/president/inventory.

Augustana College Office of the President. "The Five Faith Commitments of Augustana College." 2004, revised in 2015. https://augustana.edu/about-us/president/commitments.

"Augustana Responds to 'Racist' Action," *Illinois Lutheran*, December 1979.

Bahls, Steven. "Beyond Labels, May 1, 2019." Electronic communication, April 26, 2019.

Bartholomew, Edward Fry. "A Centenarian Answers a Question . . . What Are We Here For?" *The Lutheran Companion*, March 20, 1946, 12–13.

Bergendoff, Conrad. Letter to John W. Morland, January 7, 1944. Folder 9, box 8, MSS 5, Conrad Bergendoff Papers. Special Collections, Augustana College, Rock Island, Illinois.

Bergendoff, Conrad. "Our Lofty Destiny." Funeral address for Dr. Edward Fry Bartholomew, June 12, 1946. Biographical Information, box 49, MSS 19, Edward Fry Bartholomew Papers. Special Collections, Augustana College, Rock Island, Illinois.

"Black Minister Finds Challenge at All-White Berks Congregation." *Morning Call*, February 9, 1989. https://www.mcall.com/1989/02/09/black-minister-finds-challenge-at-all-white-berks-congregation/.

Bremer, Fredrika. *Homes of the New World: Impressions of America*. Vol. 1, translated by Mary Howitt. Harper & Bros., 1853.

Brooks, Devin. "High School Student's Nationally-Recognized Artwork Gets Turned into Rock Island Mural." WQAD, August 19, 2021.

"Bullseye Brigade." South Shore High School, 1955. Accessed through U.S. School Yearbooks, 1880–2012. Ancestry.com.

Burtis, Samuel, Sr. Will Records, 1838–1938. Iowa District Court (Jackson County), Probate Place, Jackson, Iowa.

Chief Commander Ebenezer Obey & His International Brothers Band. "Ajala-Alhaja." Track 2, *Board Members*, 1972, album.

Citizen Band of Potawatomi v. United States, 391 F.2d 614 (Ct. Cl. 1968),

April 14, 1967. https://law.justia.com/cases/federal/appellate-courts/F2/391/614/133982.

Committee on the Status of Women. Policy statement, November 1974, 1–8. Folder 1, box 1, MSS 383, Nancy Huse papers. Special Collections, Augustana College, Rock Island, Illinois.

Crouch, Michelle, et al. Report from the Working Group on Achieving a Sustainable Student-to-Faculty Ratio, Submitted to Provost Wendy Hilton Morrow and the Faculty Council of Augustana College, May 19, 2022. Google Document, Augustana Shared Drive.

Dodge, Kat. "St. Olaf Announces New Financial Aid Opportunity for Indigenous Students." St. Olaf College, October, 14, 2024. https://wp.stolaf.edu/news/st-olaf-announces-new-financial-aid-opportunity-for-indigenous-student.

Dooley, Jenny. "Augustana College Welcomes Same-Sex Ceremonies." Northern Public Radio, November 29, 2012. https://www.northernpublicradio.org/education/2012-11-29/augustana-college-welcomes-same-sex-ceremonies.

Dunbar, Paul Laurence. *The Complete Poems of Paul Laurence Dunbar.* Dodd, Mead, 1922. Project Gutenberg ebook 18338. https://www.gutenberg.org/cache/epub/18338/pg18338-images.html.

Eastern Iowa Community Colleges. "Get More Out of Your Education." Accessed June 28, 2023. https://eicc.edu/more/.

Ekberg, Kyle. "Half a Century of Growth and Success: Sports and Academics at Augie." Interview with Paul Olsen, April 7, 2021. Augustana Historical Society, Augustana College YouTube Channel. https://www.youtube.com/watch?v=9Nrq_4Wb8IA.

Evangelical Lutheran Church in America. *Social Statement: Our Calling in Education.* 2007. https://www.elca.org/faith/faith-and-society/social-statements/education.

"Five Faith Commitments: Introduction: The College's Roots for Today's Students." Accessed May 4, 2019. https://augustana.edu/about-us/president/commitments.

Glass Perez, Kristen. "Tribute to Javier Perez, Jr." Unpublished speech delivered at Augustana College Latinx Unidos 25th anniversary, October 14, 2017, Rock Island, Illinois.

Glaude, Eddie, Jr. "Keynote Address." National Network for Vocation in Undergraduate Education Conference, Dallas, Texas, March 24, 2022.

Goozner, Merrill. "Quad Cities Try to Rebound." *Chicago Tribune*, June 15, 1987. https://www.chicagotribune.com/news/ct-xpm-1987-06-15-8702150726-story.html.

Gustavus Adolphus College. "President's Council for Indigenous Relations." President's Office. Accessed November 6, 2024. https://gustavus.edu/president/pcir/.

Harper, Frances E. W. "Vashti." In *Atlanta Offering: Poems*. George S. Ferguson, 1895, 45. Project Gutenberg ebook 69248. https://www.gutenberg.org/cache/epub/69248/pg69248-images.html.

Henry Hull Estate. Estate Case Files, 1834–1959. Rock Island County (Illinois), County Clerk, Probate Place, Rock Island, Illinois.

"Holistic and Intrusive Advising Approaches for Student Retention." PowerPoint slide presentation. University of Pittsburgh. Accessed August 22, 2022. https://www.personaled.pitt.edu/sites/default/files/virtual_lunch_and_learn_holistic_and_intrusive_advising_approaches_for_student_retention.pdf.

Hughes, Langston. "I, Too." In *The Collected Poems of Langston Hughes*. Alfred Knopf, 1994. Republished by Academy of American Poets. https://poets.org/poem/i-too.

Illinois State Archives. "Illinois Public Land Tract Sales Database." Office of the Illinois Secretary of State. https://apps.ilsos.gov/isa/landSalesSearch.do.

Jackson, Ava. "The Augie Bubble." *Her Campus*, November 27, 2023. https://www.hercampus.com/school/augustana/the-augie-bubble/.

Jodock, Darrell. "The Third Path: Gustavus Adolphus College and the Lutheran Tradition." 2002. https://gustavus.edu/faith/pdf/Third_Path_Article.pdf.

Jodock, Darrell, Jason Mahn, Martha Stortz, and Mark Wilhelm. *Rooted and Open: The Common Calling of the Network of ELCA Colleges and Universities*. Network of ELCA Colleges and Universities, 2018.

Johnson, Joyce. "Recollections of My Time as Organist of Spelman College." *Vox Humana*, January 17, 2021. http://voxhumanajournal.com/johnson2021.html.

"J. Thomas Tredway (1935–2022)." Augustana College. Accessed July 1, 2022. https://www.augustana.edu/about-us/president/presidents/tredway.

King, Martin Luther, Jr. "The Birth of a New Age." Address at the fiftieth anniversary of Alpha Phi Alpha, August 11, 1956. https://kinginstitute.stanford.edu/king-papers/documents/birth-new-age-address-delivered-11-august-1956-fiftieth-anniversary-alpha-phi.

Kosnick, Kiki. "What Does It Mean That Augustana Is a Lutheran College?" Augustana Presidential Center for Faith and Learning, 2019. https://www.augustana.edu/academics/centers/faith.

Luther, Martin. *Martin Luther's Treatise on Christian Freedom [The Freedom of a Christian]*. In *Luther's Works*. Vol. 31, *Career of the Reformer I*, edited by Harold J. Grimm and trans. Helmut T. Lehmann. Muhlenberg Press, 1957 [1520].

Mahn, Jason A. "Educating Whole Persons for Wholeness." In *So That All May Flourish: The Aims of a Lutheran Higher Education*, edited by Marcia J. Bunge, Jason A. Mahn, and Martha E. Stortz. Fortress Press, 2023.

Ma-ka-tai-me-she-kia-kiak. *Life of Ma-ka-tai-me-she-kia-kiak, or Black Hawk*. J. B. Patterson, 1833.

McVey, Kurt. "How Nina Chanel Abney Is Championing the Black Lives Matter Movement with a Paintbrush." *Vanity Fair*, October 15, 2015. https://www.vanityfair.com/culture/2015/10/nina-chanel-abney-painter-always-a-winner-interview.

Meyer, Chelsea. "What's a Liberal Arts College Anyway?" *Blogustana*, November 6, 2019. https://www.augustana.edu/blog/whats-liberal-arts-college-anyway.

Office of Residential Life. "Living on Campus at Augustana College." Augustana College, n.d.

"Our Mission." Reconciling Works. Accessed September 9, 2023. https://www.reconcilingworks.org/about-2/.

"Our Philosophy." Lilly Endowment, Inc. Accessed August 27, 2023. https://lillyendowment.org/about/our-philosophy/.

Presidential Center for Faith and Learning. "Augustana Leaders in Vocational Exploration." Accessed October 2023. https://www.augustana.edu/academics/centers/faith/alive.

Pupillo, Melinda. Morning Devotion. All-faculty retreat, August 30, 2022. Augustana College.

Rae, Tushar. "Teaching the Whole Child: Longfellow-Augustana Partnership Brings the Liberal Arts to Primary Education." *River Cities' Reader*, July 29, 2009. https://www.rcreader.com/news/teaching-whole-child-longfellow-augustana-partnership-brings-liberal-arts-primary-education.

Ratified Indian Treaty 43: Sauk and Fox—St. Louis in the District of Louisiana, November 3, 1804. Record Group 11, General Records of the United States Government, 1776–2006, Indian Treaties Series, 1789–1869. National Archives, Washington, DC. https://catalog.archives.gov/id/7891102.

Ratified Indian Treaty 82: Ottawa, Chippewa, and Potawatomi—St. Louis, August 24, 1816. Record Group 11, General Records of the United States

Government, 1776–2006, Indian Treaties Series, 1789–1869. National Archives, Washington, DC. https://catalog.archives.gov/id/170281487.

Recital program. Correspondence, 1927–28, box 1, MSS 230, Augustana Conservatory of Music. Augustana Special Collections, Rock Island, Illinois.

"Reflecting on Thomas Tredway's 39 Years at Augustana." *Augustana Magazine*, Winter 2003. Republished April 11, 2022. https://www.augustana.edu/about-us/news/reflecting-thomas-tredways-39-years-augustana.

"Robert Burke: More Than I Imagined." Augustana College. Accessed July 8, 2023. https://www.augustana.edu/after-augustana/stories/2020/robert-burke.

Rockety-I yearbooks. Augustana College. All are available in their original printed form in Augustana College Special Collections, and most are digitized and available online. https://collections.carli.illinois.edu/digital/collection/aug_rocketyi.

Rubin, Bonnie Miller. "Lutheran College Opens the Door to Same-Sex Wedding." *Chicago Tribune*, January 14, 2013. https://www.chicagotribune.com/news/ct-xpm-2013-01-14-ct-met-gay-marriage-religious-colleges-20130114-story.html.

Southwestern University. "Placing Memory." https://placingmemory.southwestern.edu/.

Spencer, J. W. "Reminiscences of Pioneer Life in the Mississippi Valley." In *The Early Day of Rock Island and Davenport: The Narratives of J.W. Spencer and J.M.D. Burrows*, edited by Milo Milton Quaife. R. R. Donnelley & Sons, 1942.

Terronez, Micaela. "Iowa History Month: Iowa's Early Barrios." *Des Moines Register*, March 28, 2021.

Tributes to Andrew Woods Williamson, 1906. Box 1, MSS 122, Williamson Family Papers. Augustana College Special Collections, Rock Island, Illinois.

Trinity Church. *Manual and Directory, 1898*. Trinity Church Records, box 20, MS 407, Congregation Records. Augustana College Special Collections, Rock Island, Illinois.

Tsagaris, Ellen. "The Cables and Their Connection with Augustana," 1988. Historical Research and Writings, box 21, MSS 203, Augustana Historical Society Records. Augustana College Special Collections, Rock Island, Illinois.

US Census Bureau. Bulletin, "Population: Illinois, Composition and Characteristics of the Population." *Fourteenth Census of the United States: 1920*, 19–20. https://www2.census.gov/library/publications

/decennial/1920/bulletins/demographics/population-il-composition-and -characteristics.pdf.

US Census Bureau. "Composition of the Population, for Cities and Villages of 10,000 or More." *Fifteenth Census of the United States: 1930*. Vol. 3, pt. 1, 630–31. United States Government Printing Office, 1932. https://www2.census.gov/library/publications/decennial/1930/population-volume-3/10612963v3p1ch05.pdf.

Waldenström, Paul Petter. *Nya Färder i Amerikas Förenta Stater*. Normans, 1902.

Williamson, Andrew Woods. "The Dakotan Languages, and Their Relations to Other Languages." *American Antiquarian*, January 1882. Project Gutenberg ebook 26529.

Secondary Sources

Ahmed, Sara. *On Being Included: Racism and Diversity in Institutional Life*. Duke University Press, 2012.

Àjàlá, Olabisi. *An African Abroad*. OlongoAfrica.com, 2022 [1963].

American Council on Education. "On the Importance of Diversity in Higher Education." ACE Board of Directors, June 2012.

Anderson, Elijah. *Black in White Space: The Enduring Impact of Color in Everyday Life*. University of Chicago Press, 2022.

Anderson, Gary M., and Dolores T. Martin. "The Public Domain and Nineteenth-Century Transfer Policy." *Cato Journal* 6, no. 3 (1987): 905–23.

Anderson, Philip J. "Swedish-American 'College Mania' in the Nineteenth Century." In *Nordics in America: The Future of Their Past*, edited by Odd S. Lovoll. Norwegian-American Historical Association, 1993.

Araiza, Lauren. "Black Power and the Mills Girl: Gender and the Black Campus Movement at Mills College, 1967–69." *Journal of Civil and Human Rights* 5, no. 2 (2019): 1–33. https://doi.org/10.5406/jcivihumarigh.5.2.0001.

Arden, G. Everett. *Augustana Heritage: A History of the Augustana Lutheran Church*. Augustana Press, 1963.

Baker, Zak. "Illinois' Augustana College to Allow Same-Gender Ceremonies on Campus." ReconcilingWorks, December 3, 2012. https://www.reconcilingworks.org/news-2012-12-03/.

Bald, Vivek. "Between Hindoo and Negro." In *Bengali Harlem and the Lost Histories of South Asian America*. Harvard University Press, 2013.

Baldwin, Davarian. *In the Shadow of the Ivory Tower: How Universities Are Plundering Our Cities*. Bold Type Books, 2021.

Barton, H. Arnold. "Swedish Visitors' Views of Swedish-American Education." In *Scandinavian Immigrants and Education in North America*, edited by Philip J. Anderson, Dag Blanck, and Peter Kivisto. Swedish-American Historical Society, 1995.

Bergendoff, Conrad. *Augustana . . . a Profession of Faith: A History of Augustana College, 1860–1935*. Augustana College Library, 2010 [1969].

Berrey, Ellen. "Why Diversity Became Orthodox in Higher Education, and How It Changed the Meaning of Race on Campus." *Critical Sociology* 37, no. 5 (2011): 573–96. https://doi.org/10.1177/089692051038.

Berry, Wendell. *The Need to Be Whole: Patriotism and the History of Prejudice*. Shoemaker, 2022.

Blake, William. *The Marriage of Heaven and Hell*. 1790. Project Gutenberg ebook 45315. https://www.gutenberg.org/cache/epub/45315/pg45315-images.html.

Blanck, Dag. Introduction to *Looking West: Three Essays on Swedish-American Life by Jules Mauritzson*, edited by Conrad Bergendoff, Ann Boaden, and Dag Blanck. Augustana Historical Society, 1994.

Bluemle, Stefanie R. "Augustana and the Civil Rights Movement." 2010. https://www.augustana.edu/about-us/sesquicentennial/civil-rights.

Bluemle, Stefanie R. "GI Bill Students Change Augustana Outlook." 2010. https://www.augustana.edu/about-us/sesquicentennial/g-i-bill.

Boaden, Ann. *Light and Leaven: Women Who Shaped Augustana's First Century*. Augustana College Library, 2011.

Boaden, Ann. "Well, Well . . . Plumbing Our Depths, Telling Our Stories." *Intersections*, no. 40 (2014): 45–47.

Bonilla-Silva, Eduardo, and Crystal E. Peoples. "Historically White Colleges and Universities: The Unbearable Whiteness of (Most) Colleges and Universities." *American Behavioral Scientist* 66, no. 11 (2022): 1490–504. https://doi.org/10.1177/00027642211066047.

Booker, Vaughn A. "'Deplorable Exegesis': Dick Gregory's Irreverent Scriptural Authority in the 1960s and 1970s." *Religion and American Culture* 30, no. 2 (2020): 187–235. https://doi.org/10.1017/rac.2020.9.

Boyd, Colleen E., and Coll Thrush, eds. *Phantom Past, Indigenous Presence: Native Ghosts in North American History*. University of Nebraska Press, 2011.

Bredin, Yngve. "Ahlborg and America: The Influence of a Missionary School." *Swedish-American Historical Quarterly* 36, no. 3 (1985): 159–67.

Brolander, Glen. *An Historical Survey of the Augustana College Campus*. Augustana Historical Society Publications, 1985.

Brown, Nicholas. "They Don't Even Want Our Bones: An Interview with Johnathan Buffalo, Historic Preservation Officer, Meskwaki Nation." In *Re-Collecting Black Hawk*. University of Pittsburgh Press, 2015.

Bruning, Stephen D., Shea McGrew, and Mark Cooper. "Town–Gown Relationships: Exploring University–Community Engagement from the Perspective of Community Members." *Public Relations Review* 32, no. 2 (2006): 125–30. https://doi.org/10.1016/j.pubrev.2006.02.005.

Buechner, Frederick. *Wishful Thinking: A Seeker's ABC*. HarperOne, 1993.

Burke, Robert. "LGBTQC: Queer Perspectives on the Illinois-Iowa Quad Cities." Augustana Digital Commons, May 16, 2020. https://digitalcommons.augustana.edu/anthstudent/9/.

Calder, Lendol. "Uncoverage: Toward a Signature Pedagogy for the History Survey." *Journal of American History* 92, no. 4 (2006): 1358–70.

Carby, Hazel. *Race Men*. Harvard University Press, 1998.

Carlson, Sara-Eva Ellen. "They Tell Their Story: The Dakota Internment at Camp McClellan in Davenport, 1862–1866." *Annals of Iowa* 3, no. 63 (2004): 251–78.

Carr, Paul R. "Transforming the Institution, or Institutionalizing the Transformation? Anti-Racism and Equity in Education in Toronto." *McGill Journal of Education* 34, no. 11 (1999): 49–77.

Case, Anissa, and Bic Ngo. "Do We Have to Call It That? The Response of Neoliberal Multiculturalism to College Antiracism Efforts." *Multicultural Perspectives* 19, no. 4 (2017): 215–22. https://doi.org/10.1080/15210960.2017.1366861.

Cerezo, Allison, and Tai Chang. "Latina/o Achievement at Predominantly White Universities: The Importance of Culture and Ethnic Community." *Journal of Hispanic Higher Education* 12, no. 1 (2002): 72–85. https://doi.org/10.1177/1538192712465.

Cervantes, John. *My Moline*. Canyon Publishing, 1986.

Chilstrom, Herbert W. "What Was/Is Augustana?" In *The Augustana Heritage: Recollections, Perspectives, and Prospects*, edited by Arland J. Hultgren and Vance L. Eckstrom. Augustana Heritage Association, 1999.

Cone, James. *Black Theology and Black Power*. Orbis Books, 2018.

Dalton, Linda, and James Davis. "Campus Master Planning." *APPA: Body of Knowledge* (blog). Accessed June 7, 2022. https://www.appa.org/bok/campus-master-planning-2/.

Danns, Dionne. "Chicago High School Students' Movement for Quality Public Education, 1966–1971." *Journal of African-American History* 88, no. 2 (2003): 138–50. https://doi.org/10.2307/3559062.

Davis, Charles G. "The Indian Boundary Line Under the Treaty of August 24, 1816." *Journal of the Illinois State Historical Society* 28, no. 1 (1935): 26–64.

Deloria, Philip J. *Becoming Mary Sully: Toward an American Indian Abstract.* University of Washington Press, 2019.

Deloria, Vine, Jr. *Custer Died For Your Sins: An Indian Manifesto.* University of Oklahoma Press, 1988.

Deloria, Vine, Jr. "It's a Good Day to Die." In *For This Land: Writings on Religion in America.* Routledge, 1999.

Deloria, Vine, Jr. *We Talk, You Listen: New Tribes, New Turf.* University of Nebraska Press, 1970.

Deresiewicz, William. "The Neoliberal Arts: How College Sold Its Soul to the Market." *Harper's Magazine*, September 2015. https://harpers.org/archive/2015/09/the-neoliberal-arts/.

Deslippe, Philip. "The Hindu in Hindoo: Fake Yogis, Pseudo-Swamis, and the Manufacture of African-America Folk Magic." *Amerasia Journal* 4, no. 1 (2014): 34–56. https://doi.org/10.17953/amer.40.1.a21442914234450w.

Didion, Joan. "The White Album." In *The White Album.* Farrar, Straus & Giroux, 2009 [1979].

Dilley, Patrick. *Gay Liberation to Campus Assimilation: Early Non-Heterosexual Student Organizing at Midwestern Universities.* Palgrave Macmillan, 2019.

Drushel, Bruce E. "The Evolution Will Not Be Broadcast (or Published): Social Capital, Assimilation, and the Changing Queer Community." *Journal of Homosexuality* 66 (2019): 1756–68. https://doi.org/10.1080/00918369.2018.1511132.

Duncan, Lenny. *Dear Church: A Love Letter from a Black Preacher to the Whitest Church on Earth.* Fortress Press, 2019.

Edmondson, Mark. "On the Uses of Liberal Education," *Harper's Magazine*, September 1997. Republished in *Liberal Arts Through the AGES.* Augustana College, 2011.

Eklund, Emmet E. "Faith and Education." In *Centennial Essays: Augustana Lutheran Church, 1860–1960*, edited by Emmer Engberg, Conrad Bergendoff, and Edgar M. Carlson. Augustana Press, 1960.

Eklund, Emmet E. "Lutheran Higher Education: The Augustana Tradition." In *The Augustana Heritage: Recollections, Perspectives, and Prospects*, edited by Arland J. Hultgren and Vance L. Eckstrom. Augustana Heritage Association, 1999.

Erling, Bernhard. "Augustana's Theological Tradition: Esbjörn, Hasselquist, Olsson, Lindberg, Bergendoff, Carlfelt, Carlson." In *The Augustana*

Heritage: Recollections, Perspectives, and Prospects, edited Arland J. Hultgren and Vance L. Eckstrom. Augustana Heritage Association, 1999.

Erling, Maria. "What's in a Name? Augustana's Heritage and Prospects." In *The Augustana Heritage: Recollections, Perspectives, and Prospects*, edited by Arland J. Hultgren and Vance L. Eckstrom. Augustana Heritage Association, 1999.

Erling, Maria. "Wrestling with the Mission Mantle: Matthias Wahlstrom, Failed Missionary to the Comanche, and the Relation Between the Augustana Synod and the Covenant Church." *Swedish-American Historical Quarterly* 63, nos. 2–3 (2012): 135–57. https://dx.doi.org/10.1353/swe.2012.a939402.

Erling, Maria, and Mark Granquist. *The Augustana Story: Shaping Lutheran Identity in North America.* Augsburg Fortress, 2008.

Exum, William H. *Paradoxes of Protest: Black Student Activism in a White University.* Temple University Press, 1985.

Feagin, Joe R., Hernán Vera, and Nikitah Imani. *The Agony of Education: Black Students at White Colleges and Universities.* Routledge, 1996.

Felber, Grant. "Integration or Separation? Malcolm X's College Debates, Free Speech, and the Challenge to Racial Liberalism on Campus." *Journal of Social History* 53, no. 4 (2020): 1033–59. https://doi.org/10.1093/jsh/shz001.

Ferrall, Victor E., Jr. *Liberal Arts at the Brink.* Harvard University Press, 2011.

Flores, Judith, and Silvia Garcia. "Latina *testimonios*: A Reflexive, Critical Analysis of a 'Latina Space' at a Predominantly White Campus." *Race, Ethnicity and Education* 12, no. 2 (2009): 155–72. https://doi.org/10.1080/13613320902995434.

Forsberg, Arthur, Harry Olson, and Virgil Westlund. "The Theological Pilgrimage of the Augustana Church." In *Augustana in Retrospect: An Evaluation of Her Development.* Augustana Theological Seminary, 1957.

Foucault, Michel. *The History of Sexuality.* Vol. 1, *An Introduction*, translated by Robert Hurley. Vintage Books, 1990 [1978].

Frank, Robert. "The Storms of 69–70." In *An Adventure in Faith: A Memoir of Teaching at Augustana College, 1964–1992.* Augustana Historical Society, 2022.

Frazer, Doug, Rick Miers, and David Sebben. *Rock Solid: Our History.* CreateSpace, published by the authors, 2016.

Fur, Gunlög. "Indians and Immigrants—Entangled Histories." *Journal of American Ethnic History* 33, no. 3 (2014): 55–76. https://doi.org/10.5406/jamerethnhist.33.3.0055.

Gates, Henry Louis, Jr. *The Signifying Monkey: A Theory of African-American Literary Criticism*. Oxford University Press, 1988.

Gavazzi, Stephen. "Campus and Community Leadership in the Spotlight: How University Presidents and City Managers View Town/Gown Relationships." *Journal of Community Engagement and Scholarship* 11, no. 1 (2018): 8–19.

Gerstle, Gary, *The Rise and Fall of the Neoliberal Order: America and the World in the Free Market Era*. Oxford University Press, 2022.

Glewwe, Lois A. "Life of a Legend—Jane Smith Williamson." Dakota Soul Sisters, August 22, 2019. https://dakotasoulsisters.glewwe.biz/2019/08/.

Gonzalez, Carla, Jessica Graber, Diana Galvez, and Leslie Ann Locke. "'They Say They Value Diversity, But I Don't See It': Academic and Social Experiences of First Generation Latinx Students at a Predominately White Midwestern Institution." In *Perspectives on Diverse Student Identities in Higher Education: International Perspectives on Equity and Inclusion*, edited by Jaimie Hoffman, Patrick Blessinger, and Mandla Makhanya. Emerald Publishing, 2019.

Granquist, Mark. *Lutherans in America: A New History*. Fortress Press, 2015.

Harris, Cheryl I. "Whiteness as Property." *Harvard Law Review* 106, no. 8 (1993): 1707–91.

Harris, Daniel. *The Rise and Fall of Gay Culture*. Ballantine Books, 1997.

Hartman, Saidiya. *Wayward Lives, Beautiful Experiments: Intimate Histories of Riotous Black Girls, Troublesome Women, and Queer Radicals*. W. W. Norton, 2020.

Holguín Mendoza, Claudia, Analisa Taylor, Luz Romero Montaño, Audrey Lucero, and Angel Dorantes. "Too Latinx or Not Latinx Enough? Racial Subtexts and Subjectivities in a Predominantly White University." *Journal of Latinos and Education* 22, no. 3 (2021): 1138–53. https://doi.org/10.1080/15348431.2021.1920945.

Hoskin, Keith W., and Richard H. MacVe. "Accounting and the Examination: A Genealogy of Disciplinary Power." *Accounting, Organizations and Society* 11, no. 2 (1986): 105–36. https://doi.org/10.1016/0361-3682(86)90027-9.

Hough, Carolyn, and Adam Kaul. "Symbiosis or Entrepreneurialism? Ambivalent Anthropologies in the Age of the (Neo)Liberal Arts." In

Collaborations: Anthropology in a Neoliberal Age, edited by Emma Heffernan, Fiona Murphy, and Jonathan Skinner. Routledge, 2020.

Jackson, Philip W. *Life in Classrooms*. Revised edition. Teacher's College Press, 1990.

Jeske, Christine. "Overturning for the Common Good: Membership and Mutuality in a World of Markets and Meritocracy." In *Called Beyond Our Selves: Vocation and the Common Good*, edited by Erin VanLaninghan. Oxford University Press, 2024.

Jones, Robert P. *White Too Long: The Legacy of White Supremacy in White Christianity*. Simon & Schuster, 2002.

Jung, Patrick J. "American Indian Resistance to Settler Colonialism in the Western Great Lakes and Upper Mississippi Valley, 1815–1832." *Annals of Iowa* 81, no. 1 (2022): 3–44. https://doi.org/10.17077/0003.4827.31923.

Karma, Roger. "'The Meritocracy Trap,' Explained: A New Book Outlines How Meritocracy Imprisons Us All." *Vox*, October 24, 2019. https://www.vox.com/policy-and-politics/2019/10/24/20919030/meritocracy-book-daniel-markovits-inequality-rich.

Karpowitz, Daniel. *College in Prison: Reading in an Age of Mass Incarceration*. Rutgers University Press, 2017.

Kaul, Adam. "Critical Pedagogies of Hope: Teaching an 'Anthropological Imagination' in an Era of Unfolding Crises." In *Applying Anthropology to General Education: Reshaping Colleges and Universities for the 21st Century*, edited by Jennifer R. Wies and Hillary J. Haldane. Routledge, 2022.

Keels, Micere. *Campus Counterspaces: Black and Latinx Students' Search for Community at Historically White Universities*. Cornell University Press, 2020.

Kendi, Ibram X. *The Black Campus Movement: Black Students and the Racial Reconstitution of Higher Education, 1965–1972*. Palgrave Macmillan, 2012.

Kimmerer, Robin Wall. *Braiding Sweetgrass: Indigenous Wisdom, Scientific Knowledge and the Teachings of Plants*. Milkweed Editions, 2015.

Kosnick, Kiki, and Sharon Varallo. "Conciliatory and Queer: The Radical Love of Lutheran Higher Education." *Intersections*, no. 50 (Fall 2019): 43–46.

Kramer, William M. "The Importance of Being Turbaned." *Antioch Review* 69, no. 2 (2011): 208–21.

Lawson, James R. "Student Participation in Educational Change." *Journal of Negro Education* 40, no. 3 (1970): 282–89. https://doi.org/10.2307/2966513.

Leslie, Larry L., and Sheila A. Slaughter. "Higher Education and Regional Development." In *The Economics of American Higher Education*, edited by William E. Becker and Darrell R. Lewis. Springer, 1992.

Lopez, Cesar. "USC El Centro Chicago—a Historical Perspective." University of Southern California. Accessed November 20, 2024. https://lacasa.usc.edu/about-us/.

Lowy, Richard. "Yuppie Racism: Race Relations in the 1980s." *Journal of Black Studies* 21, no. 4 (1991): 445–64.

Lucero, Audrey, Angel Abel Dorantes, Claudia Holguín Mendoza, and Luz Romero Montaño. "Reforzando las Redes: Supporting Latina/o Undergraduates at a State Flagship University." *Journal of Hispanic Higher Education* 18, no. 4 (2019): 295–316. https://doi.org/10.1177/1538192717741.

Lund, Doniver. "Educational Experience in America: Immigrant and Native-Born." *Swedish-American Historical Quarterly* 18, no. 1 (1967): 17–30.

Lutheran School of Theology at Chicago. "History." Accessed August 1, 2023. lstc.edu/about/resources/history/.

Massey, Jennifer, Sean Field, and Yolande Chan. "Partnering for Economic Development: How Town-Gown Relations Impact Local Economic Development in Small and Medium Cities." *Canadian Journal of Higher Education* 44, no. 2 (2014): 152–69.

May, William F. "Professors: Credentialed for What?" In *Beleaguered Rulers: The Public Obligation of the Professional*. John Knox Press, 2001.

Melamed, Jodi. "The Spirit of Neoliberalism: From Racial Liberalism to Neoliberal Multiculturalism." *Social Text* 24, no. 4 (2006): 1–24. https://doi.org/10.1215/01642472-2006-009.

Menand, Louis. *The Metaphysical Club: A Story of Ideas in America*. Farrar, Strauss & Giroux, 2002.

Miles, Sam. "Sex in the Digital City: Location-Based Dating Apps and Queer Urban Life." *Gender, Place, & Culture* 24 (2017): 1595–610. https://doi.org/10.1080/0966369X.2017.1340874.

Miles, Tiya. *Tales from the Haunted South: Dark Tourism and Memories of Slavery from the Civil War Era*. University of North Carolina Press, 2015.

Misra, Tanvi. "How Turbans Helped Some Blacks Go Incognito in the Jim Crow Era." *Code Switch*, July 19, 2014. National Public Radio. https://www.npr.org/sections/codeswitch/2014/07/17/332380449/how-turbans-helped-some-blacks-go-incognito-in-the-jim-crow-era.

Montás, Roosevelt. *Rescuing Socrates: How the Great Books Changed My Life and Why They Matter for a New Generation.* Princeton University Press, 2021.

Mora, Lauren. "Hispanic Enrollment Reaches New High at Four-Year Colleges in the US, but Affordability Remains an Obstacle." Pew Research Center, October 7, 2022.

Museus, Samuel D., Varaxy Yi, and Natasha Saelua. "The Impact of Culturally Engaging Campus Environments." *Review of Higher Education* 40, no. 2 (2017): 187–215. https//doi.org/10.1353/rhe.2017.0001.

Myrdahl, Tiffany Muller. "LGBTQ+ Communities: Sexuality and the City." In *Alternative Planning History and Theory*, edited by Dorina Pojani. Routledge, 2023.

Nash, Ariana Nadia. "Realist Poetry and Paul Laurence Dunbar's Majors and Minors." *J19: The Journal of Nineteenth-Century Americanists* 10, no. 1 (2022): 121–45. https://dx.doi.org/10.1353/jnc.2022.0007.

National Center for Education Statistics. "College Enrollment in the United States from 1965 to 2022 and Projections up to 2031 for Public and Private Colleges (in Millions)." Statista. Accessed November 3, 2024. https://www.statista.com/statistics/183995/us-college-enrollment-and-projections-in-public-and-private-institutions/.

Nelson, Derek. "Unity, Ecumenicity, and Difference in the Augustana Synod." *Lutheran Quarterly* 2, no. 1 (2010): 76–96.

Ngozi-Brown, Scott. "The Us Organization, Maulana Karenga, and Conflict with the Black Panther Party: A Critique of Sectarian Influences on Historical Discourse." *Journal of Black Studies* 28, no. 2 (1997): 157–70.

Nielsen, John Mark. "Tracing Threads: N. F. S. Grundtvig, the Danish Folk High School Movement, and the Elderhostel Experience." In *Nordics in America: The Future of Their Past*, edited by Odd S. Lovoll. Norwegian-American Historical Association, 1993.

Noe-Bustamente, Luis, Lauren Mora, and Mark Hugo Lopez. "About One-in-Four U.S. Hispanics Have Heard of Latinx, but Just 3% Use It." Pew Research Center, August 11, 2020. https://www.pewresearch.org/hispanic/2020/08/11/about-one-in-four-u-s-hispanics-have-heard-of-latinx-but-just-3-use-it/.

Nordmeyer, Emma. "Using Style to Signify Injustice." Augustana Digital Commons, 2019. https://digitalcommons.augustana.edu/relgrace/2.

O'Donnell, Thomas. "Chicanas/os Begin to Organize at UC Davis." UC Davis Diversity, Equity, and Inclusion. Accessed November 20, 2024. https://diversity.ucdavis.edu/hsi/chicanasos-organize-ucd.

Olaoluwa, Senayon. "Beyond Backpacking: Solo 'Guerrilla' Border Crossing and the Penetration of Geographies of Power in Olabisi Ajala's *An African Abroad.*" *Journal of Borderlands Studies* 36, no. 3 (2021): 487–501. https://doi.org/10.1080/08865655.2019.1571431.

Olson, Oscar N. *The Augustana Lutheran Church in America, 1860–1910: The Formative Period.* Executive Council of the Augustana Lutheran Church, 1956.

Olsson, Karl A. *By One Spirit.* Covenant Publications, 1962.

O'Mara, Margaret P. "Beyond Town and Gown: University Economic Engagement and the Legacy of the Urban Crisis." *Journal of Technology Transfer* 37, no. 2 (2012): 234–50. https://doi.org/10.1007/s10961-010-9185-4.

On and Beyond The Mississippi: Essays Honoring Thomas Tredway, edited by Dag Blanck and Michael Nolan. Augustana Historical Society, 2004.

"150 Years of Augustana College: A Timeline." Accessed August 2023. http://www.augustana.net/SpecialCollections/timeline/2000s.html.

Page, Helán, and R. Brooks Thomas. "White Public Space and the Construction of White Privilege in U.S. Health Care: Fresh Concepts and a New Model of Analysis." *Medical Anthropology Quarterly* 8, no. 1 (1994): 109–16.

Patel, Eboo. *Diversity Is Not Just the Differences You Like: Multicultural Leadership in the Age of Identity Politics.* Beacon Press, 2021.

Patel, Eboo. "What It Means to Build the Bridge: Identity and Diversity at ELCA Colleges." *Intersections*, no. 40 (2014): 17–25.

Powell, Malea. "Dreaming Charles Eastman: Cultural Memory, Autobiography and Geography in Indigenous Rhetorical Histories." In *Beyond the Archives: Research as Lived Process*, edited by Gesa E. Kirsch and Liz Rohan. Southern Illinois University Press, 2008.

Pryor, John H., Sylvia Hurtado, Linda DeAngelo, Laura Palucki Blake, and Serge Tran. *The American Freshman: National Norms.* Higher Education Research Institute, 2010.

Ray, Darby. "Self, World, and the Space Between: Community Engagement as Vocational Discernment." In *At This Time and in This Place: Vocation and Higher Education*, edited by David Cunningham. Oxford University Press, 2016.

Rockenbach, A. N., M. J. Mayhew, B. P. Correia-Harker, L. Dahl, S. Morin, and Associates. *Navigating Pluralism: How Students Approach Religious Difference and Interfaith Engagement in their First Year of College.* Interfaith Youth Core, 2017.

Ronda, Margaret. "'Work and Wait Unwearying': Dunbar's Georgics." *PMLA* 127, no. 4 (2012): 863–78.

Routté-Gomez, Eneid. "The Struggle to Excel." *Homines* 10, no. 2 (1986–7). https://issuu.com/coleccionpuertorriquena/docs/mujeres_puertorrique_as_protagonistas_en_el_caribe/s/17884573.

Routté-Gomez, Eneid. "A Tale of Two Cultures." In *The Melanin Millennium: Skin Color as 21st Century International Discourse*, edited by Ronald E. Hall. Springer, 2012.

Rubin, Gayle. "Thinking Sex." In *Pleasure and Danger: Exploring Female Sexuality*, edited by Carole S. Vance. Routledge & Kegan Paul, 1984.

Russo, John, and Sherry Lee Linkon. "The Social Costs of Deindustrialization." In *Manufacturing a Better Future for America*, edited by Richard McCormack. Alliance for American Manufacturing, 2009.

Salmón, Enrique. "Kincentric Ecology: Indigenous Perceptions of the Human–Nature Relationship." *Ecological Applications* 10, no. 5 (2000): 1327–32. https://doi.org/10.1890/1051-0761(2000)010[1327:KEIPOT]2.0.CO;2.

Sánchez-Connally, Patricia. "Latinx First Generation College Students: Negotiating Race, Gender, Class, and Belonging," *Race, Gender & Class* 25, nos. 3/4 (2018): 234–51.

Sandel, Michael J. *The Tyranny of Merit: What's Become of the Common Good?* Farrar, Straus & Giroux, 2020.

Saro-Wiwa, Ken. "Trying Times." *ANA Review: Annual Journal of the Association of Nigerian Authors*, November 1993.

Schantz, Regina Trant. *The Trader at Rock Island: George Davenport and the Founding of the Quad Cities*. Heritage Documentaries, 2020.

Schock, Twila. "Accompaniment: A Model for Congregational Mission Alongside Individuals with Disabilities." *Currents in Theology and Mission* 49, no. 3 (2022): 29–32. https://currentsjournal.org/index.php/currents/article/view/362.

Schwarz, Jon. "The Origin of Student Debt: Reagan Advisor Warned Free College Would Create a Dangerous 'Educated Proletariat.'" *The Intercept*, August 25, 2022. https://theintercept.com/2022/08/25/student-loans-debt-reagan/.

Schwehn, Mark. "The Value of Evoking Vocation and the Vocation of Evoking Value." *Intersections*, no. 38, article 5 (2013): 17–25.

Sebelius, Sven Johan. *Master Builders of Augustana: Biographical Sketches, Reminiscent and Appreciative, of Great Teachers at Augustana College*. Augustana Book Concern, 1949.

Simpson, Leanne Betasamosake. *As We Have Always Done: Indigenous Freedom Through Radical Resistance*. University of Minnesota Press, 2020.

Skillrud, Harold. *Decade of Decision: A History of the Merger of the Lutheran School of Theology at Chicago*. Lutheran School of Theology at Chicago, 1969.

Smith, Monica. "Just Communities: From Liberal Arts in Prison to Racial Healing over Zoom." *Intersections*, no. 54 (2021), 11–14.

Smith, Monica. "Making Diversity Matter: Inclusion is the Key." *Intersections*, no. 50 (2019): 6–11.

Solberg, Richard W. *Lutheran Higher Education in North America*. Augsburg, 1985.

Stewart, D-L. "Whiteness as Collective Memory in Student Publications at Midwestern Liberal Arts Colleges, 1945–1965." *American Educational Research Journal* 56, no. 1 (2019): 3–38. https://doi.org/10.3102/0002831218788326.

Stoecker, Randy, and Elizabeth Tryon. *The Unheard Voices: Community Organizations and Service Learning*. Temple University Press, 2009.

Thonvold, Aubrey. "RIC Seminaries, Universities, Colleges, and Campus Ministries." ReconcilingWorks, June 22, 2017. https://www.reconcilingworks.org/ric-seminaries-universities-colleges-and-campus-ministries.

Tisby, Jemar. *Footnotes by Jemar Tisby*. Substack. https://jemartisby.substack.com/.

Tredway, Thomas. *Coming of Age: A History of Augustana College, 1935–1975*. Augustana College, 2010.

Tredway, Thomas. *Conrad Bergendoff's Faith and Work: A Swedish-American Lutheran, 1895–1997*. Augustana Historical Society, 2014.

Trouillot, Michel-Rolph. *Silencing the Past: Power and the Production of History*. Beacon Press, 1995.

Vaughan, Mary Kay, Leonard Ramirez, Marta Elena Ayala, Esther Diaz Martin, and Frances R. Aparicio. "History of LALS at UIC: A Program Birthed in a Maelstrom of Change." University of Illinois Chicago, 2023. https://lals.uic.edu/about/history-of-lals-at-uic/.

Von Robertson, Ray, Alma Bravo, and Cassandra Cheney. "Racism and the Experiences of Latina/o College Students at a PWI (Predominantly White Institution)." *Critical Sociology* 42, nos. 4–5 (2001): 715–35. https://doi.org/10.1177/0896920514532.

Williamson, Joy Ann. "In Defense of Themselves: The Black Student Struggle for Success and Recognition at Predominantly White Colleges and

Universities." *Journal of Negro Education* 68, no. 1 (1999): 92–105. https://doi.org/10.2307/2668212.

Wilson-Black, Robert. *The End of College: Religion and the Transformation of Higher Education in the 20th Century*. Fortress, 2021.

Yosso, Tara, William Smith, Miguel Ceja, and Daniel Solórzano. "Critical Race Theory, Racial Microaggressions, and Campus Racial Climate for Latina/o Undergraduates." *Harvard Educational Review* 79, no. 4 (2009): 659–91.

CONTRIBUTORS

Steven Bahls served as the president of Augustana College from 2003 to 2022. President Emeritus Bahls has written and spoken extensively about shared governance and has published articles in *Trusteeship*, the *Chronicle of Higher Education*, the *Huffington Post*, and *Inside Higher Education*. He is the author of *Shared Governance in Times of Change: A Practical Guide for Universities and Colleges*. He is a consultant for the Association of Governing Boards and a senior advisor to the Council of Independent Colleges (directing the Presidential Vocation and Mission Workshop).

Robert Burke is an AmeriCorps alumnus and urban planner whose use of geographic information systems to solve urban problems has garnered national recognition. He currently works at the Urban Data Visualization Lab at the University of Illinois Chicago and serves as the president of the Urban Planning and Policy Student Association.

Lizandra Gomez-Ramirez was the vice-president of the Latino/a Law Student Association and completed an internship with the Prisoners' Rights Project at Northern Illinois University. She is an assistant public defender for Rock Island County in Rock Island, Illinois.

Lauren Hammond-Ford is the first Black woman to earn tenure at Augustana College. She is currently the inaugural assistant vice chancellor for diversity, equity, and inclusion–academic engagement at the University of Denver. She focuses her community activism on racial equity and racial reconciliation with the church.

Sarah Lashley is an associate professor of environmental studies at Augustana College. Her research interests focus on the intersection of environmental justice and conflict management, and she has published in journals such as *Case Studies in the Environment*, *Journal of Chemical Education*, *Environmental Justice*, and *Research in Social Problems and Public Policy*.

Jason A. Mahn is a professor of religion, the director of the Presidential Center for Faith and Learning, and the Conrad Bergendoff Professor in the Humanities at Augustana College. He is the author of *Fortunate Fallibility: Kierkegaard and the Power of Sin*, *Becoming a Christian in Christendom:*

Radical Discipleship and the Way of the Cross in America's "Christian" Culture, and *Neighbor Love Through Fearful Days.*

Harrison Phillis was the assistant special collections librarian at Augustana College from 2019 to 2024 and is currently a librarian at Scott Community College in Bettendorf, Iowa.

Mark Safstrom is an associate professor of Scandinavian studies at Augustana College, where he teaches the Swedish language and Scandinavian history and literature. He is the editor of *Swedish-American Studies*, the author of several books and articles on Scandinavian religious and immigration history including *The Religious Origins of Democratic Pluralism: Paul Peter Waldenström and the Politics of the Swedish Awakening 1868–1917*, and a coauthor of the filmscript for the documentary *God's Glory, Neighbor's Good: The Story of Pietism* as well as numerous book chapters and translations.

Jane E. Simonsen is a professor of history and women's, gender, and sexuality studies and the Richard A. Swanson Chair of Social Thought at Augustana College. She is the author of *Making Home Work: Domesticity and Native American Assimilation in the American West, 1860–1919* and has recently published work in *American Indian Quarterly*, the *American Studies Journal*, and the edited volume *Gender, Race and Power in the Indian Reform Movement.*

Monica M. Smith served as the director of diversity and inclusion at Elizabethtown College and St. Joseph's University and was appointed Augustana College's first vice president of diversity, equity, and inclusion and chief diversity officer. During her five years at Augustana, her efforts led the college to be recognized with Higher Education Excellence in Diversity Awards from *INSIGHT into Diversity* magazine in 2019, 2020, 2022, and 2023. She is the vice president for inclusion and belonging at the University of Richmond.

Christopher Strunk is an associate professor of geography and the coordinator of Latin American and Latinx studies at Augustana College. His research explores immigrant and refugee organizations, urban planning, and community geography, and he has published work in *Social and Cultural Geography*, *Urban Geography*, and the *Journal of Ethnic and Migration Studies.*

Andrea Kathryn Talentino began her tenure as Augustana College's ninth president in 2022. Prior to joining Augustana, Talentino was the provost of Nazareth College in Rochester, New York. She also served as the dean of the College of Liberal Arts at Norwich University. She is the author of *Intervention After the Cold War: The Evolution of Theory and Practice* and the coeditor of *Sport Boundaries, Sports Events, and Commodification.*

INDEX

Page numbers in italics indicate illustrations.

Abney, Nina, 149–50
academic programs and departments, 52, 131, 275–77, 287, 294, 298, 300, 302; English, 52, 247, 253, 254, 258; Music, 131, 136; Political Science, 150; Sociology, 131, 143, 145; Religion (Christianities), 14, 131, 136, 145, 156, 209, 234, 288; Women, Gender, and Sexuality Studies (Women's Studies), 201, 209, 217
Adams, Phyllis, 140, 142
Aden, August, 90
advising, 61, 66, 69, 90, 104, 115, 131, 132, 136, 152, 165, 172, 180, 202, 219, 255–59, 300, 339; *see also* theology of accompaniment
affirmative action, 133, 139
African Methodist Episcopal (AME) Church, 91–93, 96, 97, 112
African Student Association, 85
Afro-American Society (AAS), 3, 109–12, 114, 116, 117, 172
Aguilar, Greg, 150, 177, 179, 181
Àjàlá, Mashood Adisa Olabisi, 13, *102*, 106, 107; early life, 99; at Augustana, 15, 99, 100–105, 119; as journalist, 98, 105
Alliance of Islamic Awareness, 145
Al-wazedi, Umme, 247, 264n8
Ahlberg School, 243–44
American Lutheran Church, 132, 142, 159n12, 277
Americanization, 33, 36, 37, 39, 105, 230, 233, 246
Andreen Hall, 2–3, 4, 6, 17n4, 19n33, 101, 213
Andreen, Gustav, 15, 242, *243*
Andrén, O. T. C., 243
anti-discrimination, administrative policy on, 137, 141–42
anti-racism, 10, 114, 125, 129, 130, 132–34
Asian students, 15, 137, 166; Asian Student Organization, 145, 182
athletics, 12, 63, 110, 111, 116, 143, 255–58, *257*, 295
Augie Acres, 63, 65
Augie Choice, 296
AugiEquality, 151
Augsburg Confession, 15, 193
Augsburg University, 11, 48, 211
Augustana College Board of Directors, 28, 50n21, 115, 195, 196, 250, 255
Augustana College Special Collections, xv, 8, 15, 169, 170
Augustana Foreign Mission Society, 101
Augustana Girls' Athletic Association, *257*
Augustana Heritage Association, 239
Augustana Historical Society, 20, 28
Augustana Hospital, 244

Augustana Leaders in Vocational Reflection (ALIVE), 302
Augustana as Lutheran Education (ALE), 300
Augustana Prison Education Program (APEP), 156, 304–5, 307
Augustana Synod, 2, 29, 30–32, 44, 90, 94, 101, 159n12, 232, 236, 240, 241, 244, 254, 255; Augustana Lutheran Synod, 230, 239; Scandinavian Evangelical Lutheran Augustana Synod, 240
Augustana Lutheran Church, 2, 230, 239
Augustana Music Conservatory, 89, 91, 93, 274
Augustana Theological Seminary, 30, *31*, 37–41, 48, 51n45, 55, 87, 89, 95, 96, 233, 239, 240, *243*, 244, 245, 275, 277
Augustana University, Sioux Falls, South Dakota, 240
Augustana Woman's Club, 89

Bahls, Steven, xiii, 76–78, 149, 150, 206, 210–12, 225n103, 235, 265n26, 280, 312, 339
Ballet Folklórico, 179, 180
Bard Prison Initiative (BPI), 304
Bartholomew, Edward Fry, 94, *250*, 250–53
Barnes, Brenda, 235
Bateman, Lane, 196–200, 208, 219n21, 219n32, 220n33
Beloit College, 241
Bengston, Tom, 192–93, 209, 218n21, 219n32, 225n107
Bergendoff, Conrad, xi, 8, 99, 195, 232, 241, 242, 252, 255, 264n19, 266n52, 270
Beta Omega Sigma (BOS), 140–42, 147
Bethany College, 242
Black Campus movement, 85, 109, 110, 118, 119, 125n80, 129–30, 133
Black church, 90, 109, 114, 116, 118, 119, 153
Black Culture House, xii, 7, 85, 111, 117, 131, 136, 145, 146, 169
Black faculty, 111, 115, 131, 132, 134, 136, 134, 150, 152, 153, 172. *See also* Hammond-Ford, Lauren; Hildreth, John
Blackface: *See* Beta Omega Sigma; Homecoming.
Black Lutherans, 86, 87, 96, 115, 132, 133–34
Black Hawk, 24–26, 49n5
Black Hawk College, 167, 168, 181
Black Hawk War, 26, 27, 50n21
Black Power Symposium, 3, 13, 112, *113*, 114, 116, 118, 134, 155; and Black Power movement, 86, 109, 111
Black Students, 3, 5, 13, 59, 114–15, 118–19, 120n4, 129–30, 133, 139, 153; and Black culture, 116, 118; institutional support for, 131, 132, 134, 136, 143–44; and BOS, 140–42; recruitment of, 2, 117, 131, 172; and safety, 145, 152; and separatism, 110, 146. *See also* Afro-American Society; Black Student Union; Routte, Jesse
Black Student Union (BSU), 7, 8, 13, 85, 110, 117–19, 131, 132,

135, 136, 137, 139, 140, 144–46, 148, 151, 152, 172, 182, 184, 314; and Black Student Orientation, 117
Blomgren, C.A., 90
Boaden, Ann, 8, 9, 264n8, 265n29
Bremer, Frederika, 29–30
Brodahl, Betsey, 201, 233, 234, 249, 250, 254, 255, 263n19, 270, *271*, 272
Brolander, Glen, 55
Brooks, Gwendolyn, 145
Brown, Carol, 145
Brown, Michael, 151
Brown, William, 131, 159n9
Buchholtz, Richard, 4–5, 16
Buddhists, 237
Busch, Mildred, 99, 100
Bush, Val, 131

Calder, Lendol, ix, 265n29
Cable, P.L., 27
Camp McClellan, 34, 42
Campbell, Evelyn, 65, 71, 204–8, 212, 213
Campus Cupboard, 269n103
Campus Ministries, 183, 208–10; and Catholic ministries, 209–10
Cantu, Sandra, 170, 171, 172–73, 180, 181
Capital University, 241
Careers, Opportunities, Research, and Exploration (CORE), 235, 268n100, 301
Carlsson Evald Hall, 57, 68
Carreno, Stephanie, 174
Casa Latina, 85, 164, *165*, 169, 172–73, *174* 179, 180
Castro, Anna, 170
Castro, Jose, 170, 180
Center for Student Life (CSL), 85, 296
Center for Vocational Reflection (CVR), 235, 272
Chicago, 29–30, 40, 143, 145, 151; Augustana in, 2, 30, *31*, 54, 240; and Black community, 3–6, 94, 111, 114–15, 133; and Latinx students, 170, 176; Lutherans in, 244, 30–31, 56, 132, 136, 142; and Mashood Ajala, 99, 106–7; Native Americans in, 40; school boycotts in, 110
Chief Diversity Officer, 10, 11, 128, 130, 340. *See also* Smith, Monica
Christian Humanism, 231, 234, 235, 237, 245, 250, 261, 262
Church of Sweden (Svenska Kyrkan), 243, 244, 266n52
civil rights, 3, 6, 38, 40, 86, 88, 97, 187; Act of 1964, 131; at Augustana, 109, 112, 113, 116, 130, 133, 142, 152, 195, 290, 295, 303; marches for, 226, 249
Civil War, 13, 30, 31, 33, 34, 36, 42, 181
Clinton, Bill, 282, 284
Coleman, Reed, 131
College/University Zone, 76, 77
College Republicans, 184
Colmenares, América, 181
Committee on the Status of Women, 201
common good, 116, 272, 273, 282–84, 290, 304, 305, 307, 313
Community Connection, 67, 187
consumer culture, 292; and education 295–97
Copenhagen University, 242

Cosmopolitan Club, 101, *102*
counterspaces, 164, 169, 171, 187, 248
Coronavirus, 53, 72, 157, 260, 298
Crouch, Michelle, 260, 264n8
Crowe, Bruce, 72
Cullen, Jack, 156

Dakota Nation, 11, 48; and U.S.-Dakota War, 30, 31; and missionaries, 20, 29, 32, 33, 35, 37; and internment, 31, 33, 34, 35, 39
Davenport (city), 4, 31, 33, 34, 57, 62, 66, 92, 101, 112, 114, 148, 202
Davenport, George, 24–27
David, Keith, 136
Davis, James, 56
Deaconess Movement, 244
Deferred Action for Childhood Arrivals (DACA), 184
Deloria Jr., Vine, 20, 22, 37–44, 41, 48, 51n45
demonstrations, 132, 142, 152, 204, 206, 249; boycotts, 110, 227; Gay? Fine by Me, 207; Rally Against Hate, 206; walkout, 150. *See also* protests; vigils
Desi House, 85
Día de los Muertos, 178, 181, 188
Diversity, Equity, and Inclusion (DEI), 13, 158n1, 169, 173, 177, 185, 188; and Justice, 128, 139, 155, 173
Dixon v. Alabama, 249
Djao, Eunice, 101
Dominguez, Domingo, 178, 185, 186
Du Bois, W. E. B., 91, 94
Dunbar, Paul Laurence, 94, *95*
Duncan, Lenny, 92

East Moline, 62, 156, 177, 304
ecological justice, 13, 14, 43, 66, 214, 273, 290, 297, 305, 307, 339
Edmondson, Mark, 292–97
environmentalism, *see* ecological justice
Erickson Elementary School, 180
Erickson, Richard, 256–57, *256*
Erickson, Stanley, 5, 18n17
Esbjörn, Lars Paul, 30, 240, 246, 265n39, 266n40, 266n43, 267n57
Evangelical Homeland Foundation (EFS), 243
Evangelical Lutheran Church in America (ELCA), x, xi, xiiin3, 2, 9, 202, 208–11, 216, 232, 237, 238, 273, 282; and Reconciling in Christ Institutions, 210; and same-sex marriage, 211

Faculty Senate, 209
faculty-student relationships, 117, 196, 197, 229, 230, 244, 249, 250, 255, 256, 261, 262, 269n109; college policy on, 197, 200. *See also* Bateman, Lane.
Fall Connection, 67
feminism, 201, 202
financial crisis of 2008, 273, 285, 286, 295, 310n44
first generation students, 167, 172
First-Year Inquiry (FYI), 267n72, 300
Fisk University, 103, 119, 131

Five Faith Commitments, x, xi, xiii, 10, 13, 128–29, 272, 210, 228, 231, 236, 238, 265n29, 280, 301
Fjellstedt, Peter, 243
Fjellstedt School, 243
Floreciente neighborhood, 152, 170, 180
Floyd, George, 7, 16, 138, 154, 156
free speech, 112, 133, 150, 184
Folk High School (Folkehøjskole), 244–45, 267n63
foreign missions, 31, 32, 36, 90, 92, 101, 115
Francke, August Hermann, 244
fraternities, 52, 101, 138, 140–42, 149, 168, 172, 202, 226, 227. *See also* BOS; Greek life
Friendship Fair, 100, 105, 107, 133

Gay/Straight Alliance (GSA), 192, 205, 206, 209, 212, 213; as Gender and Sexuality Alliance, 213
general education, 139, 233, 275, 286, 287, 290, 291, 297–99, 300, 302, 305, 306; committee on, 183
Gesling, Linda, 196, 198, 208
Gettysburg College, 241
Ghartney, James, 131
GI Bill, 233
Glass Perez, 176, 177, 179, 183, 184, 211, 259, 264n8, 265n29
Global Affect, 245
Gomez-Ramirez, Lizandra, 80, 165, 175–76, 178, 185, 186, 188
Grace Lutheran Church, Moline, 33, 92
Granado-Mohr, Rosa, 173
Great Migration, 87, 90
Great Depression, 240
Greek life, 12, 73, 110, 141. *See also* Fraternities
Gregory, Dick, 112–14
Grundtvig, N. F. S., 244, 245, 267n63
Gustavus Adolphus College, 32, 33, 48, 255, 267n63

Hammond-Ford, Lauren, 130, 149, 152, 153, 159n7, 247, 248
Harper, Frances E. Watkins, 94
Hasselquist, Tufve Nilsson, 240, 241, 246, 264n11
Hauerwas, Stanley, 116
Hero Street, USA, 173
hidden curriculum, 129, 130, 131, 146, 158n3, 167, 171
Higher Education Excellence in Diversity Award, 156, 340
Hildreth, John, 130–39, *135*, 145, 148, 152, 155, 159n12
Hispanic students, *see* Latinx students
Ho-Chunk Nation, 23, 24, 30
Homecoming, 140, 144, *203*, 204, 294
Hope, Julius C., 142
Hough, Carolyn, 285, 286
Hull, Henry Palmer, 28, 54
Hullett, John (Jack), 69, 70, 111, 112, 114, 200–202, 204
Human Relations Committee, 136, 137, 140, 141, 209
humanities, 275, 285, 306, 339
hymnals, 239

Illinois State University, 240, 265n39
Islam, 100, 145, 237, 247

immigrants, 11, 14, 33, 37, 42, 46, 47, 94, 106–8, 230, 238, 239, 244–48, 261, 262, 267n72; Mexican, 179, 181, 184; in Rock Island, 165, 313; Swedish, xi, 2, 8, 10, 22, 28–30, 34, 36, 42, 44, 50n21, 51n47, 112, 167, 230, 239–41, 242, 243
in loco parentis, 249, 250, 259, 261, 262
Inclusion and Belonging Survey (2019), 137
Indian Boundary Line, 20, 22–23, 25, 27, 28, 37, 42, 47, 54; and historical marker, 20–22, *21*, 28
inner missions, 32, 94
Innis, Roy, 112, *113*
Institute for Truth, Racial Healing & Transformation, 156
interfaith engagement, 236, 237
interfaith understanding, 151, 162n57, 231
International Club, 145
International Harvester, 59
international students, 2, 15, 90, 99, 100, 101, 105, 154, 171, 181, 247, 260, 262, 275, 302, 303, 314. *See also* Àjàlá, Mashood Adisa Olabisi

Jackson, Jesse, 112
Jensen, Paul, 208, 209
Jesus Christ, 94, 109, 114, 229, 251, 277, 278, 288
Johannelund School of Theology, 243
John Deere and Company, 59, 66
Johnson, Fenton, 94
Johnson, Harry S.B., 220n38, 249; and Mashood Àjàlá, 98–100, 102–4, 106, 107, 124n50
Johnson, James Weldon, 95
Johnson, Joyce, 131, 159n9
Jones, Jerry, 130, 139, 143–47, 149, 150

Kaiserswerth, Germany, 244, 267n57
Kalas, Taddy, 200, 225n107
Kallis, Lenny, 256–57, *256*
Kaul, Adam, 285
King, Martin Luther, Jr., 108, 143, 226,
King, Martin Luther, Sr., 226
King, Rodney, 138, 147
Knox College, 34, 181, 241
Knudsen, Sonja, *52*, *53*, 54
Ku Klux Klan, 7, 140
Kumata, Ruth, 15

Ladies of Vital Essence, 145, 148
Latinx students, 166–67; at Augustana, 2, 123n53; 164–65, 166, 167, 169, 170–71, 173, 175, 176, 179, 181, 182, 184, 185–89; college enrollment of, 164, 166–67, 170, 175, 177. *See also* Latinos/x Unidos; Casa Latina
Latinos/x Unidos (LU), 13, 80, 164–65, *165*, 166, 173, 175, 177–78, 189n1, 314; and community connections, 179–81; diversity within, 175, 181–82, 185–87; events and activities, 173–74, 176, 178–80, 182; founding of, 170–72; history of, 167, 169, 167, 169–70, 188; mission of, 174–75; and politics, 182–85, 187

LGBTQ students, 151, 154, 185, 186, 199, 208, 210, 215; and activism, 14, 164, 204, 205, 210, 213, 215, 217. *See also* Gay-Straight Alliance; Lighthouse; PRISM
Lighthouse, 145, *203*, 203–5, 209, 214, 215
liberal arts, 66, 87, 134, 147, 212, 274, 276, 278, 279, 280, 281, 286, 294, 295, 297, 301–5, 307; and Augustana identity, x, xi, 2, 10, 14, 16, 270, 272–78, 281, 286, 287, 303; colleges and universities, 69, 117, 129, 136, 147, 234, 241, 245, 271–75, 277–78, 285–86, 289, 292, 296, 299, 303, 304, 314, 316, 341; and curriculum debates, 276, 287, 288–91, 297, 298–300, 301, 307; and Lutheran, 272, 273, 278–81, 282, 287, 297, 300–304; meaning of, 241, 252, 271, 274, 278, 281, 282, 288, 294, 298, 303, 305, 306–7; and mission, 67, 75, 118, 263n4; and values, 8, 16
Lilly Foundation, 233, 264n19, 270; and Faculty Seminar, 264n19, 272; grant, 233, 235
Lincoln Park, 4, 68, 117
Longfellow Elementary School, 66, 75, 79, 168
Looney, Joseph, 110, 134–36
Lund, Anne Greve, 257, *257*
Lund University, 241, 242
Luther League, 95
Luther, Martin, 226, 178, 284, 306
Lutheran Church in America (LCA), 159n12, 208
Lutheran Church Missouri Synod (LCMS), 132, 159n12
Lutheran Companion, 251
Lutheran School of Theology, 2, 56, 277
Lutheranism, x, xi, 32, 33, 35, 86, 92, 108, 133, 194–95, 277, 313; and Augustana identity, 8, 10, 16, 36, 112, 115, 118, 129, 157, 191, 208, 227–29; and higher education, xi, xiii, 216, 231–38, 249, 262–63; 307; and students, xi, 2, 10, 11. *See also* Black Lutherans; theology.

Mahn, Jason, 10, 156, 159n7, 234, 265n29
Majestic Gents, 145, 148, 168, 172
Malcolm X, 287
Martin Luther King, Jr. Community Center, 130, 143
Martinez, Consuelo, 170, 171, 172, 173, *174*, 175
master plan, campus, 56, 57
Masterson-Algar, Araceli, 181
Mauritzson, Jules, 242, *242*
Maurus, Robert, 142
Melanchthon, Philip, 232
mentorship, 154, 255, 261, 262, 269n108. *See also* advising
Meskwaki Nation, 21, 23–28, 39, 49n5
Midwest, 10, 16, 18n32, 29, 30, 38, 43, 54, 87, 88, 92, 95–97, 99, 101, 164, 167, 209 240, 249
Minority Cultural Symposium, 136
mission, Augustana College, ix, xi, 9, 13, 14, 54, 67, 74, 78, 118, 132, 137, 150, 156, 157, 215,

mission, Augustana College, (*continued*) 237, 238, 241, 263, 284, 291, 300, 312; mission drift, 113, 217, 234, 235, 262, 270, 277, 281; mission statements, 10, 119, 236, 247, 255, 263n4, 272, 274, 277, 280
Mississippi River, 2, 23, 24, 26, 31, 56, 57, 156, 179, 191, 204, 240, 306
Morales, Cindy, 176, 181, 182, 185
Morton Jr., Chauncey Lee, 3–7, 12, 16
Monmouth College, 181, 199, 220n32
multiculturalism, 12, 139, 143, 145, 149, 150, 152, 154, 161n48, 183, 267n72, 284, 293; Multicultural Affairs Network, 182; Multicultural Coalition, 182; Multicultural Programming Board, 182
Muslim, *see* Alliance of Islamic Awareness; Islam

National Association for the Advancement of Colored People (NAACP), 140–42, 149, 150
National Association of Colleges and Employers (NACE), 155
National Congress of American Indians (NCAI), 38, 40
neighborliness, 13, 29, 53, 54, 78, 79, 81, 84n55, 313; and neighbors, 11–13, 22, 28, 31, 37, 42, 44, 46, 47, 52–54, 57, 69, 70–73, 76, 79, 80, 81, 109, 115, 149, 194, 217, 279, 281, 302
neoliberalism, 14, 161n48, 229, 234, 270, 273, 281–86, 290, 292, 295, 297, 307, 314; and neoliberal arts, 273, 285, 297
Network of Colleges and Universities (NECU), 9, 10, 18n26, 273
Network of Vocation in Undergraduate Education (NetVUE), iv, xiin3, xv, 10, 273, 298, 301
New Deal, 282, 283
New Faculty Flourishing Group, 300, 301
New Negro Movement, 87, 90
1619 Project, 156, 157
Noche Caribeña, 182
Norelius, Eric, 31
Norwegian Augustana Synod, 240

Office for International Student and Scholar Services (OISSS), 137
Office of Student Inclusion and Diversity (OSID)/Office of Diversity Services, 137, 156
Office of Student Life (OSL), 72
Old Main, 2, 27, *254*
Olsen, Paul, 145, 258–59
Olsson, Olof, 244
Our Lady of Guadalupe 173; festival of, 178, 179, *180*, 188

Palomares Social Justice Center, 180
Preparation, Awareness, Community, and Engagement (PACE), 154, 267n72; and Multicultural Mentorship Program, 154
Parkander, Dorothy, 253–54, *254*, 268n86
Patel, Eboo, 162n57, 231, 310n49
Paulson, Ross, 112, 290, 291, 299, 309n21

Paxton, Illinois, 2, 28, 30, 31, 50n21, 54, 55, 240
pedagogy, 14, 226, 230, 238, 244, 248, 262, 270
Perez, Javier, 171, 176, 177
Phillis, Tom, 72
Phroenesis (practical reason), 289
pietism, 244, 264n11, 340
political correctness, 139, 293
Pollitz, John, 172
Powell, Adam Clayton, 112–14, 126n90
predominantly white institutions (PWIs), 11, 13, 135, 136, 140, 143, 144, 146, 157, 164, 167, 173, 189n2
Presidential Center for Faith and Learning, xiiin3, xv, 10, 301, 339
Presidential Racial Justice and Equity Fund, 155, 156
Priggie, Richard, 193–94, 206, 208, 211, 214, 225n107, 265n29, 265n34
Primous-Gillon, Dezi, 130, 149, 151–52
PRISM, 206, 207, 212
property tax, 74, 75
protests, campus, 15, 112, 184, 195, 249, 255; anti-racism, 110, 133, 140, 142, 150, 184; Black Lives Matter, 184; die-in, 151; LGBTQ, 195, 206, 209. *See also* demonstrations; vigils
Pupillo, Melinda, 269n107

Quad Cities, x, 12, 14, 52, 57, 59, 62, 66, 67, 76, 78, 112, 143, 144, 148, 150, 157, 165, 167, 168, 170, 171, 172, 173, 178, 179, 215, 247. *See also* Rock Island (city), Davenport (city)

racism, 13, 16, 40, 86, 93, 95–97, 109, 112, 113, 115, 116, 118, 129, 133, 134, 136–38, 140, 144, 147–52, 157, 158, 172, 182, 184, 287, 303; and microaggressions, 143, 146, 167, 169, 171, 176; and hate crimes, 7; philosophy of, 135
Rad Fems, 201, 202, 204, 216
Reagan, Ronald, 282, 309n26
Reasoned Examination of Faith (REF, Christian Traditions), 233, 236, 237, 272, 305
Reformation, 226, 232, 278, 280, 281
refugees, 167, 340
Residential Life, 71, 72, 214, 275; co-educational housing, 195, 196, 213, 218n15, 219n31. *See also* Transitional Living Areas (TLAs); Andreen Hall
Ribbeck, James, 196, 197, 200, 219n31, 220n38, 249, 250
Ring, Marilyn, 210, 214
Robinson, Michael, 131
Rock Island (city), 4, 5, 31, 38, 63, 65, 72, 74, 77, 78, 98–101, 109, 117, 121n15, 139, 144, 146, 196, 255; Black community in, 85, 90–91, 93, 101, 111, 117, 119, 143; campus location in, 2, 12, 32, 40, 54, 164, 170, 240, 246, 277; churches in, 90, 92; Coalition of Homeowners, 70; demographics, *58*, 59–60; Development Association, 76; development of, 24 -28, 57–59,

Rock Island (city) (*continued*) 78, 81; and Hispanic community, 164; and immigrants 165, 313; Live-work program, 79; and neighborhoods, 52–53, 78; and outmigration, 61–62, 79, 257, 314; perceptions of, 61, 68; police in, 111; and Augustana, 11, 13, 53, 54, 66, 67, 69–73, 75, 76, 78, 80–81, 85, 117, 119, 142, 306, 314; schools, 75, 79, 117, 168, 180
Rock Island (island), 24
Rock Island County Assessment Office, 63
Rock Island High School, 59, 91; and Rocky Riots, 59
Rogers, Michael, 152, 156
Rooted and Open, 10, 228, 238
Routte, Jesse, 13, 86, 87, *88*, 90–98, 120n1, 120n4, 121n17
Routte, Jr., Louis, 96
Routte, Luther, 92
Routté-Gómez, Eneid, 187, 20n1

Safe Zone, 205
Salaam, Yusef, 155
Sampson, William (Bill), 111, 142
Sauk Nation, 21, 23–28, 39, 49n5
Saukenuk, 24–27, 49n9
Schwiebert, Mark, 138
Second World War, 15, 39, 59, 86, 100, 233, 254
segregation, 86, 88, 110–12, 131, 133, 227
Shipley, Neal, 214, 21, 225n107
Silvis, Illinois, 173, 179
Simpson, OJ: *Newsweek* photo, 147, *148*; trial, 147–48
Sixth Ward Neighborhoods/Augustana College Task Force, 70, 80
Skyles, Robbin, 115
Slough, Swanie, 37, 57, 168, 191, 193
Smith, C.S., 112, 114
Smith, George, 91, 92
Smith, Marsha, 145, 201, 221n45, 225n107
Smith, Monica, 10, 16, 229
Söderblom, Nathan, 242, 266n52
social justice, xi, 10, 114, 128, 132, 133, 135, 145, 150, 152, 157, 158, 180, 297, 303, 307
Sorensen, Clarence Woodrow, 115, 195, 196, 219n31, 219n32, 220n36, 220n38, 233, 277, 287; and Black Power Symposium, 112, 134; and Black students, 114, 116, 131, 133; and LGBTQ policies, 197, 198, 199, 200, 204, 208, 213, 218n21
Sorensen, Robert, 108, 138
sports. *See* athletics
Staples, David, 157, 305, *305*
strategic plans, 57, 78, 128, 182, 264, 302, 305–7; Authentically Augustana, 210
Student Action Coalition, 137
Student Affairs, 195, 196, 220n38
Student Counselling Service, 201, 202
Student Government Association, 70, 93, 172
Student Personnel Committee, 196, 202, 213, 218n15
Student Union, 100, 107
Student Volunteer Movement, 90

Students for a Democratic Society, 133
students' rights movement, 6, 195
sustainability, *see* ecological justice
Swanson, Richard, 116, 117, 168, 208, 209; and Swanie Slough, 168

Talentino, Andrea, 78, 341
Teagle Foundation, 307
Telleen, Frank, 196, 218n16
Teng, Nick, 178, 184
theology, 10, 21, 37, 118, 151, 230, 232, 237, 249, 261, 262, 269n101; of accompaniment, 230, 259–60, 262; *see also* Lutheranism
Thomas, Eric, 133
Three Fires Confederacy, 21, 23, 24, 39
Thurmond, Strom, 112
Torres, Christina, 172
Transitional Living Areas (TLAs), 63, 64 table 2.6, 71, 74, 214
Tredway, Thomas: books by, 8, 195; as Dean of Students, 75, 196, 197, 198, 200; and LGBTQ policies, 198, 202, 209, 210; presidency of, xi, 8, 75, 209, 216, 233–35, 245, 249, 250, 269n110, 279, 287, 290, 297, 307
Trump, Donald, 184, 193, 216
Turner, Reggie, 133

United States Hispanic Leadership Conference, 181
University of California vs. Bakke, 139
Unonius, Gustav, 29, 30
Upper Mississippi Center, 66
Uppsala University, 241, 242, 266n43, 267n66

Valdez, Julio, 172
VanSpeybroeck, Deb, 201, 202, 225n107
Varallo, Sharon, 156, 304
Vietnam War, 187, 303; and draft, 3
vigils, Ayotzinapa Vigil, 183–84, *183*; Vigil for Lives Lost, 154, *154*
vocation, xi, xiii, 10, 14, 42, 43, 48, 129, 132, 143, 227, 235, 236, 237, 245, 247, 250, 252, 272, 273, 276, 278–82, 284, 287, 290, 300–304, 306, 308n3, 315, 339; and calling, 238, 159, 271, 272, 302

Wahlstrom, Matthias, 32, 44
Wang, Ching, 96
Westerlin Hall, 6
White privilege, 141, 143, 151, 175, 189n2
whiteness, 45, 141, 189n2; and campus, 11–12, 86, 88, 185, and Lutheranism, 86, 97
Whitt, Christopher, 150, 152
Williamson, Andrew Woods, 22, 29, 32–37, 44
Williamson, Thomas, 33
working groups, 299, 300; ELCA, x

Youth International Party (YIP), 111